Transformations of an American County

Dutchess County, New York

1683—1983

TRANSFORMATIONS OF AN AMERICAN COUNTY

DUTCHESS COUNTY, NEW YORK

1683—1983

**Papers of the
Tercentenary Conference
April 23 and 24, 1983**

Editorial Committee
Joyce C. Ghee, Melodye Kaltz, William McDermott, & Richard Wiles

Published by
Dutchess County Historical Society
on behalf of the
Dutchess County Tercentenary Advisory Committee
Poughkeepsie, New York
1986

A *quality* product from
Heart of the Lakes Publishing
Interlaken, New York

Table of Contents

Appendix

Dedication

Less than four years ago, at the initial meeting of a group of volunteers, who had been called together to advise our County Executive, Lucille Pattison, as to the appropriate ways of celebrating our county's 300th birthday, I was first introduced to Professor Jonathan Clark—teacher, historian, American Revolutionary era scholar.

Jon, as he preferred to be called, was memorable. His rustic, easy-going manner and wild sense of humor belied the perfectionist and dedicated scholar that lurked just beneath the surface. He was pure fun to work with.

Jon deserves to be called the godfather of the Dutchess County Tercentenary—having named it, at our second meeting. While others of our fellow celebrating counties settled for the more popular and faddish "tricentennial," Jon would have none of that. "Tercentenary" was the most correct and that was what we got.

His insistence upon such high standards also won for him, very early on, the task of preparing for the first county conference (marking the tercentenary) to advance the history of Dutchess and the mid-Hudson region. The conference was agreed upon by the advisory committee shortly after I was appointed as its chairman in 1981, and when I asked Jonathan, who had been a proponent of such an event, to accept chairmanship of the conference program committee, he did so enthusiastically. Jon already had in mind a format, subject matter and participants.

He sought the best for us as always, and that extended to those whom he gathered to work with him in preaparing for the event. His enthusiasm, energy, and insistence upon the highest of quality was shared by his associates who toiled with him to put all the elements in place.

His fondest hope, shared early and often with me, was that the results of the conference, and the new scholarship which it would generate, would be preserved and disseminated for present and future generations of area students of history. To that end he worked with me to develop a proposal for a publication grant which was submitted to the Gannett Foundation on behalf of the tercentenary by the Dutchess County Historical Society early in January 1983, in the midst of Jon's sudden illness.

His untimely death in early February of that year came as a great blow to his friends and associates in the community. His was the kind of life-giving spirit which one never thought of as ending. And indeed, that spirit continues to pour forth its vitality.

I discovered, in going through his papers, how many wise decisions had been made and how very much he had already done. His choice of committee associates, Richard Wiles, William McDermott and F. Kennon Moody, was among those wise decisions for they picked up the burden and continued the job as they knew he would have expected.

Jonathan was one of the rare academics who appreciated local history. After his arrival in this area, only a decade ago, he quickly became knowledgeable about the work of local historians and familiar with the historical resources of the area. This knowledge was reflected in his work. A number of his papers done since 1975, focusing upon the American Revolution, were written from the perspective of Dutchess County history.

Jon's own paper was almost ready for presentation and was read by a dear friend and associate at the conference which was held at Dutchess Community College on April 23 and 24 of 1983.

In seeking a proper method of memorializing Jonathan, his friends, fellow-committee members from the Dutchess County Tercentenary Advisory Committee, with the approval of his wife Judy, elected to dedicate the conference to Jonathan as a living memorial.

The proposal for publication which he and I drafted was favorably reviewed, and the program committee which Jon had chaired, assisted by the Dutchess County Tercentenary Advisory

Committee, worked with the Dutchess County Historical Society, the publisher of record, to prepare conference papers for publication. The long awaited results, which you see before you, are the second part of that memorial.

To Jonathan Clark (1941–1983), who inspired it, this book is fondly dedicated.

Joyce C. Ghee, Director
Dutchess County Tercentenary
Dutchess County Historian

July 1984

To Jon

Cortland Pell Auser

Then you were free and happy under the beech trees
Around the many barns, and joyful as the plants were green.
The nights above the gables starry
Time let you live in your prime
Pleasant in the peacetime of your years.
And well-knowing your friends lived
Companions to the whole town
And once before this time, you happily had the trees and leaves,
Trailing the stone walls and seeking you biked
Down to the river of westering light.

And you were younger and free then, knowing the birds,
Above the land and singing in the fields of home
In the sun that is strong in the pre-Spring
Time let you live
And be happy with the passing of days
And young and cheery you were, seeking and reading. The thoughts
Came to your call. Outside the does in the hills ran free and wild
While the churchmen's bell rang dully
As you idled by the bright stream
All the day long, it was breathing; it was living. Early March time
Lifted you high in your house, the smoke from the chimneys you say. It was air
And breathing and sweating and being
Then on fire, bright in mind
As you fell to sleep, the thoughts coming
All the night long you heard among the trees, the night sounds
On the campus and in the streets, and the stars
Lighting in the dark, afire.

And then you awoke in the morn like a wanderer lorn
With dew on skin, your face covered with drops. It was
All Eden, with Adam in the gardens,
The sky darkening again
And the sun going behind the cloud adrift
So it must have been you mused at the beginning of simple time
In the first old places hereabouts, the farm horses not tamer then
Out beyond the neighing in the fields
And grazing in the pastures
And known to the fish and frogs of a bright stream
Under the slow climbing clouds and happy in your heart for long

---

The poem is adapted from Dylan Thomas' "Fern Hill" by Cortland Pell Auser in celebration of a delightful spirit and an unforgettable place.

As each day renewed again
You lived in simple ways
Your thoughts were only for the life of a former day
And nothing could spoil or stain a blue sky's day
And time wound down
In all its carefree passage so fast, with morning songs
Of all the birds on wing and flying
Passing with time on the edge of spring.
Nothing hurt you in those slow peaceful days when time took you
Up Takhanic hills in the shadow of dark clouds south
And the moon saw you happy again
And you sailing to sleep at the days's end
And you heard peace fly from the open fields
And you woke to the ghost marchers and men searching the land
Oh, as you were young and easy in that distant year
Time then held you live and breathing
Before it sang dirges to your destiny this year.

Dutchess County Historical Society Yearbook 1941

"View of Dover Plains, New York," by Asher B. Durand

Preface

On Saturday, April 23, and Sunday, April 24, 1983, the first of what was envisioned as an annual conference on local history took place at Dutchess Community College in Poughkeepsie. Entitled "Transformations of an American County," the conference was conceived as a broad umbrella under which all manner of subject matter dealing with local history could be gathered in a nurturing environment to be explored by any interested citizen.

That same inclusive note is apparent in the list of presenters. By acknowledging the skills gained as a result of personal interest, research and experience, the scope of the list was made broad enough to encompass local and municipal historians, genealogists, educators, activists and specialists in a variety of fields, as well as the professional scholars one would expect to find at such a gathering.

Local history has only recently been recognized by the professional historian as an appropriate area for interpretation. The general and enthusiastic acceptance of new research techniques such as oral history and the growing availability of computer technology would seem to forecast an exciting future for those of us in the field, offering the possibility of many new resources soon to be at hand.

Local history, however, is more than an exercise in scholarship. It represents our community identity. Recognition of it as such forces us to resist the temptation to become exclusive or proprietary in our historical attitudes. Dutchess County and mid-Hudson history belongs to all and must, therefore, be readily and easily available to everyone in a variety of community settings: schools, libraries, homes, historical societies, business and municipal centers, as well as colleges.

This book would seem to respond to this need for accessibility. While all those participating in the conference were encouraged to submit their works for publication, not all papers could be printed for a variety of reasons ranging from the writer's personal choices, to copyright and budgetary restraints.

Those chosen represent a fair sampling from the social, political, cultural and economic history of our valley over a period of three centuries. Because there is no one local historian who could possibly review such a wide range of topics fairly and accurately, the Historical Society and the representatives of the Tercentenary Advisory Committee have chosen to let the works speak for themselves and do not assume responsibility for statements of fact or opinion made by the authors. For this reason, too, the format of the presentations varies with the writer. Notes or references accompany some, and in others they are lacking. Copyrights for individual papers have been retained by the authors.

We are grateful for the support of the following: the faculty, staff and administration of Dutchess Community College, hosts for the conference; the Gannett Foundation whose generous grant made this publication possible; the members of the Dutchess County Tercentenary Advisory Committee and the conference subcommittee; Melodye Kaltz and the trustees of the Dutchess County Historical Society; Judy Clark for permitting us the opportunity to include her husband's work in the book; scholars Michael Kammen and Sung Bok Kim, and all the presenters and respondents whose participation made the conference such an exciting experience.

To everyone who contributed in any way to the success of the conference or to the completion of this volume, we extend a heartfelt thank you.

Joyce C. Ghee

Dutchess County Historical Society Yearbook 1979

Print by James Deyo

HERITAGE, MEMORY, AND HUDSON VALLEY TRADITIONS

Michael Kammen

Professor of History, Cornell University

Early in the 1930s, during the depths of the Great Depression, researchers at Cornell University and at Cornell's Experimental Station in Geneva, New York, developed inexpensive foods called Milkorno, Milkwheato, and Milkoato. They consisted of whole ground meal, dried skim milk, and salt. They contained lots of minerals, proteins, and vitamins; and cost very little. In February 1933 Governor Herbert H. Lehman and Mrs. Franklin D. Roosevelt visited Cornell and had a Milkorno luncheon: tomato juice, Milkorno, scrapple, cabbage salad, baked apple and cookies, all at a staggering cost of 6 cents per person.[1] I think that our luncheon today may have been *considerably* tastier; but some would say that we're in a depression once again, which makes that price tag of 6 cents sound mighty good!

Be that as it may, I'm very glad to be here; and grateful to you for inviting an "outsider" to speak on this occasion. So much so, in fact, that insiders and outsiders will be one of the themes I touch upon in discussing why a local and regional celebration—or I should say *this* local celebration, in particular— has state-wide and even national resonance.

In the year 1799, David Daggett delivered an oration in New Haven, Connecticut, that bears a charming title: *Sun-Beams May Be Extracted from Cucumbers, But the Process is Tedious*. I shall try to extract three sun-beams today, and I can only hope that the process won't be too tedious. My first attempt concerns the Hudson River Valley "school" of painters, and a certain happy lesson, or sun-beam, that I see in their story. My second involves the nature of memory and amnesia in the Hudson River Valley; what is remembered, what is forgotten, and the implications of both. My third concerns the relationship between local traditions and national heritage, once again with particular reference to the Hudson River Valley. Bear with me, and perchance the process of extracting Sun-Beams from historical cucumbers may not prove to be too tedious! We shall see.

I have always shared your affection for the Hudson River Valley school of landscape art. One never tires of those beautiful scenes; and in my opinion they have never been surpassed in the subsequent history of American landscape painting. The school is often referred to as the "first school" (meaning the earliest) in the whole history of American art. That is not quite true, of course; nonetheless you can acknowledge with pride the primacy of an earlier, less famous, yet *also* a Hudson River Valley school. I have in mind those portraits, overmantels, religious scenes and allegories ascribed to the so-called Schuyler Painter, the Gansevoort Limner, and the Aetatis Suae pictures. Many of those portraits, of course, incorporate landscapes in the background, or off to one side. An example, "Pau de Wandelaer" by the Gansevoort Limner (c.1725), shows the mid-Hudson, its mountains, and a single-masted sailing vessel with fore and aft rig.[2]

Some of the religious paintings are wonderfully naive, though perhaps "innocent" would be a better word. I have in mind "The Finding of Moses," for example, done by an unknown artist in Albany during the first quarter of the eighteenth century. Six uncorseted lovelies are reaching out to little baby Moses, whose basket seems to be not so much caught in the bulrushes as it is simply floating on Rondout Creek or the Esopus. Three of the six full-bosomed creatures are almost unseemly in their dishabille. But the painter has carefully inscribed "Exodus 2V–3" in the left foreground to remind us that Pharaoh's daughter and her handmaidens had, after all, gone to the river to bathe. Still, it seems droll to envision fleshy Egypt in the middle-distance, with the Hardenberg Hills as a backdrop.[3]

So much for the *first* Hudson River school. It was, indeed, the first American school; but exemplars will primarily be found in public galleries and homes along the Valley; and afficionadoes of these works are primarily local people plus a few professional specialists. The *second* Hudson River Valley school is a different matter, however, because it has truly become a cherished part of our national aesthetic heritage. The landscapes of Thomas Cole, Asher B. Durand, Frederic E. Church, Jasper F. Cropsey and many others are prized by collectors and art museums throughout the country—indeed, throughout the world. On October 25, 1979, I was heartbroken when Sotheby Parke Bernet knocked down "Figures on The Hudson River," by Jasper Cropsey, a brilliant October scene, for $16,000. In that very same sale "The Icebergs," by Frederic Church, went to a Texan for a cool $2.5 million. I would have been content with Cropsey's luminous vista of the lower Hudson; but it was just a bit beyond my budget.[4]

One aspect of the second Hudson River school that interests me especially is that a number of its prominent members really were not residents of the Valley. Like me, they were outsiders who found themselves attracted to the Valley: its vistas, its foliage, its people, its boats—even its cows and sheep. Precisely because they were outsiders, they helped to create a national school and a national style that was, nonetheless, place-specific. Take George Inness, for example. He was born in 1825 on a farm just two miles from Newburgh; but his family moved to New York City while he was still an infant. In 1829 they moved again, this time to a country home outside of Newark, New Jersey, where Inness spent his boyhood. At the age of sixteen he got a job with two map engravers in New York City. Then he studied with a French landscape painter in the city; and in 1845 he set up his own studio. He sketched for a while at Pottsville, Pennsylvania, where his elder brother lived, and then began a truly peripatetic career: short periods of residence in Italy, Brooklyn, France, a move to Boston in 1859, then five years in Medfield, Massachusetts, where he painted some of his greatest scenes. After the Civil War this restless man moved to Eagleswood, New Jersey, followed by four more years in Rome (1871–75), a return to Boston, New York City once again, and finally, in 1878, he settled in Montclair, New Jersey, where he spent most of his remaining sixteen years.

In 1870, however, after Eagleswood and before Rome, he painted a large oil entitled "Landscape, Hudson Valley," that now hangs in the Cincinnati Art Museum. It's a fascinating picture. Inness's emphasis is upon the Valley itself, rather than the river. Some sun is breaking through an overcast sky. Locomotive-like puffs of steam stream from the chimneys of three small homes located on the edge of a hillside in the foreground; and then farmsteads as well as a village are rather indistinct in the middle distance. The painting has a mystical quality, but not because Inness has chosen to romanticize the Hudson Valley of his nativity. Quite the contrary, his theme is as elusive on canvas as it must have become in his life by 1870. At the age of 45 he seems to have been invoking some memory of his nativity. There is no machine in this garden, no locomotives like his more famous "Lackawanna Valley" of 1855, nor a locomotive roundhouse located like an omphalos in the center, nor a field of stumps in the foreground. The Lackawanna Valley was being shaped by the hand of man, whereas "Landscape, Hudson Valley" is inhabited but remains rustic. The vast sweep of the Valley, with a limitless horizon, is viewed from a bluff on the lower edge. Inness had come home, yet he acknowledged his true situation, that of an affectionate outsider.[5]

The mysterious haze that he imposed on this Hudson Valley scene—a haze of memory, of time filtered through distance and clouds—may be contrasted with still another painting by Inness called "New England Valley," handsomely displayed for sale in the April 1983 issue of *The Magazine Antiques* (p. 723). Here the landscape is much sharper, each grove of trees stands out more clearly, and we are entering the unspecified valley behind a lone woman whose purpose in heading for the pasture and cattle in the middle distance is known only to her. The high bluff and rocky out-cropping appear *across* and above the valley. They merely define one distant boundary of it. We are, as I have noted, *entering* the valley, invited as it were by the farm woman who is preceding us. In "Hudson Valley," by contrast, one feels more like the mature Moses: permitted to observe the promised land from above and afar, but not to enter it. The viewer remains very still. Only his eye moves, drawn by a broad bend in the river, back and back and back to the hazy horizon, to a vast yet finite horizon of memory.

(I recall with great fondness a two-week trip that I made in July, 1972, while researching *Colonial New York—A History,* up and down both sides of the Hudson, from Tappan and Tarrytown at the southern end to Fort Edward and Glens Falls in the North. I considered myself an empathetic outsider then, as I do once again today, approaching the Valley with an active historical imagination.)

Although we speak of the Hudson Valley "school," each of those great artists had his own angle of vision, his own reason for recapturing some aspect of the landscape and its past. Thomas Cole wanted to comprehend awesome, sublime aspects of Nature, and sought to define the Romantic Americanness of the Valley, in contrast to the more controlled, Roman landscapes, often with ancient ruins, that he also painted. John Quidor enlivened the folklore of the Hudson Valley by using Washington Irving's tales as points of departure for such fantastic confrontations as "The Return of Rip Van Winkle" (1829) and "Anthony Van Corlear Brought into the Presence of Peter Stuyvesant" (1839).[6] Jasper Cropsey recorded the shifting of seasons in the Valley with exquisite faithfulness to each burnished or fallen leaf.

We need to consider the *entire* school if we are to savor the fullness of man's experience with nature and history in this Valley. Nor can we ignore the less famous, "naive" artists of the Valley, for their identification with it may have been the strongest of all because it was their *primary* identification. "The Hudson Valley, Sunset," a mid-nineteenth-century landscape by Thomas Chambers in which a dirt road gives way to the foreshortened river itself, reminds us that Dutch explorers and English navigators of the seventeenth century called the Hudson, quite literally, their "road."

Then we have the varied blues and greens of "Marlborough from New Hamburg" by the self-trained folk artist, Clinton W. Clapp (1831–1915). Born and raised in the Town of Wappinger, he left in 1845 to study mechanical engineering at New York University and the City Mechanical Institute. Unlike the peripatetic George Inness, however, Clapp came home in 1852, became president of a bicycle-wheel manufacturing company and the local historian for Poughkeepsie newspapers. He prepared a chapter on Wappinger for Hasbrouck's *History of Dutchess County.* Excatly a century ago, in 1883, he began to paint with oils. Sailing his steam-powered yacht down Wappinger's Creek to its mouth at New Hamburg, he noticed a fine view of Marlborough, entrepot of the local raspberry industry, which every day sent berries by steamboat to New York City. We cannot see the berries in this quaint scene; but the steamboat is at the wharf, white side-wheel and black smoke-stack ready to carry those berries down to Gotham.[7]

The second aspect of heritage and memory that I want to mention has to do with our tendency to forget as well as to remember. Since the beginning of this century, for example, New Yorkers have shown a wonderful capacity to celebrate anniversaries, but then to dismiss their historical occasions entirely. The Hudson-Fulton Celebration in 1909, for example, commemorated the tercentenary of Henry Hudson's "discovery" of the river that bears his name, as well as the centennial of Robert Fulton's invention of the steamboat. That celebration was an important landmark in our cultural history, and for many reasons, among them the first major exhibition of American decorative arts, held at the Metropolitan Museum of Art in New York City, a show that provided the genesis for the American Wing of the Met, which opened in 1924 and so richly displays objects characteristic of material culture in the Hudson Valley.[8]

That eventful tercentenary, honoring the history of discovery and technological innovation in New York, was followed in 1914 by an obscure event called The Commercial Tercentenary of New York. As its memorial booklet explained:

> The year 1614 is a red-letter year in the history of the State of New York; for it was the year in which the duly chartered commerce of the Hudson River began; the year in which the first ship was built in these waters; the year in which the first fort was built by the Dutch traders in the Hudson Valley, and the year which produced the first definite cartographical knowledge of New Netherland.[9]

I would venture the guess that virtually no one today knows about that tercentenary, even though it became a kind of prototype for comparable commercial anniversaries. In 1941, for example, Dun & Bradstreet celebrated its 100th birthday in New York by publishing a volume entitled *The Sinews of*

American Commerce. The president of Dun & Bradstreet proudly sent it to clients and other influential persons, explaining that it gave "the intimate story of the development and the evolution of credit in the irresistible progress of a vigorous people . . . ."[10]

In 1926 New York State observed the tercentenary of the founding of New Netherland: special exhibitions were prepared and appropriate publications appeared, such as a bibliography relating to the history of New Netherland, and several one-volume histories of New York, 1626–1926. Two years later the 300th anniversary of the Dutch Reformed Church in America was observed, with special homage to Jonas Michaëlius, the first dominie to arrive in New Netherland. In 1936 a Long Island Tercentenary took place; and four years later some of the towns on the eastern end of the Island, such as Southampton and Southhold, settled by Puritans who had crossed Long Island Sound from New England, celebrated their tercentenaries.[11]

Each of these occasions stimulated a certain amount of public interest; and several of them even generated publications of enduring value. Nevertheless I am impressed—or perhaps I should say depressed—by our tendency even to forget what we have re-remembered. You will not be surprised to learn that, sometimes at least, it is necessary to revive our lapses in order to recapture our heritage. I do not have individuals in mind so much as organizations. In 1935, for example, a resident of Garden City, Long Island, pointed out that in planning for the Long Island Tercentenary "some of my associates in the project believe that the best way to push our celebration is to resuscitate the dead Nassau County Historical Society . . . ."[12] Well, yes, it *does help* to have a local historical society with a spark of life to it!

Interestingly enough, I find that Dutchess County in general, and Poughkeepsie in particular, have a better record than most. Various groups, institutions, and writers have from time to time freshened our memory of the significant State convention that met here from June 17 until July 26, 1788, to consider and ratify the new U. S. Constitution.[13] The New York State Historical Association held its annual meeting in Poughkeepsie on September 15, 16, and 17, 1938, in order to mark the Sesquicentennial of New York's becoming the "eleventh pillar" of the new United States. The Dutchess County Historical Society and Vassar College served as co-hosts on that occasion.

You may be interested (or appalled) to learn that the overall cost per person for meals and lodging was $3.50 a day. Those attending could participate in a "pilgrimage" to several of the grand Hudson River mansions in the area: the Roosevelt and Vanderbilt homes in Hyde Park; and then Montgomery Place, beyond Rhinebeck, where General and Mrs. John Ross Delafield explained "the history of the house and its famous occupants, the Livingston family."[14]

On September 17th, a date observed as Constitution Day beginning in 1919, preliminary speeches were made by George V.L. Spratt, the mayor of Poughkeepsie, and Frederick H. Bontecou, State Senator from the 28th district. Dixon Ryan Fox, energetic President of Union College and of the New York State Historical Association, abbreviated his remarks because Governor Lehman was present and President Roosevelt was also waiting to deliver his address by radio from Washington. As Fox observed to the crowd in downtown Poughkeepsie, most of them had surely attended to hear Lehman and FDR supply "some fresh interpretation of our present political life and its tendencies." Fox was sagacious. Undoubtedly he did the right thing. Still, it seems at least a *bit* bizarre that on this historical occasion a distinguished historian of New York State and of American political culture during the later eighteenth century felt that he had to truncate his remarks because the audience had *really* assembled to hear two nationally prominent figures speak about current events.[15]

Yes, I do appreciate that under these particular circumstances, FDR was no ordinary American President. FDR was, in Felix Frankfurter's words, "The Dutchess County American," a marvelous appellation, in my opinion, and one that Frankfurter concocted in January 1939 in his first letter to FDR after the President had named him to the Supreme Court.[16] I'll have more to say in a few moments about the Dutchess County American.

First, however, I want to finish my point about memory and amnesia. If the Poughkeepsie Convention of 1788 provides a good example of an historical event that has remained relatively vivid, Mehitabel Wing Prendergast provides us with an instance of a wonderful woman, truly an actress in the drama of revolutionary history, who seems to be forgotten, even in the annals of Dutchess County.

Although Mehitabel is my favorite heroine in all of colonial American history—not just New York, but *all* of colonial America—she does not seem to be mentioned in James H. Smith's bicentennial *History of Duchess County, NY, with Illustrations and Biographical Sketches of Some of Its Prominent Men and Pioneers* (1882). Nor does she appear in the *Commemorative Biographical Record of Dutchess County, New York, containing biographical sketches of prominent and representative citizens, and of many of the early settled families* (1897), nor even in *County at Large,* by Martha Collins Bayne (published in 1937 by the Women's City and Country Club with Vassar College).

Some of you may know all about Mehitabel Wing Prendergast; but believing, as I truly do, that she should not be overlooked by *anyone,* allow me for just a moment or two to slip into the role of Peechy Prauw, the local historian and drinking companion to Wolfert Webber, who tells those tales in Washington Irving's *Tales of a Traveller.*

It's a complicated yarn, but here's the essence. William Prendergast led a tenants' revolt in these parts during 1766. He surrendered to a regiment of Royal grenadiers in the little town of Fredericksburg (now Patterson), and they marched him directly to Poughkeepsie, and then on to a Hudson River sloop bound for New York, where he was imprisoned. Meanwhile a Poughkeepsie grand jury indicted him for high treason, and he was brought back to a packed courtroom in Poughkeepsie on August 6, 1766, to stand trial. Mehitabel entered with him, and as the attorney general introduced damaging evidence against William, Mehitabel, a 28-year-old Quaker, maneuvered eloquently as his advocate. The Poughkeepsie correspondent for the New York *Gazette or Weekly Post Boy* explained to readers that,

> solicitously attentive to every particular and without the least Impertinence or Indecorum of Behavior, sedately anxious for her husband she never failed to make every Remark that might tend to extenuate the Offence and put his Conduct in the most favourable point of view[,] not suffering one Circumstance that could be collected from the evidence or thought in his Favour to escape the Notice of the Court and the Jury.

When the attorney general asked Justice Horsmanden to have Mehitabel removed from the courtroom, the judge responded that she was not creating a disturbance, "nor does she speak unseasonably."

"Your Lordship," the exasperated prosecutor replied, "I do not think that she should speak at all, and I fear her very looks may too much influence the jury."

He was wrong, as it turned out, because the jury found William guilty. The required sentence? "High treason against his Majesty—Friday the twenty-sixth day of September—to be hanged by the neck until you are dead."

Even as the crowds of angry, sympathetic farmers followed William back to the Poughkeepsie jail, Mehitabel swung into action. She had one last desperate recourse. Despite Quaker constraints, she borrowed her sister's best dress, a pretty white one with blue stripes, mounted a horse and galloped eighty miles to see Governor Sir Henry Moore in Fort George. As she dismounted, Mehitabel pleaded for an interview; and she got it. She explained the desperate circumstances of William and their fellow tenant farmers, and she clarified his limited role and his true intentions in the populist protest. According to Wing family tradition, her arguments were so persuasive, "and her looks so utterly appealing," that water came to the eyes of Governor Moore. Wiping away his tears, he told her: "Your husband shall not suffer."

Moore then wrote a reprieve for Prendergast, and allowed Mehitabel to draft the petition for a royal pardon. Satisfied that every legal technicality had been attended to, she then galloped the eighty miles back to Poughkeepsie, flourished the Governor's reprieve and prevented William's execution. Six months later the long awaited letter arrived from the Prime Minister himself, Lord Shelburne:

> I have laid before the King your letter of the 11th Oct. recommending W. Prendergast who was sentenced to death for treasonous Practices and Riots committed in Dutchess County, to the Royal Mercy, and his Majesty has been gratiously pleased to grant him his pardon, relying that this instance of his Royal clemency will have a better effect in recalling these mistaken People to their duty than most rigorous punishment.[17]

The coda to this complicated story goes on and on. Let it suffice to say that Mehitabel and William Prendergast lived happily ever after—pretty much. He died in 1810, and she survived him by eighteen months. Perhaps every school child in Dutchess County knows the whole stirring saga; but if—perchance—if not, then surely there's some work to be done on your local history chapbooks. The Prendergasts, but mostly Mehitabel, are what History ought to be all about.

Having talked about a local legend who may have been insufficiently honored in her own land, let me now turn to a very different aspect of heritage, memory, and Hudson Valley traditions. I have in mind the gradual, hesitant, but irrepressible process whereby Hudson Valley traditions have come to be recognized as part of our *national* heritage. In one sense that development began with Washington Irving, of course; but the process has been slow, retarded by the vagaries of regional rivalry, inadequate means of communication and transportation, etc. During the past sixty years, however, the particulars of *your* history have become part and parcel of *our* history. The transformation has been a fascinating one, and I am able to share several phases of it with you because of research that I have done during the last eight months at archives in Cooperstown, Schenectady, and Pocantico Hills, near Tarrytown.

Let's go back to the Dutchess County American. In March 1938, when the annual meeting of the New York State Historical Association was being planned for Poughkeepsie, Roosevelt declared to Dixon Ryan Fox "my deep personal interest in the early history of New York State." Earlier, in 1923, F. D. R. had published pertinent essays in *De Halve Maen,* quarterly magazine of the Holland Society of New York. In July of that year he wrote to Fox at Columbia:

> I should much like your judgment on the possibility of a publication or series of publications on old Dutch houses, portraits, etc. in New York State and vicinity . . . . In regard to the question of cooperation I am inclined to believe that other organizations might be glad to work with us—for instance, here in Dutchess County the Dutchess County [Historical] Society would, I am sure, assist us, and there are two or three people in this neighborhood who I think would be entirely willing to help us gather data, photographs, etc.

Fox responded constructively by sending, as a model, a form used by the Colonial Dames of Connecticut in recording information about historic homes. "With the multifarious demands upon your time," Fox added,

> I suppose it will be difficult for you to give very much attention to such an historical adventure, but I am sure all societies of the hereditary patriotic type will be heartened by your lively interest in such a concern. There is a great deal of energy and intelligence in the membership of these organizations that is anxious for direction in serviceable employment. I have been struck as an outsider [here's that theme once again!] with the wistfulness of some of the leaders in search of something appropriate to do.[18]

To make a long story somewhat shorter, the guidance of Fiske Kimball, a prominent architectural historian then teaching at New York University, was sought; and he offered many helpful suggestions that lifted the professional qualities of the project by enlisting expert advice. Following Kimball's suggestion, Fox stressed to Frederic R. Keator, a moving spirit behind the project, that "it is clearly desirable to have real research enter into the collection of data rather than oral tradition, unsupported by documentary evidence."[19] The outcome, eventually, was the publication in 1929 of *Dutch Houses in the Hudson Valley before 1776* by Helen Wilkinson Reynolds, with an introduction by Governor Franklin Delano Roosevelt.

Phase Two in the nationalization of Hudson Valley traditions came during the later 1930s when a batch of well-written books and essays appeared, including *The Hudson* (1939) by Carl Carmer, and "The River that Flows Both Ways" (1940) by Remsen D. Bird. The latter was partially serialized in the *Hudson River Magazine,* a journal that began in 1937 and bore the subtitle, "A monthly mirror of life along the Hudson." Carroll Osborn had established it in Hudson, New York, at the age of 22. Osborn explained his enterprise to Dixon Ryan Fox in 1940.

Concerning itself with the story of local institutions, activities, personalities, history and folklore, the Hudson River Magazine's regional theme rivals in interest the reading appeal of a daily newspaper . . . . But I am not content with my means of developing the magazine's theme or of spreading its story before the million and a half Hudson Valley people, without the support of influential valley residents who appreciate the desirability of promoting our *regional values*.[20]

Fox, in turn, commended the magazine to Carl Carmer, observing that "the whole enterprise is just about the kind of thing that you and I approve,—the sectional magazine, rich with the flavor of the locality. The Hudson River now as a social unit passing somewhat into history, it is very desirable that the history itself be kept alive."[21] When Osborn wrote to Fox a few months later to request a "guest editorial," he recommended as one possible point of departure a remark by a recent speaker that "the character of our people made Hudson valley society a stabilizing force in the nation." Fox cheerfully picked up on this suggestion and sent Osborn "a little piece" in which he embroidered what by then had become one of his favorite themes.

Nothing is more necessary in American sentiment than the defense of regionalism. Loyalty to one's homeland, by birth or adoption, now in no way diminishes our loyalty to the American nation as a whole . . . . With everybody listening to national net-work radio, looking at the same motion pictures, reading chain newspapers, we are likely to forget the special factors of our local environment which make us different, or should make us different from other people. We cannot have a truly rich national culture without cherishing a rich variety within it.[22]

In 1941, when Fox wrote those words, a transformation had already begun that would gradually complete the process whereby traditions of the mid- and lower Hudson River Valley came to be acknowledged—without any dilution of the particularities and peculiarities of those traditions—as an integral part of the national heritage. In 1939 the Tarrytown Historical Society sought the support of John D. Rockefeller, Jr., in restoring what was then called Philipse "Castle" into (symptomatic phrase) an "historic shrine." Dr. Hugh Grant Rowell, energetic president of the Tarrytown Historical Society, explained to the media that

Williamsburg has proved highly successful as covering the glamor of the South. It is proposed to restore St. Augustine, Florida, to represent an earlier period. Yet the Tarrytowns, with the story of the North, are just as rich in lore, and, in my opinion, have a richer historic background than either of the other communities—and no Northern restoration has [yet] been attempted.

What followed during the next quarter century, from about 1940 until the mid–1960s, is a fascinating story that really requires a chapter all to itself: a story involving historic preservation; the rewriting of certain pertinent state laws; a vigorous public relations campaign; and a lot of support from the region, from particular communities, and from such indispensable individuals as John D. Rockefeller, Jr. Mr. Rockefeller took Dr. Rowell's bait; and I can assure you that that represented a remarkable achievement on the part of Dr. Rowell. I have read through many boxes of Mr. Rockefeller's correspondence. Believe me, a lot of people and organizations sent him ingenious proposals for ways in which he could benefit mankind in general, or at least their pet project in particular, by the simple act of signing his autograph on a slip of paper that we, in our culture, call a check. Rockefeller was very good at saying "no;" but he said "yes" to Rowell, and by 1940 the Sleepy Hollow Restorations were underway.[23]

I would be neither original nor profound if I proclaimed to you that money means power. Nevertheless, it is endlessly fascinating to find new illustrations of the adage. In 1944, for example, at a time when Mr. Rockefeller began looking ahead to the public opening of Philipse Castle, he realized that it would help to establish the restorations as a going concern if historical societies could charge admission to their properties. According to New York law at that time, they could not. J. D. R., Jr., contacted Governor Dewey and proposed that they meet for lunch to discuss the problem. Dewey said fine, how about the Hotel Roosevelt? Oh no, said Rockefeller, if we ate in my apartment at 740 Park Avenue, "we would be quite by ourselves." That occurred on February 29th. (Yes, 1944 was a Leap Year.) On March 8th J. D. R., Jr., sent Dewey a packet of photographs of the restoration work in progress, and thanked the Governor "for your kindness in looking into this matter and advising how the interests of the enterprise could best be safeguarded." Three days later Rockefeller followed with another letter. He explained that

> I have been thinking of forming at an early date a non-profit corporation to undertake the preservation and restoration of certain historic sites and buildings in this State. During the past few years there have been brought to my attention several such sites and buildings which seem to me to be of real historic interest and significance and which will be lost to the State and to the Nation as a whole unless some steps are taken to preserve them and make them available for public enjoyment. In this connection, my attention has been called to two statutory limitations upon historical societies organized under the laws of this State. These statutory limitations are: (1) Six acres only can be held in any one locality, tax free. (2) Admission fees cannot be charged.

On April 3, 1944, the County Executive of Westchester County recommended to Governor Dewey's legal counsel that the restrictive laws be altered. A few weeks later the State Assembly obliged. Thereafter admission fees could be charged so long as the revenue was used for preservation activities and maintenance of the property.[24]

The successful sequence of events after 1944 must be reasonably familiar to you, though it is important to acknowledge that visitation figures grew only gradually. In 1952 a Temporary Visiting Committee to Sleepy Hollow Restorations, Inc., praised the work that had been done but concluded that "neither Sunnyside nor Philipse Castle are arousing the interest or attendance they deserve. They are not successfully competing for the time, attention, and support of the educators and the general public which they have earned by their inherent qualities." A visitors' survey conducted in 1959 indicated steady progress, especially by means of tours for school children. However much these visits may have helped to vivify Hudson Valley history for the kids, their noisy presence did not always please the older tourists. "We would have stayed longer," one wrote on his questionnaire, "if it hadn't been so crowded with a school tour of jumpy, uninterested small children."

Many visitors seemed more interested in the gift shops—what items were available, and for how much—than they were in the historical restorations. One also finds an unabashed admiration of wealth and social status. As a woman wrote from Toledo, Ohio: "I love to see the beauty and artistry of Colonial homes of the wealthier American [sic]. It's wonderful to keep all such shrines preserved for posterity."[25]

Well, they did, and we are the beneficiaries along with *our* posterity. That same year, 1959, Harold Dean Cater, who four years earlier succeeded Rowell as the Director of Sleepy Hollow Restorations, thanked Mr. Rockefeller for the addition of Van Cortlandt Manor. "It is a place of enchanting beauty," he remarked, "where all of us can find roots in the Hudson Valley's past."[26]

I think that we might well chime in with an "amen" to that. As an afterthought, however, we might also want to reflect upon the imperatives of swift travel and the implications of tourism for our historical vistas. "What price progress?" is a tired, rhetorical question; but there is a certain poignancy in a note that Dixon Ryan Fox sent to a Tarrytown friend in 1936. Fox expressed regret that he could not participate in the fall pilgrimage of the Tarrytown Historical Society. He requested, however, that his name be added

> to any protest which the Society makes as a whole concerning the foolish and useless bridge across the Tappan Zee. Apparently we must all be vigilant to protect the beauty of the Hudson against selfish or misguided invasion.[27]

I don't know how many of you would want to add "amen" to that utterance as well; but while we reflect upon Fox's desire to keep the status quo, and upon the mixed blessing bestowed upon us by bridges, we can be sure that the shades of Thomas Cole, Asher B. Durand, and Frederic Church are saying "amen." I don't think they would be too happy at the sight of the bridges across "the river that flows both ways." On the other hand, they surely would be pleased to learn that Hudson Valley traditions have now become securely part of the national heritage. Memory is supposed to have been the mother of the muses. After three centuries it seems reasonable to conclude that the Hudson River Valley has done well by its muses, and by our memories.

Notes

1. Morris Bishop, *A History of Cornell* (Ithaca, 1962), pg. 464.

2. Robert G. Wheeler and Janet R. MacFarlane, *Hudson Valley Paintings, 1700–1750, in the Albany Institute of History and Art* (Albany, 1959), pg. 20.

3. *Ibid.,* pg. 37.

4. Sotheby Parke Bernet sale catalog #4290, *American 19th and 20th Century Paintings, Drawings, Watercolors and Sculpture* (October 1979), nos. 25 and 34.

5. "Landscape, Hudson Valley" appears in John K. Howat, *The Hudson River and Its Painters* (New York, 1972), fig. 63. "The Lackawanna Valley" appears in Barbara Novak, *Nature and Culture: American Landscape and Painting, 1825–1875* (New York, 1980), fig. 84.

6. Located respectively in the National Gallery of Art, Washington, D. C., and the Munson–Williams–Proctor Institute, Utica. See Bryan Jay Wolf, *Romantic Re-Vision: Culture and Consciousness in Nineteenth-Century American Painting and Literature* (Chicago, 1982), pg. 131–167.

7. Howat, *The Hudson River and Its Painters,* fig. 55 and pg. 163.

8. Michael Kammen, "The Rediscovery of New York's History, Phase One," *New York History,* LX (October 1979), pg. 388–394; Michael Kammen, *Colonial New York—A History* (New York, 1975), 92–93, 109, 148, 258–263, 291.

9. [Edward H. Hall], *The Commercial Tercentenary of New York, 1614–1914: Containing a Brief History of the Beginning of the Regularly Chartered Commerce of New Netherland and the Permanent Settlement of What Is Now The State of New York* (New York, 1914), pg. 66.

10. A. D. Whiteside to Dixon Ryan Fox, October 15, 1941, Fox Papers, Schaffer Library, Union College, Schenectady, New York.

11. Clarence S. Brigham to Victor H. Paltsits, April 20, 1928, Paltsits Papers, New-York Historical Society; Dixon Ryan Fox to Byron F. Burch, January 3, 1941, Fox Papers, Union College. For the 200th anniversary of the settlement of Cherry Valley, see F. LeVere Winne to Dixon Ryan Fox, February 6, 1941, *ibid.;* and Fox to Winne, May 21, 1941, *ibid.*

12. Courtney R. Hall to Dixon Ryan Fox, November 28, 1935, Fox Papers, box 1, New York State Historical Association, Cooperstown, New York.

13. Linda Grant De Pauw, *The Eleventh Pillar: New York State and the Federal Constitution* (Ithaca, 1966), 187–254; J. F. Baldwin, "What Poughkeepsie Celebrates," *New York History,* XX (April 1939), pg. 133–141.

14. *Ibid.,* XIX (April 1938), pg. 113–115; *ibid.* (July 1938), pg. 229, 232; and *ibid.,* XX (January 1939), pg. 4. *The Historical American Building Survey* "List of Structures Recorded in Southern New York State District" (April 15, 1934), listed four structures for Dutchess County: Trinity Church in Fishkill, The Dutch Reform Church in Fishkill, the Glebe House in Poughkeepsie, and the Abraham de Peyster (or Newlin) House in Tioronda, south of Beacon. This list is in the Dixon Ryan Fox Papers, box 5, New York State Historical Association. See also William Nathaniel Banks, "Edgewater on the Hudson River," *The Magazine Antiques,* CXXI (June 1982), pg. 1400–1410. Edgewater is located in Barrytown, north of Rhinebeck along the east bank of the Hudson.

15. The six-page typescript of Fox's talk is in the Fox Papers, box 3, New York State Historical Association. Fox's books included *The Decline of Aristocracy in the Politics of New York, 1801–1840* (New York, 1919), and two on which he was working at the time: *Yankees and Yorkers* (New York, 1940) and *The Completion of Independence, 1790–1830* (New York, 1944), with John A. Krout.

16. Frankfurter to F. D. R., January 30, 1939, quoted in Michael E. Parrish, *Felix Frankfurter and His Times: The Reform Years* (New York, 1982), pg. 278.

17. I have relied on Carl Carmer, *The Hudson* (New York, 1939), pg. 89–99; and Irving Mark, *Agrarian Conflicts in Colonial New York, 1711–1775* (New York, 1940), pg. 146–150.

18. Roosevelt to Fox, March 18, 1938, Fox Papers, Union College; Roosevelt to Fox, July 9, 1923 and Fox to Roosevelt, August 8, 1923, Fox Papers, box 8, New York State Historical Association.

19. Kimball to Fox, August 9, 1923, *ibid.;* and Fox to Keator, August 15, 1923, *ibid.* William B. Rhoads, "Franklin D. Roosevelt and Dutch Colonial Architecture," *New York History,* LIX (October 1978), pg. 430–464.

20. Osborn to Fox, November 18, 1940, Fox Papers, Union College.

21. Fox to Carmer, December 4, 1940; Fox to James E. Leath, December 4, 1940, *ibid.*

22. Osborn to Fox, January 16, 1941; Fox to Osborn, March 11, 1941, with a typescript of Fox's four-paragraph editorial attached, *ibid. Hudson River Magazine* ceased publication in May 1941.

23. *The New York Times,* April 9, 1939, section 1, pg. 2; Hugh Grant Rowell to Dixon Ryan Fox, August 15, 1940, Fox Papers, box 6, New York State Historical Association.

24. John D. Rockefeller, Jr. to Thomas E. Dewey, February 11, 21, and March 8, 1944; Dewey to Rockefeller, March 10, 1944; and Rockefeller to Rowell, February 1, 1944, John D. Rockefeller, Jr., Papers, series II (Cultural), box 1, Rockefeller Archive Center, Pocantico Hills, North Tarrytown, New York.

25. The report of the Visiting Committee, October 17, 1952, is in the Sleepy Hollow Restoration Archives at the Rockefeller Archive Center, Pocantico Hills. For the visitors' survey, see *ibid.,* box 17. A male visitor from Eastport, Long Island, observed of his docents: "The women who spoke with me about Sunnyside and Philipsburg Manor were well informed, neat in appearance, and above average in class. Keep them that way!"

26. Cater to Rockefeller, July 21, 1959, *ibid.,* box 7.

27. Fox to Leslie V. Case, October 8, 1936, Fox Papers, box 1, New York State Historical Association.

Francis Rombout and the Early Settlement of Dutchess County

Henry Cassidy

Retired Newspaperman and Historian of the Town of East Fishkill

In the same year that Dutchess and the eleven other original counties of the British colonial province of New York were created by the Assembly of 1683, another event of historic significance took place—the Rombout purchase.

Francis Rombout, a respected merchant of Manhattan, and his partner, Gulian Verplanck, bought from the Wappinger Indians about 85,000 acres of land on the east bank of the Hudson River, midway between New York City and Albany. The partners adhered scrupulously to the legal principles of land transfer in the colonial period. They obtained from the provincial administration on February 8, 1682, a license to negotiate with the Indians. The negotiations took about ten months, and in later years became the subject of various legends. They made the purchase on August 8, 1683, by deed of sale, carefully signed by representative of the Indians and the purchasers. The royal patent was issued October 17, 1685, by Governor Thomas Dongan, in the name of King James II, conveying title to the land. It was the first patent granted in Dutchess County.

Gulian Verplanck had died before the patent was issued. Jacobus Kipp married his widow, Henrica, and took his place in the partnership. Stephanus Van Cortlandt, another New York merchant, purchased a one-third interest in the property and became the third partner. Under the terms of the patent, the partners were required to pay annually to the British governor "six bushels of good and merchantable winter wheat," a token payment in recognition of the sovereignty of the Crown. The new owners never lived on the land. To them, it was an investment in a hunting and trading post. But thus, they began the history of the development of Dutchess County. At the same time of the purchase, this region was not considered an attractive place. Much of it was thought to be low, swampy and heavily wooded. There was no white population. Dutch and British settlers preferred the high, dry, west bank of the Hudson River. Rombout wanted the east bank only as a source of supply for his fur trade.

Such was Rombout's reputation as a shrewd businessman that it was taken for granted he had outsmarted the Indians. According to one popular legend, he offered the Indians a price for "all the land he could see." Since they were standing on low land, rimmed by hills, so the story went, he could not see very far, and the Indians agreed to his terms. Then, the story concluded, Rombout climbed a thousand feet up to the peak of Mount Beacon, viewed an immense tract and claimed it all. Actually, the negotiations were carried out by agents for Rombout, named Anthony Brockholls, P. V. Courtlandt and John West. And if anyone got the better bargain, it was the Indians, who were represented by a brave named Sackoraghkigh, acting in the name of the Sachem, Megriesken, and the other members of the tribe.

A more likely account of the negotiations had it that a table was set out under the trees at Fishkill Landing. On one side of the rough board sat the white agents in homespun shirts, pantaloons, knee boots and broad hats with upturned brims. Across from them sat the Indians, naked to the waist, wearing leather leggings, moccasins and feathered headdress. Th white men pushed forward the Royal coins and other objects they were offering for the land. The Indians pushed them back, crying "more . . . more." Finally, the deal was made and the Indians let Sackoraghkigh sign for them. The text of the deed, is recorded in the *History of Duchess County 1683–1882*, by James H. Smith. It begins, "To all Christian people to whom this present writing shall come . . ." It names the Indians, "true and lawful owners and Indian proprietors of the land herein menchoned," and it says they send greeting.

The deed grants Rombout and Verplanck "All that Tract or Parcell of Land Scituate, Lyeing and being on the East side of Hudson's River, at the north side of the High Lands, Beginning from the South side of A Creek Called the fresh Kill and by the Indians Matteawan, and from thence Northward along said Hudson's River five hundred Rodd beyond the Great Wappins Kill, called by the Indians Mawenawasigh, being the Northerly Bounds and from thence in the Woods fouer Hours goeing. . . ." The "fouer Hours goeing" was subsequently interpreted legally to mean 16 miles, the distance a man normally would walk in four hours. The area it covered became eventually the towns of Fishkill, East Fishkill and Wappinger, the city of Beacon and parts of La Grange and Poughkeepsie. In exchange for this land, the Indians received a handsome assortment of "perticulers," including 100 Royalls, 100 pounds of gunpowder, 200 fathom of white wampum, 100 bars of lead, 100 fathom of black wampum, 30 tobacco boxes, 30 guns, 20 blankets, 40 fathom of duffills, 20 fathom of stroudwater cloth, 30 kettles, 40 hatchets, 40 horns, 40 shirts, 40 pairs of stockings, 12 coats, 10 drawing knives, 40 earthen jugs, 40 bottles, 40 knives, four ankers of rum, 10 half-vats of beer, 200 tobacco pipes and 80 pounds of tobacco.

The Indians declared themselves to be "fully paid, contented and satisfied," as well they might have been. Compared to the $24 that Pierre Minuit paid for the whole of Manhattan, the articles delivered by Rombout and Verplanck were estimated to be worth $1,250. And the Indians were permitted to stay on their land until 1756 when their last Sachem, Daniel Nimham, led them to safety in Stockbridge, Massachusetts, during the French and Indian war.

Four years after the patent was issued, Rombout had a map made to illustrate his purchase. The map was drawn by the surveyor, John Holwell, in 1689. It shows an expanse of trees north of the Highlands, between Fishkill Creek and Wappingers Creek, studded by wigwams, fields and swamps, two beaver ponds, waterfalls at the mouths of the creeks, and two little houses, labeled "ye frenchman's," at the mouth of Wappingers Creek. Raymond William Storm, in "Old Dirck's Book," the story of his family, identified the beaver ponds as the bodies of water, later known as the "Storm Lakes," on his family's farm. He said a wigwam, pictured between the lakes, was the site of an old apple orchard, and the main field was the section later called Fishkill Plains.

The original map, long in the possession of the Verplanck family, is now held by the New-York Historical Society. (NYS mss. #93) And it is a thing of beauty. The map glows with delicate colors, the trees green, the land brown. The black-and-white reproductions in history books don't do it justice. The colors have faded somewhat, the drawing is smudged and the edges of the parchment are tattered. The little houses have become barely visible, and the inscription, "ye frenchman's," can hardly be seen. But the map has survived three centuries remarkably well.

Francis Rombout was a Walloon. He was a French-speaking Protestant, living in the Flemish speaking Catholic principality of Liege, in a time of economic depression. He escaped that predicament by sailing to America in 1653, at the age of 18. There he joined a colony of Walloons, the original settlers of New York.

The first group of Walloons had sailed to Manhattan from Amsterdam in 1623 abroad the *Nieu Nederlandt,* in the service of the Dutch West India Company. They came only three years after the Pilgrims founded Plymouth, Massachusetts, but the Walloons never achieved a place in history won by the Pilgrims. Unlike the Pilgrims, who stepped from the *Mayflower* onto a rock and immediately started writing their memoirs, the Walloons waded ashore and never kept diaries. Instead of building quaint wooded houses, the Walloons dug holes and lived in the ground. Of the 32 Walloon families that left Amsterdam in March 1623 and reached New Netherland in May, only about eight persons, mostly men, remained on Manhattan. The rest sailed up the Hudson to establish Fort Orange. Other Walloons soon followed, and by 1628, there were 270 settlers in New Amsterdam, compared to the 300 in Plymouth. The first Director General of New Netherland was the Walloon, Pierre Minuit, who came from Wesel, near Liege.

Thirty years after the first Walloons landed, Rombout came to the colony from Hasselt, now capital of the Belgian province of Limburg, then a town in the Liege principality. Rombout and a young friend, Jan Visser, had made their way to the Netherlands and obtained passage on the New Amsterdam, owned by Adriaen Blommaert, a Manhattan burgher whose ship plied the ocean regularly between Holland and America. Rombout was taken on as super cargo, or freight manager. Visser served as a sailor. They arrived in 1653, the year that Peter Stuyvesant, then the Director General, proclaimed the incorporation of the City of New Amsterdam and established the Court of Burgomasters and Schepens, or mayors and aldermen. Rombout's early life in the colony can be traced in the records of that court.

Rombout and Visser brought suit September 1, 1653, against the ship owner, Blommaert, demanding payment of their monthly wages because they were about to depart for home. Blommaert replied politely that he wanted an account of their administration, meaning the ship's books, for which Rombout was responsible. The court named arbitrators in the case, but Rombout had already left, and he was not heard from again for more than three years. He was back on December 4, 1656, again demanding his wages, and Blommaert agreed to pay him whatever the arbitrators found fairly to belong to him.

The next time Rombout appeared in court, it was an entirely different case. On January 29, 1657, a young lady named Engeltie Mans brought suit against Geertie Jacobsen, charging that Geertie had accused her Rombout of doing something disgraceful. Engeltie demanded proof of her dishonor or punishment for the defendant. Geertie confessed that she had no personal knowledge of such dishonor, but had been told by someone else that Engeltie and Rombout were such people as nobody would suspect. Geertie was found guilty of gossip mongering and was fined 10 guilders. From then on, Rombout was in and out of the court frequently, as were other residents of New Amsterdam. Sometimes, he was a plaintiff, seeking payment for goods he had sold. At other times, he was an arbitrator in disputes.

Five years after he first set foot on Manhattan, Rombout signed a pledge November 22, 1658, to pay 20 florins worth of beaver pelts to the city, and he took the oath of a small burgher. He bought a stone house on Broadway. It was his home for the rest of his life. He made his last recorded appearance in the Dutch court June 17, 1664, acting as an attorney for a client who won a suit for payment of a bill. Two months later, the Dutch surrendered to the British, and New Amsterdam became New York. Rombout made the transition easily, his business flourished and he became active in the Mayor's Court. He was appointed by the mayor and aldermen in 1668 to the post of bread inspector. In 1679, at the age of 44, he was appointed by the governor and council to be mayor of New York. In that office, he succeeded his partner, Stephanus Van Cortlandt.

An unusual account of Rombout as mayor can be found in the *Journal of Jasper Danckaerts 1679–1680*, the diary of a member of the Labadist Protestant sect, who came to New York to explore the possibility of establishing a commune there. He was accompanied by another brother of the sect, Peter Sluyter. Rombout called them in to ask what they were up to, and when they lied to him, insisting that they were just tourists, he gave them a stern lecture, forbidding them to carry on trade and telling them to travel nowhere without permission from the governor. The account pictures Rombout as a somewhat pompous bureaucrat, but it still showed him to be a dignified gentleman, giving courteous attention to a couple of intruders.

Soon after he served his one-year term as mayor, Rombout was accused of treason. The charge was brought by a professional gambler named John Tuder, who was convicted in the Mayor's Court of cheating Abraham Smith at cards and ordered to return Smith's money. Tuder charged that Rombout was guilty of treason for denying him a trial by jury. A grand jury returned an indictment against Rombout in 1683, but the indictment was dismissed. The court of assizes ruled that what Rombout had done was not treason or any crime, but justice done to the party concerned.

Rombout married three times. In 1665, at the age of 30, he married Aeltje Wessels, and they had a son, Johannis. Within 10 years, both wife and son had died, and in 1675 Rombout married Anna Elizabeth Maschop, his first wife's sister-in-law and widow of Warner Wessels, a wine merchant. She bore no children, and soon died. Rombout was married for the third and last time September 8, 1683, to Helena Teller Van Ball, who had been twice widowed, and who had seven children from her two previous marriages. From this marriage, Catharyna Rombout, the future Madam Brett, was born. In January of 1691, Rombout went to the notary, William Bogardus, and made his will. He left his money to his wife. The will noted that he already given his land in the "Wappins" to his only surviving child,

Catharyna. In the spring of 1691, Rombout died at the age of fifty-six.

For years after the death of Rombout, nothing was done to develop his Dutchess County property. The new one-third owner, Catharyna Rombout, was only four years old when her father died. The Verplanck and Van Cortlandt families showed no interest in the region beyond the furs it provided for their trade.

Catharyna Brett grew up in the family home on Broadway. At the age of 16, she married Rogan English naval lieutenant and aide to the governor, Lord Cornbury. The Bretts filed a friendly suit in Supreme Court in 1707, asking for a division of the Rombout patent among the partners. There was no contest from the Verplancks or the Van Cortlandts, and the court issued a writ March 15, 1708, calling for partition of the property.

This was the first action of its kind in the province, the beginning of the break-up of great land grants, and its importance was recognized. The task was assigned to Sheriff Bartholomew Noxon. He recruited a team of 12 men who surveyed the 85,000 acres and divided them into three equal parts. Th Bretts obtained lot number 1, the southernmost section, which included about 28,000 acres bordering the Hudson River between the Fishkill Creek and the Wappingers Creek, including the fertile Fishkill valley. The Verplancks received lot number 2, the middle tier, from the Hudson east to the central course of the Wappingers Creek. The Van Cortlandts took lot number 3, the northernmost stretch from the Hudson to the head waters of Wappingers Creek.

The Bretts, short of cash and long on land, mortgaged the house on Broadway for 240 pounds June 8, 1708, and moved up the river to Fishkill Landing. They found a single white family living there, Peter Du Bois, a friendly French settler, and his wife Jannetje. Holwell's map of Rombout Patent, made in 1689, had shown two houses at the mouth of Wappingers Creek, marked "Ye Frenchman's." The next map of the area, made by Noxon in 1707 to illustrate the partition, showed the two buildings at the mouth of Fishkill Creek. This was where Peter Du Bois had settled. Apparently he was "Ye Frenchman." The Bretts made him a tenant for life.

At first, the Bretts followed the prevailing practice of leasing their land, rather than selling it outright. It was this practice of leasing to tenant farmers, rather than selling to freeholders, that contributed to the slow settlement of the region. Between 1708 and 1713, the Bretts gave leases to six tenants—John Terboss, 180 acres; Thomas Brasier, 100 acres; Peter Du Bois, 100; John Bois, 80; Casper Prince, 100, and Jurien Springsten, 60. When the first census of the county was taken in 1714, Brasier and Prince had disappeared, but the others were still there. Roger Brett still felt the need of cash for the house he was building inland from the river at Fishkill, and apparently he was building to apreciate the advantages of the sale of land to a freeholder over the lease to a tenant. On May 25, 1718, the Bretts sold 500 acres to Richard Townsend of Hempstead. The price was recorded as "a sum of money."

On a June day in 1718, tragedy struck the Brett family. Roger, sailing into Fishkill Landing on his sloop, was knocked overboard in a squall and drowned. The young widow, Madam Brett, 31 years old, with three sons, stayed in Dutchess County. She began to sell her land. Her first sale on July 9, 1718, conveyed 2,000 acres of some of the richest land in the county to Dirck Brinckerhoff for 800 pounds. Other Dutch families — the Van Wycks, the Storms, the Rosekrans, the Adriances — learned of the opportunity to own their own land. They flocked to Fishkill from Manhattan, from Long Island, from Westchester, and settlement in Dutchess County was on its way.

LAND GRANTS IN DUTCHESS COUNTY
Settlement or Speculation?

William P. McDermott
Editor, *Yearbook*, Dutchess County Historical Society

"In spite of the land system of colonial New York, or rather because of it, the great landowners were promoters of settlement, not its obstructors."[1] This conclusion by Sung Bok Kim, based on his recent reappraisal of the land system during the late seventeenth and early eighteenth century New York, is far too sweeping to describe accurately the intentions of the great landowners. It makes the same error in its sweeping reversal as was made by Spencer when he and others concluded, "Extravagant land grants to a few favorites. . . retarded the development and peopling of the province [New York] for many years to come."[2] However, Kim's three part description of the great landowners is a more precisely formulated and an eminently more testable proposal. Stated briefly, Kim described three types of landowners. The first group, the purely speculative investor, expected to improve the land only enough to enhance prospects for early sale. The second group, the developer with speculative interests, anticipated holding the land much longer to enhance its value through a combination of sales and leases. Settlement encouraged by these methods was expected to improve land values as newly created demand pushed purchase prices higher. The third group, devlopers for tenant settlement, were principally merchants whose interest in land was in its value to strengthen their primary interest, overseas trade. Products from the land such as wheat, in great demand in the colonies, provided cash with which imported goods could be purchased for resale.[3]

Dutchess County is particularly well suited to evaluate the results of New York's land grant system. Evidence from the period subsequent to the acquisitions indicates investment attitudes varied from one grantee to the next. Some of the land was simply sold in large or small parcels, while title to other tracts was retained by the landowner for settlement by tenants. These approaches to land use encompass all three of Kim's types of landwoners. The question to be considered is a simple one. Were the large tracts of land granted in Dutchess County acquired for speculative purposes, or were they acquired to encourage settlement? Kim's three part description of landowners is used in this paper to focus the question more sharply. If Kim's proposal is correct, the intensity of settlement in Dutchess County should have varied from one land grant to the next. Differences in the rate of settlement would have depended on the landowner's reasons for acquiring the grant. On the other hand, if Spencer's point of view is more accurate, settlement in Dutchess County should have developed quite slowly and perhaps even more slowly within the larger "extravagant" land grants. Land would have been, according to Spencer and others, just another commodity to sell when the price was attractive enough for profit. A quick sale would have been as likely as a land owner holding his land longer awaiting a better opportunity for profit. In either case Spencer's thesis concludes settlement was "retarded" for it was only the speculative value of land which fostered its acquisition.

Historical Perspective

Prior to Thomas Dongan's arrival in New York as governor in 1683, interest in settling Dutchess County appears to have been almost nil. The general area was thought to be too cold or too mountainous for cultivation, thereby limiting its potential for settlement.[4] However, after 1683 the need for vacant land north of New York City and the interest of some individuals in "up country" land stimulated a change in attitude toward Dutchess County as a potential area for settlement.

"Wee are cooped up" wrote New York Governor Thomas Dongan in a state of the province message to the Lords of Trade in early 1687 referring to the narrow boundaries of New York Province.[5] Four years earlier, land favorable for settlement had been transferred from New York to Connecticut to settle a boundary dispute between the two colonies. Almost two decades earlier New Jersey had been separated from New York, awarded by its owner the Duke of York to Lords Berkeley and Carteret. As a result of these changes New York had become a narrow stretch of land hemmed in by its neighbors. To further aggravate the situation, all the available land was "pretty well settled" according to Governor Dongan. However, he acknowledged the availability of "great quantities of very good [land]. . . up into the Country amongst our Indians."[6] The "Country" of which he spoke was the unsettled, largely unsold expanse of land between the half mile square village, New York City, and Albany. Just a few months earlier (1686) Governor Dongan had granted the 160,000 acre Livingston Manor to Robert Livingston for the purpose of "encouraging future settlement."[7] This grant was one of a number of grants he made to open to settlement the territory between New York and Albany.

Was the design for settlement initiated by Governor Dongan and continued by his successors successful? Governor Hunter thought not. Thirty years after the Livingston grant, Hunter commented in his report to the Lords of Trade, October 2, 1716, ". . .it is apparent that extravagant grants of land being held by single persons unimproved is the true cause that this Province does not increase in numbers of inhabitants in proportion to some of the neighboring ones."[8] This same theme was expressed again in 1732 by Surveyor General Cadwallader Colden who judged the large land grant approach to settlement, a failure. Colden believed New York was more attractive to settlement than its neighbors, New England and Pennsylvania, because of trade advantages. In spite of this New York had failed to settle as many inhabitants in proportion to the amount of land available. Complaining that the young people leave New York to settle in neighboring colonies, he pointed out, "it is chiefly if not only where these large Grants are made where the Country remains uncultivated—tho they contain some of the best of the Lands, and the most conveniently situated."[9]

Recently, early settlement has been studied in terms of the relationship between tenants and landlords. Two researchers, Bonomi and Kim independently, have drawn conclusions from their work which are contrary to the findings of the earlier research of Higgins, Mark, Spencer and others. [10] While the work of Bonomi and Kim, in a broad scope, presents a fine case for their conclusions, three limiting factors have a bearing on their findings. First, the period of study, usually the entire colonial period, is too long to conclude that original patentees encouraged settlement and were successful at it. Although Bonomi acknowledged the slow progress of settlement during the first years of the 18th century, she hastened to point to the substantial increase in population in later years. Noting the growth in Philipse Manor in Westchester county from about 20 families in 1701 to 270 families at the end of the colonial period, 75 years later, Bonomi and also Kim conclude there was significant population growth.[11] In fact, on the average, growth during that period was an unimpressive 3.3 families per year! And further, credit for population growth should not be given to the original patent owners. They had sold their land or passed it to heirs, some of whom had already died during the period studied by Bonomi and Kim. In fact, the change in population is attributable to the settlement strategies of later heirs in ony a few cases. Kim acknowledged the settlement of the Manor of Cortlandt "was quite slow until its first partition among the heirs of Stephanus Van Cortlandt in 1732."[12] In fact, Kim cited the 1712 census to compare the slow pace of settlement in the Manor of Cortlandt with the better results in neighboring areas. In 1712 the towns of Bedford, Eastchester, Rye and Westchester combined, contained 39,500 acres on which there lived 250 to 280 families. In contrast, only 20 to 25 families lived on the 86,500 acre Manor of Cortlandt.[13]

Secondly, comparison between the population growth within a particular manor and the overall population growth in New York Province was overlooked in these studies. Might not the settlement on these manors simply have been a reflection of more general population changes in New York Province? One historian attributed the increase in settlement in New York in later years to the pressure from the overpopulated, soil exhausted and land-limited New England inhabitants.[14] It is improper to attribute this or other similar reasons for migration which may actually have affected the entire province to favorable settlement strategies of a few large landowners or his heirs. Thirdly, no differentiation was made between growth from settlement resulting from immigration and growth from natural increase. While natural increase is certainly an important aspect of population growth, it should be taken into account before conclusion about settlement strategies by the large landowners are made. Neither Bonomi nor Kim made the distinction between increased settlement which resulted from natural increase and settlement which resulted from immigration. It is the latter which measures the landowner's ability to attract settlement.

While global judgements are necessary to understand the progress of an entire colony, it is equally important to understand from a more microscopic perspective the factors which contributed to the larger picture. It is with this in mind that the present study of Dutchess County was conceived.

Mandate for settlement

The purpose for which land grants were awarded by Governor Dongan and his successors was clearly to encourage settlement. In fact, the language of the patents often included specific reference to settlement. Even before Governor Dongan, the intent to settle the area between New York City and Albany was apparent. In 1683 interim Governor Brockholls licensed Francis Rombout and Gulian Verplanck to purchase land in Dutchess County from the Indians "for the future good of themselves and children to make improvements upon the plantation or farm."[15] Governor Dongan was even more specific in his wish to encourage settlement based on his growing concern about New York's economy. The decline in the fur trade, a staple in the economy of the province from its beginnings, presented ever increasing economic pressure. Recognizing the growing importance of agricultural products for export he awarded land on the Hudson (Rensselaer) in 1684 to Robert Sanders, Myndert Harmense and William Teller "to settle and manure land for the advancement and improvement of this province in the produce of corne stock."[16] The specific reference to "corne stock" indicates Governor Dongan's intent to encourage cultivation of that income-producing, exportable commodity. This was a major change in land usage. Previously land acquisition was primarily for the purpose of gathering furs, a commodity which neither encouraged nor supported permanent settlement.

Requiring settlement continued over the next several decades as each new governor awarded land. Jarvis Marshall and his partners were careful to impress Governor Fletcher with their intent to settle. In their 1696 request to purchase land in Orange County from the Indians, the land was described, "for the most part being rockey & mountainous land yet there being some thereof which your petitioners believe with great labor and [?] may be capable of settlement."[17] Although Paul Dufour and partners did not receive the land in Dutchess County they requested from Governor Cornbury in 1702, their stated intent "for the encouragement and further Peopling of this country" points to the consistency of the settlement theme almost two decades after Governor Dongan's arrival in New York.[18] Even land which might have had some questionable value was referred to in terms of its potential for settlement. Note the 1701 petition of Dirck Vanderburgh and Abraham Staats for a portion of Widow Pawling's patent. They described the land "hardly . . . of any other use than to erect a sawmill thereon."[19] Their petition was refused, perhaps because there was no reference to cultivation or settlement. However, four years later Jacob Regnier and Company were more successful in obtaining a patent for the identical tract of land. Their request recognized the "generally Rocky Mountainous" condition of the land but they also indicated "some small places are to be found therein fit for cultivation and improvement."[20] Although this might not have been the only reason these petitioners were successful in acquiring the land later referred to as the Fauconnier Patent, the reference to the intent to settle undoubtedly contributed to the success of their request.

Not to be overlooked is the attitude of reform brought by Governor Bellomont during the years of his tenure in office, 1698–1701. Although land was awarded for settlement purposes, the extraordinary size of the land grants given by Governor Fletcher made it apparent that settlement over such broad expanses of land was improbable. Therefore, Governor Bellomont's grants were fewer and much smaller in size. While not all of Bellomont's reforms were confirmed by the British government, the intended closer surveillance of land grants had an effect on some petitioners. For example, the petition of Sampson Broughton and others in 1702 for a land grant, later known as the

Little Nine Partners, was careful to include the words "for the better improvement of the said lands and that they may not by [be] wast."[21] The letter of patent awarded in 1706 specifically stated that settlement and some improvements were to be completed "within three years from the date of the Patent."[22] Two years later settlement had not yet occurred. Rip Van Dam, one of the partners who was also a member of the governor's council with special awareness of the attitude of the time, asked for an extension of the patent. In the new petition Van Dam and his partners complained the war between the French and Indians had produced hostile skirmishes in Connecticut and as a result had caused "fear which New Settlers lay under of the Eminent danger they should run by going to live and settle in the woods so fare [far] from other settlements & assistances and so near to the enemy."[23] The requested extension with a promise to settle and improve the land five years after the war was over was apparently granted, for the original patentees retained ownership.

The pressure for settlement and the dissatisfaction with landowners, particularly owners of large tracts, continued. In 1727 the Board of Trade's instructions to Governor Montgomerie pointed to "a very Great Hindrance to the peopling & Settling of our said province, that large tracts of land have been Ingrossed by Particular Persons, a Great Part whereof remain Uncultivated." The Board threatened forfeiture of land grants which did not "plant, Settle and effectually Cultivate, at least three Acres of Land for every fifty Acres, within three years, after the same shall be granted."[24] Fifty years after Governor Dongan took office, continuing concern about the lack of settlement provoked Cadwallader Colden's scathing criticism of large landowners, ". . . the Grantees themselves are not, nor never were in a Capacity to improve such large Tracts . . ." Charging the large landowners' interest was for personal gain only, he concluded ". . . the Governor who granted them [large land grants] was deceived as to quantity; but the King was deceived in all of them."[25]

While the initial intent for granting land was to encourage and even require settlement, it appears the overall result of the settlement program was marked more by failure than success. Was this the case in Dutchess County?

Settlement in Dutchess County: Growth

Settlement in Dutchess County began in the late 1680's shortly after the first land grant was awarded. The first census taken in 1703, when Dutchess was still under the administrative supervision of Ulster County, recorded approximately 70 settlers or 10 to 12 families.[26] Eleven years later in 1714 Dutchess, then with its own government, reported 330 individuals (including slaves) in 49 families inhabiting the county.[27] These statistics reflect a substantial growth in population in little more than a decade. This pattern of population growth continued through 1731 when the census recorded 1615 individuals living in Dutchess. The county assessment roll for that year corroborates that finding, listing 339 names of families.

TABLE 1
Number of heads of household in each ward 1714–1733

	1714	1718	1721	1724	1727	1730	1733
North	9	64	83	101	121	145	160
Middle	22	34	39	47	70	100	133
South	18	31	42	47	62	76	96
Total	49	129	164	195	253	321	389

Source: Book of the Supervisors of Dutchess County 1718–1733.

Table 1 lists the total number of heads of household as listed on the 1714 census and on the assessment rolls from 1718 to 1733, fifty years after the first land grant was awarded in Dutchess County. All individuals owning or leasing land were required to pay taxes. As a result the early assessment rolls can be regarded with confidence as a true reflection of the number of families residing in Dutchess each year. Evident in Table 1 is the continuous and steady increase in population over the twenty year period, 1714–1733. In fact the average rate of growth was approximately 8% annually. At that rate population doubles every decade. And in fact as Table 1 reflects, population doubled between 1718 and 1727.

In spite of its growth in population Dutchess County continued to be the least settled county through 1731, except for Richmond County (Staten Island), a county far smaller in size. During the period 1698 to 1731 the population in New York Province increased almost threefold. A population of 15,897 in 1698 grew to 43,040 by 1731. Dutchess County grew at the same rate during that period. Therefore, it appears the increase in population in Dutchess may simply have been a reflection of the general growth in population in New York Province. However, it must be noted, population growth in the province differed from county to county. In fact the rate of growth in the counties north of New York City was dramatically greater than that of New York County and the counties adjacent to or east of it, Kings, Queens, Richmond and Suffolk. These counties grew from a total of 12,099 individuals in 1698 to 24,003 in 1731. But the counties north of New York City, Albany, Dutchess, Orange, Ulster and Westchester grew from 3,798 in 1698 to 19,037 in 1731. Much of this growth occurred in Albany, 1,453 individuals in 1698 to 7,300 in 1731 and Westchester, 917 individuals in 1698 to 5,341 in 1731. In fact, two thirds of the population north of New York City in 1731 resided in the older and earlier-settled counties of Albany and Westchester. Ulster, which had also been settled at an early date, did not participate as fully in the population growth as did Albany and Westchester.

One way to appreciate the shifting rate of population growth is to compare change in each county in terms of percent of total population in the entire province. For example, note the change in Queens County. Although it grew in population between 1703 and 1731, its share of the total population in the province decreased from 21.5% in 1703 to 15.6% in 1731. On the other hand Albany which had 11.3% of the total population in 1703 had grown by 1731 to a 17% share. Dutchess also grew during the same period from a .5% share of the total population in 1703 to a 3.8% share in 1731. While its growth was less than that of Albany and Westchester, its rate of growth exceeded that of all other counties except Orange County which grew at about the same rate of Dutchess. Clearly, Dutchess, although growing slowly, was growing at a greater rate than much of New York Province.

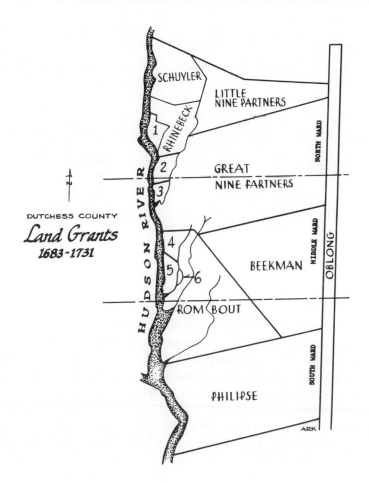

DUTCHESS COUNTY
Land Grants
1683-1731

Based on map from Dutchess County Historical Society *Year-book*, Volume 24 (1939), p. 52.

Legend of Small Patents
1. Aertson, Roosa, Elton
2. Pawling
3. Fauconnier
4. Sanders & Harmanse
5. Cuyler

31

The conclusions which can be drawn from the above discussion are as follows: 1. Dutchess County grew from an unsettled territory in 1683 to one where settlement, once initiated, grew at a steady rate. 2. The rate of population growth in Dutchess exceeded the general increase in population in New York Province. 3. Dutchess participated in the general shift of population in the province as a whole. Specifically, as the proportion of population in the southern counties declined, there was a compensatory increase in the proportion of population settling in the counties north of New York County.

Settlement in Dutchess County: the Patents

The question examined in this paper is how successful was the land grant policy in the settlement of Dutchess County. A related inquiry focuses on the individual land grants. Were they merely speculative ventures or were they used for the purpose for which they were awarded—to encourage settlement?

To begin, note Table 1 lists three wards, North, Middle and South Wards. These three wards were the civil divisions into which Dutchess County, which included Putnam County at the time, was divided during the years 1718 to 1738. Two east-west lines from the Hudson River to Connecticut divided the county into three approximately equal wards. These three wards encompassed all of the land grants in Dutchess County.

The map attached illustrates the size of all the land grants in Dutchess. Eight of the fourteen patents were substantial tracts of land. Of these eight, four were granted to individuals and four were granted to partnerships. The large patents held by individuals were: Beekman & Rhinebeck Patents, both granted to Henry Beekman, Schuyler Upper Patent granted to Peter Schuyler, and the Philipse Patent, now Putnam County, granted to Adolph Philipse. The large patents held in partnerships were the Great Nine Partners, Little Nine Partners, Rombout and the Oblong. The six smaller patents, which together did not exceed thirty thousand acres, were held similarly. Three were granted to partnerships and three were granted to individuals.

In 1733, fifty years after the first license for a land grant was awarded, 389 families were settled in Dutchess County. Table 2 tabulates the number of new families who settled during the periods specified.

Table 2
Growth of settlement during the period 1683–1733

Period	Total # of families at the end of each period	# of families added each period	Average # of families added each year	Average # of families added each year, each patent
1688–1703	12	—	.75	.10
1704–1714	49	37	3.36	.42
1715–1719	134	85	17.00	2.13
1720–1724	195	61	12.20	1.53
1725–1729	280	85	17.00	2.13
1730–1733	389	109	27.25	3.41

Immediately apparent from Table 2 is the steady increase in the number of families settling in Dutchess County during the fifty year period. Although the average growth each year as shown in column 4 was steady, it was not particularly impressive. Column 5 also points to very slow progress in settlement. This is a particularly important statistic because it sheds light on how well patent owners, on average, were living up to their agreement to settle land. In order to allow for the differences in size between the seven large patents and the six smaller ones, the six small ones were treated as one. The Oblong was excluded from the computations because it was not available for settlement until 1731. Therefore, eight patents divided into the number recorded in column 4 provides the average number of additional families settled on each patent, each year. Growth was quite slow. For example, during the period 1704–1714, on the average only one new family settled on each patent every two years. Although a great improvement is recorded for the period ending 1733, the average of 3.41 new families per patent per year is disappointing. Although some patents grew at a faster rate than others, there was almost no settlement on others. However, even taking differences in growth rates between patents into consideration, the conclusion remains essentially the same. Settlement in Dutchess County, when the number of patents and the large expanse of land available are considered, was tediously slow during the first fifty year period.

Although the growth in population in Dutchess County was slow, there were, in 1733, 389 families where fifty years earlier there were no white settlers. How much of the population growth was the result of new families who moved into Dutchess and how much of the growth was the result of natural increase? This question is significant because it serves as a basis for measuring the capability of each large landowner to attract new settlers during the period under study. To answer this question the names of new settlers were gathered from the total number of settlers found on the census or assessment rolls for each five year period between 1714 and 1733. This list of new settlers, when compared to the list of heads of households who remained from the previous five year interval, provided a list of heads of households who shared surnames in common. Genealogical information was then gathered for 80% of these heads of households with surnames in common. In this way new settlers were divided into two groups, (1) those settlers related to former and still resident settlers and (2) those settlers who were new arrivals in Dutchess County since the previous five year period. Where genealogical information was unavailable an educated guess, based on collateral evidence, placed the remaining 20% in the appropriate category. Note that even this procedure probably resulted in an underestimation of families related to previously settled families. No attempt was made to seek out those of the newly settled group who were related by marriage but with different surnames. For example, a daughter, newly married since the previous five year interval, was recorded as a new settler under her husband's name when, in fact, there was a significant relationship with a previous settler. The result is a slight underestimation of family relationships and a slight overestimation of new settlers. Table 3 records the findings of these procedures.

Table 3
Number of Settlers by Category

	1718	1723	1728	1733
Remaining from previous period	41	116	156	232
Offspring of previous settler	8	21	31	54
Brother, cousin or nephew	5	4	9	13
New settlers	75	46	66	90
Total	129	187	262	389

Several observations can be made based on the information in Table 3: (1) On the average 87% of settlers from each five year period remained in Dutchess to become part of the population recorded in the next five year period. (2) Except for the 1718 period when a large group of Palatines moved into Dutchess, about 24% of the population in any five year interval were new settlers unrelated to previous settlers. (3) Offspring and relatives accounted for 15% (12.3% and 2.9% respectively) of the new population in any given period. (4) Three of every five settlers added to the assessment roll at any given interval were new settlers while two were related to former settlers.

What conclusions can be drawn? Population growth, although slow, continued at a steady rate throughout the period studied. And further, growth from natural increase contributed to the overall growth in population almost as much as growth from immigration. Therefore, it appears the success of the large landowner to attract settlers was attributable almost as much to the procreative activity of the previous settlers as it was to the ability of the large landowner to attract new settlers. When comparing this information with that found in column 5 of Table 2, one can conclude that only 2 of the 3.41 families were new settlers. The remaining 1.41 were related to previous settlers. The results from Table 2 and Table 3 combined further strengthens the earlier conclusion—settlement in Dutchess

County as a result of the entrepreneurship of large landowners as a group was indeed tediously slow and in fact, far from being successful during the first fifty year period of Dutchess County history.

Visualizing the 389 families listed on the 1733 assessment roll living on an expanse of land containing well over one-half million acres, five decades after the first patent was awarded brings into sharp focus the sparseness of settlement in Dutchess County. A contemporary historian, William Smith, in concluding his description of the limited settlement in Dutchess wrote in 1732, "The only villages in it [Dutchess] are Poughkeepsing and the Fish-kill though they scarce deserve the name."[28]

The final purpose of this study is to determine where in Dutchess County settlement occurred. This information will disclose which of the patent grantees encouraged settlement, however sparse it was. The civil divisions of the county in 1733, wards, did not follow patent lines. For example, the Middle Ward included Fauconnier, Sanders and Harmense, and the Schuyler (Poughkeepsie) patents as well as parts of the Beekman, Great Nine Partners and Rombout Patents. Fortunately, six years later in 1739, the three wards were divided into precincts which except in a couple of cases followed patent lines. Therefore, the 1733 and 1739 assessment rolls can be compared to determine on which patents settlement occurred. Assuming the place where a family lived in 1739 was the same as it was six years earlier was considered reasonably safe, although a few small errors may have crept into the results. The names of the 389 families listed in 1733 were compared to the names of the families listed in 1739 to determine which families remained in 1739. As noted in Table 4, 293 of the 389 families remained. Ninety-six families had either left the county, died or passed their land to children so they, although still residing in the county, had no taxable estate.

Table 4
Assessment roll for 1733 separated into place of residence in 1739

Precinct	Number of residents
Not listed in 1739	96
Beekman	35
Fishkill	58
Nine Partners	19
Northeast	3
Poughkeepsie	52
Rhinebeck	119
Southern	7
Total	389

Table 4 summarizes the results. The pattern which emerges describes the relative strength of settlement in each patent. Immediately apparent is the large number of families residing in the Rhinebeck precinct and the small numbers in Northeast and Southern precincts. Identifying the patents from the precincts is especially easy because of the clear divisions. The Rhinebeck precinct included Beekman's upper patent, Schuyler's upper patent (Red Hook), the 4,000 acre Pawling Patent and two smaller patents incorporated into Beekman's upper patent. Northeast precinct included only the Little Nine Partners Patent. Southern precinct included only the Philipse Highland Patent, now all of Putnam County. To complete the identifications, Beekman precinct was Henry Beekman's interior patent. Fishkill included all of the Rombout Patent except for a small area near Poughkeepsie. Nine Partners precinct included the Great Nine Partners Patent and the approximately 6,000 acre Fauconnier Patent. Poughkeepsie precinct included Sanders and Harmense, Schuyler (Poughkeepsie), Cuyler gore and the small area east not included in the Rombout Patent. The Oblong Patent was divided between the Beekman, Nine Partners and Northeast precincts.

These findings can be summarized as follows:

1. The Rhinebeck and Beekman Patents granted to Henry Beekman appear to have played a major role in the settlement of Dutchess County. The number of families on these two patents account for more than half of all the families living in Dutchess County in 1733. The number of families who lived in the other patents included in the Rhinebeck precinct are too few to affect the conclusion.

2. Settlement on the following major patents was insignificant: Great Nine Partners, Little Nine Partners, Philipse Highland and the Oblong Patents. Only about 10% of the population of the county settled on these patents combined.

3. Although accounting for only 18% of the population, Poughkeepsie precinct, in spite of its small size, contained a greater share of the population than its size alone would command.

4. Fishkill precinct, which included most of the Rombout Patent, accounted for 20% of the population of the county—a moderate success in settlement.

One general conclusion which can be drawn from these findings is that settlement, except for Beekman's interior patent, appears to have clung to a narrow corridor along the Hudson River. And even that corridor was not settled evenly. Settlement probably clustered near the villages of Fishkill, Poughkeepsie and Rhinebeck. Confirmation of this narrow pattern of settlement is obtained from the description of Dutchess County roads extant in 1733.[29] The principle north-south road, in places barely more than a trail of blazened trees, hugged the Hudson River as it traversed the length of the county. From this there were several short roads to landings on the Hudson. Additionally there were two roads from Beekman's interior patent. The road from Poughquag, in existence since 1722, brought settlers to the landing on the Hudson in Fishkill. Approved in 1732, a new road, only a footpath in some places, traveled from Dover near the Connecticut line to the landing on the Hudson in Poughkeepsie.

A more specific conclusion which can be drawn from the findings is, Henry Beekman and son had developed a successful method for attracting and retaining settlers. Providing land on which the Palatines, abandoned by the government in 1712, could settle, provided a solid base of settlers for their two land grants thereby making a significant contribution to the early settlement of Dutchess County. Colonel Peter Schuyler, awarded the patent which occupied the northern portion of the Rhinebeck precinct, appears to have had little more than speculative interests. He sold the northernmost one-third of his land grant one year after receiving it.[30] While he held the remaining two-thirds for a longer period of time, settlement activity in the remaining portion seems to have been minimal or nil.

Failure is the most succinct way of describing the settlement activity of the owners of the three largest patents, the Great Nine Partners (Nine Partners precinct), Little Nine Partners (Northeast precinct) and Philipse Highland (Southern precinct). In fact, none of these, except for a small portion on the Hudson River of the Great Nine Partners, had been subdivided in preparation for settlement by 1733. Unlike Henry Beekman Jr., none of the owners of these patents appear to have made any provision for settlement by 1733.

Settlement on the land within the Poughkeepsie precinct seems to have succeeded because of early rentals and sales to individuals with farming or mercantile interests. They seem to have come to Poughkeepsie to stay. The patents on which most of the settlement occurred in Poughkeepsie precinct were Sanders-Harmense and Schuyler patents. Colonel Peter Schuyler, awarded his patent in 1688, had completely disposed of it by 1699, selling it in three large portions as he had done in his upper patent.[31] His interests appear to have been speculative. The absence of settlement on the patent until after he sold it confirms his speculative interest. In contrast, Robert Sanders and Myndert Harmense Van Den Bogardt seemed to have encouraged settlement through transfer of land prior to 1691 to tenants, one of whom was Sanders' brother-in-law Baltus Barentse Van Kleeck.[32] Also, Harmense built a saw mill before 1699 further indicating settlement plans for himself and others. [33] In fact, his widow and son appeared separately on the first census taken in 1714 as did Thomas Sanders, a mill owner and son of the patentee, Robert. It should also be noted that one of Schuyler's three sales was made to Robert Sanders and Myndert Harmense Van Den Bogardt.[34] These facts support the conclusion that settlement in Poughkeepsie was encouraged by Harmense and Sanders in contrast to the speculative interests of Peter Schuyler.

Settlement began on Rombout patent (Fishkill precinct), awarded in 1685 to Francis Rombout (died 1691), Gulian Verplanck (died 1684) and Stephanus Van Cortlandt (died 1700), after 1708 when it was partitioned into three parts by the heirs of the original patentees. The only impetus for settlement came from Roger Brett and his wife, Catharine, daughter and heir of Francis Rombout. Roger's untimely death in 1718 changed their initial plan from tenant settlement to land distribution through a combination of leaseholds and sales in fee simple.[35]

Some historians explain the limited settlement on the large land grants was the result of (a) the problems related to joint ownership and (b) the unavailability of settlers.[36] The problems of joint ownership were several. First, the prospective buyer had to obtain a release from all partners to be sure he had a secure, clear title. Second, reaching agreement about dividing the patent for sale was difficult after the death of one or more of the original patentees because heirs were too many or in some cases inaccessible. And finally, the law passed in 1708 permitting a simple majority of patentees to decide to partition rather than requiring unanimous agreement was not renewed in 1718.[37] As a result joint owners wishing to divide before 1708 or after 1719 were required to obtain special permission from the assembly or governor, a time consuming and expensive procedure.

How did this affect the jointly owned Dutchess County patents, Rombout, Great Nine Partners and Little Nine Partners? Of these, only the Little Nine Partners had not been divided by the owners at least once. Rombout was divided into three parcels in 1708, apparently without difficulty. The Great Nine Partners made a small division in 1699 before the number of partners swelled to nineteen.[38] An attempt made by the Great Nine Partners in 1725 to have the New York Assembly pass an act permitting further division failed. It might appear from this failure that conditions external to the partnership were responsible for retarding settlement on the patent. But five years later the one remaining original patentee, David Jamison, a prominent and very successful attorney, discovered a paragraph within the original deed for the first division in 1699 which read, "And that all further divisions to be done shall be ordered by the parties, or so many of them at least as shall be owners of the greatest part of said land . . . ."[39] Although it is difficult to ascribe intent because of the absence of personal notes from the shareholders in the Great Nine Partners company, it is equally difficult to conclude there was a great interest in division and settlement when the existence of such a significant paragraph, which essentially gave permission to divide, was overlooked for thirty years. Interestingly, Jamison was only one of two attorneys in the partnership; William Huddleston was the other.[40] The small number of settlers on the Great Nine Partners patent before 1733 attests to the lack of interest in encouraging settlement especially with a portion of the patent located on the Hudson River. And finally, settlement on the Little Nine Partners patent appears to have been absent until 1734, when the assembly approved the patentees' first request to divide the land.[41]

The remaining four large land grants in Dutchess County were owned by individuals. One is clearly an example of speculation, Schuyler's upper patent. The Philipse Highland patent was not partitioned until 1751. The remaining two large patents were Beekman's Rhinebeck patent and his interior patent, both of which were settled.

It appears the nature of the ownership was not the deciding factor in settlement. Some grants to individuals as well as to partnerships were settled. On the other hand grants to other individuals or partnerships were treated as speculative ventures. Nor was partnership a limiting factor in the Minisink Patent in Orange County. It was granted to twenty-three partners in 1704, four of whom were partners in two Dutchess County patents. The Minisink patentees were able in 1711 to reach agreement to divide a 56,000 acre section of the grant. Over the next twenty years 6,000 acres were sold in parcels ranging in size from 350 to 1,320 acres.[42] Although 6,000 acres is a small amount, the fact that partition and sales of land could occur within a complex partnership indicates partnership in and of itself was not necessarily a limiting factor in partitioning or settlement.

The question of availability of settlers is also raised in defense of the large landowner, apparently unsuccessful in settling his patent. Often cited is Philip Livingston's letter in 1741 to John De Witt in which he remarked, "its no Easy matter to gett 17 families at once."[43] Admittedly it may have been difficult to get 17 families at one time but families were available. The substantial increase in population in the province as a whole before 1733 attests to this. It was the differing attitudes toward settlement and the purpose for which land was acquired that determined success, rather than any limitation on the availability of settlers. Certainly, Henry Beekman and son demonstrated an ability to draw settlers at a time when patents adjoining theirs were considerably less successful.

Dutchess County
1737

On December 16, 1737, the county was divided into seven precincts. Precinct lines were drawn along the early patent lines. Listed below are the precints and the patents which were included in each precinct.

PRECINCT	PATENTS
South	Philipse
Rombout	Rombout excluding land west of Wappinger Creek
Beekman	Beekman
Poughkeepsie	Sanders & Harmanse Schuyler Cuyler Rombout west of the Wappinger Creek
Crum Elbow	Great Nine Partners Fauconnier
Rhinebeck	Rhinebeck Schuyler Aertson, Roosa, Elton Pawling
Northeast	Little Nine Partners

Note: Precinct lines were extended into the Oblong on December 17, 1743.

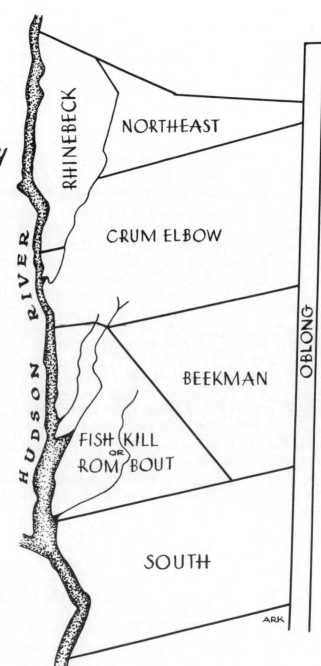

Conclusions

The manner in which the large land grants were used by their owners in the early 18th century is consistent with the model proposed by Kim.[44] Dutchess County's one commercial landlord fits Kim's model. Henry Beekman and son, although not active in overseas trade, enhanced their personal wealth through sales of agricultural products. As a result they played a major role in the settlement of Dutchess County, accounting for half the settlement in the entire county during its earliest years. The second category proposed by Kim is the landowner who developed land to enhance personal wealth by taking steps to increase its value. Into this category fall landowners such as Sanders and Harmense and Roger and Catharine Brett. Their efforts encouraged settlement in the Poughkeepsie and Fishkill areas, although at a rate considerably slower than recorded in the Beekmans' patents. The final category of landowner is the purely speculative entrepreneur whose interest in the land was no greater than as a commodity for sale without further personal or economic investment in it. Into this category fell the majority of patentees in Dutchess County. Land speculators such as Peter Schuyler, Adolph Philipse, the Great Nine Partners and the Little Nine Partners owned and controlled more than two-thirds of the land. As further evidence of their purely speculative interest one has only to note Schuyler's sales prior to 1700, the outright sale two years after receiving the patent of four of the Great Nine Partners and the failure of the speculators listed above to divide their patents. The land controlled by these speculators did not contribute to the settlement of Dutchess County until after 1740 in the Great Nine Partners patent and after 1750 in the Little Nine Partners patent and Philipse Highland patent.

Was Charles W. Spencer correct in his conclusion that the large landowners were primarily speculators and because of that they "retarded the development and peopling of the province"? By 1733 about ten percent of the land in Dutchess County was settled. Two-thirds of it was controlled by speculators; the remainder was settled only sparsely. On the basis of this study one might conclude in favor of Spencer's interpretation were it not for other factors. For example, the pool of potential settlers in New York, although growing at a significant rate, nevertheless, was finite. Competition among landowners interested in settling families from that pool must have existed. Note the great increase in population in Albany and Westchester counties. Was this the result of successful inducements from some landowners? While this may have been a factor, other conditions, some fortuitous, such as the effect on Beekman's patents of the government's failure to continue support of the Palatines, may have had a equal or more critical impact. One important possibility which may have accounted for the earlier increase in settlement in Albany and Westchester as compared to Dutchess and Ulster was the more cosmopolitan character of the culture in the former counties. Dutchess and Ulster greatly reflected the Dutch influence and as a result may have been regarded as too parochial by the newer settlers whose background was English. The common bond in the Dutch-German background must have facilitated integration and cooperation among them in Dutchess County. Nevertheless, Spencer's judgment as it relates to Dutchess County and other parts of New York cannot be discarded easily. It applies in some instances, but it must also integrate the more recent understandings which have emerged about the early land grants.

Cadwallader Colden, the harshest contemporary critic of the land system, commented in 1726, "some men in this Province own above two hundred thousand Acres of Land each which neither they nor their Great Grand Children can hope to Improve . . . ." Surely this describes some landowners.[45] Recently Kim's conclusion "the great landowners were promoters of settlement, not its obstructors", describes others.[46] The truth, as it applies to Dutchess County and perhaps to most of New York, lies somewhere between these two observations.

Notes

1. Sung Bok Kim, "A New Look at the Great Landlords of the Eighteenth Century," *William and Mary Quarterly*, 3rd Series XXVII (1970), 614.

2. Charles W. Spencer, *Phases of Royal Government in New York 1691-1719* (Columbus, Ohio, 1905), 7-8.

3. Kim, "A New Look at the Great Landlords," 595–598.

4. Sung Bok Kim, *Landlord and Tenant in Colonial New York: Manorial Society, 1664–1775* (Chapel Hill, N.C., 1978), 22–24.

5. Edmund B. O'Callaghan, ed., *Documents Relative to the Colonial History of the State of New York* (16 vols.; Albany, N.Y. 1856–1887), III, 397.

6. *N.Y. Col. Docs.*, III, 397.

7. *N.Y. Col. Docs.*, III, 625.

8. *N.Y. Col. Docs.*, V, 480.

9. Edmund B. O'Callaghan, ed., *Documentary History of the State of New York* (4 vols.; Albany, N. Y. 1849–1851), I, 384. (Hereafter cited as *Doc. Hist. N. Y.*).

10. Patricia U. Bonomi, *A Factious People: Politics and Society in Colonial New York* (New York, 1971), chap. 6, 179–228; Kim, "A New Look at the Great Landlords," 613–614; Ruth L. Higgins, *Expansion in New York with Especial Reference to the Eighteenth Century* (Columbus, Ohio, 1931), 24–25; Irving Mark, *Agrarian Conflicts in Colonial New York 1711–1775* (New York, 1940), 65–66, 72–75, 195; Charles W. Spencer, "The Land System of Colonial New York," *New York Historical Association, Proceedings*, XVI (1917), 162–163; Frederick J. Turner, *The Frontier in American History* (New York, 1920), 82–83.

11. Bonomi, *A Factious People*, 195; Kim, "A New Look at the Great Landlords," 613.

12. Sung Bok Kim, "The Manor of Cortlandt and Its Tenants, 1696–1783," (Unpubl. Ph.D. diss., Michigan State University, 1966).

13. *Ibid.*, 83 & 85.

14. Dixon R. Fox, *Yankees and Yorkers* (New York, 1940), 182–183, 191–193.

15. *New York Colonial Manuscripts, Land Papers, 1642–1803*, 63 volumes, New York State Library, II, 14. (Hereafter cited as *Land Papers*)

16. *Land Papers*, II, 31.

17. *Land Papers*, III, 30.

18. *Land Papers*, III, 71.

19. *Land Papers*, III, 15.

20. *Land Papers*, III, 175.

21. *Land Papers*, III, 93.

22. *Land Papers*, IV, 135.

23. *Land Papers*, IV, 135.

24. "Governor Montgomerie's Instructions, 20 October 1727," Instruction #38 & #36, *The Letters and Papers of Cadwallader Colden*. New York Historical Society, *Collections, 1917–1923*, (7 vols.; New York, 1918–1924), I, 211. Earlier, similar conditions and the threat of forfeiture had been included in the Board of Trade's instructions to Governor John Lovelace in 1708, *N.Y. Col. Docs.* V, 54 and to Governor Robert Hunter in 1709, *N.Y. Col.*, V, 141.

25. *Doc. Hist. N.Y.*, I, 384–385.

26. Estimate based on data from Everts B. Greene and Virginia D. Harrington, *American Population Before the Federal Census of 1790* (New York, 1932), xxiii. This estimate excludes the portion of Dutchess County transferred to Albany County in 1717.

27. William P. McDermott, "The 1714 Dutchess County Census: Measure of Household Size," *Yearbook*, Dutchess County Historical Society, LXVIII (1983), 164.

28. William Smith, *The History of the Province of New York . . . to 1762* (2 vols; London, 1757; reprint Cambridge, Mass., 1972, Michael Kammen, ed.), 211.

29. *Old Miscellaneous Records of Dutchess County, 1722–1747* (Vassar Brothers Institute, Poughkeepsie, N. Y., 1909), 154 & 160.

30. Dutchess County Clerk's Office, Deeds, Liber 2, 398; Robert Livingston Papers, Series II, Reel 28, item #26, Schuyler sale to Gansevoort, June 18, 1689.

31. Helen W. Reynolds, "Poughkeepsie: The Origin and Meaning of the Word," Dutchess County Historical Society, *Collections* (Poughkeepsie, N. Y., 1924), I, 29–31.

32. *Ibid.*, 77; Helen W. Reynolds, "How Poughkeepsie Was Founded," *Yearbook*, Dutchess County Historical Society, XV (1930), 30–35.

33. Dutchess County Clerk's Office, Deeds, Liber 1, 278.

34. Reynolds, Poughkeepsie, 29.

35. Helen W. Reynolds, ed., *Eighteenth Century Records, Dutchess County, New York: Rombout Precinct and the Original Town of Fishkill*, Dutchess County Historical Society, *Collections* (Poughkeepsie, N. Y., 1938),

VI, 1–7. Also see map made in 1728 by Robert Crooke, Deputy Surveyor, "Land in Verplanck portion of Rombout Patent," copy in Adriance Memorial Library, Poughkeepsie, N. Y., original in New York Public Library. Also note Philip Van Cortlandt, heir of one of the owners of the Rombout Patent had only six tenants on his share of the Cortlandt Manor in 1746. Kim, "Landlord and Tenant in Colonial New York," 151.

36. Kim, "A New Look at the Great Landlords," 593–594, 601; Bonomi, *A Factious People*, 197; Armand La Potin, "The Minisink Grant: Partnerships, Patents, and Processing Fees in Eighteenth Century New York," *New York History*, LVI (1975), 36–41.

37. Charles Z. Lincoln, ed., *The Colonial Laws of New York from the Year 1664 to the Revolution* (5 vols; Albany, 1894), I, 633, 882, 1006; *N. Y. Col. Docs.*, V, 527, 529–530.

38. "Proceedings of the Nine Partners 1730–1749," trans. by Clifford Buck and William P. McDermott in William P. McDermott, ed., *Eighteenth Century Documents of the Nine Partners Patent, Dutchess County, New York*, Dutchess County Historical Society, *Collections* (Poughkeepsie, N. Y., 1979), X, 3–4.

39. *Ibid*, 4.

40. Paul M. Hamlin and Charles E. Baker, eds., *Supreme Court of Judicature of the Province of New York, 1691–1704*, New York Historical Society, *Collections*, 1945–1947, (3 vols.; New York, 1952–1959), III, 104–107.

41. Passed by the New York Assembly, November 28, 1734. *Colonial Laws of New York*, II, 868–870.

42. La Potin, "The Minisink Grant," 43–46.

43. Kim, "A New Look at the Great Landlords," 601; Bonomi, *A Factious People*, 197.

44. Kim, "A New Look at the Great Landlords," 595–598.

45. "The Second Part of the Interest of the County in Laying Duties," *The Letters and Papers of Cadwallader Colden*, New York Historical Society, *Collections*, 1934–1935 (2 vols.; New York, 1935–1937), II, 268.

46. Kim, "A New Look at the Great Landlords," 614.

Early Settlers in the Beekman Patent

Frank Doherty

The Beekman Patent in Dutchess County was the second largest of the original patents, exceeded only by the Great Nine Partners and followed closely by the Rombout. The land was granted to Henry Beekman after he petitioned the Governor of New York Province for it in 1695. On April 22, 1697 he obtained a patent which is referred to as the Rhinebeck Patent, and in a report of the Board of Trade "on the affairs of the Province of New York," dated Whitehall, October 19, 1698 we read the following:

> "The next head under which we shall humbly represent to your Excellencies the rise of those difficulties which the Earl of Bellomont meets with in the administration of that government is the Grants of Lands made by the late Governor; and in order thereunto, we beg leave, in the first place, to set down a list of such grants whereof his Lordship has sent us either Copies or Abstracts: with this observation, that the lands therein mentioned are not laid out by exact measure of acres, but computed in the lump by miles. . . ."

> "A Grant to Colonel Henry Beekman for a tract of land in Dutchess County, containing about sixteen miles square; and likewise for another tract of land upon Hudson's River about eight miles in breadth and twenty miles in length."[1]

The Beekman Patent, or "Back Lots" as they were called were thus established as of the 1698 date. The man who obtained this grant which led to the settlement of a large part of Dutchess County was the son of William Beekman.

William Beekman, the father of the patentee came to New Amsterdam, now New York, with Governor Stuyvesant, in 1647. He was born in Holland, of German ancestry, on the 28th of April, 1623 and he married Catherine DeBough, of the City of New York, on the 25th of September, 1649, by whom he had seven children—three sons and four daughters. He died in the city of New York in 1707, in the 85th year of his age. In 1653, 1654, 1655, 1656, and 1657 he was elected one of the schepens (assistant aldermen) of New Amsterdam. On the 18th of October, 1658, he was appointed vice-governor on the Delaware: on the 4th of July, 1664, he was elected sheriff of Esopus, now Kingston. On the 16th of August, 1647, he was elected burgomaster of New Amsterdam, the Dutch having recovered, and restored the old name to the city during this year. The old New York records tell us that the business by which he lived and prospered was that of a brewer. His sons were Henry, Gerard and John. Henry, the eldest, was the patentee of Ryn Beck and Beekman.

Henry Beekman married Joanna DeLopes, and settled in Kingston, Ulster County, where he became county judge, member of the legislature, colonel of the militia, and deacon and elder of the Reformed Dutch Church. He never lived in Rhinebeck, but it was he who laid out the land for the "High Dutchers," and settled on his patent the Palatines who founded Rhinebeck, and gave the name to the town. He died in 1716, not above sixty-six years old; and there are very few deeds over his own signature extant. He had four children, as follows: William, born at Kingston in 1681, died in Holland, aged eighteen; Catherine, born September 16, 1683, married John Rutsen, of Kingston; Henry, born in 1688, married Janet Livingston, the daughter of Robert, a nephew of Robert, the patentee, and first Lord of the Manor of Livingston; Cornelia, born 1690, married Gilbert Livingston, son of Robert, the Lord of the Manor.[2]

In 1717 Dutchess County was divided into three wards with the Beekman Patent being in both the South and Middle Wards. These divisions made it easier to keep tabs on settlers and taxes were collected from then on. On December 16, 1737 a law was passed dividing Dutchess County into

Precincts because "the number of inhabitants is much increased and many new settlements have been made whereby it is become necessary for the ease and convenience of the inhabitants thereof, That the Said County Should be Divided into more precincts." The law further stated, "Beekman Precinct to contain all that land that was granted to Colo. Henry Beekman Deceast lying to the rear of the Patent granted to Francis Rombout & Co."[3]

Several years earlier, the heirs of Colonel Henry Beekman had subdivided the patent into 25 separate lots. These lots were then owned by Gilbert Livingston and Cornelia Beekman Livingston, Henry Beekman Jr. who married Janet Livingston and Catherine Beekman who married John Rutsen. The lots were generally 80 chains wide (one mile) and about eight miles long. The writer has completed a study of the original leases in lots 17 and 18 which were demised to Gilbert Livingston. This study involved mapping the leases in these two lots and following the settlement of the area by the various groups of immigrants who came here.

The first settlers of Dutchess County were the Dutch, who had gone from New York City right to Albany after 1625, and only began living in Dutchess County after 1680. In 1692 Fishkill was the home of less than one-half dozen families. Among these were the families of Jan Buys and Jon Ter Bos. Jan Buys had a large family and they were very influential in settling lots 17 and 18. Later, in 1710, the Palatine refugees added significantly to the population of Rhinebeck and parts of the Beekman Patent. After about 1740 the English began to come in from New England and Long Island. Many of these people were Quakers and settled in villages around their meeting houses.

Probably one of the most significant single events in the settlement of central Dutchess County occurred in 1733–1734 when Johannis Buys approached Henry Beekman about obtaining some land. Prior to this date there had been scattered squatters on the Beekman Patent, but they were few. They included the Cools, the Mastens, Josias Crego and several Palatine families on Clapp Hill and in the Clove, but no push for settlement had occurred. The land in this general area was considered poor and no one had made much effort to settle it. On February 29, 1733–1734 Henry Beekman wrote a letter to Gilbert Livingston, his brother-in-law, telling him of his meeting with Buys. The text of the letter follows:

> "Loving Brother   New York 29 Feb. 1733–34
>
> I hope these may find you and family in health as we here at present are. I suppose you have received myn with what I sent by Isaac King. I had with me Johannis Buys, who had commissioned for himself and others (to about 20) who wanted to bargain for to hyre or buy about 2000 acres on a ridge near Josiah Criegers. Told him he must apply to you. I mentioned no articles and them we should not neglect. Better to doe something when such people of the country do offer, especially since it be for land (as for my part did not know there was any good thereabout). Our paper war still goes on by the parties but the people here look only on them (being a dull time of year) as party affairs and amusements. . . .
>
>   Henry Beekman

Addressed to Gilbert Livingston Esq., at Kingston.[4]

Beekman in this letter repeats the prevalent doubt about the quality of the land in the area. He must have convinced Livingston to negotiate with Buys, however, because in 1735, two years before the accepted date of the division of the Beekman Patent into lots, Johannis Buys and a large group of other Dutch and English settlers started going into the hills of what is today Unionvale. Almost all of the people were listed in the South Ward tax lists, and the great majority of them were related to Johannis Buys by blood or by marriage. We do not know exactly how many acres were leased by the Buys group because a number of them settled in the area known as Myers Purchase which is to the east of lots 17 and 18 and includes the hill area called Mamkating Mountain. The following list shows us the names and tax records of those people in the Buys group who settled on the "ridge by Josiah Crego."[5]

Name	South Ward	Middle Ward	Beekman
Bartlett, Benjamin	1728-29—1734-35	1735-36—1737-38	1738-39—1748
Bartlett, Hendrick	1728-29—1734-35	1725-26,-37,-38	1740-41—1743-44

Dolson, Abraham	1734–35	1735–36—1737–38	1738–39—June 1753
Dolson, Jacob	1729–30—1735–36	1736–37—1737–38	1738–39—June 1748
Dolson, Johannis	1729–30—1734–35	1735–36—1737–38	1738–39—June 1748
Fontyne, Abraham	1738–29—1735–36	1736–37—1737–38	1738–39—June 1760
Schouten, Jacob	1720–1734—1735	1735–36—1737–38	1738–39—1746–47
Thomas, Hendrick	1724–25—1734–35	1736–37—1737–38	1738–39—June 1748
Wright, Gabriel	1730–31—1735–36		1739–40—June 1753
Buys, Johannis	1717–18—1734–35	1735–36—1737–38	1738–39—1765
Buys, Simon	1728–29—1735–36	1736–37—1737–38	1738–39 to John Jr.
Buys, Mathew		1736–37—1737–38	1738–39—1753
Brower, Mathew			1739–40

The first men to begin the settlement were Johannis Buys, Johannis Dolson, Abraham Dolson, Benjamin Bartlett and Jacob Schouten, all in 1735–36. The following year we saw Jacob Dolson, Abraham Fontyne, Hendrick Thomas, Simon Buys and Mathew Buys join them. In 1739–40 Gabriel Wright, and Hendrick Bartlett the next year. These men settled on the following sized farms:

Abraham Dolson	200 acres
Abraham Fountain	150 acres
Johannis Buys	215 acres
Benjamin Bartlett	150 acres
Gabriel Wright	200 acres

Hendrick Thomas settled on a farm in lot 16 that was 185 acres. Jacob and Johannis Dolson settled in Myers Purchase and we do not know the exact acreage of their farms but we could assume about 150 acres each. Jacob Schouten, Simon Buys and Mathew Buys were also in this area and we can probably assume close to the same acreage. Samuel Buys, who moved up into Myers Purchase in 1741 is listed on the Henry Beekman rent list of May 1, 1759 for 74 acres. Mathew Brower also came up here in 1739–40 and stayed one year. When we add it all up it appears as if at least 14 families moved into the area and about 2050 acres of land were settled. This was a dramatic change for an area that had only about two or three settlers previously, and none of these were in the area of this settlement which ran roughly from Oswego east into the hills. The Oswego Meeting House was later established almost in the center of this area.

To finance the settlement of these lands on the ridge, Johannis Buys approached Abraham Van Horne for money. Van Horne agreed to lend the money to Buys but Simon Buys, brother to Johannis, also had to sign the bond. On October 10, 1735 Van Horne loaned £88 to Johannis Buys to begin his settlement. Unfortunately, like most large projects, there must have been cost overruns and when the note was due one year later they were unable to pay. Van Horne retained John Alsop in 1738 to try and collect from Buys.[6]

This was not the first time Johannis had repayment problems. On June 26, 1732 he had signed a note for £12 to "Catheryne Brett, widow of Fishkill." Madame Brett was evidently in no hurry to collect because she retained Alsop at the same time Van Horne did, the May Court in 1738. One year later he again had problems, and Francis Filkin, the storekeeper from Poughkeepsie, was suing him for £10 which was owed to him.[7] Even earlier, on March 5, 1719–20 Buys gave a Promissory Note to Rudolph Philips. Buys was sued on this after Philips died, the October Court of 1752.

To help understand the movement of these families as one group we must look at the intermarriages of the early community in Fishkill.

Johannis Buys was married to Maria Brower before 1732.
Benjamin Bartlett was married to Elizabeth Buys, born 10 June 1694, sister of Johannis.
Gabriel Wright was married on 29 Dec. 1732, to Rebecca Buys, born 2 Oct. 1712, daughter of Johannis.
Jacob Schouten was married to Rebecca Buys, sister of Johannis, before 1733.
Jacob Dolson was married to Marya Buys on 12 Jan. 1734.

Johannis Dolson was married to Elizabeth Buys, daughter of Johannis.
Simon Buys was married to Elizabeth Brower.

There were numerous other intermarriages among this group in Fishkill but I think the point is made. These families constituted some of the very first settlers in Dutchess County. On June 15, 1691 there was a mortgage from Myndart Van DeBogart of Albany to Abraham DePeyster which listed 5 tenants on it. Four out of these five tenants were important to our area. They were Baltus Barents (Van Kleek), Hendrick & Jan Oostrum, Jan Buys and Symon Schouten. Grietje Oostrum married Hendrick Thomas and Jannetjen Oostrum married Jonas Slot in 1713. Jan Buys was the father of the entire Buys Clan and Symon Schouten was the father of Jacob. Baltus Barents (Van Kleek) was a very important figure in the settlement of Poughkeepsie and was married to Tryntje Jans (Buys), an aunt of Johannis Buys. Johannis Buys can rightfully be considered the father of settlement in Unionvale and his aunt Tryntje, the mother of settlement in Poughkeepsie.

The farm Johannis Buys first settled on was just east of the present location of the Oswego Meeting. The Livingston Rent Book, page 73, gives us the details of the lease given to Buys. The lease was signed March 26, 1741 and rents were to begin in 1742 with payments of 15 bushels of sweet merchantible winter wheat, 4 live fat fowls and 1 day's riding. Wheat did not have to be delivered more than 24 miles to the landlord's store or mill. The original acreage taken was 160, but this was added to later.

Johannis Buys made the following rent payments:

Year	Bushels	Fowls	Days
1747	17½	-	– at Yelvertons
1748–49	15	4	–
1749–50	17		
1752	17		
d°	17		
1754	17		
1755	17		
1756	19		
1757	17		
1759	24		
1761	15	1	4
1762	17		
1763	17		

Johannis Buys died soon after June 1765 and just the farm is listed on the tax list until June 1768 when his son Peter took over. Peter Buys resumed rent payments in 1769 as follows:

Year	Bushels	Fowls	Days
1769	17¼		
1771	11		
1772	16½		
1773	17		
1774	17		
1775	17		

Henry G. Livingston took over the lease 6 February 1781 and an accounting was made.

To rent from 1741 to 1782 is 41 @ 15 =	615
less bushels rec'd	322¾
	292¼
41 years fowls & riding is = to	68¼
1782 there remains due	360½
His rent to 1784 amounts to	£150/8.

There is further note to "April 17, 1784 all back rents satisfied and days riding £150/8."

The next tenant on this farm was Stephen Gates, who was there from 1784 until probably 1789 or so. The rent book states "Sold this farm to Stephen Gates." This was a sale of the leasehold, not a sale of the property. There are no tax listings for Stephen Gates, but he was a pathmaster in 1784 and 1786.

The following ad from "The County Journal and Poughkeepsie Advertiser" of March 7, 1787 was probably instrumental in the final sale of this property. "To be sold Farm 200A in Oswego at present tenanted by Stephen Gates near where the Friends' Meeting House formerly stood. . . . Inquire of Henry G. Livingston, Dover." Shortly thereafter, James Congden was on this farm.

The farm was actually sold by Henry Livingston and Anna of Rhinebeck to James Congden on May 1, 1798 for £400 (15:237). Congden obtained a mortgage from the local store owner Jesse Oakley (Hoxie Corners) for $1250. James Congden was a descendant of Benjamin Congden (born 1650, died 1718) of Portsmouth, Kingstown, R.I. James was the son of James who was the son of James, son of Benjamin. Congden was on the farm as early as September 1795 (12:164). His was married to Lydia Southwick.

The house on this farm is in very good condition and the farm property is unusual in that it retains its exact dimensions as when it was sold in 1798. The farm house can be seen at the end of a long driveway leading north from Oswego Road about one-quarter mile east of the Oswego Meeting. The farm was owned by Columbia University at one time and is currently owned by Trade Land Investors.

Benjamin Bartlett was born December 7, 1701, the son of Jesais Bartlett who was from New England and Cornelia Cornelise. Jesais was a descendant of John Bartlett, who was in Windsor, Connecticut by 1640. Jesais had three sons, Benjamin; Hendrick, born November 21, 1703 who married Elizabeth Palmatier, and Ephraim, born July 31, 1709 and adopted by Johannis Buys on May 7, 1715. The adoption was witnessed by Abraham Buys.

The Dolsons are descended from Capt. Van Dalsen who was a native of Workum, on the coast of Friesland, a ship carpenter. The first vessel of any size put upon the stocks in New Amsterdam was a sloop built by him for Capt. Thomas Bradley.

Teunis Dolson, the son of the captain, was born in 1664, and in 1696, he married Sarah Vermilye. He was the first male child born in New York after it was ceded to the English by the Dutch. Shortly after his marriage, he moved into the northern part of the New York Colony and established the burgh of Dolsontown, near Goshen. He lived until 1766—to the remarkable age of 102 years. Children:

Aeltie—baptized July 16, 1699 married Dirck Hegeman of Long Island, August, 3, 1738. When married, they lived in Hopewell and Stormville, Dutchess County.

Johannes—married Elizabeth Buys; moved to Marlboro, Orange County from Dutchess County. Johannes is listed with the officers of the 1st company of the Regiment of Beekman Precinct in 1739. He was a Lieutenant in the Room of John Montros under Capt. Franz DeLange.

Jacob born—married Marya Buys, January 12, 1734 (Fishkill Church record) born in Throggs Neck, Westchester County, he died at Marlboro, Orange County 1775.

Abraham—married Marytje Slot, November 10, 1734 (Fishkill Church record). After settling in Beekman they moved to Goshen, Orange County. He was born in Throggs Neck and she in Poughkeepsie.

Issac—born (Yonkers) 1707 married Marytje Hossie, April 23, 1733 (Fishkill Church Record) Moved to Goshen, Orange Co. (Dolsontown)

Annetje—married Arie DeLang June 6, 1734 (Fishkill).

Sarah—married a Wybrant.

The Fontains descend from Charel Fontain who arrived in this country on the ship the "Gilded Beaver" in May 1658. Abraham was the son of Johannes who married Catherine (Willense) Fontyn and was probably the earliest French settler in the Oswego area.

The Wrights were from Long Island and were probably English. The Schoutens were Dutch and came down from Albany and the Brouwers were also Dutch and had followed the other Dutch families in the Fishkill area up from New York.

The Verbank Mill

One of the most necessary establishments for the early settlers was a local mill, both for grinding their grain and also for supplying them with sawed wood for their homes and barns. In Verbank Village just north of the Buys settlement there is a good fall in the Sprout Creek that evidently attracted Henry Beekman Jr. as a mill site very early on. On the first day of May in "the eleventh year of the reign of King George the Second, 1739," Henry Beekman of Rhinebeck leased a parcel of land to "George Ellsworth, George Jr and Charles Ellsworth, all of Beekman Precinct in Dutchess County, Yeoman." George Ellsworth was a taxpayer as early as 1736–37 and was at this location.

The description on the lease follows:

In a patent now Beekman Precinct, beginning on the Westound or corner of John Cook by a white oak sappling tree marked standing in swampy ground, thence to run West 18° S 27C to a white oak marked *IE* standing on the south side of the mill creek then S 6C to a stone sett on the South of a wagon road, then W 1° N 11C then W 17° S 18C to an oak *111X* then S 18° E 35C then E 44C to a butternut tree marked *11X*, then N 26° W 23C then N 29° E 21C to the line of John Cook and so along his line to the first station containing 205 acres. 5 acres of which by the said Beekman being reserved for roads and also the mill creek being reserved for the said Beekman with full liberty to dam up the water and to possession and use said dam." The rent for the first 4 years was "one cupple of live fat hens payable on the annunciation of our Lady, being 25th of March. The tenant after 4 years must pay 20 bushels per year computed at 10 bushels per 100 acres.[9]

George Ellsworth was English and was married at the New York Reformed Church on November 18, 1712 to Jane Miseroll. He was the son of George and Adriantje (Rommen) Ellsworth. George Ellsworth was important in that he established the most popular mill of the time, Henry Beekman's Mill in Verbank Village which was in lot 16.

George Ellsworth, (Middle Ward Tax 1736-37—1737-38 and Beekman 1738-39—June 1747; Nov. 1753—June 1753; June 1757—June 1761) was the first mill operator, about 1740. A road dedication in 1736 mentions Ellsworth but does not mention a mill. Another dedication in 1742 mentions "Ellsworth Mill." George Ellsworth is an Ensign in the 1739 listing of military officers for Beekman's Precinct under Capt. Arie DeLong.[10]

Ellsworth remained on this mill until 1747 when Isaac Bull, a Quaker from Rhode Island, took over. We determine this as follows:

On May 1, 1747, Ichabod Boorman signed a lease for a farm on the lot 16-17 boundary, in lot 16, that is bisected by the then location of North Smith Road. The eastern boundary of this farm is listed as "Isaac Boll." There is also an old map of New England and New York, circa 1750, that lists Bulls Mill in approximately this area. This mill must have been well known to have been listed on a map of the entire new England area. Isaac Bull was off this mill by 1759 and we find John DeWitt leasing it. This information is contained on the 1759 rent list for lot 16 which states that DeWitt had a total of 276 acres with a wheat rent of 60 bushels per year and two fowls. He was in arrears 46 bushels, 2 fowls and 1 day's riding as of May 1, 1759.

The next mill operator belonged to the family who made milling famous in the area, despite the fact that they were late comers. Andrew Moore signed a lease for the mills in May 1771. Moore was actually operating the mill by 1766, however, because during that year we find wheat being delivered "to Andrew Moores."[11] This lease mentions both a saw mill and grist mill and was for the life of Andrew Moore and William, his son. The rent was the same as DeWitt paid. The acreage also remained about the same but some woodland formerly surveyed for Joseph Smith was added to the mill property.

An unusual addition to this lease reads:

". . . And it is further agreed that in case of the death of any of the persons here above named for the continuation of this lease in the hands of the leasees by paying the sum of ten pounds New York Currency within three months after such descease to the leasor his heirs or assigns, another Name shall be substituted and this lease so to continue and be perpetuated to the leasee his heirs and assigns."[12]

This renewal clause is unusual for leases in the Beekman Patent.

Mortgage 10:46 indicates that Allen Moore was still on the mill in July of 1804.

Some history on these families follows:

Isaac Bull was one of at least seven brothers, several of which also resided in Dutchess County for a time. Isaac was born in Rhode Island in 1708 and came to Crum Elbow in 1746.

By 1747 he had taken over George Ellsworth's lease on the sawmill and grist mill in Verbank. By 1757, he had left this mill and was running one in Kent, Connecticut. In 1756, Isaac applied for permission to build a house and mill in Kent.

In October, 1771, Moses Haight issued a complaint against "Isaac Bull, otherwise called Isaac Bull of Kent, Litchfield County, Ct." Bull gave a promissory note to Haight in 1761 for £30. Moses Haight was one of the creditors on Bull's insolvency petition in 1773. This is included later in this story.

A brother, Timothy Bull, also ran a mill in lot 12 and later, with his son Crisbein, was the second or third settler of Danby, Vermont. Timothy was on the Beekman Tax List June 1748–February 1763.

The father of the above was John Bull who married Mary Clausen in 1706. He was born about 1684 in Rhode Island. John Bull was the only son of Isaac Bull who was born in England in 1654 and emigrated to this country. He also had four daughters. Isaac Bull, the immigrant, died in Rhode Island in 1716.

Isaac Bull did not do well at the mill. He came to our area with a fair amount of money, his assessed value having been £6 in both February & June, 1748, which was exceeded by very few of our settlers. By February, 1753 his assessed valuation had doubled to £12 and he was among the wealthiest of the people in the area. Something went wrong, however, over the winter because by next spring he had lost 75% of his assets. During this same period his neighbors, for the most part, retained their assessments. His brother, Josiah, for example, maintained the same assessment from June, 1754 to February, £3, but he dropped to £2 by June of 1755.

In February of 1756 Isaac Bull's assessed value was back up to £5 but declined to £4 again in June of 1756 and February 1757. On September 13, 1757 Isaac purchased land in the Oblong, (3:207). Zebulon Ross of Beekman sold 100 acres of land to Isaac Bull in Lot 41 of the Oblong which bordered the river. The transaction reads, "to Isaac Bull of Oblong, miller." Lot 41 is about in the center of the Oblong, at mile post 26.

The following is from Mrs. Blanch Jack, a descendant of the Bulls.

Isaac came here to get into the iron business. He applied to the General Assembly in 1756 for "the privilege of building a saw mill or iron works." After the mill was finished he was given liberty to build a house on the highway. The family had a forge south of the Bull's Bridge and on the west side of the river. There was an ore bed on the east end of Bull's Bridge Road and they may have drawn ore from there, though I believe a good portion of their ore came from Clove; from it they made wrought iron—nails, etc. Both General Washington and Chastellux commented on the fires of the forge at "Bull's Iron Works." I have an original bill dated 1802 which Jacob Bull paid partly in iron. Whether or not Isaac, his father, had any interest in the iron business in Dutchess, I don't know.

By 1773, Isaac Bull's financial problems had become too great for him and he was incarcerated at the Dutchess County Jail as a debtor. One of the ancient documents in the very worst condition (moldy and in many pieces, #8765) is the petition of Isaac Bull, insolvent debtor. This document is priceless, however, for what it tells us about the riches to rags story of Isaac.

"To the Honorable James Smith & Henry Van Deburgh Esqs, two of the judges of the Superior Court of Common Pleas of Dutchess County.

The Humble Petitions of Isaac Bull a prisoner confined in Dutchess County Gaol for debt by reason of processes issued out of the Inferior Court of Common Pleas for said County of Dutchess.

Humbly Sheweth

That your Honors

Petitioner herewith establishes a true and perfect inventory or account of all his estate, real and personal, and of the securities relating to the same and humbly pray your Honors assistance that your petitioner may have the benefit of an act of legislation of the Province of New York passed on the 10th day of March last entitled an Act for the Relief of Insolvent Debtors within this colony with respect to the imprisonment of their persons and your honors petitioner as in duty bound shall every pray

Isaac Bull

April 29th 1773

A full and true account of all the sums of money due unto Isaac Bull from all his respective debtors viz

Captain Nath Earles	£ /8
Benjamin Stephen (?)	£ /12
Henry Livingston	£1/

James Smith and Henry Van Der Burgh Esq two of the judges of the Inferior Court of Common Pleas for the County of Dutchess do certify that a petition hath been presented unto us by the above named Isaac Bull craving the benefit of an act of the legislature of this province entitled an Act for the Relief of Insolvent Debtors within this colony with respect of the imprisonment of their persons passed on the eighth day of March last and that the said Isaac Bull hath taken the oath in and by the said act required that this inventory and account is a true and just one of all his estates this fourth day August Anno Domini 1773

James Smith

Henry V D Burgh

Know all men that I the within named Isaac Bull assign transfer and set over all my estate real and personal exhibited in the inventory here to annexed unto George Soul and Daniel Ross in trust and for the use of all my creditors to be applied as directed in and by an act of the legislature for the Province of New York entitled an act for the Relief of Insolvent Debtors within this county with respect to the imprisonment of debtors. Under my hand and seal this fourth day of August One thousand seven hundred and seventy three.

Sealed and delivered
in the presence of
G. Livingston
Peter Harris

Isaac Bull

Isaac Bull
petition
dated June 28, 1773

Inventory of Isaac Bull

A full and true inventory and account of all the estate both real and personal in law and equity of Isaac Bull and of all books vouchers and securities relating to the same excepting the wearing apparel of himself and family

1 old feather bead 3 old coverlids
1 boulester and 3 pillows
3 blanketts, 1 sheet, 1 meal chest, 1 chest of Drawers, 2 old chests and bread tray, one morter one chourn, a red barrel, 3 old barrels, 5 wooden trenchers, one sugar box, one sive, one pair bellows, one brass kettle, 3 iron kettles, one tea kettle, 2 candle, one tramble, one pair of tonge, one bead, one mold to make rake bows, smothing iron, 1 pair of stillards, 2

tables, 4 pails, 1 tub, 1 watering pot, 2 old chears, 1 pewter platter, 3 earthen platters, 3 basons, 4 plates, 1 porringer, 6 knives, 7 forks, 4 spoons, 2 teapots, 1 tea cannister, 6 cups, 6 saucers, 1 vinegar cruet, 1 pear of wool cards, 1 bowl, 1 linepin, 1 funnel, 2 tin cups, one earthen cup, 1 great Bible, 1 conch shell, 3 augers, 2 gouges, 10 planes, 6 chizzals, 1 spoak shave, 1 woman's saddle, the one half of a wheelbarrow, 1 small stone pot, 2 stone jugs, 1 stone mug, 1 stone chamber pott, 4 gimlets, 2 bitts, 1 square, 1 qurt bottle, 1 hand saw, 1 large 1/2 round phile, 2 small philes, 1 iron hold fast, 1 hammer, 1 saw and insterments to draw teeth.

Debtors - Isaac Bull

A full and true account of all the sums of money due and owing by Isaac Bull and of all creditors whom the same are due viz.

To John Hoag	£ 5.7
To estate of Isaac Thorn upon bond	35.8
To David Dutcher upon bond	18.
To John Fredericks upon obligation	20.
To David Hayes upon obligation	7.
To Abraham DeGroff upon obligation	8.
To Dirck Brinckerhoff about	3.10
To Murray Lester acct. settled	
To Leonard Van Kleeck settled	
To Clear Eveartt upon note	5.
To John Thomas	6.
To Eli Rusel acct Settled	
To Gideon Draper	.6
To Capt. Tabalon acct Settled	
To Bernard Filkin one note what is due unknown	
To Jacobus De Peyster about cost common pleas	.35.
To John Van Stenburgh about cost common pleas	.15.
To Gideon Ver Velin Deceased Obligation	.15
To Moses Haight the sum unknown cost common pleas	
To Joseph Mabbett about cost common pleas	1.2
To Samuel Mabbett on execution cost common pleas	21.15
To James Birdsall Execution cost common pleas	1.8.5
To Jacobus Roswalton cost common pleas	8.5
To William Gonroy about	1.5
To Joshua Carman about	1.

Isaac's family carried on, however, and ran other mills and forges as mentioned above. Josiah Jr. in fact was running a sawmill in Lot 16 in 1773, at the same time Uncle Isaac was having all of his problems.

The act of the legislature was actually passed on March 8, 1773 and is quite interesting. It listed all the debtors in all the prisons throughout the Colony of New York. There were 16 imprisoned for debt in the jails of the city and County of New York, three in Orange County, one in Ulster, one in Westchester, 10 in Albany, one in Kings County and 13 in Dutchess County. Isaac Bull was the only resident (farmer) of Beekman Precinct in the jail for debt at this time.

Parts of the act read as follows:

"Whereas it has been represented to the General Assembly that the several Persons herein after mentioned imprisoned in different Gaols in this Colony are destitute even of the Common Necessaries of Life, and it is conceived reasonable if their Creditors will not consent to their Enlargement or contribute to their Subsistance, that such Persons should be relieved by the Legislature. To this End. Be It Enacted by his Excellency the Governor the Council and the General Assembly, and it is hereby enacted by the Authority of the same. That such of the Creditors of the following Persons. Isaac Bull, (etc.) confined in Dutchess County Gaol, who shall insist upon such their Debtors beign detained under their respective Confinements, shall within one Month after the publication of such Advertisements as are herein after directed agree by writing under their Hands to pay and allow three shillings and six pence per Week, unto the said Prisoners respectively, to be paid the Monday of every Week so long as he shall continue in prison at his her or their Instance, and if such Agreement as aforesaid shall not be entered into or if entered into, not punctually complied with and on Failure of the payment of such Weekly sum at any Time, such of the said Prisoners whose Creditor or Creditors shall not enter into such Agreement or shall fail complying with it as aforesaid shall be entitled to the Benefit of this Act, upon complying with the Terms and Conditons herein after imposed."

The last miller in the eighteenth century was Andrew Moore. The Moore family has the honor of having a hamlet named after then in the present Town of LaGrange. Moores Mills, in the northeast section of town was named after the descendants of William Moore who first came to the area in 1735.

William Moore is listed in Middle Ward for 1735–36 and 1737–38. He is listed Beekman Tax List 1738–1753 est. to February 1759.

William Moore, a physician, was a native of the parish of Clogh, Antrim County, Ireland and was one of the earliest settlers of the Oswego area.

Dr. William Moore was born December 12th, 1705 and died November 25th, 1752. It is reported that he lived S-SW of the Oswego Meeting House on the main road to Poughkeepsie at the foot of a steep hill. This location is probably "Crossways" located at the NW corner of Barmore Road and Route 82 in the Town of LaGrange.

On June 4, 1729 William Moore married Mary Palmer in Stonington, Ct. The couple were married by David Palmer, Justice of the Peace.

Mary Palmer, born 1713, was a daughter of Moses and Abigail (Allen) Palmer. (The historian Helen Wilkinson Reynolds and Dutchess County Executive Lucille Pattison are descendants of this Palmer family.)

William Moore leased several farms in this area. His total acreage was 562.

We have been able to tell, although briefly, the story of some of the first settlers in the Beekman Precinct and the beginnings of industry there. These were great people who braved the wilderness to settle Dutchess County and start it on its way.

Notes

1. Ecclesiastical Records of the State of New York, Albany, N. Y., p. 1244.
2. Documentary History of Rhinebeck, Edward M. Smith, 1881
3. Ecclesiastical Records.
4. Livingston Papers, New-York Historical Society Library, New York City.
5. From Beekman Tax Lists by Clifford M. Buck, Salt Point, New York.
6. Ancient Documents #282, Dutchess County Clerk's Office.
7. Ancient Documents #168.
8. Buys family information from Jeanine Minisci, Lakeland, Florida.
9. Copy of Lease in Local History Room, Adriance Library.
10. Annual Report of Secretary of State, p. 500
11. Livingston Rent Book, page 98, New-York Historical Society Library
12. Copy of lease in writer's possession, from New-York Historical Society Library.

Rebels and Democrats:
The Democratization of Landholding

John T. Reilly
Professor of History, Mount Saint Mary College,
Newburgh, New York

To many historians, the American Revolution was simply and clearly a war for independence from England, a mere colonial rebellion and nothing more. It was not a revolution against an old order, a revolution in which social and political concerns were paramount. To these, Whig or neo-Whig historians, the primary concern of the American Patriots was a conservative one, the preservation of their liberty against the threat from an aggressive, distant, and perhaps corrupt, English Parliament. There was little if any interest in social or political change, both during and after the Revolution. To these historians the Revolution was hardly revolutionary at all. Other historians, however, believed the Revolution was something broader and deeper than a simple colonial war for independence. Historians writing during the Progressive Era, such as Carl Becker, Arthur M. Schlesinger Sr., Charles A. Beard, and Alexander C. Flick, and later J. Franklin Jameson and Merrill Jensen, described the conflicts and internal dynamics within colonial society which ultimately made the Revolution a great democratic movement. It was a movement which had a lasting economic, political, and social effect on American government and society. To these historians political and social issues were far more important than the conflict with Great Britain. Carl Becker, in his seminal work on the Revolution in New York aptly described this view in 1901 when he wrote the Revolution was not only over "home rule," it was also over "who should rule at home."

While this "progressive" interpretation of the Revolution was overshadowed in the post-World War II years by "neo-Whig" historians who emphasized consensus and continuity, several recent historians have resumed the earlier generation's assault on the Whig view. Historians such as Edward Countryman, Gary Nash, Jesse Lemisch, and Alfred Young have demonstrated evidence of class division, poverty, and popular discontent in Colonial and Revolutionary society that might make the American Revolution explicable in terms common to the Cuban, French, and Russian models. Writing during the turmoil of the 1960's and 1970's, these historians tried to show how expressions of discontent, coupled with the imperial crisis, led to attacks by colonial political leaders, not only on Great Britain, but on each other. They emphasized several points, such as: the punishment of Loyalists, the attempt to make freehold tenure widely available, the partial abolition of slavery, and the abolition of legal privileges which could be described as having a long term, democratizing effect on American politics and society. However, in their examinations these historians have often not fully studied the long range implications of these effects to understand how deep they really were. The attempt to make freehold tenure widely available, particularly through the confiscation and sale of the estates of the Loyalists, is one example of the need for a more careful scrutinization of the democratizing effects on the Revolution.

This question was first examined comprehensively by J. Franklin Jameson in his *American Revolution Considered as a Social Movement*. He believed the effect of the order by the Continental Congress to confiscate and sell the estates of Loyalists produced extensive changes in the pattern of landholding in the former colonies. Large estates were broken up into small parcels and sold to many different individuals. This resulted in an expansion of agricultural democracy, ultimately leading to greater political democracy.[1] However, Jameson's interpretation was open to criticism. Historians soon began to question his findings on the grounds that many of the purchasers of the Loyalist estates were members of leading landowning and merchant families, speculators, and powerful politicians, that members of the lower orders who did purchase these lands were unable to hold them during the economic dislocations of the 1780's, and it was not until the nineteenth century that freehold tenure came into existence.[2]

More recent studies, in particular those concerning New York State, have questioned these critiques. Several historians have found a strong democratizing impulse in the initial sales. Instances of land engrossment by speculators and merchants were short lived, and if they did purchase land it was quickly resold, passing into the hands of members of the lower orders. As Catherine S. Crary wrote in describing the sales in Western New York, ". . . land democratization was a by-product of the Revolution, and the redistribution of forfeited land in their long range impact contributed to bringing about significant social change."[3]

New York, as Becker discovered long ago, is an ideal colony in which to demonstrate that the Revolution was some sort of democratic transformation. By the eve of the Revolution land tenure in New York exhibited a wide disparity of ownership. On the east bank of the Hudson River, from Albany to New York City, particularly in the counties of Dutchess and Westchester, lay a series of large estates and manors. In possession of such families as the Livingstons, Van Cortlands, and Philipses, populated with numerous tenants, and the scene of several serious conflicts over land ownership in the 1750–1770 period, these great landed tracts have provided historians with much material on the political and social conditions of Colonial New York. Interspersed with these estates there were numerous small holdings. However, the landlords were not disposed to subdivide and sell their holdings. They preferred to lease them out on a long term basis.

On the west bank of the Hudson landholding patterns were more varied. On land situated near the River, the more settled areas of Orange and Ulster counties, the earlier grantees and patentees had quickly sold their holdings. There were none of the large, tenanted estates such as those which existed in Dutchess and Westchester. Freehold tenure was more characteristic of landholding in this region. However, as one moved westward, toward the Delaware River and interior New York, habitation was sparse especially in some of the great patents of Colonial New York, such as the Great Hardenbergh Patent which contained some two million acres. Settlement in this area was not to occur until after the Revolution.

Historians who have examined landholding patterns in the Hudson River Valley during the late Colonial and Revolutionary periods have displayed considerable interest concerning the east bank. Their results have supported both sides of the question: did the confiscation and sale of the estates of the Loyalists have a democratizing effect on the landholding pattern of New York State? Before discussing the views of these historians, mention should be made of the particulars concerning the decision to confiscate these estates.

The year 1779 was a trying one for the American Patriots; the British had begun their southern campaign; the economic situation, with inflation rampant and specie scarce, was desperate. To many there seemed few choices for ways to raise the funds needed to carry on the war. Taxes were a possibility, however, since the war was being fought over the issue of taxation, the patriots were reluctant to raise these funds by this means. Forced loans could be used, but this measure could also be onerous. A third method, one which had been suggested for several years, was the confiscation and sale of the estates of the Loyalists. This would serve a dual purpose; first, it would punish these supporters of the crown, and, second, it would raise the needed funds to carry on the war.[4] While there was a reluctance by some of the more conservative Patriots to take such a drastic step, eventually every state adopted this policy. In 1779, New York passed its confiscation act. There is little evidence that the decision to confiscate the Loyalist estates was motivated by a social concern, as a means of leveling society, although several historians have suggested this might be the case.[5] The act provided for the confiscation and sale of the lands of all those convicted of Loyalism. In addition it specifically convicted of Loyalism, without trial, fifty-nine prominent persons and their wives. The lands were to be sold with a maximum of five hundred acres per sale. An individual could purchase more than one lot, but no farms were to be broken up, and, if the land was inhabited by a Whig tenant, that tenant was to be able to pre-empt the land upon payment of back rents, and at a price set by appraisal. The legislature also extended credit terms to the purchasers. At first, three months were given in which to complete payment. This was later extended. While payment was initially required to be in public securities, this was later revised and various types of circulating medium were to be accepted. All of these measures point to a distinct bias on the part of the legislature toward easing the burden of purchasing on those who bought the estates, although one cannot say that the legislature intended this as a redistribution of land.[6]

The sales took place from 1781 to 1810, when the New York State Surveyor General undertook to distribute all of the remaining parcels. In all, some 425,000 acres of New York land belonging to 235 Loyalists were sold to some 1,766 persons. Although this was only a small percentage of the state's thirty million acres, it did represent some of New York's best urban and agricultural land. A considerable portion of the land lay in the Hudson and Mohawk River valleys, southern New York, Long Island and part of Washington County.[7] Historians, such as Thomas Cochrane, Frederick Tolles, and Harry B. Yoshpe described the sales as either a boon for speculators, merchants, prominent politicians, and wealthy investors, or, in more general terms, as insignificant, given the amount of land involved as compared to the total acreage of New York State. They have concluded that it was not until the nineteenth century that smaller landowners came into possession of these lands when the original purchasers subdivided their holdings. With regard to Whig tenants, Yoshpe, in his examination of Philipsburg Manor in Westchester County, concluded that many of them were well-to-do rather than from the lower orders of society. He, also, concluded the economic dislocations of the 1780's affected the purchasers because many had borrowed to pay for their lands. Unable to meet mortgage payments, these purchasers lost the land to speculators and large merchants.[8]

Other historians, such as Flick, Crary, Beatrice G. Rubens, and Staughton Lynd have argued that a number of large estates were broken into small farms and sold, often to persons of the middle and lower socio-economic order, such as artisans and yeoman farmers, many of whom were former tenants of the Loyalist landlord. This, they concluded, resulted in an expansion of agricultural democracy eventually leading to greater political democracy.[9] To the historian who wishes to reconcile these conflicting viewpoints there are several concerns that must be addressed. First, the need for an accurate description of the initial sales, for example, the location, number of acres involved, and the social and economic status of the purchasers. Second, an examination of the ability of the initial purchasers to hold on to their lands into the nineteenth century. If they had lost them through foreclosure, or had sold them in what might be described as speculative activity, then the democratizing effect of the sales would be moot.

The Middle District of Revolutionary New York, specifically the counties of Dutchess, Orange, and Ulster, with their mixture of long tenanted estates and numerous small farms has been a fruitful area of study for historians of the disposition of the Loyalist estates. First Dutchess will be examined, then Orange and Ulster. Eighteenth century Dutchess could be described as a region dominated by large landowners, such as the Philipse family in the south and the Livingstons in the north. In those areas, only leaseholds were available for settlement. Only in the center of the county, in the precincts of Rombout, Poughkeepsie, Charlotte, and Amenia were freeholds in abundance. The typical resident of Dutchess at that time could be described as a yeoman-farmer possessing a small freehold or leasehold, averaging just under two hundred acres. If he was a tenant, he probably suffered little in the way of hardship. Recent studies have found the position of the tenant in Dutchess had been better than it had generally been assumed. He could obtain a good lease and his economic condition rivaled that of his landlord. Despite these benign conditions, Dutchess was the scene of violent rebellions. Although several historians have pointed to these disturbances as evidence of social unrest among the tenantry, other historians have called for a re-examination of this situation.[10] Based on their conclusions there seems to be little evidence, if any, to connect the rebellions of the 1760's to the confiscation and sale of the Loyalist lands. In fact, the opposite may be true. Many of the tenants were to follow their landlords into battle on the side of the Crown.[11]

When the state began the confiscation process in 1779 the number of Loyalists who had their property confiscated were few. Flick put their number at 264 in Dutchess County. There were, however, only ninety-six persons who were convicted of Loyalism in the county, including Rodger and Mary Morris, Beverly and Susannah Robinson, Rev. Charles Inglis, George Folliott, and John Watt, all of whom had been named in the confiscation act. Only thirty-seven of the ninety-six had their land sold by the state.[12] The majority of the land confiscated and sold in Dutchess belonged to two men, Beverly Robinson and Rodger Morris, who married the daughters of Frederick Philipse. Their land lay in the South Precinct of Dutchess County, the Philipse Highland Patent, on which Beverly Robinson had 53,102 acres with 156 tenants and Rodger Morris had 55,954 acres with 166 tenants. Of the two, only Beverly Robinson lived on his estates, where he built his "Beverly House" near the present day city of Beacon.[13] The other major Loyalist landowners were George Folliott with 3,546 acres and no tenants, Charles Inglis with 2,739 acres and no tenants, John Kane with 1,927 acres and 13 tenants , and Henry Clinton with 1,829 acres and twelve tenants. Historians who have previously examined the sales in Dutchess have agreed that there was a growth of freeholds where leaseholds had once predominated. However, several have felt that there is evidence of land engrossment, speculation, and a loss of lands during the economic dislocations of the 1780's which mitigated the democratizing effects.[14] A re-examination of these sales, however, does not support these conclusions. By 1810, a total of 93,382 acres belonging to 37 Loyalists had been sold in 519 sales to 493 purchasers.[15] Although this does not represent the total acreage involved, Morris and Robinson reported owning over one hundred thousand acres in their claims for compensation submitted to the British government, it is enough to show that there was extensive democratization in landholding. There is little evidence of speculation or land engrossment in the initial sales, (that took place before 1788) for the number of purchasers is relatively close to the number of sales, 493 to 574, and the average sale and purchase was 161 and 194 acres respectively, close to the norm of 200 acres. While only 15 percent, or 75, of the purchasers are identifiable, 31 of whom were yeoman farmers, tax lists and rent rolls show that 376 or 78 percent of the purchasers were Dutchess residents, and were probably of the same socio-economic class as the rest of the county. As there was no large influx of outsiders in the initial sales, it must be presumed that most of the land was sold to persons who were both residents in and typical of the county.[16]

In determining the extent of land engrossment in these sales, the figure of five hundred acres, a figure which is slightly more than double the size of the average eighteenth century farm, but one which would encompass as wide a variation in individual freeholds as possible, will be used as the line of demarcation between those purchasers who may be considered as engrossers or speculators and those who bought land to establish their own homestead. There were 26 individuals who purchased 22,692 acres in amounts varying from 500 to 3,394 acres. This represents 25 percent of the total acres sold. Only 7 of these individuals purchased land in excess of 1,000 acres, and collectively they accounted for one-half of the above 20,000 acres. The two largest purchasers were William Denning, a New York merchant, lawyer, member of the Provincial Congress and State Senator, who bought 3,394 acres, and Ebenezer Boyd, a tavern keeper and militia captain, who purchased 2,012 acres.[17] There is no information concerning the remaining five. Among the other nineteen large purchasers there were several men who were wealthy merchants, lawyers or men prominent in local and state affairs. Among them were Zephaniah Platt, a local Dutchess County politician and founder of Plattsburgh, New York,[18] Comfort Sands and William Smith, New York merchants and speculators.[19] Little is known of the others. The sales in Dutchess also produced a moderate interest among men who can clearly be identified as speculators. Men such as William Duer, John Lamb, John Morin Scott, and Melancton Smith, all prominent merchants and politicians who speculated in land in other parts of the state, bought land in amounts under 500 acres from the Commissioners.[20] In general, the extent to which men of the upper social strata, investors or speculators, participated in the disposition of these estates may be considered insignificant.

An important question, and one which historians interested in the socio-economic results of the Revolution have appropriately concerned themselves with is whether or not the tenants of Loyalist landlords exercised their right of pre-emption. In Dutchess there was not as much tenant participation as elsewhere. Only 142 out of 302 tenants on the estates of Morris and Robinson purchased their lands.[21] What happened to the tenants on the estates of the other landlords is not known, as their rent rolls have yet to be found. Why is the rate of participation so low? There is no clear cut answer. Given the benign conditions of the tenants, they may have felt a loyalty to their landlords, willingly followed them into battle, and lost their lands as a result. Certainly the example of the tenantry on the estates of Beverly Robinson and Sir John Johnson in the Western District suggest this might be the case.[22]

Perhaps the landlord may have used a combination of force and fear, threatening to drive tenants out if they did not follow him and remarking that if they joined the Whigs and lost, they would lose everything. On the other hand following the landlord allowed the tenants to fall back on the crown if England lost the Revolution.[23] It is also entirely possible that many simply did nothing, neither followed their landlords nor evidenced any desire to exercise their tenant rights. The tenants, at the time of the Revolution, may have felt that they were fairly well off and had no desire to purchase land of their own. This is somewhat difficult to prove as there are several instances which may, by inference, lead to such a conclusion. The tenant, after the sale of his land by the state to another owner, was under no legal obligation to vacate his land. His lease with his previous landlord remained in force; the purchaser only bought the equity of the redemption when the lease expired. The tenant lost only the value of his improvements up until the date of sale. There were a few recorded instances of this happening in Dutchess County.[24] It is possible that some tenants remained as such under a new landlord. This new landlord could even have been a tenant of someone else. Colonel Henry Ludington, for example, a tenant on non-confiscated lands of the heirs of Philip Philipse, purchased land formerly belonging to Beverly Robinson. He leased this land to someone else and did not purchase his own leasehold until the nineteenth century.[25]

Other reasons for the lack of a large turnout by former tenants to purchase their land may have been that they were incapacitated in one way or another. Because of their Loyalism some were unable to purchase theirs; others were dead, although in some instances members of the immediate family did purchase the farm of the deceased relative.[26] This, however, was more the exception than the rule. Financial difficulty also could have kept some from purchasing their leaseholds. In the 1781–1782 period a number of petitions were presented to the legislature from Dutchess County residents complaining of financial difficulties in trying to meet payments on their estates. Their particular grievance was the necessity to pay back rents due on their lands as well as meeting the payments to the state. There were 183 names on their petitions and only 30 were identifiable as tenants of the Loyalist landlords involved.[27]

As Reubens has pointed out in the case of Westchester County, the extent of poverty among the non-purchasers must not be exaggerated. Mortgages and time payments from the state were available to all purchasers. Many of the wealthier, more substantial tenants in Westchester were either Loyalists or non-purchasers, and an examination of the tax lists in Dutchess County disclosed similar findings.[28] There were seven persons in the South Precinct, where the estates of Morris and Robinson lay, who paid from ten to seventy pounds per year in taxes. None of them purchased a confiscated estate and all except one, Thomas Davenport, a tenant of Philip Philipse, were Loyalists. In the next highest category, those who paid more than six pounds per year, there were twenty persons, but only six purchased a confiscated estate. The majority of the taxpayers paid from one to five pounds per year, with the average being about two pounds per year. Many in this category were also tenants, and it is here that a greater part of the purchasers are found.[29] There is no question that financial difficulties played a role in the decision of some of the tenants and those in possession not to purchase their estates; however, it does not seem to have been a serious, insurmountable obstacle.

In her examination of Philipsburg Manor, Reubens commented that the redistribution achieved by the Commissioners would not carry much historical significance if tenantry had been widely re-established within a few years, or if speculators had obtained a commanding share of the estate, or if a large number of the new owners had lost their farms through foreclosures of mortgages.[30] To answer this question, it is necessary to examine all of the resales, mortgages, leases, wills, and newspaper advertisements relating to these estates. The results of this study seem to indicate that the post-sale period had little influence on the landholding pattern of Dutchess County. Only 15 percent, 13,621 acres, belonging to 80 purchasers were sold to 87 buyers, a 1-to-1 ratio. Almost half of the new owners were county residents, together with a sizeable group of newcomers from Connecticut. About one-third were either related to the former owners, who were mainly of the middling sort, or could be identified as yeoman farmers or artisans, and none were identifiable as speculators or wealthy investors. There was little indication of speculation in the resales. A common sign of speculative activity is a quick turnover in landholding within one or two years after the initial purchase. In Dutchess County there was about a 10 percent turnover of land within this period. More than half, 8,000 acres, was sold from 5 to 10 years after its purchase, in small tracts of under 300 acres, the average size being 156 acres.[31]

This small turnover in land and the lack of any discernible pattern in the sales which did take place does not mean that attempts were not made to dispose of the land. Evidence of such attempts can be found in the various sources: newspapers, private documents and the like. However, with respect to Dutchess County, little indication of efforts in this area has been found. An examination of the newspapers for the 1785-1800 period found only 804 acres belonging to 5 purchasers offered for sale.[32] While the purchasers of Loyalist estates may not have been interested in turning a quick sale or leasing out their new freeholds, they were all subject to the economic dislocations of the post-war period. As the region was predominately agricultural, a decline in demand for its products, as experienced during the 1780's, could be serious. It could lead, as Lynd seems to suggest, to a return of tenantry and land engrossment through foreclosures and distress sales.[33] While the records are not complete, the situation in Dutchess was not too dismal.

The County seems to have been only marginally affected by the economic conditions. There were eleven purchasers of confiscated estates who mortgaged their lands, including two speculators, Ebenezer Boyd and William Smith, and all discharged their debt.[34] Only five purchasers, Caleb Frisby, Stephen and William Field, Jeremiah Hughson, and Daniel Ter Boss, had their lands sold for debt. This amounted to 2,517 acres, less than 3 percent of the entire land sold by the Commissioners in Dutchess, and all were sold in the 1790's.[35] The largest sale was that of 1,497 acres belonging to Daniel Ter Boss. After his death this land was sold to John DeWitt, a New York City merchant, to settle the Ter Boss estate. The remaining lands were sold to local residents.

Besides ordinary mortgages, purchasers of confiscated estates often availed themselves of the time payment provisions of the several acts which authorized disposition of these lands. In 1785 the Commissioners of Forfeiture for the Middle District listed 184 purchasers who were paying on time.[36] If payment was not met when due, the Commissioners were authorized to put these lands up for sale again. In the Middle District only ten purchasers fell into this category. Two, Moses Dusenbury and Benjamin Propean, had their lands advertised for sale due to non-payment, while 8 others, 5 from Dutchess County and 3 from Ulster County, owning 933 acres were listed by the Commissioners as having failed to make payment.[37]

What then did the sales produce in Dutchess County? There is little doubt that a wider distribution of landholding resulted, for the number of individual landholders increased twelve fold, and most of these new owners were from the lower classes. While there was a noticeable lack of widespread tenant participation, the number was high enough to indicate that tenants did take advantage of the opportunity offered. Also, there is little evidence of an attempt by the members of the upper classes or speculators to move in and take advantage of this opportunity to increase their holdings or make a purchase in the hope of a quick profit. Many of the purchasers were able to remain in possession of their lands well into the nineteenth century despite several years of economic hardship. The sales, it may be concluded, produced long term stability in landholding, setting Dutchess County well on its way toward a society of widespread freehold farming.

Orange and Ulster Counties, like Dutchess, contained a rural, agrarian society. Encompassing some of the best agricultural land in the state, the region produced mainly fruits and wheat, with some grazing on the slopes of the Schunemunk and Shawangunk Mountains, which bisected it.[38] These counties presented a different picture with regard to landholding. The area west of the mountains contained several large patents or grants from the Crown in possession of absentee owners. This region was not opened to settlement until after the Revolution. The lands located east of the mountains were made up of small patents, 82 in all, which ranged from several hundred to two hundred thousand acres.[39] While there were several prominent landlords in the region, namely William Bayard, Oliver DeLancey, Charles Inglis, James Jauncey, John Tabor Kempe, Isaac Low, and John

Weatherhead, all of whom were influential leaders of colonial New York, the general pattern of landownership in Orange and Ulster was a mixture of small to moderate size holdings and an early introduction of an agricultural democracy. Many of the patents, usually in the possession of absentee proprietors, had been divided and subdivided early in their history among the proprietors and their families and sold to others. Eventually these lands passed to those who wished to settle on a permanent basis. By the time of the Revolution the two counties were composed of a high percentage of freeholds.

An examination of the few available assessment rolls from the Revolutionary period further indicates the small freeholder character of the region. There was a noticeable lack of men who might be considered as very wealthy. Large resident landlords, such as Beverly Robinson or Robert Livingston, were not characteristic of the region either before or after the Revolution. In each town or village only a handful of men might be considered as moderately wealthy. There was some separation by wealth but not to a degree which would produce a wide disparity in the social structure.[40] Orange and Ulster had experienced a rising agricultural democracy well before the social changes introduced by the Revolution had affected some of their sister counties. A further distinguishing characteristic of the region was the absence of a large tenant class. While tenancy did exist on the holdings of several landlords, such as William Bayard, Oliver DeLancey, William Smith, and others, it was not widespread nor was it the occasion of difficulties like those which occurred in Albany and Dutchess Counties.[41]

Although Loyalist activity in the area was minimal, local authorities did manage to find 70 persons sufficiently loyal enough to the Crown to confiscate their property, selling the land belonging to 55 of them totaling 36,788 acres to 106 buyers in 126 sales.[42]

Did the sales democratize landholding in Orange and Ulster? As has been pointed out earlier, the two counties were well on the way to a small freeholder status. Only one historian, Lloyd Douglas has made an attempt to evaluate the effect of these sales, and he found it to be insignificant. Douglas, however, failed to consult all the available sources, for there were almost thirty-seven thousand acres of Loyalist land sold.[43] The effects of the sales, however, were not as dramatic as in Dutchess or Westchester. The lands of the some 55 Loyalists were sold to 94 persons, only a 60 percent increase in landholding as compared to a 200 to 300 percent increase in the other counties. The average sale and purchase, 208 and 255 acres respectively, were close to mean farm size in New York during that period. Before a definite conclusion can be made as to the extent of democratization in Orange and Ulster, there are several other factors which need to be examined. Namely, the socio-economic classification of the purchasers, the extent to which tenants exercised their right of pre-emption, and the involvement of large landowners and speculators in the sales.

About 23 percent of the purchasers indicated their standing in society. Twelve were gentlemen and merchants, 10 were artisans and yeoman farmers. It is possible , using other sources such as tax lists, militia lists, and the names of the signers of the Association, to arrive at a more representative picture of the socio-economic classification of the purchasers. From the above lists 52 persons, or 58 percent of the total number of purchasers, are identifiable as residents of the area before the sales. Of the remaining forty-two, only five are identifiable as non-residents. It is likely that the remaining thirty-seven were already residents. As noted earlier there was no great disparity of wealth in the region, and the majority of the population was of the middling sort. It is likely, therefore, that most of the confiscated land that was sold in the 1780–1788 period passed into the hands of men who were typical of the region.[44]

The question of tenant participation is more complex as there are no rent rolls in existence for the area's Loyalist landlords. Keeping in mind the absence of large, heavily tenanted estates, such evidence as does exist points in the direction of non-participation. Oliver DeLancey's lands, for example, which according to his claim for compensation contained seventy-two tenants, was sold to only seventeen persons, none of whom are identifiable as tenants.[45]

The most notable factor in examining these results is the higher degree of concentration of ownership produced, as compared to Dutchess County. There were 13 men who purchased over 13,000 acres of land, or about one-third of the total acreage sold by the state, as compared to the 25 percent in Dutchess. The above figures indicate a trend toward engrossment, and several of the purchasers such as Cornelius C. Roosevelt, a New York City merchant, are identifiable as speculators. However, these men bought only a few acres, or acreage which was like John Tabor Kemp's Dunderberg Tract, a wild, mountainous, uninhabited tract of land containing 4,029 acres of land which was purchased by Samuel Brewster. Brewster, an Orange County merchant, iron manufacturer and speculator was the largest purchaser in the area. In addition to Kemp's land he purchased 935 acres in the well settled Haverstraw section of the county.[46] Other large purchasers were prominent politicians, manufacturers, and speculators and one yeoman-farmer.[47]

While on the surface there seems to have been a higher degree of concentration of land in these two counties in the hands of men who are identifiable as wealthier than the average, or speculators, there is an important distinction to be made concerning the land involved. About eight to nine thousand acres, or two-thirds of the land in question, was located in one of the three sections, Mininsing, Dunderberg, or Wallkill, all of which were, except for Wallkill, either on the frontier or largely uninhabited. In the case of Wallkill there seems to have been some settlement, but it was not very extensive.[48] The remaining third was located in the more inhabited parts of the region, as were most of the smaller parcels which were sold.[49] Thus speculation in this area does not seem to have been particularly inhibiting to the spread of an agrarian democracy. In the well settled regions of Orange and Ulster, near the Hudson, most of the land was sold in small parcels to men who might be described as yeoman-farmers. The only exception is the nine hundred acres purchased by Brewster, more than likely with an eye to quick turnover. It is only in the sparsely settled back country and on large uninhabited tracts that one finds evidence of land engrossment. There, it was simply an exchange from a wealthy Loyalist to a rising Whig investor.[50]

As was the case in Dutchess County, Orange and Ulster experienced little change in landholding before 1800. The large unsettled or sparsely settled Loyalist tracts remained undivided. There were only 5 resales of 1,109 acres, all of which were located in the more settled areas. Only two of these resales, totaling 345 acres might be described as speculative, as they took place within a year of purchase. Orange and Ulster were affected little by the dislocations of the 1780's.[51] Few advertisements for the sale of recently purchased confiscated land were found in the newspapers. More than half of the purchasers were listed in the 1790 census as being area residents.[52] In general, there was little if any change experienced in these counties during this period.

The disposition of the Loyalist estates in Orange and Ulster did not radically alter the socio-economic and landholding patterns of the area. Taking into consideration the distinction between the settled and back country regions, it is evident that the democratization of landholding which had begun in the pre-war period was only slightly accelerated by the confiscation policy of the Whigs. However, the sales cannot be dismissed as insignificant. There were several moderately large estates which were broken up and sold to a number of purchasers. The bulk of the land did come into the possession of local residents of varying degrees of wealth. The region only needed an influx of settlers to continue the growth of its freehold character. There is little doubt that the disposition of the Loyalist estates in Dutchess, Orange, and Ulster Counties produced a distinctive change in New York's landholding patterns. On both sides of the Hudson freehold tenure was increased, much of the land in question passed into the hands of local residents, and they were able to retain possession well into the nineteenth century.

In New York State as a whole, there was an almost seven-fold increase in landholding over the pre-war period. The lands of 235 Loyalists containing over 425,000 acres were sold to some 1,766 persons. Many of these purchasers had never owned land before. A high percentage, about 70 to 75 percent, were from the lower orders of society and they came into possession of one-half of the land sold. Although there is evidence of speculation and engrossment, especially in the more rural and frontier regions, the freeholds sold by the state averaged two hundred and thirty acres, not much more than the typical eighteenth century farm. This indicates a lack of concentration of land in the hands of a few. It can be assumed that the confiscation and sale of the Loyalist lands, which involved between one-quarter and one-third of New York's one million improved acres, changed hands in the direction of a wider distribution of landownership, thereby contributing to a wider political democracy not just in the Hudson River Valley but in the state as a whole.

Notes

1. J. Franklin Jameson, *The American Revolution Considered as a Social Movement* (Princeton, New Jersey: Princeton University Press, 1926), pp. 27-36, 41.

2. Thomas Cochrane, *New York in the Confederation* (Philadelphia: University of Pennsylvania Press, 1932), p. 64; Harry B. Yoshpe, *The Disposition of Loyalist Estates in the Southern District of New York* (New York: Columbia University Press, 1939), pp. 114-117; "The Disposition of Philipse Manor after the Revolution," *The Quarterly Bulletin of the Westchester County Historical Society*, XIV (1938), 92; Frederick B. Tolles, "The American Revolution Considered as a Social Movement: A Re-Valuation," *American Historical Review*, LIX (1954), 7-9.

3. Catherine Snell Crary, "Forfeited Loyalist Lands in the Western District of New York—Albany and Tryon Counties," *New York History*, XXXV (1954), 254-256, 244-245, 247-248; Staughton Lynd, *Anti-Federalism in Dutchess County, New York* (Chicago: Loyola University Press, 1962), Chapter IV, *passim*; "Who Should Rule at Home? Dutchess County in the American Revolution," *William and Mary Quarterly*, 3rd Series, XVIII (1961), 330; Beatrice G. Reubens, "Pre-emptive Rights in the Disposition of a Confiscated Estate: Philipsburg Manor, New York," *W&MQ*, 3rd Series, XXII (1965), 437, 453.

4. Reubens, *W&MQ*, 3rd Series, XIX, 435; North Callahan, *Flight from the Republic* (Baltimore: Bobbs, Merrill, 1965), pp. 40-43, 210-211; Thomas Jones, *History of New York During the Revolutionary War*, ed. Edward F. DeLancey, (2 Vols. New York: New York Historical Society, 1879), I, 153.

5. Lynd, *Anti-Federalism*, Chapter IV, *passim*: Irving Mark, *Agrarian Conflicts in Colonial New York: 1711-1775* (New York: Columbia University Press, 1940), *passim*; Sung Bok Kim "A New Look at the Great Landlords of Eighteenth Century New York," *W&MQ*, 3rd Series, XXVII (1970), 581-614; *Landlord and Tenant in Colonial New York* (Chapel Hill, North Carolina: University of North Carolina Press, 1978), *passim*.

6. New York, *Laws of the State of New York* (5 Vols., Albany, New York: Weed, Parsons, and Co., 1886), 11th Session; Chapter LC, March 21, 1788; II, 818, 822; 3rd Session, Chapter XXV, October 22, 1779, I, 173; Cochrane, *New York*, pp. 59-60; Yoshpe, *Disposition*, pp. 18-21.

7. John T. Reilly, "The Confiscation and Sales of the Loyalist Estates and Its Effect upon the Democratization of Landholding in New York State; 1779-1800" (Unpublished Doctoral Dissertation, Department of History, Fordham University, 1974), p. 263.

8. Cochrane, *New York*, p. 64; Yoshpe, *Disposition*, pp. 114-117; Tolles, *AHR*, LIX, 7-9.

9. Jameson, *Social Movement*, pp. 27-36, 41; Alexander C. Flick, *The American Revolution in New York* (Albany, N.Y.: University of the State of New York, 1926), pp. 133, 221, 235; Crary, *New York History*, XXXV, 254-256; Staughton Lynd, "Revolution and the Common Man," (Unpublished Doctoral Dissertation, Department of History, Columbia University, 1966), p. 125; Lynd, *W&MQ*, 3rd Series, XVII (1961), 330, 334; Lynd, *Anti-Federalism, Chapter IV, passim*; Reubens, *W&MQ*, 3rd Series, XXII (1965), 437, 453.

10. E. Wilder Spaulding, *New York in the Critical Period* (New York: Columbia University Press, 1932), pp. 51-53, 57; Jackson Turner Main, "The Redistribution of Property in Post-Revolutionary Virginia," *Mississippi Valley Historical Review*, XLI (1954), 245-246; Percey W. Bidwell and John I. Falconer, *History of Agriculture in the Northern United States: 1620-1860* (Washington: Carnegie Institute, 1925), p. 115; Alfred C. Young, *The Democratic Republicans of New York: 1763-1797* (Chapel Hill, N.C.: The University of North Carolina Press, 1967), p. 92; Patricia U. Bonomi, *Factious People: Politics and Society in Colonial New York* (New York: Columbia University Press, 1971), p. 167; Kim, *Landlord and Tenant, passim*; Edward Countryman, "Out of the Bounds of the Law: Northern Land Rioter in the Eighteenth Century," in Alfred C. Young, ed., *The American Revolution* (De Kalb, Illinois: Northern Illinois University Press, 1976), pp. 37-70.

11. Lynd, *Anti-Federalism*, pp. 47, 49; Wallace Brown, "American Farmers During the Revolution: Rebel or Loyalist?" *Agricultural History*, XLII (1968), 327-339; Mark, *Agrarian Conflicts*, p. 201.

12. Flick, *Loyalism*, p. 141; Clifford M. Buck, "Dutchess County People," *Yearbook of the Dutchess County Historical Society*, LII (1967), 91-97; Lynd, *W&MQ*, 3rd Series, XVII, Note 69, 350; Edmund Platt, *The Eagle's History of Poughkeepsie* (Poughkeepsie, N.Y.: Platt & Platt, 1905), p. 30; *New York Packet*, June 22, 1780; June 22, 1781, June 13, December 20, 1782, April 14, 1783; Amount of Sale, Middle District, N.D. (1781), War of Revolution MSS, V Box 2, New York State Library, Albany, N.Y.

13. American Loyalist Transcripts, LXII, 295; LXIII, 231-234, 283, New York Public Library; William S. Pelletreau, *History of Putnam County, New York* (Philadelphia; W.W. Preston, 1886), pp. 363-364, 575: Martha J. Lamb, *History of the City of New York* (3 Vols. New York: A.S. Barnes 1896), II, 605-606.

14. Pelletreau, *Putnam County*, pp. 93–94, 106–113, 328, 578, 676; David M. Ellis, *Landlords and Farmers in the Hudson-Mohawk Region: 1790-1850* (New York: Octagon Books, 1967), pp. 4–5; Lynd, *Anti-Federalism*, p. 74; Lynd, "Revolution and the Common Man," pp. 120–133; Robert G. Livingston to Gilbert Livingston, November 22, 1786; Henry G. Livingston to Robert Livingston, March 4, 1781, Gilbert Livingston Papers Box I, NYPL; Petition of Abraham Paine, 1781, Assembly Papers, XXV, NYSL; Lynd, "Revolution and the Common Man," pp. 116, 121–123; none of the evidence citied by Lynd involved purchasers of confiscated estates.

15. These figures were compiled from the following sources: Liber 8, Dutchess County: this is the same as Liber A, Abstract of Forfeited Lands, Dutchess County Mss, New York Historical Society; Liber of Deeds, Dutchess County; Liber of Deeds, Putnam County; Deed Books, New York State, Office of the State Engineer; Account of Jonathan Lawrence, One of the Commissioners to produce a sum in specie, N.D.(1782), New York Revolutionary Committees and Commissions, Revolutionary War MSS, Box V, NYHS: Abstracts of Sales of the Commissioners of Forfeiture for the Middle District, May 20, 1785; March 21, 1788; August 20, 1789; War of Revolution MSS, Oversize, NYSL; The accuracy of some of the sales is attested to by a report by the State Treasurer, Abraham Lansing to Morris Robinson, son of Beverly, when he inquired as to the amounts of money collected by the state in the sales of his father's lands. The amounts given by Lansing corresponded to those which were reported by the Commissioners of Forfeiture and Specie, John Lansing to Beverly Robinson, Jr., September 1, 1806, Great Britain, Treasury Papers, Series T 79, Public Record Office, London.

16. Lynd, *Anti-Federalism*, pp. 27–28, 75; "Revolution and the Common Man," p. 125; Pelletreau, *Putnam County*, p. 579; Liber of Deeds, Dutchess County, *passim*; American Loyalist Transcripts, LXII, 231–234, 287–288, NYPL; Public Record Office, London; Dutchess County Tax Lists, 1771–1779, County Clerk, Poughkeepsie, N.Y.

17. Edward M. Ruttenber, ed., *Catalogue of Collections at Washington's Headquarters: Newburgh, New York* (Newburgh, New York: E.M. Ruttenber, 1874), p. 144; Pelletreau, *Putnam County*, pp. 501, 526, 529; Rodney MacDonough, "William Denning," *New York Genealogical and Biographical Record*, XXX (1899), 133–194.

18. Lynd, *Anti-Federalism*, p. 58; Young, *Democratic Republicans*, p. 46; McCracken, *Old Dutchess*, p. 424; New York, Secretary of State, *Calendar of New York Colonial Manuscripts, Indorsed Land Papers, 1647-1803* (Albany, New York: Weed, Parsons, & Co., 1804), p. 735; J. Wilson Poucher, "Zephaniah Platt," *Dutchess County Historical Society Yearbook*, XXIX (1944), 51–55; *Biographical Directory of the American Congress: 1774-1927* (Washington: U.S. Government Printing Office, 1928), p. 1461; Liber of Deeds, Dutchess County, 8, 194–195. Several Dutchess County purchasers of Loyalist estates, such as Platt, Melancton Smith and others, were involved in the Plattsburgh speculation.

19. Joseph Scoville (Walter Barrett), *The Old Merchants of New York City* (5 Vols., New York: Carleton, 1863), IV, 299–305; *Dictionary of American Biography*, XVI, 341–342. Sands bought 643 acres.

20. Lynd, *Anti-Federalism*, p. 58; *American Congress*, p. 1540; East, *Business Enterprise*, pp. 94, 108, 117–118, 146, 225, 275, 368; J. Wilson Poucher, "Melancton Smith," *Dutchess County Historical Society Yearbook*, X, (1926), 39–48; *DAB*, XVIII, 310–320, 515; Dorothy R. Dillion, *The New York Triumvirate* (New York: Columbia University Press, 1944), pp. 164–165.

21. Reubens, *W&MQ*, 3rd Series, XXII (1965), *passim*; Rent Rolls of Rodger Morris, Great Britain, Audit Office, 13,116, PRO; American Loyalist Transcripts, XLVI, 226; LXVIII, 231–234, NYPL.

22. American Loyalist Transcripts, LXIII, 225, NYPL; Mark, *Agrarian Conflicts*, pp. 200–201; Flick, *Loyalism*, p. 88; Spaulding, *New York*, p. 132; Reubens, *W&MQ*, 3rd Series, XXII (1965), 451–452.

23. Twelve tenants eventually did file claims. American Loyalist Transcripts, XVIII, 447–450, 475–480, 515–517; XIX, 173–178; XX, 107–115; XXIX, 143–162, 175, NYPL; Ontario, *United Empire Loyalists*, pp. 766–767, 771–772, 787, 790, 809, 815–817, 823, 886, 1246–1247. Bonomi has pointed out that the Crown often sided with the small farmer in a title dispute with a large landlord like the Livingstons and that this could have caused many farmers to be Loyalists, *Factious People*, Note 57, p. 210. See also Wallace Brown, *The King's Friends* (Providence, Rhode Island: Brown University Press, 1968), *passim*.

24. Comfort Sands sold 456 acres of confiscated land to Thomas Mitchell subject to a lease to Simon Wright from Beverly Robinson for three lives or 21 years. Mitchell in 1780 sold the farm to Asa Haines still subject to the lease, Liber of Deeds, Dutchess County, 11–312, 12–448; Stephen Ward bought a farm from Nathaniel Delavan, who in turn purchased it from the Commissioners of Specie; when Ward bought the farm it was subject to a thirty year lease to Archibald Campbell from Robinson. Petition of Stephen Ward to the Legislature, N.D. (1796), Assembly Papers, XXVII, NYSL; Mark, *Agrarian Conflicts*, pp. 203–204; Yoshpe, *Disposition*, pp. 32, 54, 114–115.

25. Willis F. Johnson, *Colonel Henry Ludington* (New York: Privately Printed, 1907), p. 208; Lamb, *History of the City of New York*, II, 212–213; Pelletreau, *Putnam County*, p. 692; List of tenants on Captain Philip Philipse' long lot No. 6, 1804, 1810; Philipse-Gouverneur Papers, Columbia University, New York.

26. John O'Brien purchased his deceased mother's leasehold, while Hester Van Tassel purchased her late husband's, Liber of Deeds, Dutchess County, 8, 317, 355.

27. Petition of Ruben Ferris and ninety-three others, New York Senate, *Journal*, April 10, 1782, p. 71; Petition of Alexander Kidd and 102 others, March, 1782; Petition of residents of Philipstown, March, 1782, Petition of George Lane and fifty-seven others, March 16, 1782 Senate Papers, II, 2088, Box II; XI, Box I, NYSL; New York Assembly, *Journal*, March 28, 1782, p. 81; Lynd, "Revolution and the Common Man," p. 116.

28. Reubens, *W&MQ*, 3rd Series, XXII (1965), 451–452.

29. Pelletreau, *Putnam County*, pp. 121–128: Dutchess County Tax Lists, 1777, 1779, County Clerk, Poughkeepsie, New York.

30. Reubens, *W&MQ*, 3rd Series, XXII (1965), 454.

31. Liber of Deeds, Dutchess County, *passim*; Liber of Deeds, Putnam County, *passim*.

32. *Poughkeepsie Country Journal*, May 18, 1786; December 20, 1788; April 9, November 5, 1791; *New York Journal*, December 7, 1791.

33. Lynd, *Anti-Federalism*, pp. 76–77; Lynd, "Revolution and the Common Man," pp. 121–123.

34. Liber of Mortgages, Dutchess County, 4, 414, 432.

35. Liber of Deeds, Dutchess County, 9, 209, 344; 11, 76, 224; *Poughkeepsie Country Journal*, July 7, 1789; June 26, 1790; April 20, 1793; This newspaper listed fourteen purchasers of confiscated land in the 1787–1792 period as insolvent debtors of whom only two had their estates sold., Caleb Frisby and Daniel Ter Boss, *Poughkeepsie Country Journal*, March 28, 1787; December 20, 1788; March 31, 1789; January 12, June 19, June 24, July 12, September 11, October 18, October 25, November 12, Deember 25, 1790; April 30, December 15, 1791; March 1, 1792.

36. Abstract of Sales of Commissioners of Forfeiture for the Middle District, May 20, 1785, War of the Revolution MSS, Oversize, NYSL.

37. *Ibid.*, *Poughkeepsie Country Journal*, January 7, 1787; March 12, 1794.

38. Russell Headley, *History of Orange County, New York* (Middletown, New York: Van Dusen and Elms, 1908), pp. 42, 301, 638; Alphonse T. Clearwater, *History of Ulster County, New York* (Kingston, New York: W.J. Van Dusen, 1907), pp. 17, 27; David Cole, *History of Rockland, New York* (New York: J.B. Beers & Co., 1889), pp. 17–18; Edward M. Ruttenber and L.H. Clark, *History of Orange County, New York* (Philadelphia: Everts and Peck, 1881), p. 32; Sylvester, *Ulster County*, pp. 15–17; Spaulding, *New York*, Percy G Adams, ed. *Crevecour's Eighteenth Century Travels in Pennsylvania and New York* (Lexington, Ky: University of Kentucky Press, 1961), pp. 17, 26, 30.

39. Headley, *Orange County*, pp. 35–38; Green, *Rockland County*, pp. 26–28; Ruttenber and Clark, *Orange County*, pp. 11–16; Spaulding, *New York*, pp. 51–53; Ruttenber, *Newburgh*, pp. 26–28, 112; "Rockland Record," *Proceedings and Historical Collections of Rockland County Historical Society*, II (1932), 58. *Old Ulster*, II (1906), No. II, 321–324; V (1909), No. II, 24–25; Dwight Aker, *Outposts of History in Orange County* (Washingtonville, New York: By the Author, 1937), pp. 16–17. According to Ruttenber the Evans Patent was broken up into 15 smaller ones ranging in size from 160 to 4,000 acres. Edward M. Ruttenber, *History of the Town of New Windsor* (Newburgh, New York: E.M. Ruttenber, 1911), pp. 12–16; Clearwater, *Ulster County*, p. 64; Sylvester, *Ulster County*, p. 287; Elizabeth Sharts, *Land O'Goshen* (Goshen, New York: The Bookmill, 1900), p. 5; Marius Schoonmaker, *History of Kingston, New York* (Kingston, New York: Burr Printing House, 1888), p. 188; Kenneth E. Hasbrouck, *History of New Hurley* (New Paltz, New York: By the Author, 1949), pp. 3–4; Bonomi, *Factious People*, pp. 185–186.

40. Tax Lists of the Town of New Hempstead, 1794, "Rockland Record," *Proceedings*, III (1940), 64–65; Ruttenber and Clark, *Orange County*, pp. 520–521; Tax List of Marbletown, *Ulster County*, N.D. (1790), Clearwater, *Ulster County*, p. 64; Tax List of Esopus, 1791, Sylvester, *Ulster County*, p. 109; Orange County Tax Lists, 1775, 1780, 1787, Lansing Papers, NYSL. The road lists of the period which indicate how many days a man must labor on the public roads correlated to his economic standing in terms of property owned show only a few fairly large landowners with no great disparity between levels of property owned. Marlborough Road List, 1788, Ulster County, Sylvester, *Ulster County*, p. 75; Douglas "Confiscation in Ulster County," p. 40; Assessment Roll, Town of Orange, Orange County, 1796, Budke Collection, XLVII, NYPL; Main, *Social Structure*, p. 24.

41. Richard Smith, *A Tour of Four Great Rivers* (New York: Charles Scribner & Sons, 1906), p. 6.

42. These figures were compiled from the following sources: Liber of Deeds, Orange County, County Clerk, Goshen, New York; Liber of Deeds, Rockland County, County Clerk, New City, New York; Liber of Deeds, Ulster County, County Clerk, Kingston, New York; Abstract of Sales by Daniel Graham, Commissioner of Forfeiture, Middle District, May 20, 1785, August 20, 1787, War of Revolution MSS, Oversize, NYSL; Abstract of Sales of forfeited estates of Commissioner of Forfeiture for the Middle District, N.D. (1785); Abstract of Sales of Commissioners of Forfeiture for the Middle District, Report of Daniel Graham's sales, March 2, 1786; War of the Revolution MSS, Miscel. NYSL; Abstract of Sales of Commissioner of Forfeiture for Middle District, December 13, 1793; Assembly Papers, XXII, NYSL; Abstract of Sales of Commissioner of Forfeiture for the Middle District, 1784, War of the Revolution MSS, LXIV, Box 2, NYSL.

43. Douglas, "Confiscation in Ulster," pp. 35–37.

44. Orange County Tax Lists, 1778, 1780, 1787, Lansing Papers, NYSL; Other tax lists in Sylvester, *Ulster County*, pp. 173, 572–573; Schoonmaker, *Kingston*, p. 324; Ruttenber and Clark, *Orange County*, p. 376, 614, 666, 668; Cole, *Rockland County*, p. 342; "Day Book, Charles Clinton," *Historical Society of Newburgh Bay and the Highlands*, XXVI, (1929), 23–27; Militia Lists are contained in James A. Robert, ed., *New York in the Revolution* (2nd Edition, Albany, New York: Brandow Printing Co., 1898), *passim*.

45. American Loyalist Transcripts, LXI, 101–276, NYPL.

46. Cole, *Rockland County*, pp. 150–151, 161–162, 320, 343; Ruttenber and Clark, *Orange County*, pp. 18, 57; Green, *Rockland County*, pp. 37, 391; Arthur S. Tompkins, ed. *Historical Record of Rockland County* (Nyack, New York: Van Dusen and Joyce, 1902), p. 558.

47. "Day Book of Charles Clinton," *Historical Society of Newburgh Bay and the Highlands*, XVI, 23–27; Sharts, *Goshen*, pp. 87–88; Cochrane, *New York*, p. 20; Ruttenber and Clark, *Orange County*, pp. 376, 440; Nathaniel S. Benton, *History of Herkimer County, New York* (Albany, New York: Joel Munsel, 1856), 373–377; John Nicholson to Evans Whorry, February 7, 1781; February 12, 1785, John Nicholson Papers, NYHS; Writ of Trespass against Evans Whorry by James Monnal, February 24, 1784, Aaron Burr papers, NYHS; Orange County Tax Lists, 1779, Lansing Papers, NYSL; New Hempstead Tax List, 1794, "Rockland Record," *Proceedings*, III (1940); Cole, *Rockland County*, pp. 92, 232, 261–262, 317, 318; Green, *Rockland County*, p. 42; New York, Secretary of State, *Calendar of Colonial Documents-Indorsed Land Papers*, pp. 787, 869, 888, 895, 897, 900, 928; Suffern bought 142 acres with 5 other persons, Liber of Deeds, Rockland County, 8, 182; Article of Agreement between Gilbert Cooper, John Suffern, Thomas Russell, Benjamin Coe, John D. Coe, and Thomas Coe, December 24, 1784, February 12, 1785, Budke Collection LXXVII, NYPL.

48. Wallkill Precinct in 1754 contained only forty to fifty families. Description of Wallkill Patent, N.D. (1760), Ulster County, New York.

49. Robert J. Rayback, ed. *Richards Atlas of New York State* (Phoenix, New York: Frank E. Richards, 1965, p. 34. A breakdown of the population according to 1790 census indicates that the area in Ulster and Orange Counties between the Shawangunk Mountains and the Hudson River was well populated, as high as forty-three to fifty persons per square mile in Orange County, while the area west of the Shawangunks was relatively unsettled with about one to ten persons per square mile. Herman R. Friis, "A Series of Population Maps of the Colonies and the United States: 1625–1790," *Geographical Review* (July 1940), 463–470.

50. Flick, *Loyalism*, pp. 257–261; George D. Wickerham, Record Book, NYHS; Manilton Child, *Gazetteer and Business Directory of Sullivan County, New York* (Syracuse, New York: By the Author, 1872), p. 147.

51. Liber of Deeds, Rockland County, 141, 15; Liber of Deeds, Ulster County, KK, 416.

52. Bureau of the Census, *Heads of Families, 1790, passim*.

The Founding Fathers and the Constitutional Confrontations of 1973

Jonathan Clark
Professor of History, Vassar College
(1941–1983)

We have a cat, large and black, nearly nine years old. As a kitten he spent a great deal of time outdoors, chasing butterflies, swatting bees, crouching in the uncut grass ready to pounce on any unsuspecting leaf that blew by. But as he grew older, we discovered he had an insatiable thirst for power. Not satisfied with his own yard, he tried to extend his domain to the whole block. Unhappily, other cats considered those yards as their turf. During the next few months we were subjected to concerts of cat-wails, throat-rattles and to veterinarian bills we could not afford. We finally settled the issue of dividing up the turf, at least as far as it concerned us, by having our cat's physical constitution surgically altered. We renamed him Jake, after the Hemingway hero in *The Sun Also Rises*. He does not go outdoors anymore.

My explanation of why Jake lost his cathood, if that is the right word and the constitutional confrontations arising from Watergate affair have in common one important ingredient: the central theme of power.

Because the White House has been at the center of much of the constitutional controversy, the powers of the presidency have become the focal point of that debate. When, for example, President Nixon chose to withhold the Watergate tapes, he stood his ground on the doctrine of separations of powers, on, so to speak, his definition of the boundaries of presidential turf. While Judge Sirica disagreed with Mr. Nixon's position, he, too, based his decision on an interpretation of the amount of power the Framers of the Constitution intended to lodge in the executive branch.

Unfortunately, the Constitution itself does not say whether the President must or must not turn over evidence to either Congress or the courts. Thus, much of the debate concerning the limits of executive power has rested on the intentions of the Founding Fathers, since for one reason or another they failed to specify in any detail all of the things a President shall or shall not do.

In fact, the entire Constitution is, by later standards anyway, a model of brevity. This has been one of its great virtues, allowing the document to survive vast changes in society, and giving gainful employment to generations of constitutional lawyers, jurists, historians, and political scientists. That same virtue has also resulted in doctrines like executive privilege and the inherent powers of the President, doctrines about which the Constitution contains nothing. It neither forbids nor endorses them. It simply stands mute. And where the letter of the Constitution is lacking, men turn to its spirit, to the words and actions of the Founding Fathers.

President Nixon has invoked the names of George Washington and Thomas Jefferson on his behalf, two men who had a pretty fair idea of the intent of the Framers. Washington had actually served as president of the Constitutional Convention at Philadelphia as a kind of prefatory act to presiding over the new nation. And though Jefferson was in France in 1787, he could be as well-informed on the meaning of the Constitution as most people through the offices of his good friend, James Madison. Citing Washington's actions in the debates over the Jay Treaty and Jefferson's during the Burr trial, Mr. Nixon has stressed what the Founding Fathers *did* with presidential power. Judge Sirica, meanwhile, quoted statements made by Madison and South Carolina's Charles Pinckney, both of whom had a hand in framing the Constitution, to support his interpretation. Judge Sirica concentrated on what the Founding Fathers *said* about the limits of executive power.

I am no lawyer and this is no brief, but I think this preoccupation with the power of the presidency, especially with regard to the constitutional issues raised by Watergate, is as incomplete, if not as misplaced, as my explanation of why our cat is now a eunuch. It also does a disservice to the records, incomplete and unreliable as they may be, left by those who framed and debated the Constitution.

The Founding Fathers provided America with a rare phenomenon. They were politicians who took political ideas seriously. So of course they worried about executive power and the kind of men who would wield it. Members of the Convention discussed whether the president should be given an absolute veto, a conditional veto or no veto at all. They debated to what extent he should have power to appoint federal officers. They wanted, as Madison wrote in a letter to Jefferson, "to unite a proper energy in the Execuitive."

But if the records of the Convention are to serve as a guide, a particular emphasis should be placed on the word "proper." For the delegates spent comparatively little time considering how much power belonged in the executive branch. Many more hours of thought—and anguished debate—were given to what the Framers considered the more fundamental problem of making the President responsible for his actions. The issue of executive responsibility cropped up time and again. On whom should the President depend for his election, Congress, the states, the people, or some combination of all three? How long a term in office should have? Should the President be elegible for re-election? Should an executive council be annexed to the presidency? Should the executive office consist of only one person, or would three offer greater safety? These questions, and the answers finally arrived at, reflected a concern central to the deliberations of the Framers, to make a President responsible for the way he used the power granted him by the people, to make authority inseparable from duty and accountability.

This theme of responsiblity seems to have gone underground recently. Yet it was crucial to the whole concept of separation of powers, at least as the Founding Fathers envisioned it. They had no intention of setting up an all-powerful President, no matter how popular, against as all-powerful Congress, no matter how representative. Such a government would have smacked too much of England's King and Parliament, and the Constitution was written a short eleven years after Americans had decided they wanted no part of Kings and Parliaments, period.

In 1776 England had demostrated once again the truth of a maxim revolutionary Americans found evident throughout human history: powerful men are dangerous men. Though worldly-wise in several matters, eighteenth century Americans remained thoroughly paranoid about politics. When in office they cried out against those who would destroy free and orderly government. When out of office they denounced and exposed the tyrannical designs of those who governed. They spent what seems an inordinate amount of time trying to demonstrate, in effect, that all the world was Watergate. We like to remember the Declaration of Independence as a magnificent statement of revolutionary hopes and principles, which of course it was. We tend to forget, though, that its main purpose (which the bulk of the text reflected) was to expose to a candid world the diabolical conspiracy attempted by King George III. In the America of 1787, as in 1776, only a fool would grant political power without demanding responsiblity in return. And the Founding Fathers were not fools.

George III was only a man, not the kind of creature the Founding Fathers placed much confidence in. Alexander Hamilton, with no great delicacy, said simply, "Take mankind in general, they are vicious." Hamilton has a reputation as a conservative, so perhaps we should expect that reaction from him. Moving across the spectrum, though, we find Madison writing that government itself is the greatest reflection on human nature, and Patrick Henry, whose popular image as a fire-eating radical remains almost untarnished, lived, he said, in dread of the depravity of human nature.

Not everyone was as pessimistic—realistic, some would say—as a Henry or a Hamilton. The venerable Benjamin Franklin, from the wisdom of his eighty-one years, scolded some of his fellow delegates at the Constitutional Convention for casting aspersions upon the moral capacity of the common man. Franklin did not deny the truth of the aspersions. He merely wished to observe that some of the greatest rogues he had known happened also to be the richest rogues.

While the Founding Fathers did not believe that all politicians were crooks, they also knew of no way to guarantee that crooks—or worse—might not govern. As Madison worded their dilemma so aptly, "In framing a government which is to be administered by men over men, the great difficulty lies in this: you must first enable the government to control the governed; and in the second place oblige it to control itself."

Under the Articles of Confederation each of the thirteen states had been more or less master of its own destiny. By 1787 a number of respected Americans feared the Confederation to be in danger of dissolution. The inability of that government to control the governed had brought the delegates to Philadelphia in the first place. Their primary task, to state it with beguiling simplicity, was to transfer to the federal government some of the powers enjoyed by the states, to invest Congress with enough power to legislate for national concerns, while still leaving the states in control of their internal affairs. The completion of their work required more than three months of argument, back-room dealing and compromise.

The result of their labors met with as much criticism as it did praise. New York's Melancton Smith, for instance, insisted that the Constitution "gave too much power to the central government, however it might be organized." Other Antifederalists, as opponents to ratification were called, predicted the new and now powerful federal goverment would drive the state governments out of existence. A Virginian feared the coming day when Congress would force him to obey the blue laws of Massachusetts. Folks in Massachusetts, meanwhile, shuddered at the prospect of being exposed to, even infected by, the loose morals and dissolute manners of the slave-holding South. Many Antifederalists wondered out loud if the men who framed the new government might not have designed it that way on purpose, if the Constitution itself was not the work of conspirators who intended that only the rich and powerful should rule.

More relevant to the current constitutional conflicts than the question of governmental power, though, was the second part of the difficulty Madison had pointed to, that of obliging the government to control itself. Here, too, Antifederalists found the Constitution wanting. They considered the powers given to Congress too loosely defined, and the branches of government not sufficiently independent of each other. Some Antifederalists predicted the rise of a monarchy under the Constitution, others foresaw the creation of an aristocracy, and this in republican America.

Even if the Framers had not deliberately constructed an engine for tyranny, they had, according to Antifederalists, foolishly forgotten the nature of the human animal. They had failed to frame the government around the first law of human motivation, that, as William Grayson phrased the platitude, "mankind are governed by interest." Otherwise, the Constitution would never have granted so much power to so few people in such a sloppy fashion.

Patrick Henry, who vehemently opposed the ratification of the Constitution, capsulized the thrust of such criticisms as well as anyone in a speech before the Virginia ratifying convention. "My great objection the Constitution," he said, "[is] that there is no true responsibilty—and that the preservation of our liberty depends on the single chance of men being virtuous enough to make laws to punish themselves." Patrick Henry knew, in his own words, "the absolute necessity of energetic government." But in return for power, he demanded responsibility.

What Henry wanted was precisely what the Framers had tried to provide. They, too, believed man to be a creature of self-interest. They, too, knew that untrustworthy men would likely be elected or appointed to positions of high trust. So they formulated a complex series of checks and balances, they provided the means to remove from office men judged unfit to govern, and they separated powers. But they did not create this obstructing labyrinth to promote the use of power. They did so to prevent its abuse.

In the recent constitutional clashes among the President, the courts and Congress, with each branch proposing its own interpretation of where the line should be drawn demarcating the limits of executive power, all sides have placed the terms of confrontation in an anachronistic context. They have interpreted the Constitution they revere from the same perspective as Patrick Henry, and Henry did not like the Constitution at all. Henry also thought of the Constitution almost solely in terms of power. His analysis, and it was one employed by the Antifederalists, boiled down to a very simple proposition: when one governmental power contests another governmental power, no matter which side wins, power still prevails.

These critics of the Constitution failed to realize, and too many of us fail to remember, that the separation of powers was not an end, only a means. The Framers never intended to establish independent bailiwicks of authority within which those who held office could do and dispose as they pleased. The powers of government were separated for essentially the opposite purpose: to restrain self-interested men whose ambition and avarice could lead to tyrannical government. Seperation of powers was only an artifice, one means among many, dedicated toward the end of creating a government responsive to and accountable to the American people. What else, after all, is representative government all about.

That the terms of the current debate should be set by the issue of executive power and not executive responsibilty, while predictable, at the very least warps the spirit os the Constitution. But perhaps such warpage is inevitable. Historians write glowingly about strong presidents, not responsible ones. Americans admire results, and we are often not particular how politicians get those results, unless they make fools of us in the process, which surely accounts in parts for Mr. Nixon's drastic droop in popular stature.

Just as George Washington was first in war, peace, and his countrymen's hearts, so was he the first president to employ the doctrine of separation of powers to defend his interpretation of the Constitution. In March, 1796, the House of Represenatives requested President Washington to supply it with the papers relating to the controversial Jay Treaty, Washington denied the request. In a message to the House defending his refusal, Washington noted his own attendance at the Constitutional Convention (Who could know more of the intentions of the Framers than one of their number?) and went on to cite the secret journal of the proceedings of the Convention (entrusted to him for safekeeping). When it came to one-upsmanship in interpreting the Constitution, George Washington obviously had few peers.

But it so happened that in 1796 one of the leaders in the House of Representatives who opposed Washington's foreign policy was none other than James Madison. If for no other reason than the copious and now classic notes he took at the Constitutional Convention, Madison evidently knew at least as much as (if not more than) Washington did concerning the intentions of the men who framed the Constitution. In a letter to Jefferson, Madison described Washington's message as "improper & indelicate." Later, and in more measured tones, he offered a reasoned rebuttal of Washington's position in a speech before the House. One portion of his speech dealt with the materials men used to support their interpretations of the Constitution. Madison there made a point which has not received too much attention. It deserves to be quoted in full:

> But, after all, whatever veneration might be entertained for the body of men who formed our Constitution, the sense of that body could never be regarded as the oracular guide in expounding the Constitution. As the instrument came from them it was nothing more than the draft of a plan, nothing but a dead letter, until life and validity were breathed into it by the voice of the people, speaking through the several State Conventions. If we were to look, therefore, for the meaning of the instrument beyond the face of the instrument, we must look for it, not in the General Convention, which proposed it, but in the State Conventions, which accepted and ratified the Constitution.

The delegates to the state conventions decided whether or not the Constitution would become the law of the land, not the men who wrote it. Those delegates knew full well their decision would affect the lives of their children and grandchildren as well as themselves. Furthermore, several of the Framers also served as delegates to the ratifying conventions of their respective states. There they had the opportunity to explain publicly the kind of government the Constitution was intended to provide. And the new government was ratified not on the basis of the private deliberations that took place in Philadelphia during the long, hot summer of 1787, but on the public discussions that occured throughout the following year.

If the fragmentary records are at all indicative, in many states surprisingly little time was given to discussions of the executive branch. Where the Presidency was discussed, supporters of ratification were not shy in admitting that they wanted a strong President. But they also stressed how carefully the Constitution provided for a responsible President. James Wilson, who had contributed more than most men to the making of the Constitution, talked to the Pennsylvania ratifying convention about the office of the President. What he had to say merits a careful reading:

> The executive power is better to be trusted when it has no screen. Sir, we have a responsibility in the person of our President: he cannot act improperly, and hide either his negligence or inattention; he cannot roll upon any other person the weight of his criminality; no appointment can take place without his nomination; and he is responsible for every nomination that he makes.

Nor was that all Wilson had to say concerning the Presidency:

> *We secure vigor.* We well know what numerous executives are. We know what numerous executives are. We know there is neither vigor, decision, nor responsibility in them. Add to all this, that officer [the President] is placed high, and is possessed of power far from being contemptible; yet not a *single privilege* is annexed to his character; far from being above the laws, he is amenable to them in his private character as a citizen, and in his public character by *impeachment*.

So much more for executive privilege.

I am unaware of any defenses of the Presidency made in 1787 or 1788 which refute Wilson's views. Even Alexander Hamilton, who probably would have preferred a limited monarchy for America rather than a republican government, completed his discussion of the powers of the presidency in *The Federalist Papers* by asking if the executive branch combined the requisites of republican safety, "a due dependence on the people, a due responsibilty." He answered in the affirmative.

Such evidence suggests that we should redefine the terms of today's constitutional conflicts. Instead of asking if the President has acted within his authority, perhaps we should ask the more pertinent question of whether he has acted responsibly.

I do not know how James Wilson would have reacted to President Nixon's fine distinction between blame and responsibility. But I think that neither he nor the other Founding Fathers would have been especially shocked at recent revelations: that a Vice President did not mean for his stance on law and order to apply to himself, that crimes were committed to help ensure the re-election of a President, that some men tried to cover up those crimes, or that the President attempted to withhold evidence that might help establish who was guilty of wrong-doing.

The Founding Fathers could have anticipated as much. They realized that free government was built on a paradox, that power had to be invested in men who could not be trusted with power. Thus they had created mechanisms designed to make such men responsible.

The Founding Fathers were a singular group of men. Yet they knew that no government, no matter how wisely constructed, could be any better than the people for whom it was constituted. For freedom to flourish in America, an additional ingredient was necessary. Some men called that ingredient republican virtue, others signified the same thing by a different term, that much maligned word, patriotism. But when the Founding Fathers spoke of patriotism, they did not envision its perversion, the unthinking and unblinking loyalty to those in authority, which the phrase "my country right or wrong" has come to imply. Rather, they had in mind the patriotism exhibited by a salty Antifederalist from New England who said he would not trust a flock of Moseses and declared that the people had a right to be suspicious. That man loved his country enough to care that it be protected from the men with the greatest potential to destroy it, those who governed.

Only the American people have the power to decide if the paradox of the Founding Fathers will turn into a contradiction for us. No one saw that more clearly than James Madison. The man who earned the title Father of the Constitution, knew full well that responsible government ultimately depended on the American people having the patriotism to make politicians accountable. "I hope,"

Madison told the Virginia ratifying convention, "the patriotism of the people will continue and be a sufficient guard to their liberties."

I hope so, too.

Transportation and Changing Patterns of Settlement
in Dutchess County

Richard P. O'Connor

Professor of Physical Sciences, Dutchess Community College

At the beginning of the nineteenth century, the overwhelming majority of Dutchess County's citizens lived in small isolated communities spread more or less evenly over the County. Furthermore, many of these communities were little more than collections of isolated farms bound together by a few small social institutions, such as a school, a store or a church. Subsistence farming dominated the economy. Each community was, for the most part, a self-contained economic unit producing most of the goods and services necessary for survival within its boundaries. To be sure, cash crops for export from the community were produced; but their delivery was hampered by the very poor transportation system in the County at the time.[1] The economic and social isolation was imposed on the residents by the inadequacies of the transportation system of the day. Vast improvements in transportation technology presented new opportunities which were aggressively adopted by the County's citizens. With each new change in transportation came new economic and social opportunities. As the people of Dutchess County embraced these opportunities, the patterns of settlement, the sense of community, and the very fabric of everyday life underwent accompanying changes. This paper is an analysis of those changes.

In 1840, the population of Dutchess County was about 50,000. Its economy was firmly based upon its agricultural land. In 1840, there were no communities that claimed the title of city, and only two townships had more than 10,000 souls. One was Fishkill, which at that time contained all of what was to become the City of Beacon, the Town of Wappingers, and the Town of East Fishkill. The other was the Town of Poughkeepsie, which at that time still contained what was to become the largest city in the County. Of the remaining sixteen townships, the smallest was Pine Plains with 1,300 inhabitants and the largest was Red Hook with 2,800. Roughly, three quarters of the County's population lived outside of the areas that would later become the cities of Beacon and Poughkeepsie and these were fairly evenly distributed over the entire county.[2] But in 1840, the forces of economic and technological change were already beginning to destroy the relatively homogeneous distribution of population and consolidate both population and economic activity in just a few communities. Of these forces, the most important were the mechanization of the farm and the railroad.

The revolution in agriculture seems to have had a twofold effect in Dutchess County during the nineteenth century. It obviously freed people from the land. On the other hand, it also permitted the more intensive use of the better agricultural land and the evolution of a more extensive cash crop system. When one compares the population of the poorly connected towns of Pine Plains and Milan to the towns of Red Hook and Rhinebeck which were close to the river and the mainline Hudson River Railroad, differences are notable. The steamboat and the railroad probably permitted Red Hook and Rhinebeck to shift their agriculture to the production of perishable cash crops such as fruits, dairy products and even fresh flowers for the New York City market.[3] (One of the most unusual industries to develop in this area was the violet industry of Rhinebeck.) The more intensive use of the land in the communities near the river not only created an increased demand for agricultural labor, but it also created an increased demand for labor in transportation, packing and the general service sector of the economy. As a result, the populations of Red Hook and Rhinebeck grew in the early days of the railroads and the agricultural mechanization, whereas the population of Pine Plains and Milan showed no growth.[4] But, by 1880, further improvements in agricultural efficiency and competition from other areas made possible by an ever-improving transportation system and new techniques for storing food caused the populations of these communities to peak.[5] From 1880 until the automobile began to have its effect in the early twentieth century, the population of Red Hook and Rhinebeck decreased as did the majority of the towns of the County.

Between 1850 and 1920, the population of Dutchess County increased by about 55 percent. During the same period, fourteen of the seventeen towns for which sufficient data exist actually lost population.[6] Only three towns, Hyde Park, North East, and Pawling gained in population and one of these gained more than twenty-five percent. By comparison, the town of Milan lost sixty percent of its population. Clearly, the population of Dutchess County was shifting from the farm to the city, and Dutchess' first city was Poughkeepsie.

Poughkeepsie's reason for being is obviously the Hudson River. The river, the first artery of commerce in the area, brought the first Europeans to the region, and later it served as their connecting link with the world. Over the years, it enabled supplies to come and products to leave. When the sloop and steamship were replaced by the steam locomotive, the new rails, clinging to the shore of the river, simply re-enhanced the role of the river valley as the transportation corridor servicing Poughkeepsie. Undoubtedly, the city of Poughkeepsie is focused on the river. But, why is the city located exactly where it is on the river? Why not a few miles to the north or on the other side? The answer to this is found in the nature of the river bank's topography. Poughkeepsie, like all commercial cities, is located at the intersection of two transportation routes. The first is obviously the river, and the second is the natural land transportation corridor originating at the river and extending inland as far as Connecticut. Most of the banks of the Hudson are steep and hemmed in by low but rugged mountains which made transportation to the interior difficult. Wherever a break in this barrier was found, a town or village developed. Poughkeepsie was no exception to this rule.

Poughkeepsie's artery to the interior was one of the best in the Mid-Hudson Valley. The usually low-lying hills which flank so much of the river are broken at Poughkeepsie, and the more imposing Appalachian ridge is far to the east. This made possible a system of roads fanning outward from Poughkeepsie which serviced the fertile interior of the county. At first the network of roads emanating from the river at Poughkeepsie developed informally to satisfy the immediate needs of the residents of the agricultural interior rather than the entrepreneurial aspirations of Poughkeepsie's businessmen. As the village grew, however, the connection between prosperity and transportation to the interior become more and more obvious and the city's businessmen became the promoters of transportation improvements. In 1802, Poughkeepsians were caught up in the wave of turnpike fever then sweeping the country. With the financial support of many of the village's leading citizens, a stock company was organized to build the Dutchess Turnpike. It began at Poughkeepsie and proceeded eastward through the towns of Pleaant Valley, Millbrook, Millerton and eventually crossed the New York State line into Connecticut. While the Dutchess Turnpike failed to reward its investors financially, it benefited the growing community of Poughkeepsie by funneling trade from inland communities through its growing warehouses and across its docks.[7]

Throughout the nineteenth and twentieth centuries, Poughkeepsie's booster citizens labored to improve the community's transportation advantage. The building of the Hudson River Railroad is a case in point. In 1841, the New York and Albany Railroad (later the Harlem division of the New York Central) planned to construct a railroad from New York City to Albany along a route that passed through eastern Dutchess County. This was a serious threat to Poughkeepsie's prosperity because a railroad through eastern Dutchess County threatened to siphon off much of the trade passing through Poughkeepsie's docks. Not to be outdone, the local boosters, lead by Matthew Vassar, began a campaign to build a competing railroad along the east bank of the Hudson. In 1842, Vassar called a convention of delegates from the towns and villages along the river to be held in the Poughkeepsie Village Hall. Attendance was poor, however, and none of the other towns were willing to supply any money for a preliminary route survey. It was left to the Poughkeepsie boosters to go it alone. It was Poughkeepsie businessmen who raised the money for the initial survey of the route and led the political battle in the state legislature for a charter. Their efforts were successful and by 1849 the line was completed from Poughkeepsie to New York City, and Poughkeepsie's importance as a transportation hub was greatly enhanced.[8]

Over the years, the Poughkeepsie booster-businessmen continued to agitate and campaign to intensify the community's role as a transportation focus. They promoted several feeder railroads which radiated from the city to eastern Dutchess County and western Connecticut. Their crowning achievement, however, was the building of the railroad bridge across the Hudson. While the idea of a railroad bridge across the river had been informally discussed for many years, the first serious attempt was begun in 1871 under the leadership of one of Poughkeepsie's greatest boosters, Harvey G. Eastman. It took seventeen years, two bankruptcies, and a campaign that ranged from Philadelphia to Albany to Boston to complete the project. But complete it they did, and the last pin was driven home in the cantilever span on August 29, 1887. Since that time the massive span has been the physical symbol of Poughkeepsie's prominence as the transportation hub of the Mid-Hudson Region.[9]

Poughkeepsie's growth, however, slowed to a near standstill in the 1870's and 1880's indicating a basic change in the region's economy. During the first half of the 19th century, the main theme of Poughkeepsie's economy was the exploitation of the natural resources of the region. Agricultural products destined for the port of New York, native timber and iron ore from the interior but processed in Poughkeepsie were shipped from its docks. This dependence on primary industries stagnated Poughkeepsie's growth in the post-Civil War period for two reasons. First, the ability of the hinterland to supply resources had reached its limit by the Civil War. Second, the competition from other regions such as the mid-western farm belt made possible by improved transportation, decreased the relative value of Dutchess County's raw materials. Poughkeepsie could no longer expect the limited hinterland to foster growth. Growth would have to come from some other source and manufacturing was the natural and only choice.[10]

Poughkeepsie institutionalized its efforts to achieve growth through the establishment of factories in a series of chamber-of-commerce-like organizations. The first of these was the Board of Trade, organized in April of 1872. Its most outstanding success was the case of the De Laval Separator Company. The De Laval Company was started in Sweden and established its first American plant in Bloomfield, New Jersey. Fortunately, through the efforts of the Board of Trade, the company was convinced to move to Poughkeepsie in 1892. To facilitate this, the Board of Trade raised ten thousand dollars from private citizens to purchase an abandoned site along the river which they gave to the De Laval Company. De Laval's arrival in Poughkeepsie must have been a relief to the local boosters, who were well aware of the loss of business in their town as the primary resource exploiting industries of the past began to fade.[11]

Throughout the first half of the twentieth century, Poughkeepsie's boosters actively campaigned to attract new industry to the city. Advertisements were placed in the New York City papers and a whole series of promotional pieces aimed at industrial leaders was prepared.[12] The campaign was reasonably successful, judging from the number of firms that opened plants in Poughkeepsie during the period. The Schatz-Federal Companies, a major manufacturer of bearings for automobiles and general use, located in the city in 1908. At its peak it employed over one thousand people. The Fiat Company built a plant in the area in 1909. At this time Fiat was noted throughout the world for its racing and luxury automobiles. A group of American entrepreneurs purchased the right to manufacture Fiats in America and they chose Poughkeepsie as the location of their production facility.[13] On the other hand, many of the new manufacturing firms springing up in Poughkeepsie were home-grown affairs. Fargo, Dutchess Trousers, Smith Brothers Cough Drops and dozens of other firms started by local people all contributed to the industrialization of the city.

The statistics of the era demonstrate in another way the success of the city in attracting new industries. The population of Poughkeepsie almost doubled during the period from 1890 to 1930, clearly showing the city had successfully made the transition from a regional port and market town limited by the size of its hinterland, to a modern industrial city producing goods for national and international markets. Relative to the County as a whole, the growth of secondary manufacturing in Poughkeepsie and to a lesser extent in Beacon, Wappingers Falls, and several smaller centers had profound effects. The manufacturing centers provided new economic opportunities for displaced agricultural workers. They also absorbed most of the immigrants filtering into the area. Furthermore, the shift to the cities heightened the contrast and cultural separation between the older agricultural areas of the County and the growing manufacturing centers.

At the dawn of the age of the automobile, Dutchess County was in the midst of a dynamic shift of its population into its growing urban areas. Between 1850 and 1920 the population of the County increased by nearly 33,000 people. All of this growth could be accounted for in the regions that were to become the cities of Beacon and Poughkeepsie.[14] Between 1860 and 1920, the City of Poughkeepsie increased its share of the County's population from 23% to 38%, and by 1920, fully half of the County's residents lived in the cities of Beacon and Poughkeepsie. On the other hand, nearly every other town in the County had been losing population over the preceding seventy years. The automobile put an end to this long established trend and replaced it with a new dynamic; the full effects of which we have yet to experience.

In many ways, the urban shift of the nineteenth and twentieth centuries did not radically affect the fabric of life in the rural regions of the County. To be sure, the shift from subsistence farming to cash crop agriculture must have been profound, but without the pressure of population increase, the social institutions and the rural sense of community probably remained more or less intact. The slow pace of travel tended to protect the hundreds of small hamlets of the County. Each one had its post office and general store, its blacksmith shop, perhaps a church and a mill. It may even have had a railroad station. Most importantly, however, it had a school. The 1876 Atlas of Dutchess County lists nearly two hundred school districts each with its own building and each with its own board of education.[15] Around these small institutions existed a myriad of small communities many of which have been all but forgotten in the age of the automobile.[16]

As the Model-T invaded the countryside, new possiblities for consolidation became available. The larger marketing centers began to absorb the business of the rural general stores. Rural Free Delivery via the automobile eliminated the need for the scores of post offices scattered across the County, and most importantly, the school bus made the old one-room school house obsolete.

As early as 1910, the State Education Department had adopted a policy of school consolidation, but without motorized road transportation, their efforts met with only modest success. To be sure, some consolidation did occur before the age of the automobile, but this was usually just a combination of two adjoining districts. As late as 1935, Dutchess County still had 146 common school districts.[17] It was during the thirties that the old common school begin to give way to the modern central school. Motivated by favorable funding from the state and availability of federal funds for building construction, Dutchess County began to use the school bus as an instrument to consolidate its many small common schools into just twelve central school districts and two city systems. Pine Plains led the way by centralizing in 1931, but the process was not completed in the County until around 1960.[18] It is my belief that many communities resisted centralization because they knew that the loss of their school meant a loss of their sense of community. On the other hand, I am sure taxes had something to do with it. It took coercion and sometimes catastrophe to bring many of the common school districts into the fold of centralization. Red Hook is a good case in point. In April of 1936, the Red Hook School, which had been serving as a high school for eleven common school districts of the region, burned. Only then did the area consider taking advantage of the very favorable state aid formula for central schools and the federal funds available for school construction. In 1937 eleven common schools of the Red Hook region were closed, and the students were bused to the new central school building in the Village of Red Hook.[19]

As the smaller villages and hamlets lost their schools, post offices and businesses, they also lost their identities. To the under-forty crowd, names like Schultzville, Lafayetteville, and Rock City are virtually meaningless and at best, conjure up an image of a place where there is a cluster of older houses and a drop in the speed limit. The automobile transformed these once healthy social systems from real communities to just places.

Ironically, just at the time when the smaller communities of the County were fading, the long decline of population in the rural towns started to reverse itself. At first glance this seems inconsistent. Why should a community die when its population was increasing, or conversely, why should the population of a dying community increase? The answer to the first question has already been given. Without social institutions to bring the people together, there can be no community. The answer to the second question lies outside these communities, and for it we return to the City of Poughkeepsie.

As indicated earlier, transportation has always been a major force in the shaping of the City of Poughkeepsie. The city itself grew around the intersection of two transportation routes, the river and the eastward corridor followed by the early Dutchess Turnpike. However, it is the internal transportation system that led to the rise and fall of the core of the city. In the early nineteenth century, there was little specialization and differentiation in the use of land in Poughkeepsie. With the exception of the docks, none of the region was used exclusively for any one function, and people worked, shopped and lived more or less in the same place. There were no neighborhoods which were reserved exclusively for residences or for stores or for any other purpose at that time.[20] As the city grew, however, the land closest to the hub of transportation became too valuable to be used as residential land, and the city began to experience an extensive differentiation of land use. The waterfront became almost exclusively used for shipping and manufacturing while Main Street became the commercial hub of the city. Residences were forced out of these areas to the periphery by the prevailing economic value of commercial property as compared to residential property. The resulting residential neighborhoods also began to sort themselves out along class lines, and their location was determined by a mixture of social and technological forces. By the time of the Civil War, the pattern was well established. The best residential neighborhoods ringed the commercial district along Main Street and the quality of the housing, in general, decreased as the distance from the commercial hub increased. This pattern can still be seen in the fine early Victorian homes that still stand along Mill and Church Streets above Market Street. The poorer neighborhoods were closer to the bustling waterfront or on the fringe of the city. This was probably due to two reasons. The first is that in a time when even the well-off walked, having your house close to the business district was a decided advantage. Secondly, there was a certain status associated with being close to the center of a dynamic town like Poughkeepsie. One must remember that without automobiles these streets were quiet and civilized. Also, the farm and the countryside were being abandoned in favor of the excitement and opportunity of the city.[21]

The land use pattern established in the middle of the nineteenth century was, to some extent, inverted by the introduction of the streetcar and trolly system. As Poughkeepsie evolved from a walking to a mass transportation city, new housing opportunities were presented to the wealthier classes. The new trollies permitted the wealthier people to move to the more spacious and prestigious neighborhoods developing along the city's fringe. Hooker Avenue with its collection of fine old houses is a good example of such a neighborhood. However, the residents of these new outlying neighborhoods were still tied to the core of the city by the trollies. These residents still commuted into the center of the city to work, shop and entertain themselves. The less affluent classes were left in possession of the residential neighborhoods closer to the expanding business-industrial core. As the pattern intensified, the middle classes joined in the move away from the hustle bustle of the core, leaving the center of the city to the groups at the lowest end of the economic spectrum. By the First World War, Poughkeepsie had segregated itself into three basic types of land use. The industrial-business core was located along the river and Main Street. The working class neighborhoods were generally located closest to the center of the core which was the intersection of Main Street and the river. In general, there was more lower class housing on the north side of Main Street. This was probably due to the effect of the railroad bridge over the Hudson which tended to give the north side a more industrial and utilitarian air. The better residential sections were found in the southeastern section of the city far from the noise of the docks and safely removed from the smoke of the railroad bridge and northside factories. The most elite neighborhood was centered along Hooker Avenue on the southside.

While the trollies permitted the middle and upper classes to flee the growing unpleasantness of the core of the city, they did not ruin its economic health. The corner of Main Street and Market Street became the hub of the trolly system and was, therefore, the only place to which everyone could get. The Main Street line, the Hooker Avenue line and the northside loop all met at the intersection of Main and Market. In addition, the two inter-urbans, one from New Paltz and the other from Wappingers Falls, also led to the corner of Main and Market. Since everyone living on the urban fringe depended upon the trolly to some extent, the corner of Main and Market became the most valuable piece of real estate in the city. As businessmen and merchants crowded together at this intersection, the buildings became taller and the area more and more congested. The area around this intersection became the most exciting in the city. The big stores, the theaters, and restaurants and the best hotels were all located within a few blocks of the intersection of Main and Market. It became the "great white way;" the "Broadway" of not only Poughkeepsie but of all the surrounding territory. In addition, it was accessible to all classes of the society. The wealthy had more money to spend, but the poorer classes could get a thrill just being there. During the days of the trolly, the center of Poughkeepsie was at its peak, never equalled before or since.[22]

When older Poughkeepsie residents talk of their town, they usually reminisce about the city in the old days. They remember with warmth and pride the schools, the clean streets, the stores, the movies, the ice cream parlors, the trollies, the ferry, the parks and the host of other things too numerous to mention. Shaking their heads they wonder what happened to their beautiful, boosterish town. What changed Poughkeepsie from a proud, growth-oriented booster town to a city of decreasing population and decreasing economic health? The cause of Poughkeepsie's decline can be summed up in one word, the automobile.

The mass produced automobile is America's great freedom machine. At first Poughkeepsians used it to see the world and as an instrument of entertainment. The Sunday drive, the picnic in the countryside, and the visit to rural relatives were all part of its early use. Increasingly, however, in the period around the Second World War, it became a substitute for the trolly and bus system. Here for the first time was a transportation system which was truly under the control of the individual. He could go where he wanted, when he wanted. The individual was no longer confined to trolly routes and timetables. Furthermore, the auto was relatively inexpensive. Even the blue collar workers of the city could afford to own and operate a car. The relatively low cost of the automobile was complemented by the fact that it gave dependable access to the large region surrounding the city which was formerly reserved for agriculture by the limits of the old transportation system. With an inexpensive automobile, just about everyone could acquire a relatively inexpensive piece of rural land and build his dream house amidst pastoral splendor. These economic forces came into full bloom after World War II, accelerated by a rapidly expanding national and local economy. Almost overnight, new suburbs of the city began to sprawl over the southwestern section of the County. Hyde Park, Pleasant Valley, Wappingers and Spackenkill all experienced rapid growth while the City of Poughkeepsie declined in population. The automobile gave people the freedom to flee the city, and they have been exercising that freedom in increasing numbers since the Second World War. Note the number of automobiles registered in Dutchess County increased from 20,000 in 1945 to over 130,000 in 1980.

On one hand, the effect of the automobile can be viewed as an extension of the trend to move away from the core of Poughkeepsie which was begun a half century earlier by the street car system. However, the differences are profound relative to the economic health of the city. While it is true that the trollies permitted the population to flee to the urban fringe, it did not damage the economy of the central business district. In fact, it did just the opposite. The old street car system permitted urban growth but at the same time tied all of that growth to the central business district of the city. Since all of the mass transportation routes emanated from downtown, it was the one place in the region to which nearly everyone could travel. Therefore, it became the ideal location for stores, offices and factories. Real estate values rose in the central business district as a result of the trolly system rather than declined. As the values of the land around the hub rose, it became used more and more intensely. Open space was rapidly built upon, and after all of the land was occupied by buildings, future growth was accommodated by building upward into the sky. The skyline of Poughkeepsie still attests to the fact that the area around the hub of the trolly system was one of the most valuable pieces of real estate in Dutchess County.

The shift away from mass transportation to the private automobiles spelled doom for the economic core of Poughkeepsie. At first the early owners of cars used their vehicles to travel into the core to shop, do business and work. However, as the number of autos entering the downtown district swelled, the resulting congestion began to become an annoyance. The private automobile was proving itself technologically incompatible with central Poughkeepsie. The very intense use of the land which was encouraged by the former trolly system was at the heart of the problem. The narrow streets were unable to cope with the burgeoning flow of vehicles, and the lack of open space made it impossible to meet the parking needs of this new transportation system. The population of southwestern Dutchess County was faced with a choice. They could abandon their automobiles and keep their Queen City, or they could abandon Poughkeepsie and keep their freedom machines. They chose the latter.

By 1950 the emerging new pattern of retailing was well established. Supermarkets with large parking lots were springing up on the fringes of Poughkeepsie and in the new suburbs. In 1950, the first true suburban mall, Poughkeepsie Plaza, was constructed along the once bucolic South Road, ironically right next to the Poughkeepsie County Club. The Poughkeepsie Plaza was the harbinger of the nearly complete shift of retailing from the central business district of Poughkeepsie to the twenty mile strip of Route 9 from the southern boundary of the city all the way to Fishkill.

During the 1950's and 1960's, the factories and work places also joined the exodus from the central region of Poughkeepsie. Once their workers had cars and they began to rely on truck transportation to ship their goods, the congestion of the central city became a net disadvantage. One by one the factories left the old manufacturing districts along the Hudson and around the Smith Street rail yards and moved to the urban fringe. Most notable among these firms were Lumb Woodworking, Fargo and De Laval Separator. Other industries such as the button industry simply closed their doors and were not replaced by new industries within the city. New firms, most notably IBM, coming into the region could see no advantage in locating in the center of the city, so they set up shop in the suburbs. The advantages of cheap land, lower taxes and adequate parking favored overwhelmingly the location of new plants outside the city. By the 1970's the abandonment of the City of Poughkeepsie had probably reached its peak. The homes, the stores and the work places had all more or less left the center of the city. Only the seat of the county government remained, and it retained the usual number of lawyers, businessmen and clerical workers. Had Poughkeepsie not retained the governmental function, it probably would have become a bleak place indeed.

The old structure of the central region of Poughkeepsie is gone but it has been replaced by a new structure of the greater Poughkeepsie area. The compact and highly focused community of the past has been replaced by a diffuse and sprawling region which includes most of southwestern Dutchess County. At the geographic heart, but not the economic heart, of the region is the central section of the old city. Most of the better jobs have left this zone, and the housing has been occupied, for the most part, by the more economically disadvantaged members of society. Around this central core is a ring of middle and upper class residences. In addition, this inner ring contains most of the retailing and the work places that offer the better jobs to be found in the area. It should be noted that this inner ring also includes some of the outlying residential districts of the city proper, most notably the still affluent southside. People who live in the inner ring work, shop, go to school, and find their entertainment within the ring itself. Rarely are they motivated or forced to venture into the old center city. They have everything they need right within the ring. Outside of the inner ring is still a third zone, the outer ring. This ring includes areas such as Millbrook, Stanfordville and several towns on the west bank of the Hudson. Large numbers of people living in the outer ring travel to "Poughkeepsie" to find employment and to make major purchases. However, when a resident of the outer ring says he works in "Poughkeepsie" to find employment and to make major purchases. However, when a resident of the outer ring says he works in "Poughkeepsie," he usually means he works in the inner ring rather than in the city proper. Thus, we find that the once-thriving City of Poughkeepsie has been replaced by a larger structure which, on the whole, is economically healthy. On the other hand, the old city has been more or less isolated from the mainstream of the economy by the changing technology of transportation, and its future survival may be severely threatened.

NOTES

1. For a discussion of farm life and economy in the nineteenth century see: Ulysses P. Hedrick, *A History of Agriculture in the State of New York* (New York: New York State Agricultural Society, 1933.)

2. "Population of Dutchess County by Towns & Cities 1840–1940," a table prepared by Paul J. Miller, County Treasurer from the U. S. Census data and revised through 1970. In the files of Adriance Memorial Library, Poughkeepsie, New York.

3. The summary of agricultural statistics in the N. Y. S. Census for the township of Red Hook clearly indicates that Red Hook was well on its way in the transition from subsistence to cash crop agriculture by 1865. The significant fresh fruit crop is the best evidence of this. See the manuscript copy of N. Y. S. Census: 1865, Dutchess County Clerk's Office, Poughkeepsie, New York.

4. Red Hook and Rhinebeck are unique among Dutchess County towns in their late nineteenth century population patterns.

5. For example, the fresh meat industry begins to centralize in the 1880's. G. Swift began the refrigerated shipment of dressed meat from Chicago in 1881. See: Daniel J. Boorstin, *The Americans: The Democratic Experience.*

6. The population trends of the towns of Fishkill and Poughkeepsie are difficult to access because they were subdivided, and portions were annexed to the growing cities of Beacon and Poughkeepsie.

7. Edmund Platt, *The Eagle's History of Poughkeepsie* (Poughkeepsie: Platt & Platt, 1905), pp. 77–78.

8. *Ibid.* pp. 139–143.

9. *Ibid.* pp. 214–216, 219–221.

10. To a large extent, the casualty implied in this paragraph relative to the stagnation of Poughkeepsie's population is difficult to support. Clearly, the general slow down in the nation's economy following the panic of 1873 must have had a major effect on Poughkeepsie. Be that as it may, the author views the 1870's and 1880's as a watershed period relative to the shift toward secondary industries. Edmund Platt, writing around 1905, clearly shared this view. See: *The Eagle's History of Poughkeepsie* (Poughkeepsie: Platt & Platt, 1905), pp. 230–234.

11. *Ibid.*, p. 234.

12. The most elaborate of this promotional literature is: Poughkeepsie Chamber of Commerce, *Industrial Survey of the City of Poughkeepsie* (Poughkeepsie, 1930).

13. Michael Sedgwick, "The Pride of Poughkeepsie: A Look at American Fiats," *The Upper Hudson Automobilist* (Jan. 1980) pp. 9–14.

14. "Population of Dutchess County by Towns & Cities: 1840–1940," a table prepared by Paul J. Miller, County Treasurer, from the U. S. Census data and revised through 1970. In the files of Adriance Memorial Library, Poughkeepsie, New York.

15. H. L. Kochersperger, *The New Historical Atlas of Dutchess County, New York: 1876* (Reading, Pa: Reading Publishing House, 1876).

16. The sense of community which existed in the smaller hamlets of the county is difficult to document by traditional means. However, scores of interviews with older residents of the county conducted by the students of Dutchess Community College leave no doubt that it existed. See for example: Elizabeth Catalino, *Mary Alley,* unpublished manuscript of an interview with Mary Alley of the town of East Fishkill, 1983. In the files of the author.

17. Bayne, Martha Collins, *County at Large* (Poughkeepsie: The Woman's City and Country Club with Vassar College, 1937), p. 126.

18. Charles D. King, History of Education in Dutchess County. Cape May, New Jersey, by the author, 1959.

19. Author unknown, *Dedication Exercises: Red Hook Central School* (Red Hook, New York, Red Hook Board of Education, 1939), p. 6–7.

20. Before cities became densely packed, it was the custom for a businessman, his employees and his family all to live on the work site. This is a carry-over from the era of agriculture. Dutchess County mill towns with their company housing such as Wappingers Falls or Glenham reflect this tradition. The fine old house at the mouth of the Fallkill, an important mill site since the colonial period, also attests that this pattern existed in Poughkeepsie. Platt also discussed this pattern. See: Edmund Platt, *The Eagle's History of Poughkeepsie* (Poughkeepsie: Platt & Platt, 1905), p. 86.

21. The main evidence for the fact that the wealthier classes were in possession of the area immediately surrounding the commercial hub of the city is to be found in the buildings themselves. Platt also indirectly

supports this view in his descriptions of real estate development. *See* for example: Edmund Platt, *The Eagle's History of Poughkeepsie* (Poughkeepsie: Platt & Platt, 1905), p. 218–219.

22. Numerous interviews with old Poughkeepsie residents done by the author and the students of Dutchess Community College contains accounts of the business area around Main and Market Streets. *See* for example: Richard P. O'Connor, *Steve Tkazyik,* unpublished manuscript of an interview with Steve Tkazyik, lifelong resident of Poughkeepsie, 1981. In the files of the author. The history of the Main and Market Street area before World War II is also recorded in the surviving buildings and in numerous post cards and photographs in the collection of the author.

The Impact of the Hudson River Railroad on Tivoli and Germantown

Richard C. Wiles
Director, Hudson Valley Studies, Bard College
Annandale-on-Hudson

Much of the evidence for assessing the impact of the Hudson River Railroad on localities along the River from mid to late nineteenth century has been lost in visions of writers—contemporary and later—who stressed what I will call the "romantic" version of the place of the railroad in American life. Later historians have not helped to define the picture; they have often taken such a cosmic view of the technological development that their generalizations are difficult to apply to the local scene.

It has been assumed for years in the writing on American economic history that the railroad was a keystone in the transformation of vast regions of the U. S.—the opening of the west, changing settlement patterns, structural changes in the location and mix of agricultural production, etc. In recenty years, economic historians have challenged such views. Robert Fogel maintains, for example, in his work *Railroads and American Economic Growth* that such assessments have been accepted as "axiomatic truths."[1] The questions raised are interesting to keep in mind even when dealing with a topic as parochial as the one discussed in this paper. Were the railroads indispensible to economic development and, further, were they the only way? An economic historian would maintain that they were only if their contribution to U. S. economic progress during the nineteenth century was sizeable when compared to the next best alternative. What would towns like Tivoli and Germantown have lost if the railroad had not invaded their boundaries?

Indirect effects of such a technological change are also of importance. Much of the literature again assumes a major impact on the coal, iron, machine and lumber industries as inputs. Fogel and others view this impact as overstated or, at best, as having such an effect much later than is usually assumed. Coal, for example, was not used extensively as railroad fuel until after the Civil war and the major impact of wood for both fuel and ties was not a product of the lumber industry but a result of hapazard cutting of readily available rough timber. The iron industry, Fogel maintains, was more impacted by the rising demand for nails than by the growth of rail orders. In short, while growth was taking place all about the mid-nineteenth century, no single factor such as the railroad can explain either its diretion or its rate.

The question then arises: can one take some of these hesitations and look at a small microcosm such as Northern Dutchess and Southern Columbia Counties and test the phenomenon's social and economic impact? I think that it can be done, particularly in the case of employment impacts on railroad villages. It seems that the overall employment effects are easier to document in small communities than to assess the overall impact as Fogel tries to do upon inputs of supplies and raw materials.

It is interesting to note that early opinions as to the probable impact of railroads on economic development were not as sanguine as they were later to become. Even railroad executives and boosters, at least initially, seemed to have a limited conception of the role of the railway in the future, seeing its profitability stemming from passenger traffic, provision of service to small localities and as feeders to waterways. Canals were still assumed to be the most efficient freight carriers. However, it is clear from statements made in the formative years of the Hudson River Railroad that John Jervis—

chief engineer for construction—reversed this outlook, expecting freight to be the major source of revenues, perhaps due to the projected route's parallelling the waterways of the Hudson-Mohawk system. The winter months they saw as their competitive edge with differential rates charged when water routes reopened.

With these observations as a setting, what benefits and limitations faced the growing rail network in our sector of the Hudson Valley? Secondly, what impact did the railroad's expansion have on the economic and social pattens in the hinterland? In short, I would like to proceed from the global view to a minute focus upon two towns on the main line; were they railroad towns in the broader sense?

In the immediate Tivoli-Germantown area, the potential impact of the Hudson River Railroad on village and town development was far more limited spatially than was the case with the neighboring settlements across the Hudson. For example, in Tivoli, formerly Upper Red Hook Landing, land availability was severely restricted as the Landing was hemmed in by the three large estates at the River's edge—Callendar House, Rose Hill and the Pynes—so that a tight space was utilized to the fullest; only a few hundred yards of river front remained open for devleopment. This fact, in addition to the precipitous land configuration on the Hudson's bank restricted the possibilities. North from Tivoli only Gemantown and Linlithgo stations had similar space, though far less developed.

The image of such early nineteenth century Hudson River communities and their economic and social, i.e., pre-railroad, is in many cases drawn from the large number of travellers' accounts of the Hudson. Though these are of interest, they, like the work of earlier historians of the American scene, are biassed in their viewpoint. First, they are views of the wealthy. For example, the steamboat passenger accounts—especially those drawn from foreign visitor diaries—present an entirely different sense of the area than the view of the residents. As one commentator has recently written: "Americans operated with a different map of the River than these accounts portray—with virtually no mention of life in Newburgh, Poughkeepsie or Hudson beyond the boat landings."[2] Thus the life and feel of such river front communities have to be painfully reconstructed over time.

The coming of the railroad to our riverbank in 1851 changed things a bit, though the accounts present a vision comparable to those of steamboat travel. Ironically, where before the estates had cut off the ordinary resident from the River, so the estates themselves were now cut off, with some major objections from the landowners. Thus the "rich man's bank" first saw the railroad, while the "wrongside" was not opened to rails until 1883. An example of the response of the estate owners is (the problem met by Washington Irving) as the railroad threatened his "Sunnyside" in Tarrytown. Irving suggested ". . . if the Garden of Eden were now on earth, they would not hesitate to run a railroad thought it."[3] After the initial shock of the railroad's placement so close to his homestead, Irving like so many other landowners finally resigned himself to the inevitable, reducing his complaints to the President of the line to a rather weak objection to the blasts of the steam whistle from the passing engines.

The push for the railroad on the Hudson's shores came out of fear that the Harlem Valley line in eastern Dutchess and Columbia counties, already under construction, would divert trade from the river towns. In fact, Poughkeepsie boosters and capital provided a real catalyst in the railroad's completion. To the complaints of estate owners and early day environmentalists that the Hudson River Railroad would ruin the landscape and beauty of the river banks, John Jervis replied:

> To a very great extent the construction of the Road will improve the appearance of the shore; rough points will be smoothed off, the irregular indentations of the bays be hidden and a regularity and symmetry imparted to the outline of the shore; thus by a combination of the works on nature and of art adding to the interest, grandeur and beauty of the whole.[4]

It is interesting to note in passing that one concession to the estate owners early in the railroad's presence was the provision of drawbridges for access to estates hemmed in from the open Hudson by the roadbed. These were manned and operated at railroad expense as shown in the 1860 Red Hook Census, and not for years were those rights denied the more powerful landowners.

There is little question as to the negative impact of the railroad west on New York State farming. The question of how they reacted and why is not so clear. Agriculture in eastern New York and the

Hudson Valley had already experienced competitiveness from western New York products, especially grain, with the Erie Canal; the farmers somewhat adapted by a switch to dairying and milk production, fruit farming and the like. Now the railroad made the advantage of closesness to the New York City market a thing of the competitive past. Transformations were again called for and some response was made. Yet to the canal and railroad must be added the already existing problems of poor farming methods in the Hudson Valley with continuous cropping and resultant soil exhaustion.

In any event, agricultural interests in the Hudson and Mohawk Valleys resented the coming of the Canal and expressed this resentment. Yet, in the later period, the farmers' reaction was much more varied and they never gained the solidarity they needed to carry the legislative day. Diversification had grown by this time and intrastate factions and jealousies were present. As Lee Benson has pointed out: "Hostile attitudes of Genesee Valley wheat farmers toward Illinois wheat farmers may be compared to those of Orange County milk producers toward Delawre county dairymen."[5] This is not to say that agriculture did not recover from this second blow in the 1850s. For in our region, Dutchess County did not peak in terms of agricultural output until the 1880s. Yet farm output diversification was the result, and the heterogeneity of New York farmers—regionally and in terms of their farming interests, made a solid political front versus the railroad difficult indeed. One is tempted to mention here in passing an observation made in comparing the pattern of the industrial revolution in England with that of the United States. In the former case, agricultural and industrial progress had taken place to an extent where the railroad was a necessary satellite or complementary technology needed for further growth; in the U. S. case, agricultural and industrial patterns, not as well developed in the 1840s and the 1850s, were changed dramatically, at least in terms of loction, with the railroad almost a leading factor in the transformation.

This mixture of power, prestige and romance in the early days of the railroad is worth musing over. Again we turn to foreign travellers' accounts for a flavor of early railway travel—as misleading parhaps as the accounts of steamboat journeys before the concurrent with them. The reaction here is much more clearly a class one, with European visitors expressing shock that the American railway carriage—a mode of travel they had experienced earlier in England—in this new world setting they viewed as a social leveller, with no classes in the cars. A Livingston could thus ride next to a worker from Germantown or Tivoli, at least theoretically and until parlor and sleeping cars shortly provided segregation by at least income class. The American poet John Godfrey Saxe caught this spirit in his poem, Rhyme of the Rail:

> Men of different "stations,"   High and lowly people,
>   In the eyes of Fame,   Birds of every feather,
> Here are very quickly   On a common level
>   Coming to the same.   Travelling together.[6]

The accounts differ in one sense from the boat journey statements; as the faster travel changed the sense of the landscape, in much the same way as Dickens presents in his novel *Hard Times* the romantic vision of factories as "fairy palaces" when viewed from the window of a speeding train.

Beyond such vision, however, there were hopes for the railroad; hopes that since that time have solidified into Fogel's axiomatic views of the railway's inpact in the past. Some of these hopes were poetic, some simply overblown puffs of promoters' attempts to seduce capital from potential investors. Both the hard sell and the romantic aspects of this new technological phenomenon produced a common belief that the presence of a line would convert a hamlet into a thriving community, and in the course of this boom, land values would double or triple. The railroad was hailed as the key to prosperity and as a remedy for all manner of economic ills. Much of this stemmed from the process of trying to win public support for bond issues and public subsidies. In our region, public aid was not a a major issue with the Hudson River Railroad; but later in the century the push becomes more intense with the construction of the cross county lines—the Rhinebeck and Connecticut, the Poughkeepsie and Eastern and the Dutchess and Columbia. The town of Rhinebeck, for example, subscribed $100,000 to the Rhinebeck and Connecticut. At this time officials of the proposed route from Hudson River at Rhinecliff to the Massachusetts and Connecticut borders threatened leaders in Columbia

County that if they did not contributed funds for the railway construction, they would be bypassed. One official noted: "Let them, the towns of Livingston and Clermont be told that unless they cooperate the Pleasantville cut-off will be made and thus they will lose the road. The line thence to Hudson may be mentioned to aid in waking them up."[7]

But these are concerns of romance, finance and alleged benefits. Technological transformation is never this simple and takes its toll and provides its benefits on other levels. Railroads, unlike the steamboats before and concurrent with them, depending upon a right-of-way that had to be created from the river bank, filled in across bays and then—a point crucial for my topic—they had to be maintained. This obviously required much more labor than did the free right-of-way of the Hudson, and local labor would not suffice. The fact that travel in a day coach was classless was not a fact that carried over to the construction and continued operation of the railroad itself.

One of the best ways to assess the most direct impact of the railroad on a region is to study the demographic patterns before and after the introduction—not only the size of the workforce but its distribution, the origins of the workers and their occupational changes over time. By so doing, often romance and supposed impacts are placed in a different light. The last major portion of trackage completing the link between New York City, Albany and the west were difficult miles, spanning the bays near Hudson, Tivoli and Annandale. This last link opened October 1, 1851; the Harlem Valley route a few months later. The competion of the water level route allowed villages such as Tivoli and Germantown to be hours closer to Albany or New York City, a least four closer than was possible *via* the venerable steamboat. This, of course, allowed the railroad to win out in the competitive transportation battle over the next few decades.

It is indeed fortunate for out topic that the Federal Census takers began to record occupations in the 7th Census of 1850. For we are thus allowed to see the dramatic changes from 1850 to the first Census after the Hudson Valley Railroad's completion. The shift of occupations is dramatically seen, pointing to the social setting alterations that technology can bring about. the 1850 Tivoli–Madalin Census (still separate villages at that time) shows the impact of the River on the village work and life. Fourteen persons list themselves as boatmen, several more involved as workers or proprietors in commercial fishing, freighting and the like. The 1860 Census shows the shift in abrupt terms—62 workers in Tivoli–Madalin listing their occupations as laborer on the railroad, with a liberal sprinkling of other railway jobs thrown in—engineer, station agent, telegraph operator, conductor, brakeman, fireman, etc. As a basis for comparison, the Germantown Census for that year shows the same pattern on a reduced scale, with 29 railroad laborers, and engineer and station agent listed. This data reflects the situation nine years after the railroad's completion and seven years after the roadbed was doubled tracked. I mention this latter point since in May 1853 a second track was being laid north from Tivoli to Albany to speed up operations and increase traffic density. Double tracking was completed from New York City to Poughkeepsie in 1854. It is clear from these figures that Tivoli was more the way station in 1860, and the large amount of railroad-induced employment cannot be explained by the construction boom in 1851 or 1853. It is not clear, however, when or why the Hudson River Railroad officials centered on Tivoli as a major railroad point. Perhaps it was due to the ferry to Saugerties, perhaps the element of space, though this was not overly generous; or was it because Tivoli is almost exactly 100 miles from the City? Were there more accomodations available here for work crews, etc? In a diary account in 1853, Charles H. Beach, civil engineer for the double tracking, notes that in that year the superintendent of Track is based in Tivoli and is buying supplies for the project locally, especially from Saugerties across the river. He also notes that 40 men are employed on the project.[8] This item presages an event that explains many of the impacts of Tivoli, that is that the village at least by the 1870s was made a division point with the divisional superintendent a resident of the Village.

The activity in the Tivoli area is further attested to in a most detailed diary kept during the 1850s by Edward S. Johnson, a sloop captain from Schodack, who presents interesting accounts of his continual deliveries of crushed rock, railway ties and iron rail to the construction sites at Tivoli—some of the materials picked up in Kingston across the river. In an ironic vein, he writes of his difficulties with the River's tides and tells of his being forced to leave his sloop stranded in the mud flats and to take the train home![9]

In any case it is evident that the Tivoli area was inundated with railroad workers and, in proportion to the population it was a substantial flood. Clyde and Sally Griffen point out in their work on Poughkeepsie that 124 railroad workers can be identified in the county directory as living in the city in 1879 when the population of Poughkeepsie was about 20,000.[10] At about the same time in the Village of Tivoli it is clear that railroad employment had grown so that the 1800 Census listed 75 residents as railway laborers and the more prestigious occupations are now much more noticeable with 44 men employed in the standard railroad jobs. Thus 119 workers out of a total populatin of the now combined villages of Tivoli and Madalin of 1254. By this time, although the exact year is in doubt, Watson D. Otis, Division Superintendent is living in Tivoli. The prestige of his position is shown by the fact that he was elected eight times as "President" of the Village—the term mayor not being used until the 1920s. Living on Montgomery Street in the village, Otis named his victorian frame house "The Maples," not only perhaps, as a sign of prestige but in ironic imitation of the Livingston estates whose lands were a mere 100 yards from his door.

The important social aspect of this growth, however, is the ethnic mix that dramatically appears. By far the largest number of railway laborers are of Irish origin. Thus it is not by chance that St. Sylvia's Catholic Parish in Tivoli was officially established in 1852, presumably with the promise of a larger clientele.

The dominance of Irish names for railroad workers in the 1860 Census is, or course, not surprising. Nor is it surprising that the higher positions in occupational categories—the more prestigious positions—are held by the non-Irish. If we create a rough "pecking order" the only Irish non-laborers I note in 1860 are a flagman and one switchman, barely higher on the ladder, while the more skilled occuaptions bear more familiar Hudson Valley names: engineer, Clinton Van Buren; track foreman, S. F., Stotenberg; telegraph operator, James Ashdown. The picture is identical in the same census for Germantown, though on a smaller scale.

By the 1870s and 1880s the situation changes with some upward mobility appearing. John Kelley is a brakeman, Thomas Conway a railroad foreman, Phillip Harrington a brakeman, John Sweeney a flagman and Joseph Higgins a conductor. This definitely is not the case in Germantown. By 1900 the apex is reached with a Joseph Malloy recorded as a railroad engineer.

The numbers thus show an important and continuing impact on the Village and its character; but what of turnover? Of the 78 names of railroad workers listed in Tivoli in 1860, 16 are still recorded in 1870, 14 in 1880. The Germantown story is similar: the 1870 accounts show 27 workers employed on the railroad; by 1880 only 4 of these remain. The interesting difference in pattern compared with Tivoli–Madalin is the smaller percentage of railroad workers of Irish origin. Of the 27 names in 1870, only 5 are from Ireland, while 14 of the total are listed as railway laboreers. The remainder—non-Irish—are job titles higher on the occupational ladder. This deserves a comment, for an interesting pattern appears attesting to the character of the two villages. The 1870 Census for Germantown shows 7 men living those who are Hudson River Railroad engineers, more than the entire Tivoli–Red Hook–Barrytown area. This difference continues to be true until 1900 though the number diminishes to 4. Predictably, these are all non-Irish names. It is clear that there seems to be a difference between the two areas. Was Tivoli too Irish by this time to be an appropriate residence of an engineer? Or was it simply too much of a "railroad town?" Probably a mixture of both; for while we do not know a great deal about the social life of Tivoli before its incorporation as a village in 1872, scattered evidence pointing to the tone of the railroad town might provide an explanation. One piece of evidence that has come to light in recent years is a memoir of the village in those days written by the daughter of Rev. James Starr Clark—the first President of the Village and Pastor of the Trinity Church in Madalin. This remembrance points clearly to the fact that neither Tivoli nor Madalin were sleepy rural villages. She recalls her father's being at the ready every Saturday night with a heavy headed cane prepared for the walk to Morey's Bar to restore order. In the first village minutes after Clark's election, along with a modern sounding theme of the lack of law and order in Tivoli, the first items of Clark's agenda are his plan to close the bars on Sunday, closely followed by a request for public funds to erect a jail in the village as well as establish a police force. It seems fair to say that the non-Irish railroad engineers sought perhaps a quieter and more genteel atmosphere in the Germantown area. Only Clinton Van

Buren, the sole engineer living in the village, seemed able to brave the rigors of the lively village. Things must have calmed by 1900 for that census lists three engineers as residents of Tivoli. Morey's remains; the railroad is gone.

If we had data on the passenger ticket sales for the Tivoli station as well as records of freight shipments to and from the village, a finer assessment could be made of the indirect impacts of the railroad on the area. Without such statistics, we must read into the development of commercial establishments in Tivoli. One of the most obvious impacts would be evidence of the growing need for lodging places for workmen—especially with a relatively settled workforce which included not only track workers but also the manpower for such support services as storehouses, freight facilities and work train personnel. It is certainly clear that the growth of hotels parallelled closely the coming of the railroad. As an example, James Outwater, the long time ferry owner, freighter and shad fisherman, in 1850 built the Tivoli Hotel on the river, perhaps speculating on the arrival of the railway. The second major hotel, the Farmers' Hotel, was built in the 1860s, also at the Landing. The same was true in Madalin with the conversion of a store to the Howard Hotel about 1870. Even James Ashdown, long time station agent and telegraph operator in Tivoli and Germantown gets into the act by opening the Dutchess Hotel in the 1860s as a moonlighting opeation.

One could also document the indirect growth of retail and service enterprises as the population grew to the highest point in Tivoli's history—1350 in 1890. The 1880s saw an expansion of the railroad's facilities at Tivoli—extension of the railway dock and freighthouse and the exapansion of siding capacity. Though 52 railroad employees still are listed in the 1900 Census, the peak was past as population and economic activity began to decline. Village totals show a fall of approximately 100 people per decade until reaching a plateau of 700 in 1930, where it has remained until the present day.

One, of course, can imagine the exaggerated claims by proponents of the railroad for rising business, flows of income and wages and the inevitable carrot of increased property tax revenues from the right-of-way. In the case of Tivoli, by the time of incorportion in 1872, the President of the Village, after dealing with the law and order issue, refers to the large sums of money collected from the railroad by the taxing jurisdiction—Red Hook. These funds, Clark maintains, "should have been expended by the officers appointed by the town upon your highways and your board have been unable to discover what has been done with the money." He continues in his report with an understatement: "It is plain to see that the tax levied was only a small part expended upon the roads."[11]

While I feel that quantitative data—slim though it is at times—is an absolute necessity to gain any semblance of a comprehensive view, bits and pieces of more qualitative material should be added to give hues and tones to the picture. As usual in local history, this is fragmentary. In this case I was indeed lucky to come across the journal I cited earlier of Edward S. Johnson, an incredibly detailed account of the years 1851–56 during which the writer never missed a day's entry. As mentioned, Johnson ran a sloop out of Schodack and spent much time on both the Hudson River and the railroad, as passenger and observer. Much of the material refers to our area. His accounts escape the romance that I mentioned at the outset that is present in many early visions of the railway. Johnson documents, in passing, more than he probably intended. In February 1851, as the last link is being completed, he states: "Irishmen are on strike and are driving the men working in gravel pits away from their jobs." In March of the same year, he notes: "Irishmen went to work on our section today;" not simply workers, note, but Irishmen. On November 22, 1951 another entry reads: "I came across an Irishman today—a boss on the railroad whose name was Rutledge, a very uncommon name for an Irishman and he was a strong Wesleyan Methodist."[12] These entries could be duplicated for early railroad construction in general. For the Hudson River route it is clear that trouble was brewing from the start in Tivoli. The Superintendent of Track at Tivoli writes his superiors for instructions about the wages to pay his men for he simply states: "They want more pay." Presumably this was happening all through the valley. Matthew Vassar, Jr.'s diary records in 1848 similar problems in Poughkeepsie: "The Irish on the railroad are becoming troublesome" and recounts riots between the workers and the military, helped along with purchases of ale at the Vassar Brewery. There also was a work stoppage in Rhinecliff in 1850 to which the sheriff called the military which fired on the laborers, killing three.

Tivoli Railroad Tower during the early 1900s

Tivoli Revisited: A Social History by Richard Wiles

Such vignetts are not surprising in terms of our country's early labor history. In terms of the Irish influx to areas such as Northern Dutchess and Southern Columbia Counties, however, the tone of the situation must have been dramatic at times. The accounts of Johnson, in addition, point to something basic to my theme of the employment extending beyond the early years of construction. Covering the first four years of Railroad operation from the city to Albany, the entries almost prosaically recount the almost continuous accidents along the line. Not only was technology in its early and somewhat crude phase responsible, but the engineering of right-of-way also left a good deal to be desired. Large quantities of stone from the crude rock cuts falling on the track and "stopping the cars" or throwing engines off the rails. For three years the limitations of the single track main line led to several head-on collisions. And finally, Johnson tells of the low lying "water level route" roadbed being inundated by the ice breaking up in the river in the spring resulting in the demolition of the trackage. In December, 1851 Johnson notes "The up train which left New York at 12:30 o'clock stopped at Schodack while the conductor went up with a team of horses to see something about the train coming down—he was afraid of a collision. I honour his judgement but I condemn the idea of the passengers sitting all night in the cars, the weather as cold as 'tis now; there are bad arrangements on this road."[13] Entries of this sort abound in the diary., In April, 1852, rocks fell and threw the engine off the track requiring 200 men working for 5 days to right the engine after disassembling it in part.

The point of citing such accounts is that the laborers needed, at least in the early years, explains the continuous presence of such a relatively large number of workers in a center such as Tivoli for much of the nineteenth century. This requirement definitely trails off in our area about 1900. Tivoli was very hard hit, Germantown had less to lose. It is clear that improved technology, longer distance travelled by train crews and faster schedules limited to passenger density made the labor requirements far less than the last three decades of the century. But it is clear from the census that economic activity in villages like Germantown and Tivoli was declining as well—the small factories no longer viable, the pattern of employment shifts from the northern part of Dutchess either southward or inland to post road towns. In a few years the automobile will complete the transformation and free the local population—already 50% less than the late nineteenth century—from both the river and the railroad. Though Tivoli enjoyed passenger service until 1960 it is no longer a "railroad town" in the real sense of the term. The fact that Divisional Superintendent Watson D. Otis' son opened the first automobile dealership in Tivoli is symptomatic of the change. Transformation was taking place.

Notes

1. Robert W. Fogel. *Railroads and American Economic Growth* (Baltimore: John Hopkins Press, 1964), p. 7.

2. Roger Haydon, editor. *Upstate Travels: British Views of Nineteeth-Cenutry New York* (Syracuse: Syracuse University Press, 1982), p. 31.

3. Washington Irving. *Life and Letters* (New York: G. P. Putnam, 1864), Vol. IV, pp. 26–37.

4. Alvin Harlow. *The Road of the Century* (New York: Creative Age Press, 1947), p. 143.

5. Lee Benson. *Merchants, Farmers, and Railroads* (Cambridge, Mass.: Harvard University Press, 1955), p. 83.

6. John G. Saxe. *The Compete Poetical Works* (Boston: Houghton, Mifflin & Co., 1982), p. 19.

7. Harry H. Pierce. *Railroads of New York* (Cambridge, Mass.: Harvard University Press, 1953), p. 53.

8. Charles H. Beach. *Journal* (Feb. 15–May 28, 1853) Unpublished manuscript in the New York State Archives, Albany.

9. Edward S. Johnson. *Journal* (1851–1856) Unpublished manuscript in the New York State Archives, Albany.

10. Clyde and Sally Griffen. *Natives and Newcomers* (Cambridge, Mass.: Harvard University press, 1978), p. 219.

11. Margaret Clark. Unpublished manuscript in the Bard College Archives, Bard College, Annandale-on-Hudson, N.Y.

12. Johnson, *Journal, op. cit.*

13. *Ibid.*

F. D. R.: Neighbors and Politics in Dutchess County

F. Kennon Moody
Dean, Dutchess Community College

In the decades following the close of the Civil War, the United States witnessed an extraordinary increase of productivity and prosperity.[1] Changes confronted the nation as each decade brought the continuing challenges of industrialization and urbanization. John Sproat, writing in his book *The Best Men—Liberal Reformers in the Gilded Age,* saw post Civil War America as a time that "laid down a revolutionary challenge to reponsible men."[2]

These challenges of rapid industrialization and urbanization were not easily met. The result described by Richard Wiebe in his book *Search for Order* was a "society of island communities," a society "without a core."[3] Island communites found that growth exceeded their abilities to administer the effects of change productively. In the island communities men reacted in different ways. Some clung more tightly to the old-fashioned values of the small town.[4] Others moved restlessly from one island to another.[5] The search for order through geographical change was felt by many. Still others reacted by leading the nation in "the quest for goodness in bigness."[6] According to Wiebe, "For lack of anything that made better sense of their world, people everywhere weighed, counted, and measured it."[7]

There was, however, one group that found a method of coping with the all-pervading change that was successful. Those described by various writers as "aristocrats" were so able to compartmentalize their lives that change would be met in a variety of ways. Through such paths as common educational experiences and intermarriage, the aristocrats "made peace with an impersonal world by extending their families' patterns of life."[8] The mid-Hudson River valley provides an outstanding example of the manner in which one group of aristocrats were able to find order in their world and mediate the conflict between social change and everyday life.

Seventy miles north of New York City, on the east bank of the Hudson River, lies the upstate county of Dutchess, an area of 816 square miles that seemed to some a place of escape from the turmoil of change that swept over post Civil War America. With the exception of the developing urban center of Poughkeepsie, the county remained quietly rural and overwhelmingly agricultural. By 1880 95% of the land or 490,620 acres were used for farming in Dutchess County.[9] The original patents covering Dutchess County had, in the late 17th and early 18th centuries, been issued to less than forty men.[10] The concentration of large land holdings in the hands of a few men was nowhere in Dutchess County more evident than in the Town of Hyde Park. In the last quarter of the 19th century one fourth of all available land in Hyde Park was owned by thirteen men, proprietors of the large river estates— estates varying in size from 39 acres to 2,000 acres.[11] In essence, another world had been created in the Town of Hyde Park which would shield the river estate rich and their employees from the upheaval and turmoil of an America. Instead they created conditions which would lead to a life of comfort, wealth and riches.

This was the world into which Franklin D. Roosevelt was born on January 30, 1882. It can only be described as a world of landed aristocracy which was most easily characterized by such terms as graciousness, security, property and roots. It was a world of privilege and implied wealth, although actual wealth was never the controlling factor.[12] It was a world of class lines, fully insulated from the realities of life as it was experienced by the great mass of Americans. Franklin Roosevelt's life was deeply rooted in the ancestral landed society of the Hudson River Village of Hyde Park. His life was also deeply established in American soil, reaching back into the early past of the American nation.

F. D. R. was the 7th in a direct line of descent from Claes Martenson Van Rosenvelt, and until that seventh generation the family was, in the words of Gerald Johnson, "remarkably clear of both scandal and glory."

Long residents of Manhattan, the Roosevelts, in the 5th generation, arrived in Dutchess County in 1819 when F. D. R.'s great grandfather James purchased 75 acres in the Town of Poughkeepsie on the site of the present Hudson River Psychiatric Center.[13] In 1882 Isaac, F. D. R.'s grandfather, actually purchased land in Hyde Park—the town that was to become almost synonymous with the Roosevelt name in the 20th century. Eventually in 1886, F. D. R.'s father James purchased the estate known as Springwood, the present Roosevelt homesite—one hundred and ten acres of rolling, wooded land two miles north of the original purchase and reaching from the Post Road (present Rt. 9) to the Hudson River.[14] Within a year two additional purchases enlarged the Roosevelt farm by 372 acres. In 1871 additional acreage was purchased. Thus the estate that F. D. R.'s imagination would christen "Crumb Elbow," and always erroneously referred to as "Hyde Park" by his father, although neither name was accurate, was essentially formed prior to F. D. R.'s birth in 1882.[15] Eventually F. D. R. would make sufficient purchases to enlarge the estate to approximately 2,000 acres.

Jacob Cohen, writing in *Dissent,* notes that:

> . . . man is inextricably rooted in historical circumstances. . . . whatever truth he perceives about his own destiny is therefore relative to his circumstances, whatever actions he takes to implement that truth must be mediated through it.[16]

F. D. R. was rooted in the historical circumstances of his birth and the land. There is no doubt that all his actions and his relationships (particularly to those people whom he called his neighbors) were mediated through the circumstances that were his by inheritance and place of birth.

F. D. R. was not only the intense young state senator fighting the Tammany political machine over the nomination of "Blue-eyed Billy" Sheehan, nor the brilliant young politician struck down in his prime with crippling poliomyelitis, nor the American Moses leading his people through the devastating wilderness of the depression years, nor the heroic Allied wartime commander fighting the scourge of the Axis powers—he was also a man who defined himself with his relationships to the aristocrats of the Hudson River Valley, the tradesmen of the village of Hyde Park, and the residents of the upstate county of Dutchess. He was a man of global fame and immense power who was infinitely complex and to many almost incomprehensible. Existing in the two worlds of global politics and small town values, F. D. R. has been most often studied and analyzed as if he existed only in a framework of national and international activity. Too often his relationships to the insular world of Dutchess County have been ignored in favor of the more inclusive global frame of reference. Such an approach has severely limited the portrait of Franklin D. Roosevelt presented to the world.[17]

In order to understand some of the complexity of the man and the myth he must be seen in relationship to the time, the place, and the people which provided his roots—roots that could withstand the tempestuous political storms of the first half of the twentieth century. We want to examine the place, the time, and most of all the people—those to whom F. D. R. habitually referred as his "neighbors." In hundreds of speeches and radio broadcasts the voting public heard him speak of his friends and neighbors in such a unique manner that the use of these terms was to become a characteristic almost totally identifiable with the political life of Franklin D. Roosevelt. So total was the identification of F. D. R. with these phrases that Richard Hofstadter, writing after F. D. R.'s death, would claim that "Roosevelt could say 'my old friend' in eleven languages."[18] To fully understand how F. D. R. came to see the residents of Dutchess County as his "friends and neighbors" we must understand him as one in whom a particular portion of the American tradition was peculiarly and vividly alive. To understand F. D. R. and his relationship to those he called "neighbor" is to understand that part of the American tradition that has sought to explain the very special place that agriculture has had in American society—that part of the American tradition that has emphasized the special virtues of the farmer and the inherent values of the rural life.

Whether one speaks of the agrarian myth (Hofstadter), agricultural fundamentalism (Paul Johnstone), agrarian democracy (Grant McConnell), or the pastoral ideal (Leo Marx), the speaker essentially is claiming that the farmer was the ideal man and the ideal citizen.[19] From the early days of the American nation when Thomas Jefferson would claim that "those who labor in the earth are the chosen people of God"[20] to a time in the 20th century when F. D. R. could tell a reporter of the New York Globe that "the political salvation of the country lies within the country men and boys," the agrarian myth remained a part of American life.[21] Even the editors of *Fortune* magazine would refer to the agrarian myth as they tried to explain the new president in 1933:

> . . . it is a tradition of individual responsibility; and its guiding principle is the principle that a man must control and direct his own life, that he must take full responsiblity for the well-being of the community in which he lives.[22]

His inheritance of the values implicit in the agrarian myth, and his periodic affirmations in later years of those values, provided him with a sense of community with those who lived on the land, and/or who made their living from the land. So accepting was F. D. R. of the agrarian creed that he saw all people as members of a community living in harmony with the land.

In July, 1940, Franklin D. Roosevelt had just been nominated to run as the Democratic candidate for a third term as President of the United States of America. On the 24th of that month he drove to the small Dutchess County hamlet of Salt Point to speak with Hardy Steeholm, a Justice of the Peace, in Salt Point. As the judge later told the story, F. D. R. spoke: "I come here first of all as a neighbor and to talk a little politics"[23] From his days as a fledgling New York State Senator, to his last tragic days as President, F. D. R. carried a perception of his Dutchess County neighbors that had a profound effect on his politics. Even today, in 1983, when one speaks of Franklin D. Roosevelt in Dutchess County, one must speak in terms of "neighbors" and "politics." An understanding of these "neighbors" is essential if we are to talk of F. D. R. and politics, either in Dutchess County or the nation. Conversely, any study of F. D. R. and his politics is impossible without an understanding of the role played by his Dutchess County "neighbors."

Throughout an unsuccessful campaign for the Vice Presidency, two successful campaigns for the Governorship of New York, and four successful campaigns for the Presidency of the United States, the residents of Dutchess County were to be known and dealt with by Franklin D. Roosevelt as his "neighbors." Returning from San Francisco where he had just been nominated to run for the Vice Presidency on the 1920 Democratic ticket with James M. Cox of Ohio, F. D. R. encountered the first in a series of many ritualistic expressions of his relationship to his "neighbors"—the first of the Hyde Park parades, traditionally torch-light parades on election eve. Roosevelt was accompanied by his friends John E. Mack and Tom Lynch. According to one biographer:

> Hyde Park was dressed in gala attire and the residents, regardless of political lines, were out to wave and cheer him . . . . Senator Newbold called him "our Hyde Park boy."[24]

Similar receptions were held after each Presidential election, and F. D. R.'s response in 1940 was representative of his approach to these affairs: "You've got another four years in which to know your neighbor is living in the White House, but I can tell you I'd much rather live here (in Dutchess County)."[25]

Not only was F. D. R. a recipient of these ritualistic expressions of neighborliness, he also actively maintained some similar expressions of his own. On each Monday before Election Day of each presidential years, F. D. R. undertook his election pilgrimage—north to Rhinebeck and Red Hook, west across the Hudson to Kingston, south to Newburgh and across the Hudson once more to Beacon, with a final campaign rally in the City of Poughkeepsie. At each stop he spoke little on the campaign issues, but always reaffirmed his relationship to the County of Dutchess and its residents. His remarks at Rhinebeck on November 7, 1932, were typical: "I don't have to tell you, my neighbors, that in all the years to come, no matter what happens tomorrow, I shall be coming back to Dutchess County where my only home is."[26]

It is true that the verbal affection so often expressed by Roosevelt toward his fellow residents of Dutchess County was not always reciprocal in nature. Yet often the same affect the F. D. R. projected flowed in turn to him from his neighbors—neighbors as diverse as a plumber from Fishkill and the Dean of Vassar College. After traveling to the Springwood estate to change the threads on the fire

Franklin D. Roosevelt at Hyde Park School site (Hyde Park Post Office mural by Olin Dows)

plug, J. A. Craig wrote to F. D. R.: "Since I met you in person, I feel like calling you neighbor as we live only 18 miles south of you."[27] Similarly on election eve in 1944, on the steps of the Poughkeepsie Post Office, Dean Mildred Thompson of Vassar College introduced F. D. R. to the assembled crowd with these words: "We in Dutchess County have advantages over voters in other parts of the country, for we know our President as neighbor and as friend."[28]

The simple fact is that the relationship of Roosevelt to his neighbors in Dutchess County was an enigma. Nowhere is that enigma more evident than in the election returns of Hyde Park and Dutchess County in the gubernatorial elections of 1928 and 1930, and the Presidential elections of 1932, 1936, 1940, and 1944. Even when F. D. R. won the governorship in 1928 with a plurality of approximately 25,000, both Hyde Park and Dutchess County voted in their traditional Republican manner.[29] Newspaper headlines proclaimed, somewhat sarcastically, that "Neighbor Franklin did not carry his home town and county"—a fact which caused his former employer, *The Beacon Standard,* to lash out editorially at the home town "neighbors" of the new governor: "Dutchess County should be ashamed of Hyde Park."[30]

The presidential elections of 1932, 1936, 1940, and 1944, continued the pattern of voting that first appeared in the governor's race of 1928. In each of these elections, Franklin D. Roosevelt won not only the majority of votes of the Electoral College, but also the majority of popular votes cast.[31] In none of these elections did he "carry" Dutchess County or his home town of Hyde Park. In fact, the plurality by which he lost the presidential election in Dutchess County increased from 5,433 in 1932 to 10,185 in 1944. Even in his home town of Hyde Park his political rejection was complete. Roosevelt did carry his own election district during each of these four elections. However, the pluralities were small, 5 in 1932, 29 in 1936, 85 in 1940 and 14 in 1944.[32] With the exception of a few districts in the cities of Poughkeepsie and Beacon, F. D. R. did not consistently carry a large number of election districts in Dutchess County. Although F. D. R. was never successful in capturing the political affection and votes of his Dutchess County neighbors, he was involved in the political life of Dutchess County throughout his long and turbulent political career.

The life of Franklin Delano Roosevelt was a life full of dramatic and abrupt changes—from a limited number of childhood friends to the enforced camaraderie of a prep school at Groton, from health to the devastating sickness of poliomyelitis, from a bed-ridden recuperative young man at Warm Springs to a successful politician as the Governor of New York State. But perhaps the greatest change in his life occured in 1910 as he changed from the quiet life of a private citizen to the excitement of political life as a public figure. As one biographer described the change, "the amiable, admirable and useful, but patently second-rate Roosevelt would turn into a very different sort of man."[33]

Almost exactly twenty-three years later, on a summer afternoon in August of 1933, F. D. R. would attempt to explain that change to an audience at Vassar:

> I want to go back for a minute to the old days before I got to know the United States. . . . It is just twenty-three years ago that I chanced to be in Poughkeepsie on a Saturday morning in August. . . . In front of the court house I ran across a group of friends of mine. . . . [who] took me out to the policeman's picnic in Fairview. . . . On that joyous occasion of clams and sauerkraut and real beer I made my first speech and I have been apologizing for it ever since. . . . And also on that same occasion I started to make the acquaintance of that part of the county that lies outside of the Town of Hyde Park.[34]

These were the neighbors who lived in the towns and villages and rural areas of Dutchess County. Actually the event happened in a slightly different manner than F. D. R. remembered. John E. Mack, the district attorney of Dutchess County, visited Roosevelt on a legal errand and asked if F. D. R. would be interested in running for the state assembly seat that was then held by Lewis Stuyvesant Chanler, a great-great-grandson of John Jacob Astor. According to James McGregor Burns, Roosevelt was highly responsive.[35]

Eventually Chanler decided to run again and suggested that F. D. R. run for the Senate seat in the Twenty-sixth District which included the counties of Dutchess, Putnam and Columbia.[36] The magic of the Roosevelt name to gain votes, the possibility of the Roosevelt money to finance the campaign and the absence of any other viable candidates were thoughts that probably helped the county party leadership to accept F. D. R. as a candidate. Summoned to meet with the county leaders in the office of Edward Perkins, local bank president, state Democratic committeeman and Tammany Hall's man in Dutchess County, F. D. R. showed his neighbors the chasm that existed between him and most of the county. According to one of his biographers:

> Roosevelt strode in bareheaded and dressed in boots and riding breeches. The leaders look him over. "You'll have to take off those yellow shoes and put on some regular pants," said Perkins.[37]

By late October the campaign had begun. The average student, and the not-so-brilliant lawyer, had begun the transition to a masterful political campaigner. Each morning at approximately 8:00 a. m. a bright red Maxwell touring car turned from the gates of Springwood onto the Post Road, not to return there until late in the day. Accompanied by Thomas Jefferson Newbold and Harry T. Hawkey (Dealer in All Kinds of Musical Instruments—Reliable Makes Only), F. D. R. began a daily tour of the dusty backroads of Dutchess County.

For twenty-eight days, at a rental fee of $20 per day, F. D. R. and his two companions covered the 26th District in a manner that was innovative and eyecatching—perhaps even vote-getting.[38] Beginning at Millerton on October 24th, the party stopped, and speeches were made at Wassaic, Dover Plains, Wingdale, and Pawling. At each stop the government in Albany was denounced as extravagant and corrupt while F. D. R. assured those present that he "would like to know every voter personally.[39] Basically the same speech was given in Poughquag, Beekmanville, Green Haven, Stormville, and Hopewell Junction on October 25th. Once again on the 26th there were speeches in Gay Head, Wiccopee, Fishkill Village, Wappingers Falls, New Hamburg, Hughsonville, Chelsea, Fishkill Landing and Matteawan.

As F. D. R. closed the gap between himself and his rural constituents, the gap between him and a rival Republican aristocrat would widen until by the late 1930s it would be unbridgeable. Congressman Hamilton Fish, a Republican party power, and the scion of a prominent Hudson River political family, accused Roosevelt of not being a bonafide resident. Unable to defend himself, possibly because he did remember his pre–1910 life away from Dutchess County, F. D. R. launched into paeans of praise of his life along the Hudson:

> . . . my heart has grown glad and I have thanked my God that it fell to my lot to be born and to have lived as one of the people of this Hudson Valley.[40]

The antagonism between Roosevelt and Fish developed into a life-long affair, even being the subject of a memorandum after F. D. R. was elected president—from F. D. R. to Charley Michelson, 26 September 1935, President's Personal File #905, FDRL:

> Here is a gem! In Dutchess County, New York, my county, also the congressional district of Congressman Fish, the Republican candidates were endorsed by and received the official Communist party designation. This is something that ought to give a big laugh to the whole country in view of Fish's attitude towards everything red.[41]

On one of these early political trips through the Harlem Valley of Dutchess County (along the present Rt. 22), F. D. R.'s enthusiasm in seeking votes led the group into foreign territory. Morgan Hoyt related the story:

> One day our party, including Roosevelt, had been campaigning in the Harlem Valley, stopping at various settlements and meeting people. About dusk we came to a settlement, drove up to the hotel and asked those present to have a cigar or their pleasure. As we were partaking our refreshment, one of our party asked "What place is this?" "Sherman, Connecticut," was the reply.[42]

Roosevelt's first venture into the arena of political life was a successful one, as he defeated John F. Schlosser of Fishkill Landing by 15,708 to 14,568. On that damp and chilly fall day of 1910, he ironically accomplished a political feat that he was not to accomplish again during a political career unmatched in American politics—he won both Hyde Park (by 469) and Dutchess County (by a plurality of 850) votes.

It was only natural that the neighbor and self-proclaimed farmer who had become a state senator would continue his earlier interests once he journeyed to Albany to represent Dutchess County. In his first term he was selected as Chairman of the Forest, Fish and Game Committee; in his second term he was to chair the Agriculture Committee. His committee memberships also reflected his interest— Agriculture, Codes, Conservation, Military Affairs, Railroads, and a special committee to investigate the New York City Police Department. A sponsor of approximately 75 bills and resolutions, Roosevelt mostly concerned himself with the development of a comprehensive conservation program for the State of New York.

These few short years in Albany were a learning experience for the young politician from Dutchess County. For example, there had been a possibility of locating a state prison on a portion of the 700 acres of land owned by the state in eastern Dutchess County in the village of Wingdale. On March 26, 1912, F. D. R. introduced a bill calling for the abandonment of that site for purposes of a prison, pointing out that it had been discovered to be a swamp and unfit for such an institution. The Dutchess County neighbors perhaps did not want a prison in their midst at Wingdale but they did want the jobs involved. Therefore, about two weeks later there appeared in print a public letter noting that state lands at Wingdale should be used for other state purposes—the present Harlem Valley Psychiatric Center was constructed in 1925.[43]

In May 1911 the secretary of the New York City Conference of Charities and Correction wrote asking F. D. R.'s support for a vagrant farm in Dutchess County. By early 1912 the citizens of East Fishkill petitioned the Governor to locate such a prison at Hopewell Junction; the letter being signed by the Town Supervisor, the Town Clerk and four Justices. Once again, to F. D. R. there seemed to be a solution to the Wingdale prison problem: "I will do all in my power to support your efforts to locate the new prison at Hopewell Junction."[44]

If F. D. R. was making the acquaintance of the county, such an acquaintance had not yet ripened into a knowledgeable relationship. He had forgotten to find out what the rest of his county neighbors were thinking. An ad in the Poughkeepsie *Sunday Courier* on October 13, 1912, listed fifty-five property owners united against such a "tramp farm" as it was called. Hopewell Junction ultimately would have to wait until 1948 for the Green Haven prison to be built.

Elected again to the State Senate in the fall of 1912, F. D. R. would not complete that term—but would be selected to fill the position of Assistant Secretary of the United States Navy. During his tenure as the Assistant Secretary of the Navy his influence in Dutchess County would be mainly in the area of patronage—the distribution of governmental jobs to the deserving and the not-so-deserving, particularly postmasterships. At this period of the century the post office controlled most of the federal spoils in a county like Dutchess. And in Washington F. D. R. found himself closer to the source of those jobs—the office of Albert S. Burleson, the Postmaster General. In a satirical letter from his old friend Harry T. Hawkey F. D. R. caught a glimpse of both the power and the problems involved in post office patronage. In October 1913 Hawkey wrote:

> I am carefully holding a basket to catch that postmastership in case you should throw it my way . . . . Have gone so far as to lay in a supply of silk hose, and cravats of suitable shade, to properly harmonize with the interior color scheme and mural decoration of the above mentioned office and have acquired an "official smile" with which to deal successfully with any misguided "kickers."[45]

In a battle over the postmastership in Poughkeepsie, F. D. R. found himself aligned with John E. Mack and James Townsend, the Sheriff, against Tammany Hall. F. D. R.'s political infighting expert, Louis Howe, reminded him to rise above such a bad fight. To one politician involved he wrote that "I cannot take an active part in this matter as it would be interference in the affairs of another department of the federal government.[46] At other times the patronage system controlled by these three did not operate efficiently. Periodically Mack and Townsend would complain about their lack of influence:

The Post Office department is making appointments of Rural Free Delivery carriers without giving either the postmaster or the county chairman the opportunity to aid them with information as to the character and qualifications of the applicants.[47]

And he might have added "information about the political affiliation of the applicants."

Other patronage requests also arrived at F. D. R.'s office. Thomas Pendell, for whom the road next to the college is named, wrote asking to be appointed ambassador to Austria. F. D. R. worded his response in such a manner as to imply that he was taking the request seriously even though the man was not qualified. The desire for patronage even, at times, threatened to interfere with some of his most cherished projects even after he became president. After the Roosevelt Library was completed the county chairman, James Townsend, and the first library director, Fred Shipman, would argue concerning the chairman's desire to give local citizens patronage jobs at the library.[48]

Late in the second decade of the century F. D. R. seemed to put together his strategy for future involvement in the political life of Dutchess County—he would take a more active interest in local elections and involve himself to a greater extent with the selection of the county democratic chairman. When first elected to the state senate, F. D. R. had worked primarily with John E. Mack and James Townsend, although Thaddeus Herrick (a Rhinebeck lumber dealer) was the county chairman. In time, while Roosevelt was away in Washington, Herrick was succeeded in that position by Fred H. Vandewater. As his illness re-focused his attention on the county, F. D. R. was instrumental in having Philip A. Mylod elected to the post as Democratic County Chairman, on July 29, 1923.

As charming as he was on a personal basis, and as committed as he was to gaining Democratic control of the county, F. D. R. always seemed to approach his county conflicts with the Republicans on a pragmatic level. The building of county roads is illustrative of his approach. Apprised by Jim Townsend that the state was planning a farm-to-market road to be built in the Town of Washington and running through the property of Mr. Bontecou (the Republican County Chairman), F. D. R. wrote to Governor Herbert Lehman to intervene. He placed the blame for his failure to get roads for "Democratic towns" on the county engineer and proceeds to describe the engineer and his affiliations to Governor Lehman:

> . . . he is an excellent engineer, but his social and other affiliations are extremely close to Bontecou, to the rich Millbrook crowd—all Republicans—and to the Amrita Club in Poughkeepsie—not all Republicans, only 97.5%.[49]

The role that Roosevelt played most easily with his county neighbors and his political power is to be seen most easily during his presidential years. The difficulties of the depression and the average citizen's inability to cope with the bureaucracies of a New Deal alphabetic government resulted in many Dutchess County citizens seeking aid and assistance from the one neighbor whom they felt could be of help. Mr. Alfred E. Bahret was a resident of Dutchess County, Master of the Chapel Corners Grange and the owner of a small florist business in Poughkeepsie. In the midst of the depression, Mr. Bahret wrote to his neighbor the President, seeking relief from his mortgage indebtedness.[50] The request was referred to the Farm Credit Administration, who advised that relief could be obtained from the Home Owners Loan Corporation, who in turn felt help could be from the Farm Loan Association. Finally, in January 1935, F. D. R. wrote to Governor Myer of the Farm Credit Administration indicating of Mr. Bahret that "this man is a neighbor of mine in Dutchess County."[51] As Roosevelt attempted, most often successfully, to charm the members of the county committee, his political mentor and guide, Louis Howe, was often not so charming. At one point in time his frustration with the local county committee was so great that he wrote to F. D. R. suggesting that there was a solution to this problem:

> My own remedy for the lackadaisical attitude of your own county committee would be to invite them to a picnic—offering them free food or free anything. . . . drop them into the creek with a weight around their necks like so many sick kittens. This would do a world of good for the Democratic party in your county—think it over.[52]

F. D. R.'s remedy was not so drastic—he would only replace the chairman, not drown the committee. While still recuperating he wrote to Mylod suggesting a change. After informing Mylod that Dutchess was one of the few counties in the state where the Democratic vote had declined instead of increased, he suggested that it was time to "try out something new." He notes that the weakness lies in the outer part of the county, in the "country districts." James Townsend succeeded Mylod as chairman.

By the early months of 1940 he was again hoping for a Democratic county victory and the political blessing of his neighbors. Once again he sought to manipulate the county organization to gain those goals. James Townsend was to resign in favor of Jim Benson of Dover. After talking with Townsend he wrote to Benson as if his selection was not already an accomplished fact:

> I hear that there is talk in Dutchess County of your succeeding Jim Townsend as chairman of the Democratic County Committee and I just wanted you to know personally that, of course, I should be very happy if this were done.[53]

The selection of Benson, a resident of the Town of Dover in the eastern part of Dutchess County, was only the latest revival of F. D. R.'s long standing dream that someday the Democrats could penetrate the Republican strongholds in the outlying towns of the county.

The label of neighbor was able to bring forth instant positive response. Governor Myer replied that he was asking President Thomson of the Federal Land Bank of Springfield, Missouri, to make a careful investigation of the loan application. The careful investigation by a Missouri Bank resulted in the authorization of a first mortgage loan of $6,700 for Mr. Roosevelt's "neighbor" in Dutchess County, New York.[54] Other, and more slightly affluent, neighbors also sought the help of their neighbor in the White House to secure government contracts and scarce machine parts. In May 1943 the president's office aided the Lumb Woodworking Company to secure machinery needed to fill an order from IBM to produce gunstocks and handguards for the M–1 carbines.[55] Another corporate neighbor, Sedgwick Machine Works was aided in their attempt to gain approval for a plant expansion project.[56]

Time will not allow to tell of his multitudinous involvements with the residents of the county— through his interest in local history, in his role as Hyde Park Town Historian, in his interest in establishing the first radio station in the county, his sponsorship of baseball games between the White Hopes (White House correspondents) and the Saints & Sinners, sponsored by Lowell Thomas of Pawling.[57]

By the time that the Fireside Chats carried F. D. R.'s unique personal style to "friends and neighbors" his neighborhood had become all inclusive. To all men he began to speak the same message he had earlier to his county neighbors that "one day they might all live together as neighbors." His involvement with Dutchess County had taught him an invaluable political lesson. He had become convinced that his Dutchess County neighbors were totally representative of the country and even the world community. They became the prototypes for Roosevelt's verbal images as he explained the problems that would be the heart of the New Deal. These neighbors were the originals upon which later images and designs were based. With the beginning of the Roosevelt presidential years, the neighbors in Dutchess County had become representative of the millions who had inherited the stresses and pains of the depression and for whom Roosevelt sought relief.

Not only did they provide the prototypes for his verbal images, his Dutchess County heritage provided the nourishment for the growth of ideas that would eventually result in the programs of the New Deal—the Civilian Conservation Corps, the Resettlement Administration, the Agricultural Adjustment Administration, the Tennessee Valley Authority. In all of these the agrarian myth so accepted by F. D. R. was evident. In the words of William Leuchtenburg: these were a reflection of "the reformers' faith in the Jeffersonian dream of the yeoman farmer."

In a political career without parallel in history, F. D. R. was never able to carry his home town or his home county after the first two elections to the New York State Senate. But any survey of his relationship to the residents of Dutchess County will show that the political rejection of Roosevelt by his "neighbors" is not the important fact of their relationship. The important and significant fact of that relationship is that his perception of it was to mold his public and private life throughout his career. His perception of his neighbors gave him roots in Dutchess County. These roots gave him in turn stability when all about him the winds of change were sweeping the landscape.

With his Hudson River Family neighbors, Roosevelt had shared a heritage that would mold his values and tie him forever to the land. With his Hyde Park neighbors he had shared a concern with the institutions that filled their lives—the church, the library, the school system, the public services. However, not until he had made the acquaintance of the neighbors who lived in the county of Dutchess did he begin to emerge as the political figure later known to the rest of the world. With his county neighbors Roosevelt engaged in the multitude of activities that would polish and hone his political skills. With them he would be involved in the political minutiae of local campaigning. With them he would continue to manipulate events and people—always hoping for the Democratic victories in Dutchess County politics that would forever elude him.

NOTES

1. Many writers agree that such an increase in productivity did exist. For example see, Stephen Salsbury, "The Effect of the Civil War on American Industrial Development," in Ralph Andreano (ed.), *The Economic Impact of the American Civil War* (Cambridge, Massachusetts: Schenkman Publishing Company, 1962), pp. 161–168. There are some, however, who contend that the war did not provide the increase of productivity but actually retarded pre-War industrialization. See Thomas C. Cochran, "Did the Civil War Retard Industrialization?" *Mississippi Valley Historical Review,* XLII, (September 1961), pp. 197–210.

2. John Sproat, *"The Best Men"—Liberal Reformers in the Gilded Age* (New York, New York: Oxford University Press, 1968), p. 279.

3. Robert W. Wiebe, *The Search for Order,* (New York, New York: Hill & Wang, 1967), pp. xiii, 12.

4. Ibid., pp. vii-viii.

5. Ibid., pp. 3–4.

6. Ibid., p. 40.

7. Ibid., p. 43.

8. Ibid., p. 111.

9. Martha Collins Bayne, *The Dutchess County Farmer* (Poughkeepsie, New York: Vassar College Norrie Fellowship Report, 1936), p. 31.

10. *American Guide Series: Dutchess County* (Philadephia, Pennsylvania: William Penn Association, 1938), p. 117.

11. Bayne, *The Dutchess County Farmer,* p. 11.

12. Editors, "What's to Become of Us?" *Fortune,* Vol. VIII, No. 6 (December, 1933), p. 114.

13. H. Schriftgiesser, *The Amazing Roosevelt Family* (New York, New York: Macmillan Company, 1922), p. 177, entitles his narrative of James Roosevelt (1760–1847), Isaac Roosevelt (1790–1863), and James Roosevelt (1828–1900), in Chapter XVIII, "Back to the Hudson."

14. James and Rebecca had been in England when Mount Hope burned—their home being occupied by a renter at the time. See Kenneth Davis, *F. D. R.: The Beckoning of Destiny* (New York, New York: G. P. Putnam's Sons, 1971), p. 30; Clara and Hardy Steeholm, *The House at Hyde Park* (New York, New York: Viking Press, 1950), pp. 39–40, for more extensive discussions of the move from Mount Hope to Springwood.

15. F. D. R. insisted that his estate was known as "Crumb Elbow" although there is no historical foundation for such a claim. Mr. Howland Spencer, whose estate was on the west bank of the Hudson across from Springwood also called his estate "Crumb Elbow." F. D. R.'s feelings about this controversy can be found in a letter to a friend—FDR to Bevill-Champion, 20 July 1937, President's Personal Files #234, Franklin Delano Roosevelt Library. James Roosevelt called the estate "Hyde Park," which was also inaccurate, for "Hyde Park" was actually the name of the Bard Family home which originally occupied the site of the present Frederick W. Vanderbilt mansion owned by the U. S. Park Service, and for which the Town of Hyde Park was named.

16. Jacob Cohen, "Schlesinger and the New Deal," *Dissent,* Vol. 8, No. 4 (Autumn 1961), pp. 461–472.

17. Such an approach has left a distorted view, an F. D. R. who was, in the words of his son "legendary . . . of heroic size, immune to frailty or human passion . . . a demigod, beyond the reach and touch of the people who elected him." Elliott Roosevelt and James Brough, *The Roosevelts of Hyde Park: An Untold Story* (New York, New York: G. P. Putnam's Sons, 1973), p. 9.

18. Richard Hofstadter, *The American Political Tradition* (New York, New York: Alfred A. Knopf, Inc., 1949), p. 316.

19. Richard Hofstadter, *The Age of Reform* (New York, New York: Alfred A. Knopf, 1955), p. 24; Paul H. Johnstone, "Old Ideals Versus New Ideas in Farm Life," in *Farmers in a Changing World: The Yearbook of Agriculture 1940* (Washington, D. C.: United States Government Printing Office, 1940), p. 117; Grant McConnell, *The Decline of Agrarian Democracy* (New York, New York: Atheneum Press, 1969), pp. 6–7; Leo Marx, *The Machine in the Garden* (New York, New York: Oxford Univeristy Press, 1967), p. 142.

20. Quoted in Grant McConnell, *The Decline of Agrarian Democracy,* pp. 6–7.

21. Quoted in Rexford G. Tugwell, *In Search of Roosevelt* (Cambridge, Massachusetts: Harvard University Press, 1972), p. 67.

22. "What's to Become of Us?", *Fortune,* Vol. VIII, No. 6 (December 1933), p. 111.

23. Olin Dows, *Franklin Roosevelt at Hyde Park* (New York, New York: American Artists Group, 1949), p. 150.

24. Ernest K. Lindley, *Franklin Roosevelt: A Career in Progressive Democracy* (Indianapolis, Indiana: Bobbs Merrill Company, 1931), p. 193. Similar receptions were held after each Presidential election victory. The meetings of the Roosevelt Home Club during the 1930's should also be seen as such ritualistic expressions of the relationship of F. D. R. to his neighbors.

25. *Poughkeepsie* (New York) *Eagle-News,* 11 November 1940, p. 1.

26. Franklin D. Roosevelt, President's Personal Files, #1820, FDRL.

27. F. D. R. to J. A. Craig, 3 October 1934, *PPF #1852,* FDRL.

28. Mildred Thompson, "F. D. R.—A Recollection and Appraisal," An unpublished manuscript, C. Mildred Thompson Papers, FDRL.

29. For an analysis of the elections of 1928, see Frank Freidel, *Roosevelt: The Ordeal* (Boston, Massachusetts: Little Brown and Company, 1954), pp. 257–269; Kenneth Davis, *FDR: The Beckoning of Destiny,* pp. 819–853; Edward J. Flynn, *You're the Boss* (New York, New York: Charles Scribner's Sons, 1947), pp. 64–72.

30. Donald Scott Carmichael, *F. D. R.: Columnist* (Chicago, Illinois: Pelligrini and Cudahy, 1947), p. 100.

31. Harold F. Gosnell, *Champion Campaigner* (New York, New York: Macmillan Company, 1952), p. 226.

32. Results of the 1932, 1936, 1940 and 1944 presidential elections tabulated by election districts in Dutchess County are to be found on microfilmed copies of the *Poughkeepsie Eagle News,* located in the Vassar College Library, Vassar College, Poughkeepsie, New York.

33. Gerald Johnson, *Roosevelt: Dictator or Democrat?* (New York, New York: Harper and Brothers, 1941), p. 71.

34. Harold F. Gosnell, *Champion Campaigner,* p. 28.

35. James McGregor Burns, *Roosevelt: The Lion and the Fox* (New York, New York: Harcourt Brace and Company, 1956), p. 30.

36. Slightly varying versions of this incident are given in Burns, *The Lion and the Fox,* p. 30; Joseph Gies, *Franklin Roosevelt: Portrait of a President* (Garden City, New York: Doubleday and Company, Inc., 1971), p. 18; Davis, *FDR: The Beckoning of Destiny,* p. 221.

37. Ernest K. Lindley, *Franklin Roosevelt: A Career in Progressive Democracy* (Indianapolis, Indiana: Bobbs Merrill Company, 1931), p. 28.

38. Harry T. Hawkey to FDR, 12 November 1910, New York State Senate Papers, Bill for Services, FDRL.

39. Robert L. Jacob, Compiler, *Calendar of the Speeches and Other Public Statements of Franklin D. Roosevelt, 1910–1920* (Hyde Park, New York: General Services Administration, 1952), pp. 1–2.

40. *Hudson* (New York) *Valley Register,* 28 October 1910.

41. FDR to Charley Michelson, 26 September 1935, *PPF #905,,* FDRL.

42. An undated news column found in the Mylod Papers, FDRL.

43. Robert L. Jacoby, *Calendar of Speeches,* p. 25, "Will you allow me to add that in my humble judgment the land owned by the state at Wingdale is eminently suited for a state institution." The present Harlem Valley Psychiatric Center was finally constructed in 1924.

44. FDR to Seaman, 22 February 1912, *NYSS,* Box 45, FDRL.

45. Harry T. Hawkey to FDR, 10 October 1913, *Assistant Secretary of Navy Papers,* Box 146, FDRL.

46. FDR to David Spratt, 14 February 1913, *ASN,* Box 147, FDRL.

47. John E. Mack to FDR, 28 March 1918, *ASN,* Box 148, FDRL.

48. William D. Hassett, *Off the Record with F. D. R. 1942–1945* (New Brunswick, New Jersey: Rutgers University Press, 1958), p. 3.

49. FDR to Governor Herbert Lehman, 18 January 1935, *PSF* #145, FDRL.

50. Alfred E. Bahret to FDR, 7 March 1934, *PPF,* #1853.

51. FDR to Governor Myer, 14 January 1935, *PPF,* #1853.

52. Louis M. Howe to FDR, 24 October 1928, *Howe Papers,* FDRL.

53. FDR to James Townsend and FDR to Jim Benson, 12 April 1940, *PSF* #145, FDRL.

54. FDR to Governor Myer, 14 January 1935, *PPF,* #1853.

55. William Hassett to Brigadier General W. H. Harrison, 24 May 1943, *PPF,* #8230, FDRL.

56. Charles Booke to FDR, 6 July 1943, *PPF,* #5661, FDRL.

57. FDR to H. N. W. Magill, 29 June 1914, *ASN,* Box 108, FDRL, explained his concept of the work of the Dutchess County Historical Society: "It seems to me that the Dutchess County Historical Society has two fields in which it can be of real service, not only to the county, but to historical students generally. . . . The first is the collection of original records, memorabilia and other original historical material. . . . A second is in the publication of vital, historical statistics relating to Dutchess County." In July 1926, the town supervisor of Hyde Park, E. S. Foster, submitted a letter of nomination to Alexander C. Flick, State Historian for New York, nominating F. D. R. as Town Historian for Hyde Park. Quoted in Albert Corey, "Franklin D. Roosevelt—Local Historian," *New York History* (October 1947), p. 511; Lowell Thomas to FDR, 4 September 1939, *PSF* #145, FDRL, and FDR to Lowell Thomas, 7 September 1939, *PSF* #145, FDRL.

Dutchess County Adopts A Charter

Jack Lippman
Professor of American History and Government,
Dutchess Community College

Many students of county government in the U. S. saw county governments as the "dark continent" of American governments. Few people felt its presence and fewer understood its function. Its ancient origins in English history need not detain us, but suffice it to say that it was one of the governmental units brought over with the English colonizers and with minor adaptations to regional colonizing methods, remained essentially the same for most of our history. In New York State, the county, a unit of the state government, was the government responsible for roads, care of the poor, keeper of the peace, tax assessor and collector; the county also maintained a judicial system with the sheriff and the courts as its principal agencies.

In 1683, the first representative assembly under English rule, divided the colony into counties. Each county was administered by a coterie of officials who were appointed by the governor, or by the county court. This format was "democratized" with the authorization for the election of town supervisors (one for each town) who were empowered to assist the county court justices in the administration of the county. The town supervisors, in each county, were constituted as a "board of supervisors" serving as an administrative-legislative body for the county. This change meant that towns would be in the hands of an elected executive. At the town meeting the landowning, taxpaying subjects of the crown, could, and did elect the array of government officials for the operation of town government, and what was more significant, they had an elected administrative-legislator governing the county. From a vigorously democratic town, there developed a democratically directed county government. It is important to note that this model was to be widely duplicated in the development of the Middle West in the wake of the westward migration of Americans. New York's contributions to our democratic heritage is worthy of note and pride.

Dutchess County Adopts a Charter

As of January 1, 1968, the government of Dutchess County operates under a charter adopted in a special election on April 17, 1967. The transfer from a general law form of government to a charter form represents nothing short of revolution for Dutchess County. It constitutes the aboliton of a form of government that had existed with very few changes in Dutchess County from the 18th century until December 31, 1967.

To understand the change in the governmental form of Dutchess County, one needs to first understand the changes that have occurred in the county since World War II. Unquestionably, the economic changes from a predominately agricultural to a growing industrial complex played a major role in providing the proper atmosphere for change. The old Board of Supervisors form of county government, with its monthly meetings, might well have served a county in which change was gradual and almost never dislocating, in which the day to day operation of the citizen's life was barely touched by county government. A rural population, whose contact with the county tended to be for occasional highway construction and repair and small services, could exist with the township government as its major instrument of governance. World War II changed that.

During World War II, the economic potential of the Poughkeepsie area began to attract large industries into the area. Firms in such fields as ordnance, electronics, and machinery, found the locale ideally suited for industrial sites. Its proximity to New York City's services and markets, immediate access to main roads and rail lines, and available labor forces within commuting distance brought the impact of the industrial age to the Mid-Hudson region of Poughkeepsie and Dutchess County. Slowly, economic development took over what had once been essentially a single agricultural industry, and with the change, the concomitant services, such as wholesale, retail, and service trades developed.

Since World War II this growth of industry has been accelerated and Dutchess County is the center of the IBM empire. Clearly, the populations that flowed in with the industry, and the industries themselves, required governmental services which were more responsive to change than the old Board of Supervisors could possibly be. The population statistics of Dutchess County also revealed some of the dramatic changes in the county:

DUTCHESS COUNTY POPULATION STATISTICS

Year	Population
1950	136,781
1957	167,449
1960	176,008
1967	202,000*

*estimated

In seventeen years the population of Dutchess had grown almost fifty percent. With this increase in population came a growth in housing and increasing demands on government for other services, and recently, welfare. These demands were met with varying degrees of efficiency by the Board of Supervisors, but the basic governmental structure could not respond with the speed, economy, and efficiency needed. More than that, the growth, while clearly providing positive benefits, portended great danger, if not directed.

The Board of Supervisors form of government could not provide the necessary coordination and planning to keep the growth constructively controlled. Most objective viewers of this phenomenal growth could see the impending danger in unstructured and unplanned growth. The dangers of water pollution by industry, and air pollution as well as an intrusion into the beautiful landscaping of the Hudson Valley caused by unplanned industries and unzoned housing stood as a constant and eminent danger. Acting as a bridge for federal and state mandated programs, the county's responsibilities grew with alarming speed. While many individuals recognized this potential threat, the established power structure resisted any dramatic changes which might, in any way, seriously alter the status quo.

Traditionally, Dutchess County has been, in a political sense, a staunch conservative Republican community, and it saw in change a threat to its control of the establishment. In response to the growing demands placed upon the county government, the Board of Supervisors, operating through committees, attempted to meet the burdens imposed. With no long range planning capacity, the Board tried to cope. What emerged was therefore less than a comprehensive or coordinated effort, and it became clear that the danger of being overwhelmed was real. There was a rumor that gained credibility by 1964, that New York State might take over many of the functions then carried out by the county! This was believed to be the case because of the large sums of money flowing from the State to the county, and the fears by the State that there would be much waste occasioned by the absence of any full time responsible supervision of county government! This fear was expressed by several responsible county officials several times and by some State officials as well.

Dutchess County consisted of twenty towns, two cities, and eight villages. The governing body of the county was the County Board of Supervisors. The Board consisted of the supervisors of each town and a supervisor from each ward of the two cities. The town supervisors were the executive officers of their individual township elected by the township in that capacity, and as ex-officio members of the County Board of Supervisors. The city supervisors, elected by wards in the city, had no satisfactory city function, but merely represented their wards on the County Board of Supervisors.

Under the rules of the Board of Supervisors, the Board met once a month and functioned as an administrative and legislative body. The operation of each department of government was presumably controlled by a committee of the Board. This meant that, under normal circumstances, once a month the Board would meet to resolve the problems of the county and to expedite this function. It would delegate authorities to committees of the Board who would then meet with department heads and recommend to the Board legislation to provide for the effective operation of their respective departments. In essence, individuals responding to, and only to, a parochial electorate, their township, were involved in making decisions about county-wide operations. The degree to which they might be inclined to act would be in direct proportion to the advantages they could see to their own electorate, in their town. While there are many services that were county-wide in their impact, there were also a great many services which might not touch more than one or two townships. Therefore, there was a greater incentive for the committees to retard rather than to advance county-wide services.

Another criticism was that not only was the existing form of county government not responsive, it was an anomaly in the traditional expectation that government has built into it separation of powers, and checks and balances, to assure high quality of performance as well as a means to prevent errors and waste, not to say undue influence by privileged special interests. In its simplest form, it meant that it was unwise to permit the body that raises funds, to spend it without having some other body serve to check the propriety and accuracy before the spending! The absence of such a check also meant the absence of clear lines of responsibility.

That the departments of the county government functioned at all attests to the ability of individual department heads. Clearly there was absent an overall administrative head to coordinate and to oversee the operation of these departments; a failing of the supervisors form of county government. These criticisms apply not only to Dutchess County, but to other general law counties in New York State. In Dutchess County, the crisis became irresistible in the spiraling expenditure for government in the county; specifically, increases in the budget for 1960 to 1966 at the rate of $1,000,000 a year. Change was not only desirable, but necessary.

In 1961, the Dutchess County League of Women Voters undertook a systematic study of the problem of county government, and turned for information to the author of this paper in his role as professor of American Government at the local community college. He had been interested in county government, and in his course on State and Local Government, students were required to examine how county government might be made more efficient. Charter possibilities were studied, including existing charters in chartered counties. Efforts were made to develop charter provisions for some of the departments of Dutchess County's government. At the request of the League, summaries of the findings from the classroom study and other research material needed were delivered to the League for its deliberations. The League of Women Voters publicized its belief that the county governing structure needed to be changed. Surveys and various charter options under state law were printed for public consumption. Efforts were directed towards publicizing the need and presenting the options available. In this effort, the League performed commendable civic service in keeping with their long and honorable career.

While the Republican party, secure in command, became aware of the growing problems in government, it nevertheless chose to resist change for the reasons already stated. The Democratic party which existed in the county tended to be small and disorganized, and there appeared to be a working agreement between the parties to allow Democrats certain appointed positions or patronage rights. This served as a safety valve for the privileges of an "organized" second party opposition that could not seriously threaten the status quo. The Democrats did field candidates as rivals for Republicans seeking office, but with little hope of success at the polls. There were notable exceptions in the two cities and in one or two of the towns.

In 1963, in a political upset, the Democratic party seized control of the Board of Supervisors. When the Democrats were out of power, the political campaign of that party could make open criticism of the in-power Republicans; and, therefore, the Democratic party tended to be a vehicle for critics of the Board of Supervisors form of government. Now in temporary command of government, the Democratic Party might have felt a strong desire to forget its campaign slogans, but it was forced to act on some of them in regard to the operation of the Board of Supervisors form of government.

The Board created a study committee charged with the responsibility of examining itself and the various options available to county government for change. The committee traveled to other chartered counties, interviewed officials and department heads, and wrote reports which reluctantly showed that the charter form of government provided for more efficiency. These reports, however, were tinctured with cautions and provisos which revealed how quickly these reformers had developed vested interest in the status quo. Acting on these reports, the Board created a citizens' committee of twenty-two members representing various regions, industries, and institutions in the county, and charged them with the responsibility of a study in which this committee was to determine whether:

1. the existing form of county government was effective enough to be continued;
2. if not, should a charter form be adopted;
3. if a charter was to be adopted, should there be an elected or appointed executive.

The chairman of that committee was an industrialist with a baccalaureate degree in economics, and some work in history at that time. The vice-chairman of that committee was professor of government of the local community college. The report that this committee submitted to the Board unanimously agreed that the existing form of government had outgrown its utility, that a charter form was long overdue, and that, for reasons of separation of power and efficiency, the executive should be an elected one. It was recommended that the Board create a charter commission of citizens empowered to write the charter with a strong and separate executive head. This report was received by the Board in August, 1965. A resolution was introduced empowering the chairman of the Board to create such a commission, but no action was taken on the matter for several months. In November of that year, the normal voting pattern in the county was re-established, and the Republican party was returned in overwhelming control of the county Board.

At the last meeting of the lame-duck Board, the chairman of the Board created a bipartisan citizens' commission empowered to write a charter and submit a re-apportionment plan for the county. The last act of this Board, then, fulfilled its campaign pledges for change, but did so only when it became apparent that it could not retain control of the existing majority of government. It should be clearly understood that many of the Democrats on the Board and some of the Republicans strongly felt the need for this change, and had authorized action for such changes before the results of the election. But the fact remains that this action was not taken until the Board was about to change hands.

The newly appointed commission consisted of nine citizens appointed by the chairman of the Board of Supervisors, to represent some of the developing interests and regional background of Dutchess County. The commission was composed of a professor emeritus of economics from Vassar, an executive from a large printing corporation in Dutchess County, an executive from IBM, two practicing attorneys, the president of a local chemical dye manufacturing outfit, who was also a trained lawyer, an insurance executive representing the Grange, and a professor of American History and Government from the local community college, and for a time a professor of astronomy from Vassar, who was replaced by a representative of the League of Women Voters. The members, listed in alphabetical order, were as follows:

Henry Albers (resigned)	G. Stuart Mansfield
Anne Blake (replaced Albers)	Margaret Meyers
W. Carlton Bernard	Robert L. Ostertag
Jack Lippman	Henry Pitcher
Joseph MacAvery	Geriaco M. Serino

Arnold Baratta also became a member of the commission after the charter was submitted.

The original resolution creating the commission provided that there should be three ex-officio members of the commission: a Democratic and a Republican supervisor, and the county attorney. They were as follows: Samuel H. Morrison, Jerome Stuetzle and William Welch. The Chairman of the Board of Supervisors, David C. Schoentag was also an ex-officio member. The intent of the ex-officio status by the architect of the resolution was to provide the commission with *liaison* between the commission and the Board and the legal advice from the county attorney, but it was apparently not intended that the ex-officio members would vote on the commission's actions. The failure, however, to specify this prohibition created the first major obstacle to be surmounted before the commission could begin its operation.

In its first organizational meeting, the commission members were introduced to each other by the incoming chairman of the Board of Supervisors, given copies of the creating resolution, and a discussion followed in which the basic problems confronting the commission were outlined. It was agreed by the commission that at its next meeting, its officers would be elected.

The commission met one week later, and unanimously elected the following officers: Chairman Jack Lippman, Vice Chairman G. Stuart Mansfield and Secretary Joseph MacAvery. After assuming the chair, the chairman outlined the problems confronting the commission, and suggested methods for procedures. It was agreed that the commission would maintain minutes of their proceedings, and that the minutes would be in broad terms, serving as a kind of outline of action. It was also decided that all meetings would be held in executive session. This last decision was also to create some problems. Then the issue of ex-officio was raised, and the county attorney allowed that ex-officio implied all rights for all members to participate and, unless otherwise stipulated in the resolution, this ought to apply here too. Another member of the commission, a practicing attorney, agreed to research arguments against the county attorney's position, and the county attorney would research precedents for his position. Both arguments would be presented at the next meeting. The commission also agreed to meet once a week on a regular basis, and more frequently if necessary.

Until the members understood what county government was about and what options were available for selection, no creative choices would be made. With this in mind, the clerk of the Board of Supervisors was instructed to write for copies of the charters from the eight counties in New York State that were chartered counties. Communications were dispatched to the State Department for Local Government in Albany for literature on county government charter forms, and invitations were extended to representatives of that office to speak to the commission at its next meeting.

The first few meetings were open to discussion of the literature provided, examining the options, and arguing the value of various aspects of different charter forms. The only members who had any understanding about the existing form of county government were the chairman and the ex-officio members. The issue of the ex-officio was resolved in favor of allowing the ex-officio members the right to take part in the voting. This later turned out to be a very fortunate decision.

The commission members, because of their positions, professional associations, and backgrounds, were much inclined toward the concept of a managerial head of government. The chairman explained his objections, based upon political theory as well as on practical consideration; absence of separation of powers, the lack of a responsible head of government to oversee the daily functions of a growing and increasingly expensive operation. As to the attractiveness of a "professional" manager to head the government, the notion of "hired expertise" needed to be examined more carefully. Even if one could agree on what experience and or training would qualify as credentials for "expertise," one had to remember that the applicability for Dutchess County might not be so easily established, but even more of a sticking point was the method of appointment. The argument on behalf of a manager as head of government is based upon the idea that such an expert is non-political and his/her responsiveness is guaranteed by virtue of the fact that he/she has no tenure; he/she serves at the pleasure of the appointing body. In the end the "expert," beholden to a body of non-experts whose policy decisions were bound to be based upon political considerations, would have political curbs upon his/her judgements. The absence of a political base would, therefore, reduce the independence of that position and not provide for a genuine separate executive head of the county government. Since politics could not be removed, was it not better to open the government to the political control of a county-wide constituency, the voters, directly? The logic of the argument carried the commission to the position that the Citizen's Committee had suggested in their final report, namely that what was called for was a popularly elected executive head of county government.

Once having crossed this Rubicon, the commission had to concern itself with the actual structure of a charter. The method used was, first, to take all those obvious administrative functions out of the hands of the Board and structure these functions into an executive branch of government. Working from other charters and interviews with the department heads in Dutchess County, the commission was able to outline these areas and dictate in rough draft the suggested sections of the charter, which each member was asked to study. By the summer of 1966 there emerged a realistic executive branch of government in charter form. The commission had agreed to keep its deliberations among its members so that all members could change their views about any issue of the charter. It would be very difficult if information leaked about half-formed opinions of the charter commission members, to then present a document which, at its completion, might have been dramatically different. The chairman was empowered to create a subcommittee which would provide weekly releases in general terms to the communictions media in Dutchess County about the commission's activities; and this was carefully followed.

Throughout its existence, the commission also held several public hearings for the purpose of having interested citizens and citizens' groups address the commission on the changes and as to the most effective changes that might be made in county government. The commission wrote letters to the department heads of government asking each to provide, in writing, information on the applicable state law and local law under which they operated, their yearly budget, and the monies taken in, if any. The letter also contained a request for their view on how their department might best be organized under a charter. These department heads were assured of the confidential nature of their responses, and appointments were made for their personal appearances before the commission.

In the personal appearances, the chairman of the commission attempted to allay their fears on the nature of the impending change with varying degrees of success. But what was important was the conviction among many of these department heads of the opportunity they would have to help shape this change. This tended to neutralize what was a potentially dangerous opposition.

The commission's mandate required it to provide a draft of the charter and a re-apportionment plan by August 1 of 1966. The commission had concluded in June that this was an unrealistic deadline, and its chairman appeared before the Board of Supervisors in the July meeting to ask for an extension, having submitted an interim report on the progress to date. The Board extended the deadline through December, giving the commission four months more of effective deliberation. This deadline would have been an easy one to meet were it not for diversions of a citizens' suit on re-apportionment, which drew the commission's efforts from the charter to the necessity of providing an acceptable re-apportionment plan. This was done, and the plan was placed before the courts and the voters in the November election, and both affirmed this plan.

Nevertheless, the commission was able to complete its assignment and submit the charter to the Board in December at its last meeting of the year. The chairman was asked by the Board to appear with the Board at a public hearing to be held in January. As a matter of fact, the public hearing was not held until the February meeting, but the chairman and two members of the commission spoke with the Board, answering questions at the public hearing. The Board adopted the commission's draft charter after one serious attempt to amend it in order to limit the power of the emerging county executive. With the adoption of the charter, the board had to apply for special legislation from Albany to provide for a special election in April of 1967. This special legislation was forthcoming, and the special election was set for April 17. The charter commission assumed that it had fulfilled its function, and expected to be discharged; but this was not yet to be.

The commission had publicly stated several times its willingness to meet with interested groups to explain its proposed form of government and to respond to questions; and by the middle of February, an impressive calendar of meeting dates from all quarters of the county had emerged.

The chairman and two other members of the commission were called upon to speak throughout the county. It was agreed that, wherever possible, two or three members of the commission ought to appear at each speaking engagement so that, confronting large numbers of questions, or even hostile groups, what one member might not be able to deal with, the others might. For several weeks this practice was followed. But as the requests for speakers grew, it became necessary to divide the group, the chairman usually speaking by himself, and the other two together. Between the end of February and the special election of April 17, some 60 speaking engagements took place. This entailed luncheon speeches before service groups, dinner meetings before civic organizations, evening meetings before town political groups, and church groups, League of Women Voters meetings, and so on. This was interspersed with radio interviews and telephone answering programs, as well as one live cable TV program. Nothing in the mandate had indicated that the commission would be responsible for promoting the charter. Both political parties left the charter in their hands. The number of speaking engagements left no time to plan strategy for campaigning. Nevertheless, these members of the commission took part in mobilizing public opinion on the charter's behalf.

It became apparent to the commission members that their operations throughout the county would have to be the major effort in promoting the charter. The one major newspaper in the county was enlisted on the people's behalf through personal discussion with the managing editor, who was finally convinced of the charter's value and future, and who actively supported the commission by giving prominent coverage to the various speeches made by its chairman and his two fellow commission members throughout the county. In the appearances throughout the county, some opposition was sensed. This opposition could be divided into two types: one type, which felt that the existing form of government had served the county well and could continue to do so and, therefore, opposed changes. It also felt that the existing form provided closer contact with a "non-political" official, the town supervisor, which would result in a convenient way in which favors could be exacted. The second type that emerged was based on an assumption that no one individual or group could be actively engaged in promoting change unless they were personally going to gain from it. This type assumed ulterior motives in the charter commission's actions and in the support given the charter commission by any of the civic groups in the community. It was important to convince the first group that the improvement in government would actually offer more chance for communication and pressure to the citizens than the existing form. This was done by an analysis before these groups of the one route of pressure that citizens could apply in the town to a failure of county service and a demonstration to the effect that, under the new system, it would not only be the town supervisors, but it would be the county representative and a full-time county executive. The commission hammered home the argument that, while costs in government would continue to spiral in the foreseeable future, it was important to provide an efficient instrument to assure that tax revenues were properly expended, that it made no sense to have a business whose expenditures increased at the rate of $1,000,000 controlled by a part-time, once-a-month committee form of government. If some in the group remained unconvinced, there was, however, evidence of conversion.

From the second group there emerged an organization dedicated to the defeat of the charter referendum. The membership of this group was never made public. The group claimed erroneously that, "the full-time executive would be permitted to hold outside employment," "that the charter could not be changed once adopted," "that the charter created a large number of new departments, and therefore, patronage," "that it was the end result of vested interests, and that the unseemly haste for its adoption was proof of the bad faith of the commission and of the establishment which seemed to be underwriting it." This group called itself "GOAL," which was supposed to stand for Government Answerable to Law. The group printed a pamphlet which was widely circulated, in which it made these charges. Although the commission was provided with $10,000, none of these funds were used for its promotion. Therefore, the commission, without funds, had to rely upon the newspapers and radios for its publicity and its responses to the "GOAL" accusations. Two of the commission members met with the head of this committee in public on a radio debate in which the commission proved that the accusations made were incorrect and forced the chairman of the "GOAL" committee to agree with this. He was then publicly asked, now that his position was proved wrong, would he support the charter, and he responded with an emphatic "no." There was some evidence which indicated support for "GOAL" may have come from small segments of ultra-right wing groups who sought to convert the opposition to the change into a political crusade. It was generally believed that the newspaper account and the radio debate severely damaged the opposition's position, and was responsible for, if not completely, countering it and reducing its effectiveness.

On Monday, April 17, in a drizzling, driving rain, the county of Dutchess went to the polls; and the charter was adopted. The total vote cast was less than ten percent of the eligible voters of the county, and the margin of victory was something like 1,000 votes; but it was sufficient, and the charter had been carried. A congratulatory telephone call from the Laverne committee, which was the joint legislative committee for Urban Problems in the state of New York, to the chairman of the commission included a question as to how so strong a charter could have been adopted by so essentially conservative a county. While it was perfectly obvious that the electorate stayed home "in droves," nevertheless the charter was adopted.

The real success of the charter's adoption lay in being able to get the tacit support, if not active work for the charter, from the political structure in the county, and from the ability to gain approval for change from those directly involved in the change: the political structure. To a great extent, this was possible because of the obvious apolitical functioning of the commission and of the respect this engendered. The commission's chairman had established a reputation for knowledge on the subject of county government and a strict nonpartisan view in his leadership of the commission. Being asked to speak several times before the Board of Supervisors, the chairman was particularly careful in affording the Board its due respect and credit for past performances. Having gained the confidence of the Board, it was possible to gain support for a dramatic and sweeping change and for the Board to accept a loss of something like 75% of its former power in the process.

It ought to be understood that for many members of the Board, the implications of the changes were not clear at all. The chairman of the Board, who had functioned in an ex-officio capacity on the commission, was very effective in convincing the Board of the desirability of change. He and the two supervisors on the commission worked as missionaries with their colleagues. They provided significant help in overcoming what would otherwise have been a very serious obstacle. The opposition on the Board continued to come from two supervisors who resented the commission's functioning in executive session, and who also saw how the authority of a strong executive would impact the Board. Nevertheless, this opposition was countered, and the commission was upheld.

In retrospect, the commission was successful because of a number of circumstances, some controllable and some not. The make-up of the commission provided for some talent in the area of county government and the reputation for impartiality. It was fortunate in having both a Democratic and Republican supervisor who had accepted the commission's view on the need for change, and who were respected in the body of the supervisors enough to carry weight. It was also fortunate that the commission was able to convince the major source of information, the one daily newspaper, of the value of its deliberations. Also important was the fact that the chairman of the Board of Supervisors, who joined in the deliberation with the commission, began to see himself in the role of county executive.

These factors are essential to the ultimate passage of the charter by the electorate. Even the developing opposition from the "GOAL" committee provided a forum for controversy which gave publicity to the charter and ultimately turned out to be useful. Finally, one cannot overlook the driving spring shower of April 17 as a factor. It is my premise that, in an election such as this, there are three identifiable types of voters; those who are in favor of change, those who are emotionally opposed to change, and the bulk of the electorate who are neutral, but who, when asked to support change, are more likely to vote against. The driving rain storm kept this third group out; and the emotionally opposed group always tends to be small, and fortunately, was so on April 17.

Dutchess County's adoption of a charter has opened the door to change in the Mid-Hudson Valley. Neighboring counties Ulster, Orange, and Putnam have created chartered counties, but what is significant in Dutchess County is that this county now has a modern instrument for a modern age.

A revision of the charter has recently been submitted for approval by the County Legislature, but the basic structure has not been disturbed. And with a few, very few exceptions, no one has seriously suggested the dismantling of the charter, which speaks well for the efforts of the charter commission.

As a post script, the task force charged with proposing charter changes is presided over by one of the original shapers of the charter together with the former chairman of the charter commission.

THE AFRICAN (AMERICAN) IN THE MID-HUDSON VALLEY BEFORE 1800: SOME HISTORIOGRAPHICAL CLUES

A. J. Williams–Myers
State University of New York at New Paltz

History—Where is the African (American)?

A striking thing about most of the literature on the History of the Mid-Hudson Valley is an absence of a more detailed picture of the African (American).[1] One wonders whether this is as a result of the so-called marginal role he may have played in the development of American society in the valley or perhaps an oversight on the part of those who wrote most of the literature. One is also taken by the question that if history is the process of humans humanizing the world, or men in search of themselves and their rightful positions in the historical stream of humanity, then why is the African viewed by some as peripheral to that process or even excluded from it? If it is a given that by the laws of nature man is interdependent, then why is the role of the African in the ultimate outcome of that interdependence, which is the making of history, given such little attention? Answers to these questions I pose could probably be debated *ad infinitum*. But my intent is only to raise these questions at this time, not to answer them. But what I propose to do in the paper is present historical evidence, both primary and secondary, to indicate that if such evidence had been sought by those who wrote the literature on the Mid-Hudson, then perhaps they could have written a history that was more inclusive of all ethnic groups, and one that painted the African in a more dynamic role than that of a mere slave.[2]

Historiography and Methodology

In a preliminary article on the African presence in the Mid-Hudson Valley before 1800,[3] I stated that perhaps one reason for the African's marginality in the history of the valley had to do with the historian's use of a macrocosm in his/her approach to an examination of the African presence in the whole of New York, rather than the use of a microcosm in any regional study of that presence.[4] In a macrocosmic approach, relevant primary data may be overlooked, and as a result there is the tendency to peripheralize the African's role and deny him historical substance. To remedy this, the use of a microcosm would address the issue of marginality as well as the so-called a-historicity of the African in the annals of New York history.[5] With such a methodology it is possible to obtain a more personable look at a topic (the African presence) which heretofore has been historically short on evidence and much too broad. The methodology calls for a reexamination of the primary sources (potentially rich with data), the ferreting out of published material long forgotten, and an interpretation of some of the secondary sources that could carry their arguments even farther. One end result of this approach is the possible historiographical contributions such a study could make to the history of African Americans and that of the state of New York towards filling in the so-called *historical* gaps.

Why this move to reexamine the primary sources, the ferreting out of published material long forgotten, and an extended interpretation of secondary sources? My position on this is based on what appears to have been an accepted American mind set among historians, and other writers, prior to the middle of this century, which "required that Blacks (and Native Americans) assume an anonymous image bereft of fully human capacities for thought, feeling and the comprehension of social experience."[6] As examples of this with respect to the Mid-Hudson Valley, it is possible to resort to works such as the *Journal of Jaspher Danckaerts 1679–1680*, J. Lossing's *The Hudson from the*

Wilderness to the Sea, Philip H. Smith's *Legends of the Shawangunk*, Richard Smith's *A Tour of Four Great Rivers*, and Henri and Barbara van der Zee's *A Sweet and Alien Land*, and not once find the African mentioned in any substantive way.[7] But despite what is absent in these works, and others, and the existence of an American mind set, they were forever confronted by the truth. In line with this, the American historian Wesley Frank Craven once wrote: "We tend to preserve or restore only that which by some artistic or other standard seems worth preserving, and so the picture can be distorted. Who among us wander down the street of Williamsburg, with promptings on every side to remember Washington and Jefferson, and still remember that it all rested originally on the back of a Negro?"[8]

Methodology and the Revelation of History

Wesley Frank Craven's statement also holds true for the African in the Mid-Hudson Valley; and although his numbers never reached those of his brethren in the southern seaboard states, he nevertheless was instrumental in the opening up of the valley to settlement and the sustaining of its white population.

If this is true, then what are the historian's sources to support such a role? It is this writer's contention that the evidence is there, and that it is simply a matter of dedication and perseverance in ferreting out this information from the primary and secondary sources. To give an inkling of this picture, I will draw on material either from the already existent primary and secondary sources or little known material such as personal correspondences, travellers' accounts (journals), reminiscences, and biography. Some of the archival material is now available in published form, having either been translated and edited from Dutch or simply compiled and edited from English documents.[9]

Primary Sources: Censuses, Court Records, and Probated Wills

There is still much work to be done in working with censuses, especially in determining exact or, if possible, relative population counts for Africans. But certain facts do come to life with the available data. For example, before the Federal Census of 1790, it was possible to get a picture of the growing African slave population in the Mid-Hudson counties. In a preliminary examination of the data, it is noted that there are census figures for Africans for 1702, 1714, and for 1720 in the counties of Orange, Dutchess, and Albany. There is also an "Account of the Number of People" in the entire New York Province for 1723 including an African head-count, and a slave census for 1755 which list all slaves above the age of 14 years, their first name only, and the names of their owners.[10]

In an interpretation of the data what is evident, especially from the Federal Census of 1790, is that Africans, both free and slave, in the counties of Columbia, Albany, Orange, Ulster, and Dutchess, were estimated to be approximately 12,303 as opposed to approximately 184,491 whites. Prior to 1790, in 1746, Africans in Ulster County alone accounted for one of every five inhabitants. As a matter of fact, by the time of the 1790 census, in the Mid-Hudson counties of Albany, Dutchess, Orange, and Ulster, their African populations were estimated to have been 5.2, 4.1, 5.4, and 9.9 percent respectively of the total populations. Further, because of the need for labor or simply the desire to gain wealth through the resale of Africans, and contrary to the belief that slavery as an institution declined rapidly after the Revolutionary War, and by the end of the first quarter of the nineteenth century was almost non-existent, African slavery in New York actually showed an increase in certain areas. In both Dutchess and Ulster counties there were marked increases in their slave populations between 1723 and 1790, with each gaining 1,813 and 2,340 additional slaves, respectively. Between 1771 and 1790, the Revolutionary period, both had respective gains of 496 and 952, small but significant increases for the region and for an institution considered to have been in decline at the time.[11]

Like the population censuses, the court records are quite revealing as to the civil and social positions of Africans, first obtained under the Dutch and later continued under the British during the second half of the seventeenth-century.[12] Yet much of what the African may have been granted under Dutch rule was to be eroded by laws enacted by the British in the beginning of the eighteenth century to confine him within a more dehumanizing condition of servitude.[13] But until the beginning of the eighteenth century, free Africans under British rule appeared to have been able to achieve a degree of social and economic success, although on a number of occasions they might end up in court as defendants in cases involving financial default. One African, Dominikus Manuel, or who was often referred to as "Mingus the Negro," created a reputation for himself as having the potential to be a good businessman but who often ended up in court for financial defaults. On one occasion, December 23, 1670, Dominikus appeared in court twice that day to seal an agreement between him and two gentlemen with whom he had agreed, in the first instance, to sell his labor in exchange for the purchase of a mare, and in the other to pay in Dutch currency for a stallion. According to the *Kingston Records:*

> Appeared before me. . .Dominikus Manuel who declare having bought of Thomas Harmansen a mare named "de boute Koe" for which Dominikus is to work eight months in the service of Thomas Harmansen. . .Harmansen shall deliver the aforesaid mare as soon as he, Dominikus enters his service, and in case the mare should have a colt, he is to have the same with the mare. . .[and later that day]. . .Appeared before me. . .Dominikus Manuel declares having bought of Reynier van der Coden a stallion named "Dredalov" for which Dominikus is to pay an amount of 300 guilders, in grain, vis., all at current prices, to be paid on Nov. 1, 1671. But van der Coden is to deliver the aforesaid horse at the beginning of April, 1671.[14]

There is also the case of Barendt the Negro, who had been purchased by Dominie Schaedts in New York and who had made a reputation for himself as a "drunk and a thief." Prior to his appearance in court, Barendt had previously been publically whipped in Albany for theft. On February 18, 1672, Barendt appeared in court on several counts of theft and having broken the law against drinking on the Sabbath. The lack of an executioner in Kingston forced the court to put the onus of punishing Barendt on the African community. The *Kingston Records* read:

> . . .public theft cannot be tolerated in a place where justice is supreme, and for the purpose of preventing further evil, and this being a case of evil consequences, therefore the justice of the peace besides the hon. Court at Kingston, dispensing justice in the name and by the authority of his royal majesty. . .the hon. Court resolves whereas the negro is to be whipped, therefore, the negroes shall draw who shall whip the negro. Wessel Ten Broeck's negro drew the lot, and he is to receive 25 gldrs. for his trouble.[15]

Probated wills are equally revealing as to the business of slavery itself in the Mid-Hudson Valley and the positions of some slaves as inheritors in the estates of their owners. In addition, one interesting point that stands out in these documents is that manumission for some slaves was an established fact long before the Revolutionary War and/or before the enactment of the New York Manumission Acts of the late eighteenth century. Further, because slaves were property it is possible to get some idea what the so-called "going-rate-of-sale" was for Africans. In one Will dated September 26, 1708 of Gritie Hendrix of Kingston it was recorded:

> My negro named Pieter shall be free from slavery, and no body shall use him for sake or for any other reason; I also give him one third of my house and land in Kingston, a bullock three years old, 12 1/4 pieces of eight. . . .[16]

In the Will of William West, also of Kingston, and dated May 28, 1738, it is possible to read of another example where the benefactor wills most of his/her estate to their slaves.

> My negro girl Pegg to Mary Danport, daughter of John Danport, as soon as I am dead and buried. All the rest of my negroes by name Saser and Betty, his wife with their children, are to be free. My house and all my land to my negroes Saser and Betty, his wife. . .and make them heirs of all my estate. . . .[17]

Finally, and as an example of sale prices for slaves, it was recorded in an inventory of the estate of Thomas Garton of Marbletown in 1703:

> . . .Negro woman, man and sucking child £108, 1 old woman £15, 1 woman about 32 years old £40, 4 male negroes, aged between 10 and 18 years £180, 3 males between 6 and 8 years £80, 3 females ye eldest 5 years old £36. . . .[18]

The Combining of Primary Sources with Biography, Journals-Reminiscences, and Personal Correspondences to Produce a More Dynamic and Vivid Picture of Africans in the Mid-Hudson Valley

In addition to a number of censuses from the eighteenth century which are now available in published form, there is also other material available that can be used in reconstructing the day-to-day work regime to which Africans were subjected, as well as other roles they may have assumed prior to the end of the first quarter of the nineteenth century.

A. African Allegiance

From this material it is assumed that for much of the eighteenth century the Mid-Hudson region was part of what was then referred to as the hostile frontier of bloodthirsty savages and Frenchmen. Albany (Fort Orange) which had been established on the "Far Frontier" in the early part of the century, was later joined by the town of Kingston (Wiltwyck) and together were constantly besieged by attacks from the Esopus Indians for much of that century. Because of the problems of the frontier, and coupled with the fact that such problems tended to discourage large white settlement, the few who had already settled found themselves dependent upon the African for more than simply to clear and work the lands as well as various forms of domestic work. Many Africans were used as auxiliaries in the campaigns against the Indians, and later in the French and Indian War. In the campaigns against the Esopus, the African was first used in 1660, after the then Dutch Governor of New Amsterdam, Peter Stuyvesant, had written to Dutch officials on the Caribbean island of Curaçao requesting aid. Stuyvesant requested: "Clever and strong" African slaves to "pursue the Indians," adding that it is "evident that in order to possess this country in peace and revenge affronts and murders we shall be forced into a lawful offensive war against them [the Indians]."[19] A Lt. Martin Creiger in the second campaign against the Esopus in 1663 gives an account of African auxiliaries, both in numbers used and casualties.[20]

Although there is still much to be researched with respect to the American Revolution, the little that is available is enlightening.

In Ulster County, the names of four Africans come to light as having served with the Continental Armed Forces during the Revolution. Both Cuffy Baer, a slave of Adam Baer, and Cato Dederick, a slave of Gilbert Dederick, served in the 1st Ulster Regiment and upon completion of duty were emancipated. Jack Gaul, a mulatto and slave of Isaac Fowler-Jansen, and Jack Roosa, a slave of Guysbert Roosa of Marbletown, both served in the Revolution but data as to regiment and whether or not they were emancipated has yet to be ascertained.[21]

In Dutchess County during the Revolutionary period there are the tales of Norma and Dina who, in 1777 at Fishkill Landing (now Beacon) and Poughkeepsie respectively, preferred to remain at the side of their owners during the British bombardment of the cities from the Hudson rather than seek safety further inland. Norma was the slave of the Van Voorhis family whose house stood about a mile north of Fishkill Landing, and Dina, who was said to have been born in Africa and purchased in New York, was the slave of Theophilus Anthony of Poughkeepsie. It is reported in the literature that it was Dina's freshly baked bread which she offered to the British soldiers sent to burn her owner's home that made them change their minds. Dina is buried with the Anthony family in their plot in the Poughkeepsie Rural Cemetary. Norma and Dina, together with an African named Tome also of Dutchess County, who was manumitted from John Warring because of his enlistment in the Revolutionary Army, and with those valiant souls in Ulster County were simply a few of the many Mid-Hudson Africans who contributed to the maintenance of early American society in the region.[22]

B. African Labor

The combining of primary and secondary sources with personal reminiscences and biography permits the methodology to reveal a more vivid and constructive role for the African in the work place. Heretofore, our knowledge of the African's work regime has been limited to a few published sources.[23] This paper, in addition to resorting to those few sources, draws upon some little-known material, quite rich with evidence, to paint a fuller and richer picture of the African's work regime as it may have existed first under the Dutch and later under the British.

Of all the little-known material on African labor in the Mid-Hudson Valley that of the Frenchman, St. John de Crévecoeur is the most comprehensive and detailed. In his *Sketches of Eighteenth Century America*, written during the middle of the eighteenth century and with much of it pertaining to his own estate, Pine Hill, in Newburgh, Orange County, it is revealed that the African was an indispensable element in the efficient operation of the farm. Not only was it a crucial task of the African to clear swampy areas for future farm land, but he was that "essential cog in the wheel" that kept the farm solvent.[24] It is possible to discern from de Crévecoeur that the African was instrumental in the care of the oxen, cows, colts, sheep, horses, ducks, and all other barnyard animals as well as farming the land. As to the importance of African expertise in the area of animal grooming, the *Correspondence of Jeremias Van Rensselaer* and the *Cadwallader Colden Papers* are important supportive evidence.[25] Writing to his brother, Jan Baptist in Holland in May of 1659, Jeremias wrote:

> Your negro, Andries, has this winter taken care of the horses alone and has done it so well that during my time [there] the horses have never looked so fine. . .[Jan responded in that same year]. . .please send him [Andries] over on the first ship and contract for his passage at the lowest price possible. I need him very much at Carlo to take care of my horse [which is full of worms. . .][26]

It is from the journal of William Strickland, a late eighteenth century traveller through the Mid-Hudson Valley, that it is possible to get some idea of the number of slaves on some of the larger estates in the region and the enormous responsibilities some Africans had in the overall operation of those estates. In his journal he wrote:

> Many of the old Dutch farmers in this country, have 20 or 30 slaves about their house. To their care and management everything is left. . .without consulting. . .the master can do nothing. . .[the African] is in fact in general the more intelligent of the two; and so as the master can but exist in the enjoyment of contentment and ease, his is content to become the slave of this slave. . . .[27]

There were other, more prestigious, roles which Africans were able to acquire. For example, among some of the wealthiest Dutch families on the Mid-Hudson was the tradition of traveling in an open carriage pulled by exquisite stallions and manned by African coachmen who sat on an elevated seat decked out in fine livery. The African slaves of Madam Brett, wife of Roger Brett, held such an enviable position. During the decades of the mid-eighteenth-century, these African coachmen handled Mrs. Brett's coach-and-four as she would ride about Beacon on church and gala days.[28] In addition, at what was then Fishkill Landing during the second half of the eighteenth century, a slave named Quam of Martin Wiltse and Son captained a ferry of theirs serving that area and Newburgh. Quam conducted the boat from Fishkill Landing by "means of a row boat and a piraqua, a two-masted vessel without a jib."[29]

C. Black and White Interpersonal Relationships:
Paternalism, Obedience, Fear, and Violence

The further corroboration of primary and secondary sources with that of biography and personal reminiscences can also produce a more realistic picture of interpersonal relationships established between black and white in the valley.

One could assume that where the number of Africans held as slaves by a particular household was small, genuine, close relationships could develop. In line with this, what we find is that the typical white owner, together with his African slaves, was involved in the overall operation of a small, self-contained farm on the frontier, and the smallness and intimacy of the setting tended to aid the development of a close relationship. No doubt similar relationships were harder to establish on the larger plantation-type farms where slaves could total as many as forty or more. On the smaller farms where Africans resided in the same house with whites, either in the basements or attics, de Crévecoeur could write: "The few negroes we have are at best our friends and companions. Their original cost is very high. Their clothing and their victuals amount to a great sum, besides the risk of losing them. . . ."[30] Further on, when all in the household were drawn around the fire to comfort one another during a fierce snowstorm in Newburgh, he wrote:

"The negroes, friends to the fire, smoke and crack some coarse jokes; and, well-fed and clad, they contentedly make their brooms and laddles without any further concerns on their minds, thus the industrious family, all gathered together under one roof, eat their wholesome supper, drink their mugs of cider, and grow imperceptibly less talkative and more thoughtless, as they grow more sleepy. . . .[31]

Both Cadwallader Colden, his family, and Jeremias Van Rensselaer expressed disappointment and pleasure in some of their slaves, but the overall impression is one of necessity, i.e., the need for African labor. In the *Calwallader Colden Papers* there is this special sense of need but also the concern that the African remains obedient. To insure this, Colden was not adverse to breaking up the slave family. As early as 1717, and in order not to have one slave "corrupt" others on his farm at Newburgh, he made the decision to return the mother of some of his Africans to Barbados. In a letter to a friend in Barbados he confided:

I send by this vessel the Mary Anne Sloope Capt. Edward Harely Commander a negro woman and child . . . she is a good house negro . . . . Were it not for her abusive tongue her sullenness . . . . I would not have parted with her . . . . I have several of her children which I value and I know if she should stay in this country she would spoil them . . . .[32]

The concern for obedience as well as to make the African "stand in fear" drove the whites to severely punish Africans in such a manner that it has been approriately described as having been "diabolic". These acts of punishment against the African were as a result of a continuous atmosphere of fear and violence that engulfed the institution of slavery: fear on the part of whites because of the potential destructive power of humans they held in bondage against their wills, and fear and violent acts on the part of the Africans because of the oppressive and dehumanizing nature of the institution of slavery. In the eighteenth century much of this fear and violence was exacerbated by reverberations impacting the Mid-Hudson region as a consequence of the slave rebellion of 1712 and the slave conspiracy of 1741 on the lower Hudson.[33]

In the Newburgh area, de Crévecoeur referred to one means of punishment which involved tying the African naked to a stake situated in a salt meadow. While in such a position for a long period of time, the African "was attacked and bitten by green and blue flies." As a result the body would swell to a prodigious size, with the consequence being either death or some severe trauma to the body.[34] In line with this the Catherine Schuyler biographer wrote:

. . .no slave being sold unless he proved unmanageable or to be a corrupt influence; and in this case, the threat to send the refractory one to Jamaica or Barbados was usually sufficient. Later in the more demoralizing days following the Revolution, there were negro troubles at Albany similar to those in earlier times in New York. Such a period was in 1793, when the "Bet of Philip Van Schaick, a handsome wench," and Dinah, prompted by Pomp, a favorite Albany negro, carried coals in a shoe and occasioned one of the famous fires of Albany. The two girls were tried, sentenced, and speedily executed, in accordance with the summary judgement of the times. Pomp, from his great popularity, had a stay, but subsequently suffered the same fate. . . .[35]

Many of the so-called "diabolic" acts of punishment meted out to Africans had the sanction of law, and with an imprint that was peculiarly British. Although the Dutch took measures to punish unmanageable African slaves, further research is needed in this area. But there was a marked growth of laws under the British in the eighteenth century to specifically define the parameters of slavery within which the African was bound. Any unlawful traversing of those parameters was dealt with harshly.

D. The Development of a Free African Community, the Retention of Africanisms, and Manumission

If the attitudes of such slaves as Andries (spirit unbroken) of Van Rensselaer and the Negro woman of Cadwallader Colden are examples of the African's fierce determination to be free and assume his/her rightful place in the midst of humanity, then there is every right to believe that those who eventually acquired their freedom held on to it tenaciously and sought to prosper where possible.

The literature, to date, discloses the past existence of at least three predominantly black towns in the County of Dutchess, and with only oral traditions of one or two in Ulster County.[36] The first appears to have been situated somewhere in the vicinity of present-day Beekman and called Freemanville after its founder, Charles Freeman, a mulatto. It was also referred to as Guinea, perhaps in reference to the West African Coast from which many may have been taken as slaves.[37] The second was near Fishkill and named Baxtertown. It was populated by freed Africans and Wappinger Indians. Later on white families were to settle within the town.[38] The third town was called Lithgow and was located near Amenia in eastern Dutchess County.[39]

Now if these kinds of things could happen in the historical development of the Mid-Hudson Valley, and with the data revealing more and more that the African was right in among others in the stream of humanity, then why not carry it farther and argue that like other ethnic groups who came into the valley to settle, one's retentions of old world traits was as possible for the African as they were for others. Though there is still much research to be done, what the data already reveals is substantial enough to indicate a possible high degree and extent of Africanisms in the Mid-Hudson region prior to the end of the eighteenth century.

The most astonishing evidence for the retention of Africanism in the Valley was the week-long lenten observance celebrated by Africans and called Pinxter Day, i.e., Whitsuntide. This was a very colorful, gala event in which a syncretism of rituals emerged over time as a result of the combining of Africanisms with Christian traditions. This celebration, allowed to take place under both the Dutch and the British, is still observed today in regions like New Orleans, the Caribbean, and in Brazil. The event is recorded both in the works of James Fenimore Cooper[40] and the biography of Catherine Schuyler. Catherine witnessed the event yearly in Albany during the eighteenth century, and her biographer wrote:

> Pinxter, one of the three Dutch fetes of the year, belonged to the negroes. It was observed the Monday following Whitsunday, and generally continued through the week. There was a colored harlequin. For many years this was personated by a well-known Guinea negro known as King Charley. Dressed in a cast-off coat of the military, decked out with colored ribbons, his legs bare and a little black hat with a pompom on one side, he was seated on a hollow log, which had each end covered with skins and served as a drum for dancing. Other negroes had eel pots covered with skin which they beat with their hands while they sang a song that had a refrain "Hi-a bomba bomba", which it was supposed was brought over from Africa. To this music the negroes danced. There were also gingerbread booths and side shows, and under the charge of the elderly women all the young gentry were taken out to see the sights.[41]

The idea that the "New World African" on the Hudson River could retain African traditions was given added support when Fenimore Cooper wrote:

. . .The features that distinguish a Pinkster [also Pinxter] frolic from the usual scenes at fairs, and other merrymakings, however, were of African origin. It is true there are not now, nor were there then, many blacks among us of African origin; but the traditions and usages of their original country were so far preserved as to produce a marked difference between this festival, and one of European origin. . . .[42]

As stated above, acts of manumission of the African occurred as early as the seventeenth century, with many done by owners in their wills while the shadow of death lingered over them. But not until the general laws of manumission were enacted in 1788, 1799 (for gradual emancipation), and 1817 was there a rush to take out such papers. What is interesting about this period are the instances of free Africans who sought manumission papers for a relative or for their own personal slave. In the *Eagle's History of Poughkeepsie* it was recorded that "one record shows that Negroes themselves might hold slaves". That of "Toney Fox, a black man of the town of Poughkeepsie, who [in 1801] received a certificate for the manumission of his wife and slave, Margaret.[43] Even before the end of the eighteenth century, a mulatto, Frances Jansen, appeared in a Dutchess County court in August of 1756 to take out manumission papers for his son, Cornelis Jansen.[44]

Conclusion

One of the first things that can be concluded about the material presented here is that the "stream of humanity" is undoubtedly the embodiment of all men in the process of "humanizing the world". The problem for some, with respect to the writing of history, is that they have been made to appear tangential and/or sidelined to that "stream of humanity". But if the historian is really about the business of writing a more substantive and inclusive history of the African in the Mid-Hudson Valley, and if he or she does a thorough examination of the data, what will turn up is that the African is there and in more of an interdependent role rather than in one that solely characterizes him as dependent.

In a reassessment of the above sources what is evident is that the initial settlement of whites in the valley necessitated the use of Africans both in clearing the land and the maintenance of farm life. Within such a setting, black and white, in spite of the institution of slavery, could develop a degree of human trust and admiration between one another. Yet at the same time because of the constant fear and violent nature of the institution, such interpersonal relationships were always threatened by the desire of humans to be free and the use of force to make them stand in fear. But in face of such longings and severe consequences, it does appear that Mid-Hudson society was open enough for such relationships to develop between slave and freeman.

In support of this, the evidence reveals that not only were Africans bequested property by which to begin a new life of freedom, but also that some of those who were manumitted may have been either a progeny of a white owner and/or a relative and slave of a black owner. The idea of the existence of mulattoes in the Mid-Hudson society demonstrates a degree of racial interbreeding.

The revelation in the evidence which gives support to the retention of Africanisms within Mid-Hudson society, is a challenge to those who would deny the "New World African" his ability to retain traditional African cultural traits in face of such dehumanizing conditions to which he was subjected during slavery. E. F. Frazier was so sure of an absence of Africanisms that he once wrote, "Probably never before in history has a people been so nearly completely stripped of its social heritage as Negroes who were brought to America".[45] Echoing a similar position R. E. Park could write:

My own impression is that the amount of African tradition which the Negro brought to the United States was very small. In fact, there is every reason to believe, it seems to me, that the Negro, when he landed in the United States, left behind him almost everything but his dark complexion and his tropical temperament. It is very difficult to find . . . anything that can be traced directly back to Africa . . . .[46]

But such statements should no longer hamper the efforts of the historian in his/her search for the historical position of the African in Mid-Hudson society. Because in spite of the traumas suffered by the African in his capture in Africa and The Middle Passage, he was resilient enough to integrate old

114

beliefs brought from Africa with those encountered in The New World. He reinterpreted "both to fit a pattern of sanction and value that [functioned] effectively in meeting the psychological needs of life [within the institution of slavery],[47] and thus preserved for himself, his rightful place in the "stream of humanity."

Notes

1. Breaking tradition, The Negro-Afro-Black-American is here referred to as the African because culturally that is what he remained up to and beyond the 14th Amendment to the U. S. Constitution.

2. There is still this tendency among some intellectuals to view the Africans in this fashion.

3. "The African Presence in the Mid-Hudson Valley Before 1800: A Preliminary Historiographical Sketch." *Afro-Americans in New York Life and History* (1984).

4. Such macrocosmic histories are those of Edgar J. McManus, *A History of Negro Slavery in New York* (Syracuse, 1966) and Samuel McKee, Jr., *Labor in Colonial New York, 1667–1776* (Port Washington, New York, 1963) a reprint.

5. Cf. Barbara Sheklin Davis, *A History of the Black Community of Syracuse* (Onondaga Historical Association, 1980) as an example of a microcosmic study.

6. Cf. C. J. Robinson, "Class Antagonisms and Black Migrations: A Review Article", *Race and Class*, XXIV, 1 (1982), 49–50.

7. B. B. James and J. F. Jameson, (eds.) (New York: Barnes and Noble, Inc., 1946); L. Lossing (Virtue and Yorston, 1866); P. Smith (Syracuse, 1965); R. Smith, F. W. Halsey, (eds.) (New York, 1906); Van Der Zee (New York: The Viking Press, 1978).

8. W. F. Craven, *The Legend of the Founding Fathers* (Ithaca: Cornell University Press, 1965) 121–22.

9. Cf. *New York Manuscripts: Dutch Kingston Papers.* translated by Dingman Versteeg, and edited by P. R. Christoph, K. Scott and K. Stryker-Rodda (Baltimore: Genealogical Publishing Co., Inc., 1976). 2 Vols.

10. E. B. O'Callaghan, *The Documentary History of the State of New York* (Albany: Weed, Parsons & Co., Public Printers, 1849), Vol. I, 366–69, 693–97; Vol. III, 844–68.

11. Thomas J. Davis, "New York's Long Black Line: A Note on the Growing Slave Population, 1626–1790." *Afro-Americans in New York Life and History.* II, 1 (January, 1978), 48–49. The white populations of Dutchess and Ulster Counties in 1771 were 21,044 and 11,996 respectively: *Documentary History of New York,* I, 697.

12. *Dutch Kingston Papers,* op. cit.

13. Cf. E. B. O'Callahan, ed., *The Colonial Laws of New York from the Year 1664 to The Revolution* (Albany: James B. Lyon, 1894), vols. I and II.

14. *Dutch Kingston Papers,,* vol. II, 691.

15. *Ibid.* vol. II, 494–96.

16. Gustave Anjou, *Ulster County N. Y. Probate Records from 1665,* American Record Series A (New York, 1906, 2 vols.) Will of Gritie Hendrix, widow of deceased Dirck Hendrikse of Fox Hall, dated September 26, 1708. Written in Dutch, vol. I, 75–76.

17. *Ibid.* Will of William West of Kingston, dated May 28, 1738, vol. II, 124.

18. *Ibid.* Thomas Garton, Captain, late of Marbletown. Inventory of Estate, 1703, vol. II.

19. Quoted in R. Ottley and W. J. Weatherby, (eds.), *The Negro in New York: An Informal Social History* (Dobbs Ferry, New York, 1967), 12.

20. *Documentary History of New York,* Vol. IV, 42, 53.

21. Cf. B. M. Brink, *The Early History of Saugerties 1660–1825* (Kingston, 1902), 349; J. A. Roberts, *New York in The Revolution as Colony and State* (Albany, 1898) 2nd edition, 187; *History of Ulster County New York* (Kingston, N. Y. 1907).

22. H. W. Reynolds, "The Negro in Dutchess County in the Eighteenth Century." *Year Book Dutchess County Historical Society, 26.* (1941), 97–99.

23. McManns and McKee, *op. cit.*

24. St. John de Crévecoeur, *Sketches of Eighteenth Century America,* edited by H. L. Borndin, R. H. Gabriel and St. Williams (New Haven, Conn.: Yale Press, 1925).

25. J. E. Van Laer, ed., *Correspondence of Jeremias Van Rensselaer, 1651–1674* (Albany: State University of New York, 1932; *The Letters and Papers of Cadwallader Colden, 1711–1775,* 9 vols. (New York: The New York Historical Society, 1918), Collections, L-LVI, LXVII-LXXVIII (1917–23, 1934–35).

26. Van Laer, *op. cit.,* "To Jan Baptist, May 11, 1659", 159; "Fran Jan Baptist Van Rensselaer, December 20, 1659, 197.

27. Rev. J. E. Strickland, ed., *Journal of a Town of the United States of America 1794–1795,* by William Strickland, (New York: The New York Historical Society, 1971), 163–64.

28. *Dutchess County,* Federal Writers Project (Philadelphia: William Penn, 1937), 75.

29. Frank Hasbrouck, ed., *The History of Dutchess County New York* (Poughkeepsie, N. Y.: S. A. Matthieu, 1909), 347.

30. de Crévecoeur, op. cit. 83.

31. *Ibid.* 46.

32. *Cadwallader Colden Papers, op. cit.,* "To Mr. Jordan, Philadelphia, March 26, 1717", Vol. I, 1711–1729, 39.

33. Cf. K. Scott, "The Slave Insurrection in New York in 1712, *New York Historical Society Quarterly,* XLV (January, 1961), 43–74.

34. de Crévecoeur, op cit. 110.

35. Mary Humphreys, *Women of Colonial and Revolutionary Times: Catherine Schuyler* (New York: Charles Scribner's Sons, 1897), 38–39.

36. Both Gardiner and Eagle's Nest in Ulster County are alleged to have been founded by Africans and Indians. See *Ulster County Gazette,* Feb. 4, 1983.

37. Philip H. Smith, *General History of Dutchess County from 1609 to 1876, Inclusive* (Pawling, New York, 1871), 135.

38. *Dutchess County, op cit.,* 127–28.

39. H. M. MacCracken, *Blithe Dutchess: The Flowering of an American County from 1812* (New York: Hastings House, 1958).

40. J. F. Cooper, *Santanstoe or the Littlepage Manuscripts* (New York, 1860) 69–75.

41. M. Humphreys, *op. cit.,* 39.

42. Cooper, *op.cit.,* 74–75.

43. E. Platt, *The Eagle's History of Poughkeepsie from the Earliest Settlements: 1683–1905* (Platt & Platt: Poughkeepsie, 1905), 63–64.

44. Reynolds, *op. cit.,* 93.

45. Quoted in M. J. Herskovits, *The Myth of the Negro Past* (Boston: Beacon Press, 1958), 3–4.

46. *Ibid.* 3.

47. *Ibid.* "Preface to the Beacon Press Edition", XXV.

BLACK SCHOOLS IN THE MID-HUDSON REGION

Carleton Mabee

Professor Emeritus of History, State University College, New Paltz

The story of black schools in New York State is a long one, reaching back into the early colonial period.[1] But the sources available are often thin. To piece the story together one must pore over old school records and old newspapers to find only scattered bits of information. Much remains to be done to develop the story; more local investigations of the black schools where they existed would help. And, further, it is important to relate the history of black schools to the general history of black-white relations.

During and after the colonial period, when most blacks in the colony of New York were slaves, the mid-Hudson region had a rather large proportion of blacks in its population in comparison with the rest of the state north of New York City.[2] Accordingly, the mid-Hudson region had more black schools than most upstate regions. The black schools in the mid-Hudson region, like those in the rest of the state, were of different kinds, established by different kinds of people for different purposes, at different times in history. Only a few of the various kinds of schools will be mentioned here.

During the colonial period, the only black schools in the colony of New York which I have been able to discover were run by the Anglican Church, the church we now call Episcopal. This church felt an obligation to Christianize the slave, and doing so meant teaching them to read, so they could read the Bible and participate in church services. The church taught a few slaves even though many slave owners were afraid that educating slaves would make them rebellious or at least more insolent than they already were. When the number of blacks was small, the Anglicans simply accepted them along with whites into small church part-time classes, which met in the evening or Sundays. But in a few places where the number of blacks was large enough, separate part time evening or Sunday classes were created for them. This was the approach in Manhattan in 1704 (considered to be the first black school known in the history of the colony), and later in other places in the state such as Rye and Phillipsburg (Yonkers), in Westchester County. Why the Anglicans, who were never in the majority in this polyglot colony, were the only church which pushed significantly to educate blacks is an intriguing question; even at that the Anglicans only reached a small proportion of the slaves.

During the American Revolution, some whites became convinced that fighting for liberty for themselves was not consistent with keeping blacks in slavery. For this and other reasons, Northern states gradually freed their slaves. New York State, with an unusually high proportion of slaves for a Northern state, was among the last to free its slaves. It freed them by gradual steps which were finally completed in 1827. The ending of slavery in the state meant that the position of blacks was not as clearly defined as it had been before. And this helped intensify a trend toward segregation, in education as well as in other aspects of life, which had begun in the colonial period. In the early 1800s in the South there was a tendency to adopt laws prohibiting the education of blacks out of fear that educating them would lead to slave revolt. In New York State, education for blacks was never legally prohibited; whites tolerated it reluctantly, only a little less reluctantly than in the colonial period. Still, most blacks who grew up in the early 1800s in the state never attended any school, nor for that matter did large numbers of whites. Sojourner Truth, an Ulster County slave, was typical of the great majority of blacks in the early 1800s in never having been to any school. In spite of the fact that she became a famous lecturer for the abolition of slavery and for women's rights, she never learned to read or write.

From the American Revolution into the 1830s, when there were only a few public schools in the state, there was a movement by societies of benevolent whites to encourage black education. These whites were organized not so much through churches as through charity societies. These societies ran schools to educate the children of the white poor, but they sometimes included the black poor as well. These charity societies tried to educate children to be orderly citizens, to develop good work habits, and to support themselves. When there were only a few blacks in these charity schools they were taught along with the whites. However, when there were enough blacks to justify a separate class or school, they were taught separately. Such was the case in New York City, Albany, and in the mid-Hudson region, in Catskill, Hudson, and Poughkeepsie.

These black charity schools were often short of money. They often campaigned for public contributions—individuals and churches might donate private funds, town officials might give public funds, and societies of black women might contribute clothing for the pupils. Pupils who were able to pay tuition fees were expected to do so, but often it was difficult to know who was able to pay and who was not, and this caused tensions. A basic reason why it was difficult to raise money for such black schools was that many whites still questioned whether blacks were capable of much education. Moreover, as a Poughkeepsie paper explained in 1837, many whites feared that educating blacks would make them insolent. As a result they would forget that whites expected them to do lowly work. Another reason, according to a black New York City paper, was that blacks "have as yet sacrificed nothing for the purposes of education." Unlike whites, blacks "have not even denied themselves the luxuries of life."[3] Most whites and most blacks expected very little of black education at this time, except those blacks who were active abolitionists. A few teachers pushed their black pupils. As a result some black leaders came out of these black schools. Quite a few blacks were becoming teachers and preachers during the 1830s and 1840s in contrast to the colonial period.

Meanwhile, a few blacks were becoming significantly educated, and blacks were gradually attaining their freedom during the period from about 1800 to the 1850s. Blacks were taking more initiative for themselves, as in establishing churches of their own, newspapers, temperance societies, anti-slavery societies, organizations to improve their status and education. As part of this, they sometimes established their own private schools, organized by one or two black teachers, as they did in Poughkeepsie, or they established charity societies of their own to run black schools, as they did in Albany, Troy, Brooklyn, and Manhattan. Also, often encouraged on by white abolitionist allies, a few blacks began to ask for higher standards of black education, and the training and appointing of black instead of white teachers for black schools. In the New York City area, blacks tried establishing black high schools to help train their leaders—previously, black schools had been almost entirely elementary. But these high schools never survived very long. However, blacks were often successful in pointing out where schools were needed. They offered the use of their own buildings, especially churches, for schools to meet in. They helped show that some blacks cared about education. The private black schools they created along with the more numerous schools for blacks that whites created—helped to prepare the way for black public schools.

By the 1840s black public schools were becoming common in the state. By law, blacks were neither specifically excluded nor included in public schools. The custom simply developed in some places in the state for blacks to attend the same school as whites, and in other places the custom developed, perhaps from fear by blacks, and from dislike by whites, for them not to attend. Where the numbers of black pupils were considerable, there was a trend to start separate black public schools. In some cases existing private or charity schools for blacks were transformed into black public schools— this happened in Poughkeepsie. In other cases new black public schools were founded—at the request of blacks or whites or both. Once a black public school existed, local school officials usually required all the black children of that district to attend that black school. In the 1850s to 1870s the black public schools reached their height in the state. There were black public schools in this period in the mid-Hudson region in Hudson and Kinderhook in Columbia County, in Catskill in Greene County, in Poughkeepsie and Beacon (then called Fishkill Landing) in Dutchess County, in Newburgh, Middletown, and Goshen in Orange County, in Haverstraw in Rockland County, in Harrison, New Rochelle, and White Plains in Westchester County. The quality of education in these black schools was better than it had been in the previous black schools. There was more money available, better public expectation of what the schools could accomplish, better teachers.

Who were the teachers of the black schools, whether church schools, private schools, charity schools, or public schools? While the teachers of the black church schools of the colonial period had all been white, gradually more and more blacks taught in the black schools. In the 1820s, 46% of the teachers whose racial identity was available were blacks, but by the 1890s, 76% were blacks, and by the 1930s and 1940s, over 90%. In the nineteenth century, downstate, where the black population was especially concentrated, the teachers in the black schools were mostly black, in the Hudson region about half of them were black, and in the rest of the upstate—where the proportion of blacks was small, the teachers were mostly white.

How much freedom did the black teachers who taught in the nineteenth century in the black schools have? In particular, how many of them took some significant action against inequality or discrimination on the basis of race, and did so either before or while teaching, so that school officials in hiring them or rehiring them could have found out about their being protesters and refused to hire or rehire them? Of the 390 black teachers of black schools in nineteenth century New York State 27% can be identified as protesters. This is remarkably high, especially since most of the teachers were women, and in much of the century women were expected to leave public affairs to men. The proportion of the teachers who were protesters who taught in the Hudson region was only moderate; there were more of the protesters among the teachers the farther one moved upstate, north and west, fewer in proportion downstate. Why would white school authorities in the state—and particularly in the mid-Hudson region—allow black protesters to teach, since in much of the nineteenth century, New York State whites seemed determined to keep blacks in their place?

This is a particularly interesting question to relate to the Mid-Hudson region because this region was more hostile to blacks than most of the rest of the upstate region. This hostility can be judged by noting the relatively small number of antislavery societies in the region before the Civil War; by the low popular vote in the region in 1844 for the abolitionist Liberty Party; and by the low popular vote in the region in favor of an amendment to the state constitution to give blacks the equal right to vote in the states, in popular referendums taken in 1846, 1860, and 1869, an amendment which failed each time to carry the state.[4] Samuel R. Ward, a black who had taught in a black school in Poughkeepsie, said in 1851, when he was the editor of a black abolitionist paper, the "most places on the Hudson River" are "thoroughly and hopelessly pro-slavery."[5]

A probable factor in the greater hostility to blacks in the mid-Hudson region compared to most of the rest of upstate is that the Dutch who were traditionally strong in the Hudson region had themselves held slaves in considerable numbers and seemed unsympathetic to black rights, and were generally conservative, whereas few of the New Englanders—especially from Massachusetts and northern New England—who flooded across the upper part of New York State in the period before the Civil War had ever held slaves, and they often made their churches—commonly Congregationalist or Methodist or Baptist—into engines of zealous reform of all kinds—educational reform, temperance reform, and antislavery reform, and they were generally sympathetic to black aspirations. Another factor probably was that there were more blacks in the Hudson region. So the farther one went from the Hudson region north and west upstate one found fewer blacks, less prejudice, more abolitionists, more Republicans, and more white institutions, including schools and churches open to blacks. This difference makes it all the more interesting to ask: why in the Hudson region did white school officials tolerate black teachers who were protesters?

An example of a black protester who was allowed to teach in the mid-Hudson region is Nathan Blount. He taught the colored school in Poughkeepsie through most of the 1830s. During part of this time his school was operated by a white charity society, the Lancaster Society, and was located upstairs in the society's school building on Church Street, where the white school was held downstairs. At the same time that Blount was teaching school in Poughkeepsie, he was also an agent for William Lloyd Garrison's famous weekly paper, the Liberator, published in Boston, which was widely regarded as a seditious, treasonable newspaper; and also an agent of the New York Colored American, which was a black newspaper which vigorously worked for equal rights for blacks. At the same time Blount was also a member of the executive committee of the Dutchess County Anti-Slavery Society. As such he helped to raise money for the society, helped locate speakers, and with other officers, most of them whites, refused to support the candidates for public office of either major party because they refused to oppose slavery, and instead endorsed the candidates of a tiny, radical, abolitionist party. But doing all this seemed to make no trouble for Blount as a teacher. The white trustees who operated his school said that they were much pleased with the order in his school and the improvement of his pupils. A white newspaper, the Poughkeepsie *Telegraph*, said of an exhibition program at his school, the pupils were neatly dressed, gave attention, and were spirited.[6] Why were whites, who were generally virulently anti-abolitionist in the Hudson region in this period, so tolerant of such a radical black teacher?

An example of a black teacher in Newburgh who was a protester is Elizabeth Waters who taught the black public school there from just before the Civil War in 1859 to about 1862. She and a cousin of hers who had been born in the slave state of Maryland gave lectures against slavery. Her cousin did most of the speaking, while she showed pictures with the aid of a magic lantern, and commented on the pictures, and sang slave songs. *Frederick Douglass' Paper* recommended their anti-slavery presentation, and a black New York City newspaper said that Miss Waters' comments on the pictures were "well-timed, eloquent, and full of pathos," and she "bids fair to become distinguished in the cause of the oppressed."[7] Why would white school authorities allow her to teach a black school without making any issue of the matter, at a time when the state was deeply divided over slavery?

One can never be sure about such complex questions as why white officials tolerated black protesters as teachers, but possible reasons can be suggested. (1) Despite occasional claims that the North was at least as prejudiced against blacks as the South, in fact I believe the North was less so. In New York State less prejudice was fostered by comparatively few blacks being in the population, and by the proportion of blacks either declining or remaining stationary through the century. (2) White school officials, like white leaders generally, often ignored black protest. Some officials may have done so in part because they felt guilty about it, and hoped that by ignoring it, it would go away. Others may have felt able to ignore it because it came from blacks who were inferior, un-influential, and could be be isolated; they did not ignore such protests from whites, but could from blacks. (3) Finally, if school officials were to employ well-educated black teachers at all, they could scarcely avoid employing protesters. The better educated black teachers were more likely to be protesters than non-protesters. In addition, many of the well-educated black teachers were likely to be protesters simply because the milieu of New York State's more articulate blacks was one of protest against slavery, against segregation, and against inequality.

Turning to an allied question, how were black teachers educated? Generally in the early and mid-nineteenth century blacks could not get into the white academies or high schools where many teachers were educated at this time, nor into the white normal schools which were beginning to be established in the mid-century, nor into colleges. There were however a few exceptions. Blacks were admitted into two colleges that abolitionists controlled, one near Utica in the 1830s and 1840s, and another in Cortland County in the 1850s and 1860s; but because these colleges admitted blacks they became known as "nigger" schools, had trouble raising money, and staggered painfully into closing. Many more black teachers, however, were educated in New York City where the public school system maintained special teacher training classes in the black schools, and eventually established a Colored Saturday Normal School which was taught by two especially outstanding black principals. But there was no such public black teacher education upstate. In the 1870s, during the post-Civil War Reconstruction, when black hopes for their advancement were high, black leaders in five mid-Hudson counties met together in Poughkeepsie to try to improve the opportunity for advanced education for blacks, including teachers. The presiding officer of these meetings was Isaac Deyo, a black Poughkeepsie cartman who believed that education was the way to elevate blacks above their usual menial position in society. The meetings decided that blacks should found a black college in Poughkeepsie. They chose all-black trustees for their college, which may have been a mistake considering that other black colleges of the time like Howard and Lincoln had few black trustees. Moreover, they chose a rather defiant name for their proposed college, Toussaint, after the Haitian black revolutionary. This group incorporated their college and tried to raise funds to get it started. Even though a local Poughkeepsie Republican newspaper encouraged their drive to raise funds, and even though among the black trustees they chose were some of the best known black leaders of the state and nation, including the politically influential black barber of Troy, William Rich, the militant black minister of New York City, Henry Highland Garnet, Dean John M. Langston of Howard University, and Senator Hiram Revels, the first black to serve in the U.S. Senate, they failed to raise the necessary funds. Many blacks believed that establishing a black college in New York State at this time would encourage segregation which would be unfortunate when there was hope for progress toward unsegregated education. New York State had never had a black college, though some nearby states like Pennsylvania and Ohio had. The proposed Poughkeepsie college never opened, and even today New York State has still never had a black college.

In fact, from the 1870s on, there was a trend, though slow and painful, for blacks to be admitted more and more into colleges in the state. In the 1870s, the Republican administration in Washington directed West Point Academy to admit blacks, and New York City opened a Normal College, later called Hunter College, which from its beginning admitted blacks; however, blacks at both of these colleges met serious hostility and doubt about their capacity to learn well. By the 1880s four blacks were already studying at Albany State Normal. But still in 1900 Vassar College announced that "the conditions of life here are such" that we "strongly advise" blacks not to enter.[8] In the early 1900s the number of blacks attending Columbia University's Teachers College began to zoom, moving it towards becoming a center for the education of black teachers from around the nation. But in the mid-Hudson region progress was much slower. It was only in 1934 that Vassar announced that it was ready to accept black students. At about that time the first black student attended the State Normal School at New Paltz—she was a Poughkeepsie girl, later Mrs. Julius McLean. But when she tried to find a place to live in New Paltz, as other students did, in private homes, she was unsuccessful, and so had to commute from Poughkeepsie. In 1965 there were still only a few black students at New Paltz, and significantly, most of them were foreign students from Africa.

Returning to the nineteenth century, from the Civil War on, there was a strong movement among blacks and their white allies to abolish black separate public schools. The movement was fostered by such factors as the high cost of separate schools for blacks; the declining proportion of blacks in the state so that whites felt less discomfort in being associated with blacks; the upsurge in confidence which the freeing of slaves in the South gave to blacks generally and the impulse to equality nationwide which it fostered, including the giving of blacks the equal right to vote everywhere by U.S. Constitutional Amendment in 1870. In 1873 the state legislature adopted a law providing for equal education for blacks and whites, which seemed to some people to outlaw separate schools, but the courts later interpreted it as not necessarily doing so provided equal facilities were given to blacks in separate schools. In 1900, however, the state flatly outlawed separate schools in cities, and in 1938 also in rural areas.

Blacks were divided among themselves as to whether closing black schools was better for them or not. Those opposed to separate education argued that it humiliated blacks and provided inferior education; those in favor argued that it kept black teachers in jobs and black schools were more able to teach black children what they really needed than white schools were. In the long run, an important force in closing the legally separate black schools in the later 1800s and early 1900s, was that many black parents in effect boycotted the separate black schools when they could, choosing to send their children to the white schools instead.

For instance, in Newburgh, after the passage of the 1873 law requiring equal facilities for black and white children in school, the black D. B. Alsdorf, who ran a private music and dancing school, wrote the local school board asking that his three children be admitted to the white public schools in order for them to enjoy the advantages of equal facilities, instead of being required to attend the less-than-equal black public school. After fuming for a while, the Newburgh school board decided to interpret the law as requiring that the black school be discontinued at once, and the board admitted all the black children to the white schools.[9] About the same time the school boards in Albany, Troy, and Schenectady acted similarly, closing their black schools. In contrast, the school board in Poughkeepsie, as well as most blacks in Poughkeepsie, seemed reluctant to close their black school. However, one black family decided to force the issue—the family of Joseph Rhodes, the owner of a

Poughkeepsie business for dyeing cloth. Rhodes had sent his children out of town to the Finger Lakes region so that they would not have to attend the segregated Poughkeepsie black school, but when he saw Newburgh and other Hudson Valley cities opening their white schools to blacks, he decided to send his children to the Poughkeepsie white schools whether most Poughkeepsie whites or blacks liked it or not. He did so, and this caused turmoil in Poughkeepsie for several days.[10] Eventually the school board decided that the new law would not permit the board to keep blacks out of the white schools, so they let the Rhodes children stay in the white school. But they also decided that it was not clear that the law required them to close the black school. So the board kept the black school open for those who wished to attend it. But then so many black children gradually dropped out of the black school to attend the white schools that a year later the board closed the black school. Elsewhere in the Hudson Valley, with blacks themselves as well as whites often divided about whether they wanted the black schools to remain open, black schools remained open longer: in Hudson until later in the 1870s; in Kinderhook and New Rochelle into the 1880s; in Catskill, Beacon, and Haverstraw into the 1890s; in Brooklyn and Manhattan into the early 1900s; in Goshen into the 1930s; in Hillburn into the 1940s.

By the 1930s and 1940s, of course, the proportion of blacks in New York State was rapidly rising as a result of immigration of blacks from the South, and segregated housing was leading to a new kind of segregated school, particularly downstate. But that is another story, with which we are more familiar.

In conclusion, when we look at the problems in education in our state in recent years, from the short perspective we may sometimes doubt whether the education of blacks or whites is improving, but when we take the long perspective from the colonial period until now, then I think we can confidently say that education for both blacks and whites has improved immensely. This can give us hope for the future.

But when we ask, "Did education do a great deal to raise the status of blacks in New York State?" then caution is necessary. In the latter half of the nineteenth century, education for blacks was clearly improving, but at the same time, as white immigrants from Europe poured into the state, they took jobs that blacks had formerly held, and opportunities for jobs for blacks declined. I think we have to say that education alone has limitations as an agent of social change. Education needs to be combined with other agents of change to effect a great deal of significant change in society.

Notes

1. This paper generally follows Carleton Mabee, *Black Education in New York State: From Colonial to Modern Times,* Syracuse University Press, 1979. However, this paper includes details about the Mid-Hudson region which are not in the book.

2. For the purpose of this paper, the Mid-Hudson region is considered to be the New York State counties which are contiguous to the Hudson River and which lie between Bronx County on the south and Albany County on the north.

3. Poughkeepsie *Telegraph,* in New York *Colored American,* October 28, 1837; New York *Colored American,* November 11, 1837.

4. American Anti-Slavery Society, *Annual Report,* 1837, p. 130–134; *New York State Register,* N.Y. 1845, p. 106; *Tribune Almanac,* New York, 1870, p. 53.

5. Boston *Impartial Citizen,* February 1, 1851.

6. Dutchess County Anti-Slavery Society, Minutes, 1838–1839, manuscript, at New York Public Library; New York *Colored American,* June 1, 1839; Poughkeepsie *Telegraph,* Aug. 9, 1837.

7. Rochester *Frederick Douglass Paper,* March 4, 1859; New York *Weekly Anglo-Africian,* August 27, 1859.

8. W. E. B. DuBois, *The College Bred Negro,* Atlanta, 1900. p. 34.

9. Newburgh *Daily Journal,* April 17, May 3, 5, 6, 8, 10, September 3, 1873.

10. Poughkeepsie *Daily Eagle,* September 2, 3, 10, October 9, 1873.

The Development of Public Education In Dutchess County

From One Room Schools to Centralization
Education Comes to Dutchess County
Charles D. King, Jr.

In 1716, thirty families from Columbia County settled in an area near present day Rhinebeck. Near a hill, they cleared the land and constructed log houses. Higher on the hill, they erected another structure, the church, which was their center of community life.

These newcomers were German and their church was called St. Paul's Evangelical Lutheran Church. Some were Calvinists, some were Lutherans, but they were united by a common language.

These settlers held a strong belief in education and in teaching their children the German language, thus their log church served as the school. This was the first "school" in Dutchess County. This type of church-school continued well into the 1800's, teaching the ways of the church and other essentials deemed necessary for the time.

By the 1760's, people began to develop the idea that education should be received outside the church. The American Revolution brought this idea into reality with the separation of the Church and State.

There were several small non-church village schools established before the Revolution, located wherever a community was well settled. They were built and financed by the village and Poughkeepsie set the pace for this type of educational facility:

These village schools were of simple construction, heated by a wood stove, where the older boys prepared the wood and made the fire. The room was generally plain with the exception of a map or two on the wall and a so-called "blackboard."

The teacher was a revered member of the community and was paid about $20.00 to $25.00 per month. He lived with the family who had a child in school, his length of stay was determined by the number of children the family had on the basis of one week per child.

The first law encouraging public education was the one of 1795 called "An Act for the Encouragement of Schools." It was passed at a legislative session held in Poughkeepsie and was passed in response to a recommendation from Governor George Clinton. This law became the foundation of the state system of aid to schools and the state regents.

Under this act, Dutchess County (which then included Putnam County) received 2,100 pounds as state aid. In this period, a school district was called a society. North East (which prior to 1818 included Pine Plains and Milan) had at least seventeen such societies by 1795. By 1819, after splitting from Pine Plains and Milan, North East still had eleven full districts and four fractional ones "imparting instruction to 456 children between the ages of five and fifteen."

The act of 1795 did not give rise immediately to a public school system in the modern sense, meaning free schools, but aid was extended to incorporated schools or academies, and there may even have been a few lower grade schools receiving financial aid. The act caused a good deal of discussion as to its real meaning and intent, but good, bad and mixed, it was a new departure in the school system.

Some of the first schools involved with this new act included: District 14 in West Pine Plains, District 18 near Josua Hamblin's Oblong, both in North East; District #1 in Pine Plains, located on the west side of North Street. Rhinebeck did not come under the district school system until 1805 and Hyde Park entered the system shortly after 1806.

123

As the private and village schools were being established in the county, so was Poughkeepsie developing schools of its own. The reputation of being "the city of schools" came to Poughkeepsie largely through the institutions founded during the Improvement Party's best days, but these were private schools.

In 1841 a survey was made in Poughkeepsie, which revealed that 383 children between the ages of five and sixteen did not attend any schools. In 1843, therefore, an act was passed creating a special village board empowered to borrow $12,000 to build a school, and to raise $7,000 a year by taxation. The establishment of free schools was bitterly opposed, on the grounds "that which costs nothing is lightly prized." However, in the face of this opposition, three free schools were opened in 1843, each accommodating one hundred and fifty pupils.

Until 1843, it must be remembered, there were no free schools, entirely supported by taxes, in the entire county. The so called "common school" occasionally furnished free tuition to those who could not afford to pay, a plan similar to the pauper schools of Pennsylvania. These common schools were supported partly by private subscription, and partly by taxation.

Such schools as the Dutchess County Academy in Poughkeepsie received a share of state money, and were under the supervision of the Regents, but they were not truly public schools. These academies charged a tuition to most pupils, and these charges usually amounted to about four dollars a quarter.

When the climactic news came from Albany that the Senate had approved a bill creating a public school district in the village of Poughkeepsie, there were thirty-two schools within its corporate limits, which had a population of 8,158. The act as presented by the State carried an amendment that the villagers must vote to determine the final fate of the proposition. They had one month before the election was to take place to discuss the pro's and con's, which as previously mentioned, was hotly disputed.

A total of 976 went to the polls and the law was carried by a majority of 168. Approximately one month later, on June 13, 1843 the first board of education was elected.

Its duties, in addition to governing the administration of the school system, included a visit to each school at least once a week to render such assistance to the teacher and advice to the pupils as was considered expedient. However, that responsibility was quickly repealed as the Board members found it too much of a chore to be assistant teachers along with their personal obligations.

The village corporation in 1843 owned no school building, so the board supplied the need by renting a building formerly occupied as a theatre in Market Street for a term of three years and nine months, at $80.00 a year. A room was also rented in the building located at Clinton and Thompson Streets, on the same terms. They also rented a room in a coach factory at the junction of Mill Street and Dutchess Avenue. Thus, the free public school came to Poughkeepsie. Soon, the county followed Poughkeepsie's start and established free schools for all throughout the county. A new era was about to start. Education was finally to become available for all, and on a uniform, tax-paid basis as opposed to a tuition paid basis.

With the free school system now firmly established in Poughkeepsie, the village was rapidly growing, and on March 28th, 1854, it became a city. The public schools established in this period were basically mechanistic and rudimentary, and included only training in reading, writing, arithmetic, English grammar and spelling. There were no high schools yet established, in the sense we know them today, and there were no vocational or trade schools.

The purpose of formal higher education of this period was training of the mind along so-called "classic" lines (Greek, Latin, etc.), and college training was primarily along philosophical and literary lines. However, in this period of 1843 to 1900, educational opportunities were greatly expanded. A new subject was added to Poughkeepsie's public school system in 1854—music—and more new courses were to follow later in the century.

On March 14th, 1856, a motion was offered at the Board of Education's meeting that the upper floor of the new building in Church Street, school number 2, be devoted to the use of a "high school," for the admission of students of both sexes. The motion, after some discussion, was tabled. Subsequently a high school was established there and continued until 1865 when a resolution was adopted discontinuing the school for one year. At a meeting held June 6, 1866, it was unanimously resolved that "the high school again re-open on the first of September, 1866."

Meanwhile, to the north, Rhinebeck's school conditions were becoming crowded. The number of children of school age in the district in 1865 had nearly doubled since 1860. At the annual meetings, commencing with 1865, the question of better school accommodations and facilities was raised. This was repeated in 1866 and 1867. Nothing, however, was done except talk. In 1868, Captain Van Wagenon, the president of the Board of Education, and Dr. William Cross, Board member and clerk, convinced of the necessity for favorable action on the subject of improvements, consulted with several village leaders of the district to find out what was the best thing to do under the circumstances. Parents sending children to school wanted better conditions. Taxpayers were not for this movement, because of the fear of a higher tax rate.

After much discussion at Board meetings it was finally agreed that a new school house was to be built at a cost of $8,000. It, in fact, cost about $9,000, additional sums being appropriated. Plans and specifications were prepared and approved by the Board. The contract for the erection of the building was awarded to Peter M. Fulton, a well known architect and builder residing in the village. He was the lowest bidder on the project. The work progressed rapidly, and on the 22nd day of February, 1870, the spacious new building was dedicated with the appropriate ceremonies to the cause of education.

In 1860 Rhinebeck abandoned the Oak Street school and the district consolidated with number 5, making a district covering the entire village. This school of district #5 became the most important school in the town, and for nearly sixty years very little change had been made in the school accommodation. This little oblong, one-story, two-room structure answered all the requirements of teachers and students.

By 1869, after much controversy, a Union Free School was erected in the village, which later became Rhinebeck High School. Again you can see this opposition by the general public regarding free education. There were always taxpayers fearing a higher tax rate, thus trying to abolish the idea before it ever got started. Nevertheless, by the close of the Civil War, the general population in the county, as well as in the rest of the nation, was beginning to agree that there was some value in free schools, and that they should become part of the American educational system. Thus the period beginning at the close of the Civil War was marked by the advance of public schools, and the gradual decline of private institutions.

Throughout the county, state and Nation, this was the time of transition from Academies to high schools. Feeling the force of this movement, the old Dutchess County Academy closed its doors in 1866. The trustees sold the building and turned the money over to the city Board of Education. With this money a high school and library building were erected at the corner of Washington Street and LaFayette Place, a building that later served as the School Administration Building, prior to the present one on College Avenue.

At one time students attended classes on the second floor of the Mulreain Building on Market Street until the new high school was ready in April, 1872. Many other academies were also closed in the next ten to twenty years; by 1900 there were few academies or private schools in Dutchess County.

After the Panic of 1873, school budgets were drastically cut and the buildings became increasingly ill suited to their purpose. For a short time after the panic a unique program was developed by St. Peter's Church, called the Poughkeepsie Plan, whereby a public school system was set up in both city and parochial schools. This was a decided financial gain for both church and town, but was naturally abandoned when the enlargement of public school funds were made available.

Poughkeepsie created the office of Superintendent of Schools in 1878. This was a time when schools were becoming more aware of the child and they realized new subjects had to be added to the curriculum. Art instruction by a special teacher was begun in September, 1883, in the Poughkeepsie School System. The annual report for 1893 states that the position of a writing teacher was established, as a special branch of instruction in 1890. Academies by this time were converting to high schools rapidly, such as the Seymore Smith Academy of Pine Plains which became the Pine Plains Union Free School in 1894. The one-room school house was rapidly disappearing from the scene and

LaGrange, a Historical Review, 1959

District School #10 at Billings

being replaced by larger schools. Districts were converting scattered schools to a more consolidated area, and were forming Union Free Districts. In Poughkeepsie, in 1899, a new central grammar school was built, and the high school began to prepare students for college. High schools were becoming important. This trend was reflected nationwide when prior to 1900, the rate of increase in high schools was greater than that of any decade in the twentieth century.

It was also in the late 1800's when teacher education became established, and although it had not yet reached the height of popularity that it would enjoy in the 1900's, men and women were getting some training in the fine art of teaching.

During the late 1800's no unusual precedents were established in the city or county. However, some noteworthy accomplishments of this period included compulsory school attendance laws and increased curriculum, and it should be pointed out that time spent in school increased during this period. It can be safely stated that the county, educationally, grew up in this era; a new century of county education was about to begin.

It was about the turn of the century when the Poughkeepsie school district converted schools by name, rather than a designated number; a plan that was developed by Superintendent Ward C. Moon.

In spite of the progress so far accomplished, conditions of the public school system at this time were not in any way similar to our present day standards. This is pointed out in the following excerpts from the first annual report of J. L. Williams, president of the newly appointed Poughkeepsie Board of Education, December 31, 1900:

Gentlemen, as you are aware, this board was organized May 16, 1900, under provisions of Chapter 659 of the laws of 1900.

The responsibility and duties charged upon it were and still are grave, important, and serious. These duties have been assumed and met, it is fair to say with full appreciation of this truth.

You found a condition which has existed for forty years, during which time our school facilities had not materially improved, but have been permitted to fall into a deplorable condition. Contrary to the law and policy of the State, six of our schools were maintained in rented buildings.

Most of these, as well as buildings owned by the city were without systems of ventilation, with little or no provisions for heating except by coal stoves, with an almost entire absence of proper provisions for hanging children's wraps, with dangerous and unsanitary closets, or those maintained in the school yards, together with school rooms with narrow aisles and dangerous outside stairways as well as many other serious defects."

This is the way the twentieth century began in Poughkeepsie and it was similar in the rest of the county.

It was in 1901, that the union free school built in 1869 in Rhinebeck was enlarged and became the Rhinebeck High School. In this period the Rhinecliff School was the second largest in the Town of Rhinebeck.

A new Union Free School at Dover Plains was established March 19, 1908. The building was estimated to cost about $10,000 and the land, purchased from Mr. Hanna and Mr. Wing, about $12,000, with $1,500 voted for furnishings.

The Arlington School district was also becoming established in this early period. Actually the Pleasant Valley School was built in 1830 and torn down in 1904, to be replaced by a modern four-room school. Also a forerunner of the Arlington district was the College Avenue School, built in 1857 and which later had several additions before being converted to other uses. The Davis Avenue School was built in 1903. At this time they were not called Arlington Schools, but were the nucleus of the present Arlington district.

Educational authorities in Poughkeepsie realized very early that the education of children was much more than a training of the mind through mental discipline. Manual training and construction work for boys and sewing for girls was offered in 1903, but no general elementary manual training courses with special teachers and equipment were offered until 1920. Physical education was incorporated into the curriculum in 1907, and summer play grounds were made available that same year.

It was through the early 1900's that the one-room school houses vanished from the scene, becoming part of the union free school districts of the county. Various reasons contributed to their decline, including advanced forms of transportation. It was now no longer necessary to walk to school or to take a horse and carriage; the school bus and the motor car were coming into general popularity. It was also noted that a large school with many teachers could offer more advantages than could a small one-room school. Taxpayers would prefer to pay often smaller taxes for a large union free school than to support the many small schools scattered throughout the town. However, it was basically the educational opportunities that were offered in the larger school that finally forced many of the old one-room school houses to close. The one-room school, with few exceptions, could not offer such things as physical education, art, music, drama, vocational opportunities, or even a teacher specialized in fields such as writing, similar to those established in the large schools of Poughkeepsie.

Arlington Union Free School District No. 7 was formed in 1920 by the incorporation of the Pleasant Valley School, Gothic School, Washington Hollow School, Sunnyside School, and the Gretna and Davis Avenue schools. The first school acquired was the Davis Avenue School which was used until 1930. In 1924 the Raymond Avenue School was built and opened to serve both as a high school and a grade school. When this new district was first established, only one year of high school was offered. In 1922 the course was expanded to two years, and in 1924 the district offered three years of high school work.

Arlington High School was granted a charter as a six-year high school in 1926, and its first commencement was held that year with nine pupils graduating.

In 1933, a new high school was built on Route 44. The school opened in 1934 and is now serving as a junior high school. It was at this time the Raymond Avenue School became a grade school. As part of a PWA project, the wings were built on this school in 1938. In 1933 the Pleasant Valley School became the modern school it is today, with an addition built in 1938. It was also in 1938–39 that an auditorium and an addition were built on the former high school on Route 44.

Public educational developments in Dutchess County during the 1930's featured the formation of consolidated and centralized school districts. It has been said that President Franklin D. Roosevelt had more to do with this trend than any other individual resident of the county. He was deeply interested in county activities, particularly education. President Roosevelt spent much time in Hyde Park and neighboring townships discussing plans for new schools for the county.

Because President Roosevelt had such an interest in the county's educational development, he had the honor of dedicating the three field stone schools of the Hyde Park Central School District, October 5, 1940. The Public Works Administration had supplied forty-five percent of the funds for the $1,300,000 project. The three schools were the Franklin D. Roosevelt High School in East Park, the Violet Avenue Elementary School and the smaller grade school in Hyde Park village, known as the Hyde Park Elementary School.

One of the murals in the Hyde Park Post Office depicts President Roosevelt discussing plans for the Roosevelt High School. The land for this school was purchased from Benjamin Haviland, a farmer and old friend of the President.

In his dedication speech, President Roosevelt reminded the listeners that the Town of Hyde Park could claim "a kind of sponsorship of school education in New York." For it was in Hyde Park, he said, "nearly a century and a half ago," that Governor Morgan Lewis, "who lived on one of the river estates, was chiefly responsible for the starting of the Union Free School system for the children of New York State."

The President also paid a tribute to the taxpayers of the towns of Hyde Park, Poughkeepsie, Pleasant Valley, and Clinton for having backed a school centralization movement and made the construction of new schools, "rather than a repair job," possible.

During the same period when the new schools were being built in Hyde Park, another combination elementary and high school was being provided for the Wappingers Central School District in southern Dutchess, which is now one of the largest school districts in the entire state.

Wappingers was one of the earliest schools to centralize in Dutchess County. Before centralization, the village and town of Wappingers had practically no school facilities of a modern type. In 1938, Wappingers Falls had a population of 3,500. The village was a small mill town. The parents of the children in school were mostly foreign born, and the subjects taught in school were commercial and vocational in nature, for the most part. It took considerable effort to get the people of Wappingers Falls to realize the value of a centralized school, but the final vote was 1,259 for and only 819 against centralization. In September, 1940, the new central school was ready for occupancy. The pioneer for school centralization was Pine Plains, followed closely by Wappingers and Hyde Park.

Many districts in addition to Hyde Park took advantage of WPA funds, among them Red Hook and Arlington. However, Rhinebeck and Poughkeepsie failed to utilize these grants. Rhinebeck applied too late, and in Poughkeepsie the idea was defeated in taxpayers' elections.

One of the last districts to become centralized was Arlington in 1951. Until this time, Beekman, LaGrange, and other outlying districts were not included as part of the Arlington School System, but the children of these areas were attending Arlington Schools. Because of this, Arlington schools were becoming rapidly overcrowded, which gave the school district only two alternatives: (1) Not to allow students from these outlying areas to attend Arlington schools, or (2) have these areas permanently join with Arlington and become centralized. This would mean increased State Aid; it would also give the students in these areas a definite school. This, in other words, would eliminate the threat that they would be stopped from attending Arlington Schools.

In 1950 a commission studied the possibilities of centralization and on June 30, 1951, it became effective. The vote was approximately 800 for with only about 100 against. One and three-fourths million dollars was appropriated for school buses, a bus garage, and the LaGrange School. In 1956 Beekman and Overlook Schools were built and an addition was made to the Pleasant Valley School.

A few small one-room school houses survived to the 1950's in the county. These included the Shenandoah School which closed in June, 1958. The Shenandoah School District taxpayers voted to close the school and to sell the property at public auction. The students were transferred to the Fishkill Plains Elementary School in the Wappingers School District.

In 1958, a five pupil one-room school in Bull's Head was closed and these pupils were transferred to Rhinebeck Central School.

The last major hurdle in public education in this county developed in the late 1950's. This was the junior school concept, which many teachers' associations strongly opposed. The New York State Department of Education had already mandated that junior high schools be organized. After much discussion and opposition the idea was gradually accepted, and by the late 1950's, this movement became a standard part of our educational system.

Thus we have seen the educational system of this county evolve from the first small church-school to our large, modern centralized districts. The history of public education in Dutchess County reflects the development of public education in the United States in general. The pattern for any period has been set by its needs. In the early days, the population was small and scattered, communication facilities were primitive, economic security was solely the responsibility of the family, and community life was restricted to isolated neighborhoods. We have changed from rural-agrarian to an urban-industrialized society.

Problems have been shifted from the family to the community. Social and physical health, welfare, safety, sanitation, communication, transportation, etc. are all now problems of the community. In particular a tremendous change has come in the operation of the enterprise of public education.

There have always been problems in public education, and we have seen them as they developed in the county. Educational opportunities in America in the mid–1800's were confined to the mechanistic and rudimentary study of reading, writing, arithmetic, English grammar and spelling. College training was almost exclusively along philosophical and literary lines.

We have seen the great expansion of educational opportunity which occurred during the period 1850–1900, with the development of the high schools and professional schools. Compulsory school attendance laws were passed, and time spent in school was increased. Many new subjects were being taught.

Dutchess County citizens are aware of the importance of education for their children; they are, and have always been, willing to assume the burden of its support; they are increasing alert to progressive trends, and we do not think they will change. Education should continue to be an exciting development in the years to come in historic Dutchess County.

INFORMAL EDUCATION IN ANTEBELLUM
RURAL DUTCHESS COUNTY

Melodye Kaltz

The word education usually conjures up images of perfectly aligned rows of desks in classrooms embracing either side of a long, beckoning hallway. Whether the students are contained within the ivy-covered walls of colleges or universities, or whether they pour forth at the 3:00 bell to fill the playgrounds or the buses of the public schools, we still see them as the recipients of a formalized education, that hopefully prepares them to take their place in society. We all know, however, that much of our education is not the product of a formalized system. We learn our values at home and from the community, we learn from our associations with others, we learn through the communications media, and we learn from life itself. While these methods of learning are certainly not as structured or formalized as school systems, most of us would agree that many of our best lessons were outside the classroom. Mr. King and Dr. Mabee have beautifully examined the more formal aspects of education in Dutchess County, and so, it seems left to me to try to examine the other types of education that helped to shape this county. To do that I have decided to examine a Dutchess County community in a given year. My decision was prompted not by any great conversancy with any one town in any one year, but rather by the existence of two diaries kept by two young men who resided in Pleasant Valley in 1844.[1] They afforded a rather unique look at Pleasant Valley and a singular opportunity to examine the social and cultural forces that were part of the informal education of a Dutchess County rural town in antebellum New York State.

New York, like much of the rest of the United States in the antebellum period, was being swept by the tide of great change. To understand if and how Pleasant Valley, Dutchess County, was affected by these changes, we ought first, perhaps, to take a general look at the forces that were transforming society and educating its people in the ways of a more modern world.

The period, first and foremost, was characterized by the rapid development of new forms of transportation. Old roads were improved, new roads were laid down, and turnpikes appeared. Robert Fulton's 1807 successful production of the steamboat transformed river transportation. A trip to Albany, that had formerly taken anywhere from 3 to 9 days depending on wind conditions, now was available at least three times a week via Fulton's boat.[2] Even these major improvements were surpassed, however, by the 1825 opening of the Erie Canal and the emergence of the railroad. The transportation revolution that resulted from these developments made travel much easier and opened up newer and greater markets for the produce of the state. Greater mobility of both people and produce also tended, however, to break down certain elements of the traditional society that had previously dominated American culture. Instead of a society based on a rural way of life, more and more emphasis was being placed on urban commercial centers. Additionally, rural residents were no longer isolated, but were becoming increasingly more integrated with the other parts of society.

The availability of better and faster transportation, and the accessibility of an ever-growing market place had a great impact on agriculture. During the second quarter of the nineteenth century, the agricultural economy of New York went through the most profound change ever. The 1825 opening of the Erie Canal had made available the more fertile western lands, and eastern New York farmers were forced to diversify in order to survive. While wheat remained the most important cash crop until after 1850, it began to be displaced by corn, oats, barley, rye, hay, dairy products, sheep and wool and fruit orchards.[3]

As farming became more and more competitive and complicated, farmers realized they needed more skills and there was a concurrent rise in interest in scientific agriculture.[4] Fruit growing became highly technical and the nursery business emerged. There were substantial advances in the spread of agricultural knowledge and its appreciation via publications such as Jesse Buel's *Cultivator*. Additionally, New York State undertook support of agriculture. A New York State Agricultural Society had been established in 1832 and in 1841, state legislators agreed to subsidize county societies and to underwrite county fairs. A state fair was authorized, the first occurring in 1842.[5]

The antebellum period was also marked by the beginnings of a factory system. Elements of mechanization were showing up at the work place, mass production was replacing the filling of individual orders and there was a tendency toward the centralization of capital. The first businesses to be affected included flour milling, cotton and wool manufactories, tanneries, and distilleries.

Applied technology did not stop its onslaught of society at the edge of the fields or the doors of the factory, however, but entered directly into the homes of the citizenry. Medicine in particular became more technical with the emergence of such ancillary professions as pharmacy and dentistry. In 1840 the American Society of Dental Surgeons and Baltimore College of Dental Surgery were founded.[6]

Evangelical revivalism emerged in the 1820's and 1830's. With its leadership directly tied to the churches, it stressed the "perfectibility" of American life and the notion that a "saved" Christian must, to make his salvation complete, apply his religion to the world around him and make his faith a practical matter.[7] Social reform became a moral imperative for many fresh from the revivals resulting in an era of reform.

The major objectives of the Era of Reform were the promotion of women's rights, the expansion of public education, the improvement of conditions for prisoners and the insane, and the elimination of slavery and alcohol from society.

The period was also marked by an increased urge for self-improvement, not surprising considering the climate of reform, and the idea of perfectibility. People were reading more; newpapers and books were more readily available. The Lyceum circuit introduced everyone to the marvels of oratory and all it had to offer. The editor of the United States *Literary Gazette* wrote in 1826 that the "art of public address occupies a distinguished place among the departments of our literature and contributes greatly to form the taste, guide the opinions and increase the information of our people." The age abounded in talk.[8]

But the age also abounded in increased leisure time particularly for the middle class. The advances of technology made life easier for most and there was increased opportunity for socializing and for the forming of organizations.

But what about Pleasant Valley, New York in 1844; just what kind of a community was it and who were our diarists? Were they mainstream Pleasant Valley? Can we trust their record?

Pleasant Valley is an interior town of Dutchess County. Its major village, Pleasant Valley, lies seven miles northeast of Poughkeepsie on Route 44, formerly the Dutchess Turnpike, laid out in 1806 and one of the most important turnpikes in the development of the county. The village had been settled as early as 1740 by both Quakers and Presbyterians from Connecticut and Rhode Island. Agriculture played an important part in the development of the town, but its proximity to the Wappingers Creek and the numerous streams that flowed into it gave impetus to the early establishment of mills. The location of the village on the crossing of the turnpike and the creek was an ideal location for the development of a mill center, and by 1844 there were at least eight mills located close to the village including grist mills, fulling mills, woolen mills, cotton mills and flour mills.[9]

By using both the 1840 and the 1850 Census records, we are able to paint a fairly accurate picture of 1844 Pleasant Valley. The total population for the town in 1840 was 2219 and included 83 free blacks, 4% of the population. 412 families are represented by this number. The white population was fairly evenly divided between male (1044) and female (1092) and 47% of that number represented children to age twenty. Eighty-seven percent of the population was under the age of fifty and had consequently seen most of the growth of the new era. According to the statistics provided, 78% of the population claimed to be involved in agricultural pursuits, 20% in manufacturing and trades, and 1% each in commerce, and learned professions/engineering.

The 1850 Census is the first to give specific information relating to the families polled and as such gives a clearer picture of the make-up of the citizens. The population had only increased from 2219 in 1840 to 2226[10] in 1850 so it can still be accepted as a fairly accurate representation of 1844 Pleasant Valley. The proportion of males to females and blacks to whites had remained relatively the same. The census indicates there were by then 386 dwellings housing 433 families. The town included 152 farms and eleven business establishments. Not all of the business establishments were located in the village of Pleasant Valley as there were community centers at both Salt Point and Washington Hollow. The occupational statistics for the town are revealing, and at the same time a little confusing. The bulk of the population claimed to be either farmers or laborers. Nine people claimed to be manufacturers and are probably only those people who owned mills or factories. The laborer category can therefore be expected to be divided between those doing day labor and those involved in mill or factory work. It is impossible given the category to define it in any clearer way. There were several persons who claimed specific skills relative to mill operations such as spinners, dressers, weavers, and millers, but the bulk of the remainder provided goods or services to the community. Craftsmen included shoemakers, blacksmiths, masons, carpenters, wagonmakers, basketmakers, saddlers, and corders. The business community included merchants, butchers, bakers, hotelkeepers, tailors, and bartenders. Professional services were available through clerks, justices, physicians, lawyers, and clergy. The town claimed one teacher and three students.[11]

The majority of persons listed in the census claimed to be native to Pleasant Valley. Of the rest, the greatest proportion were immigrants from Ireland and England. The massive 1840's Irish immigration to the United States doubtless accounted for the former and the latter were probably attracted by the availability of textile mill jobs in the area.

By 1844 there were four churches in the town, a Baptist, a Methodist, two Presbyterian, and in addition one Friends Meeting, and all of them were dissenting in their origins and transplanted from New England. Each of these religious groups were also among those who were most affected by the advance of evangelicalism that swept the country during the early nineteenth century. The most active of the religious groups was the Pleasant Valley Presbyterian Church whose membership in 1845 totalled 425.[12]

The diarists are representative of the Pleasant Valley citizenry of 1844. Alson Ward, a member of the agricultural community, is 22 years old when he begins his diary in 1844. He is white, an Anglo-Saxon Protestant (Presbyterian), unmarried and living at home with his parents and two sisters. The Ward family, originally from England, had been among the earliest settlers of Pleasant Valley. From the beginning, they had been farmers and mill owners and such was true in 1844. Alson's father, Joshua, owned a mill and farm lands on what is today Traver Road.[13] Although they owned extensive millworks the Wards perceived themselves to be farmers and listed agriculture as their occupation in the 1850 Census. The family appears to have been quite comfortable, one indication being the variety and number of vehicles they owned. While the extent of Alson's formal education is unknown, his writings are articulate and he served as Secretary of the local school committee.

John Bower represents the other type of citizen who was most common in Pleasant Valley at that time, the laborer. He had been born in Yorkshire, England, in 1814 and at the age of twelve had immigrated to America with his father and two brothers.[14] In 1844 he worked for his brother, Joseph Bower, who in 1837 had purchased a textile mill east of the village. The mill, the Pine Grove Factory, was located one mile east of the village on the Dutchess Turnpike and manufactured wool, satinett or flannel work. The factory also included an indigo vat.[15] John Bower had been married in 1842 and with his wife resided on North Avenue in a house built by Rodman Mead, a member of his wife's family. Probably not as well off economically as the Wards, John Bower seemed always to be borrowing transportation from Uncle Rodman. He, too, listed his occupation as farmer although he spent much of his time at the mill.

A diary offers a unique opportunity for those of us in the present to make inquiries of those who lived in another time. The question I chose to pose to Alson Ward and John Bower was, "Were your lives in a rural Dutchess County community in the mid-nineteenth century influenced at all by the informal educational forces of the day and if so, in what way?" For both of them the answer was a resounding "yes."

Joshua and Ann Ward House, Pleasant Valley

The transportation revolution allowed both the Ward and the Bower families to travel a great deal and consequently to be exposed to a greater variety of people and experiences. The Wards, who were apparently more affluent than the Bowers, had access to more vehicles such as sleighs, cutters, carriages, and wagons, and both Alson and his father traveled frequently to Poughkeepsie, usually at least once a week and sometimes three to four times.

Besides business trips, there were also a great many pleasure excursions. Without movie theatres and television, "visiting" was the most popular form of social entertainment and provided an ideal forum for the exchange of ideas on nearly every topic. The weekday routines of farming and millwork were frequently broken by visitors from as far away as Hopewell and Fishkill or by trips to visit friends and relatives. In September 1844, Alson takes what would today probably be called a vacation, although he himself does not call it that. He leaves at 6:00 one morning to travel to Columbia County to visit relatives, arriving before sundown. He spends the next three days still "on the road" visiting and traveling to a nearby lake for a "picnick." He returns home on the fifth day spending another ten to twelve hours on the road. He, by the way, decides, without giving a reason, not to go to church the next day, an unusual choice for him.

Interest in scientific agriculture and acceptance of its importance in an agricultural community such as Pleasant Valley is seen repeatedly in the Ward diary. Alson and his father spent most of March 1844 working at establishing a peach orchard. In one week alone, Alson's father went to Poughkeepsie three times returning with a total of 600 peach trees. They were careful to buy only inoculated trees and Alson makes a point of desribing in some detail the method for planting the trees. A January 3, 1844, advertisement in the Poughkeepsie *Telegraph* for the Fishkill Hook Nursery near Johnsville gives some indication of the choices available in the area. One could buy apple, apricot, cherry, pear, peach, and nectarine trees at prices that ran from 20 cents for a small apple tree to 25 cents for a medium tree, to 37½ cents for a large tree. All other varieties were sold at reduced prices. While John

Bower did not have extensive orchards, he too spent time planting plum trees and inoculating the others.

September 1844, much like today, was Fair time and the diaries indicate that fairs then generated much the same enthusiasm that they do now. In this year, however, there was double the excitement; the Annual County Fair was held at Washington Hollow and the State Fair was being held in Poughkeepsie. The location of the infant State Fair in Dutchess County was an honor to the agricultural community of the area and they had been planning for it all year. The Poughkeepsie *Telegraph* refers frequently to the committees meeting to plan the fair. Both the Ward and Bower families attended, the Wards even entered produce in the judging. The fair grounds covered ten acres and included such buildings as the Ladies Home, Floral Hall, Manufacturers Lodge, Farmers Hall, and Farmers Implements. There were agricultural trials, exhibitions of stock, ploughing matches, and traditional awarding of premiums.[16] Alson reports that it was the greatest gathering Poughkeepsie had ever experienced, and estimated the total crowd to be 140,000–150,000 based on ticket sales. The Poughkeepsie *Journal* and *Eagle* reported a more modest 25,000 or higher.

The value of medical science in Pleasant Valley is more difficult to evaluate. Physicians are reported to have been in the Valley as early as 1770 and by 1850 there were five practicing doctors in the town. Both Alson and John were ill in 1844 and both availed themselves of medical assistance, but neither of them was willing to rely solely on medical science. When Alson became sick with what sounds suspiciously like a common cold, fever, headache and sore throat, he soaks his feet for the purpose of "taking a sweat." When this does not work, he drinks paregoric. Eventually he cures himself with proper rest. While he does not mention a doctor he talks about being under the influence of medicine. John's illness is beyond self-cure and a little medicine. On the first day of his illness, he is visited four times by the doctor who bled him, immersed him in a warm bath and applied brandy and red pepper to his back and side. The following day the doctor visited twice and within two more days he was feeling "rather stouter." The malady was recurring, however, and over the next month he is stricken twice more. The first time he treats himself with an application of boiled oats and is visited by the doctor. The third occurrence apparently called for more than home remedies, however, since the doctor this time prescribed opium pills that left John in a "stupor and quite unwell for three days."

If both the Ward and Bower families were inclined to cling to the traditional in medicine, they had no hesitation in availing themselves of the advances of modern dentistry. Pleasant Valley had no dentists at this time, but Poughkeepsie did and the Poughkeepsie newspapers contain a variety of advertisements.

In the January 3, 1844, Poughkeepsie*Telegraph*, W. A. Palmer, dental surgeon, announced that his "silicious, incorruptible teeth, from the best selections now in use, (were) inserted on the most recent and improved principles." R. C. Holmes, surgeon dentist, was "inserting whole sets of teeth by either atmospheric pressure or springs. All operation warranted." Alson and his sister Mary both traveled to Poughkeepsie to have their teeth plugged and John takes his wife, Amanda, to Poughkeepsie to have her teeth fixed.

The advances of technology and its applications to daily life must have affected Pleasant Valley. Although neither of the diarists mention it directly, there is internal evidence that suggests its influence on their lives. Alson mentions once in passing that he is writing directions for using Ward's Patent, a clear indication that the family was interested in employing modern methods and techniques. The most obvious effect of the advances of technology, however, seems to be increased leisure time and an increased involvement in organizations and self-improvement.

To judge from these two diaries the most important social activity in Pleasant Valley in 1844 was singing. Both Alson and John belonged to the Singing Association and attended singing school. Mr. Bartlett's singing school was held weekly and concentrated on such things as learning the minor scale. The Association, which also met weekly, concentrated more on business matters; it purchased notebooks and had the authority to set up new schools and obtain subscribers. When people were not singing at meetings, they were apparently singing at church or singing at home. John and Amanda Bower frequently returned from all-day worship services to have their own singing services.

The greatest boon to self-improvement and self-education in the nineteenth century came with the Lyceum circuit and traveling orators. People flocked to hear them and learn about the marvels of modern society.

In early April 1844, a man "professing sleight of hand" entertained the locals, but it was Professor Bronson, who arrived two days later, that was the major attraction. From Pleasant Valley, he moved on to Poughkeepsie and advertisements in the Poughkeepsie *Journal* and *Eagle* give the specifics.

"Mr. Bronson (who has been engaged in teaching in our principle colleges, cities and towns for the last ten or twelve years) proposes to deliver a popular course of six lectures, if properly sustained, interspersed with readings and recitations, accompanied with dissections of that splendid masterpiece of human science and ingenuity, the manikin, representing nearly 2000 parts of the body with wonderful accuracy and chasteness, and without unpleasant associations or anything to offend the most fastidious."[17]

Bronson appears to have been a walking jack-of-all-trades as he promised to "convey a practical knowledge of the philosophy of mind and body . . . to develop and train the voice and ear for reading, speaking and singing," and, "also to show, incidentally, how to prevent as well as cure, dispepsia, liver and lung complaints in their incipient stages and diseases of the throat and spine." He also promised to help one improve their personal appearance.

A single ticket for the course of six lectures was $1.00, $2.00 for two ladies and one gentleman, and $3.00 for a family of five. A local reviewer called the series an intellectual treat and Alson and John must have thought so, too, for they attended every lecture, especially marveling at Bronson's manikin.

Valley residents also educated themselves by reading. Both men make reference to traveling to the post office to pick up newspapers and when Alson was overwhelmed with work, his grandfather would deliver the papers. John mentions buying the *Christian Parlor Magazine* and recounts that he is reading *The Life and Biography of John Summerfield* and a history of the reformation.

The most important force in the educating and molding of society in the first half of the nineteenth century was the church. In 1831, Alexis de Toqueville concluded that "religion is the foremost of the institutions of the country."[18] Nineteenth century faith, derived principally from awakening theology, was deeply evangelical and intuitive. Although this evangelicalism cut across sectarian lines, it occurred most frequently in Congregational, Presbyterian, Methodist, and Baptist churches, those who theologies were the least ritualistic and who most emphasized the role of the individual in attaining salvation.[19]

The churches of Pleasant Valley all fell within this definition and the Ward and Bower familes both attended the Presbyterian Church. For both of them the church was probably the single most influential factor in their lives. Sundays were unequivocally given over to church and nothing else except perhaps Sunday dinner with relatives. Frequently, one attended morning services at the Presbyterian Church, dinner, afternoon services at the Episcopal Church, tea, and evening prayer or temperance meeting at the Methodist Church. Occasionally, a missionary would visit.

While the church clearly influenced the life and behavior of its members, its greatest influence on society was through its espousal of reform movements. The directors of the American Bible Society explained the philosophy thusly: "It is part of Christian duty" to rescue one's fellow-man from "thoughtlessness, ignorance, and peril; it becomes Christians to imitate their master and to seek the good of those who are careless of their own good."[20]

For most, involvement with reform ideas came through the church and this was true in Pleasant Valley. All the churches there seem to have been involved in reform movements, but the Presbyterian Church, under the direction of Rev. Benjamin Wile, seems to have been the leader.

In 1811, the General Association of Presbyterian Churches had declared drinking an evil and Wile, who was installed in the Pleasant Valley Church in 1829, was an earnest advocate of this philosophy. He is reported to have been a persuasive and convincing speaker who is credited with securing more than 5,000 signatures to the total abstinence pledge and almost entirely abolishing liquor traffic from Pleasant Valley during his 38 years there.[21] Indeed, temperance activities and the church are so intertwined, it is sometimes difficult to separate them.

Alson Ward and John Bower were both members of the Juvenile Franklin Temperance Society and both attended the Sunday night temperance meetings that were frequently held at the Methodist Church and addressed by various ministers from around the county. Alson reports that he attended the first Anniversary Celebration of the Sons of Temperance. It was held in Poughkeepsie and two chartered steamboats brought other divisions from Hudson and New York City. Alson himself was heavily involved in planning the Temperance Meeting and County Convention held that year in Pleasant Valley. Alson's diary recorded the following:

"Temperance Convention, went to the village early in the morning by eight o'clock to prepare to dinner the delegates and others, met the committee and a number of ladies making the necessary arrangements, prepared the dinner in Mr. McChord's wagon shop instead of the grove on account of the unfair prospect of the weather which proved to be the better as it rained part of the afternoon and very hard in the evening. There were about 400 took dinner and tea. The wood sawer general from Hudson, Mr. Haddock who has been a reat sufferer by the use of alcohol gave from the platform in front of shop an artillery of truths that will not be easily forgotten by the rumsellers. While he was speaking which could be distinctly heard at the hotel, there came a drunken man and called him a liar, etc., but he was so drunk that he came under the platform to sit down which he did and soon fell asleep giving ocular demonstration that rum destroys the reason. The day passed off pleasantly all things in order, the tables prepared in exquisite style with flowers and the luxuries that the animal and vegetable kingdom of this community could provide. In the evening the meeting came off in the church. Mr. How and Van Loon were the speakers. During the meeting Daniel Anson and our Free notorious drunkards came in the church with each a bottle of liquor and placed it on the platform and told the gentlemen to help themselves but were so drunk that they were of no service to their employers for they sat down as mute as could be. They took the bottles of rum, one red, the other colourless and placed them on the tables by the sides of the pitcher of cold water. Mr. Van Loon made some very entertaining and happy remarks on the incident."

While Temperance was not the only reform issue inspiring citizens of this time, it seems to be the movement that most involved residents of the Valley. Both John and Alson mention an abolition meeting at the Presbyterian Church at which there was some rioting, but neither appears to be involved in the movement or much interested in anything other than its sensational value.

Women's rights appear also not to be an issue in the Valley. In both diaries wives, mothers, and sisters are only mentioned in passing and there is no way to evaluate their impact on the family or society.

Pleasant Valley in 1844 seems to be then a community that was affected, shaped and educated by the prevailing forces of the age, forces that would propel Pleasant Valley into a more modern age. Although still primarily rural and agricultural in both reality and self-perception, the successes of the mill operations and the steady onslaught of mechanization is eroding that. Once isolated from other parts of the county, Pleasant Valley is now structurally integrated with other parts of the county via improved transportation and communication. Indeed, frequent trips to New York City by members of both the Bower and Ward families enlarged their experiences by exposure to life in major metropolitan centers. What was once a fairly homogeneous town is by 1850 more and more influenced by an influx of Irish and English.

Still, however, for all its tendency toward modernity, Pleasant Valley still stood with one foot in the traditional past. Despite all the new-fangled farm and mill equipment, Alson's diary tells us that he frequently operated according to a rural clock and had "gone fishing." Pleasant Valley had not given up its rural character and the sense of community that bound it together., The diaries still exuded a small-town hominess where everybody knew everybody else. What secular influences were in existence were usually outweighed by those of a more hierarchial nature.

John Bower and Alson Ward have told us what forces were affecting and changing their lives in 1844 and never once do either of them seem perplexed or distressed. Technology was apparently freeing them but not overwhelming them. They seem, rather, to take it all in stride and integrate into their own personal lives the informal education that surrounded them.

Notes

1. The Alson Ward diary was given to the Dutchess County Historical Society by the family of Baltus Van Kleeck. The John Bower diary is owned by Mrs. George L. T. Bauhan and was loaned to the Society for study.

2. David M. Ellis, et al, *A History of New York State* (Ithaca, New York: Cornell University Press, 1967), p. 179.

3. *Ibid.,* p. 272.

4. Chancellor Robert R. Livingston in particular was instrumental in the promotion of scientific agriculture.

5. Ellis, *A History of New York State,* pp. 275–276.

6. Russel B. Nye, *Society and Culture in America 1830–1860* (New York: Harper and Row Publishers, 1974), p. 343.

7. *Ibid.,* p. 36.

8. *Ibid.,* pp. 136–137.

9. A number of publications discuss statistical information concerning Dutchess County towns. See: Frank Hasbrouck, ed., *The History of Dutchess County, New York,* Poughkeepsie, 1909; James Smith, *History of Dutchess County,* Syracuse, 1882; Philip Smith, *General History of Dutchess County, 1609–1877,* Pawling, 1877; J. H. French, *Gazetteer of the State of New York,* Syracuse, 1860; Horatio Gates Spafford, *Gazetteer of the State of New York,* Albany, 1824.

10. The extremely small population increase is significant when compared to New York State and the nation in general which during the period between 1825 and 1855 had doubled. Specific causes for the lack of population growth in Pleasant Valley have yet to be examined.

11. The students referred to in the census were not those being educated in local district schools but rather those receiving an advanced education elsewhere.

12. *This Earthen Vessel; A History of the Pleasant Valley Presbyterian Church 1765–1965* (Pleasant Valley: 1965), p. 19.

13. Dutchess County Historical Society, Ward manuscript.

14. Clifford Buck, Bower Genealogical Notes.

15. *Poughkeepsie Telegraph,) January 3, 1844.*

16. *Poughkeepsie Journal and Eagle,* September 21, 1844.

17. *Ibid.,* April 27, 1844.

18. Nye, *Society and Culture in America 1830–1860,* p. 297.

19. *Ibid.,* p. 285.

20. Clifford S. Griffin, *Their Brother's Keepers: Moral Stewardship In The U. S., 1800–1865* (New Brunswick, 1960), 46ff.

21. *This Earthen Vessel: A History of The Pleasant Valley Presbyterian Church 1765–1965,* p. 16.

Teaching Local History in the Secondary School

Joseph J. Lombardi

High School Teacher, Arlington Senior High School

The teaching of local history at the secondary level is a relatively new dimension in the social studies. Ten years ago, if one attended a statewide conference for social studies teachers, one would be at a loss to find any reference to local history or local studies. Today's professional conferences are replete with presentations, workshops, and tours, exalting the values of local history programs and covering both the substantive and procedural aspects of the topic. The study of local history has come of age.

Why study local history at the secondary level? How does one incorporate it into the existing program, a program already overburdened with topics in the 10th and 11th grades? Should it be left only to the 12th year elective program? Questions abound on this subject and yet we know that creative forces both in the community and in the schools are succeeding in making local history one of the most stimulating and innovative areas in the secondary curriculum.

Let us address ourselves to some of these questions. Why study local history at the secondary level? Why not? The thrust of the existing 10th grade Modern European History program is to explore in an essentially chronological fashion the roots of western civilization especially as they relate to the foundations of American society. One would expect that at the conclusion of a course in the 10th grade that the student should be able to detect within his or her immediate environment those manifestations of European culture. I submit that it is entirely possible for that student to see in our local architecture reflections of European architectural movements, or to view our local courts as institutions that evolved out of an English system of adversary justice. Does not "due process" have its origins in the Magna Carta, and yet evidences itself every day in every court in the land, changing from time to time depending on decisions by those courts? Does not the business community and industrial concerns of our area reflect an organization and set of values that developed during the Commercial Revolution? The intrinsic logic of local history then, lies in the fact that it offers an opportunity to give meaning and purpose to the traditional course. It can justify a year's study right in one's own community. One no longer is just looking at architectural masterpieces thousands of miles away, but one now can see in one's own community reflections of those very structures that have impressed the world ever since man began to build. A study of European history is truly incomplete if it ignores the proximate as it is evidenced in the locality. The question that should be raised, and seldom is, is how can one justify the teaching of 10th grade European history *without* referencing the locality?

The same analogy may be applied to the teaching of 11th grade American studies. Do not most communities within our area reflect some of the ethnic diversity of our nation? Do not our local governmental institutions experience the same agonizing budget-making procedures as the federal government? Is not the economic mix and pattern of activity in the locality to some extent a reflection of the national economy? Is not a study of justice on the local level as valid as its study on the Federal bench? Again, the question that should be asked is how can one come to understand his nation and society *without* peering into the locality? If good citizenship be a goal of the social studies, then is it not logical to study the locality as part of the nation, especially at the time that one lives within it? I am personally and professionally convinced that the social studies at the secondary level must contain elements of the locality if it is to be a meaningful experience for our students.

My experiences in teaching local history stem both from efforts to infuse local history into established courses and from teaching a senior year elective that develops topics in local studies. My first experience was in 1970. I had been assigned a non-academic section of European History. I had taught non-academic students before and I knew the frustrations of trying to water down the content of the course so that these students could function successfully. Instead, with the permission of the building principal and my coordinator, we set aside the textbook as our main source and embarked upon one of the most exciting years in my teaching career.

The rationale underlying the course was simple. If European civilization provides the underpinnings of American civilization, then is it not possible to see those connections within a 10 mile radius of the Arlington High School? The community would become the laboratory, the textbook only a guide, and the students, teacher, and community resource people the creators of the course content. Armed with little more than our ideas and the help of the Historian of the Town of LaGrange, Emily Johnson, to whom I shall always remain indebted, we moved into the uncharted waters of our locality.

The class took up many of the traditional topics covered in a European history course, only some of which I shall explore here. For example, in studying the classical civilizations of Greece and Rome we focused on the more visible manifestations of those societies. Architecturally, the dome, the arch, the use of columns, the variations of the facade of the Parthenon, the concept of beauty, of proportion, of harmony were all evident in local structures that reflected elements of classical civilization. One does not have to go far to see those structures. The idea that a society preserves and retains what it values cannot be lost in this exercise. To tie the classical past with the present, the students filmed both, using photographs of the originals. I do not recall the film as being spectacular artistically, but it was something they created and stated eloquently.

The Industrial Revolution provided some of the most fertile fields for exploration. The idea of change, especially change that is induced by technological development, is an area of high interest. I, too, was unaware of the significant changes that had taken place within a few miles of the high school until I began to look. For example, a textile industry developed, flourished, and disappeared on the Wappingers Creek in the nineteenth cenunty to the more populous villages and emerging cities. The remains of cottages used by the mill workers are still evident alongside existing homes. We have the remains of a "company town" right within the confines of the Arlington school district. We discovered photographs of one of the mills, taken before it was destroyed by fire. We were also able to obtain copies of old maps that showed the location of these structures, and through careful copying and enlarging by means of the over-head projector, we were able to super-impose a present day map on the nineteenth century copy. It then becomes patently clear that technological change has in fact induced substantial demographic change.

The same changes were evident when one examined a series of nineteenth and twentieth century maps detailing the expansion and demise of the railroad network in the County. One could see how population shifted once the railroads came through, and since the railroads have disappeared, these small centers of settlement are no longer hubs of activity. The railroad boom and the rise of industry on swift bodies of water are not unique to Dutchess County, and if one were to look for similar developments in other parts of the state or nation, they would yield similar results.

In addition to maps and existing structures as tools for discovering the past, the interviewing of prominent and not so prominent senior citizens revealed a different way of life, 50, 60, or 70 years ago. This technique added words to the graphic images and provided answers to many of the questions. In addition to exposing students to the wealth of information that the senior citizen possesses, recording their conversations makes the students part of the historical process. In a sense, they are assembling the raw material of the historian. There is a certain thrill that goes along with creating history, and a valuable lesson to be learned in the process.

Short field trips were an integral part of the course, and since we focused on subjects close by, we could accomplish our objective in just a few periods. We visited some of the one room school houses that were used in some cases until the 1950s. Students who know only the schools they attend are overwhelmed by the stark simplicity of the one room schoolhouse. It again states eloquently the value that society places on education, and the rapidly changing nature of the process. The class had an opportunity to meet with a retired teacher who had spent most of her teaching career in a one room schoolhouse. Describing the before-school chores of a teacher, teaching eight grades in one room, and handling discipline problems within a totally different format provides great insight into the nature of an earlier society. Another senior citizen described how he would take the train from LaGrangeville to Hopewell Junction, and then change to a train that would take him to Poughkeepsie High School since that was the only high school in the county. That trip would be impossible by train today.

One also never knew what one would encounter. On that field trip to the one room schoolhouses, we met an individual who lived across the road from the school who brought a large saw out of his barn and asked if anyone knew what it was used for. It turned out to be a saw that was used in cutting pond ice, an activity that modern refrigeration has totally displaced. Research on the topic of ice harvesting revealed not only a great deal about the winter activity of the farmer, but also a totally different economic dimension to his life.

Our town historian continually provided us with documents that lent an element of discovery to the course. For example, clerk's records kept by the one room school districts detailed not only the costs, but also the types of supplies used in those districts. They could easily be contrasted with the minutes of any board of education today. Other materials that were available included tax records, voting lists, minutes of town boards, dispositions of cases by town justices; all of which shed light on an earlier society and documented the changes that have taken place. The list of sources is endless, and I will have more to say about this later on.

What I have described above relates to my effort to teach European history from an American and purely local perspective at that. One need not be as categorical in the process. Certain units lend themselves more readily to local history than others. Where the liaisons can be established, they ought to be tried. Teaching an elective course on local history at the 12th grade level also presents opportunities as well as some problems. While integrating local history as part of the traditional course on the 10th and 11th grade level serves to maintain the needed perspective, local history taught as a self-contained course runs the risk of being detached from the larger context. One can become so preoccupied with locally oriented topics that the opportunities for integrating the locality into the broader context may be ignored. Care must be taken to avoid this pitfall.

The great value in teaching local history as an elective is, of course, the freedom one has in defining the course of study. For example, one can focus on the history of land use, comparing existing practices with those of the past. A variety of resources are available for this study including the maps, first hand observations, community resources including Conservation Advisory Councils and Cooperative Extension. The study also can become multi-disciplinary which further enhances its scope. Although it may be somewhat unorthodox, the topic provides an opportunity for sound learning and life long understandings about man and his environment. Such learnings are essential if we are to maintain the quality of life in our society. Further, the elective course allows students to develop, in an independent study format, topics of interest. An example that comes to mind is a former student who was interested in architecture. He used drawings and photographs of a now demolished historical building to recreate an exact scale model of the structure. The student has gone on to become an architect.

The teaching of local history as an elective need not be limited to those topics that are normally considered part of that discipline. Opportunities exist within all the social studies for local studies. For example, the Anthropology class at Arlington is about to undertake a supervised dig at Bowdoin Park at one of the primitive rock shelter sites. There are many such sites, both within the park and within the county that could be uncovered by students working with proper supervision. Opportunities exist for all the social studies to become much more involved in the locality.

It should be obvious, then, that it is not only possible but most desirable to infuse local history into the traditional courses at the secondary level, but it is also possible to explore its applications in an elective program. Possibilities for truly creative teaching exist, waiting to be tapped by the willing teacher. The rewards offered for those who venture are some of the most substantial in the profession. The discovery of new materials, the gaining of new insights into the past, the satisfaction of seeing meaningful learning take place are worth the additional time and planning required.

How does one go about developing local history correlations to their existing program? One of the best sources is a recently published book by Fay Metcalf and Matthew Downey entitled *Using Local History in the Classroom*. The book is a "how to do it" manual and treats both the infusion of local-oriented topics in established curricula and the development of independent courses in local history. Also the New York State Education Department has distributed curricular materials on the topic, and these should be available in each school district.

The real key to using the locality successfully is getting to know your town historian. If they are as helpful as the historian in the Town of LaGrange, you should have no problem developing materials. The Adriance Memorial Library has a wealth of information in its Local History collection. The Library should be contacted before dispatching students on research projects. The Regional History Program at Marist College conducts seminars and workshops on local history and these provide not only an introduction to the topic but also solid content. The various town halls, the Records Room at the County Clerk's Office and the Dutchess County Historical Society all contain a wealth of information. Displayed on the walls of the County Office Building, and also in collections, are maps of the county that go back to the eighteenth century. Nursing homes and Senior Citizen Drop-In centers should not be overlooked. Louise Tompkins at the Dutchess County Infirmary in Millbrook is one of the most resourceful and inspiring persons that any student could ever encounter. Sources seem to multiply and are only limited by the amount of time one can apply to their discovery. Every community contains these ready resources, all of which are waiting to be tapped.

In addition to the obvious joys of using local history in the classroom, an unexpected reward is one's professional growth. Information can never become stale, for it is constantly being developed. Both the teacher and the students are continually learning, becoming more sensitive to their environment, and better able to relate to facts that are normally distant and abstract. The teaching of local history can be one of the most thrilling experiences in one's teaching career.

Songs That Tell Our History: Music as Historical Resource

Joyce Ghee
Dutchess County Historian

Between 1764 and 1775, Benjamin Franklin resided in London as the agent, at different times, of the states of Pennsylvania, Georgia, and Massachusetts. During this period, upon the eve of the American Revolution, his brother Peter sent him a poem from America requesting him to find an English composer who could set it to music. Franklin's reply, in part, follows:

Dear Brother:

I like your ballad, and think it well-adapted to the purpose of *discountenancing expensive foppery,* and *encouraging industry and frugality.* If you can get it generally sung in your country, it may probably have a good deal of the effect you hope and expect from it. But, as you aimed at making it general, I wonder you choose so uncommon a measure in poetry that none of the tunes in common use will suit it. *Had you fitted it to an old one, well known, it must have spread much faster than I doubt it will do from the best tune we can get composed to it.* I think too, that if you had given it to some country girl in the heart of Massachusetts who has never heard any other than psalm tunes, or 'Chevy Chase' 'the Children in the Wood', 'The Spanish Lady', and such old simple ditties but has a naturally good ear, she might more probably have made a pleasing popular tune for you, than any of our masters here, and more proper for your purpose, which would best be answered *if every word, as it is sung be understood* by all that hear it, and if the *emphasis you intend* for particular words *could be given by the singer* as well as by the reader; *much of the force and impression of the song depending on these circumstances . . .*

You in the spirit of some ancient legislators, *would influence the manners of your country by the united powers of poetry and music.* By what I can learn of their songs, the music was simple, conforming itself to the usual pronunciation of words, as to measure, cadence or emphasis, etc. . . . . Their singing was only a more pleasing because of a melodious manner of speaking; it was capable of the graces of prose oratory, while it added the pleasure of harmony. . .[1]

Musicologist Elie Seigmeister points out in *The Music of America* that the roots of American music stem not only from the traditional sources, such as those referred to by Franklin but also from local events colored by regional characteristics which he calls "a vast body of music with distinctively American traits. Besides its sheer musical fascination, it tells us much of the life and spirit of the plain people of this country."[2]

These distinctive regional characteristics and the use of local lore as poetic source for song to which Seigmeister refers, combined with the deliberate employment of music as a tool for editorial expression and education, which Franklin encourages, are precisely the elements which make the music of an area a useful resource for historical research.

The traditional historian gleans material from original documentary sources: newspapers, journals, diaries, minutes, business, census, and court records, eg. These provide facts and the raw material of historical events and trends. As an interpreter, the historian develops his theses and draws his conclusion from these documents.

Written and composed, copyrighted music is well within this form of documentation. Some regional music falls into this category and as such is acceptable to the most conservative of historians. Other forms of regional music, traditional and folk music are also valid areas of research, providing insight into the attitudes, feelings, and values of a people over and above basic data from documentary sources.

For point of discussion, a clarification of several terms which are used herein is necessary. Within the context of this paper the terms traditional, regional, and folklore will be used as follows:

Traditional music is shaped by community preference. It encompasses folk, popular, composed, secular, and liturgical music.

Regional/Regionalism pertains to a broad, homogeneous geographical area. Dr. David Wisnant, Fellow in Residence, the Smithsonian Folklife program, in a recent lecture at Vassar, entitled, "The Politics of Culture in Appalachia," speaks of an emphasis perhaps less on geography than upon shared local characteristics in art, literature or speech.[3] In what may seem a contradiction in terms, the basic regional characteristic of the Hudson Valley in both geography and culture is variety. This area, the Mid-Hudson Valley has been, from earliest recorded history, a pathway to and from the interior for successive waves of newcomers, all of whom have left their mark upon the valley. This cosmopolitanism contributes to the richness of the musical heritage of the region, making it all the more valuable from the standpoint of the researcher.

Folklore is the collected traditions, customs, wisdom of a people, preserved orally; a comparative science that investigates the life and spirit of a people. In its pure state folklore is not written down. A *folklorist* is one who collects and passes on folklore. *Collector* is a useful alternative term for someone, including those folklorists who make a point of writing down or recording folklore, (another contradiction in terms.) A *folksinger* is anyone who sings music from his/her own oral tradition. We are all folksingers when we sing that lullabye or ditty that we learned as babes at our mothers' knee or when we recite uncertainly the sing-song games we passed along to each other as school children. Such materials reach deeper into unrecorded history than many of us would ever suspect.

Interpreters or *revivalists* take the process a step further by interesting themselves in the sources of folk songs and by trying to place them culturally or historically within a context. In our mid-Hudson region, the interpreter, allied to the historian fulfills a useful role, making the music of the area comprehensible to each successive wave of new "natives."

Benjamin Franklin was most certainly an unique person, however, his view of music as an appropriate editorial/educational tool was not original. This view has been forthcoming from educators, philosophers and political leaders from time immemorial, going back to Homer. What one learns in examining the music of an era and an area is not the progress of events, but how those involved in events felt about them. The music acts as a barometer, revealing attitudes, feelings and values.

Regional music then becomes history in human terms, fleshing out the bare bones of fact and putting it into human context. This music, or primarily the lyrics, becomes a valuable tool in the search for history.

Examples of composed music and popular music are easily come by. Old popular music, manuscripts, concert programs and announcements can be found in the stacks and local history collections of many area libraries and historical societies and even in the attics, cellars and closets of many private homes. Harder to come by, but equally useful to the researcher is the folk music of the area. It is part of the oral history or folklore of the valley.

In the more remote sections of the mountains and rural backroads, there are still traditional practitioners of the area folklore existant, but in these times of split second communications, their folkways are imperiled daily by the constant spectre of an homogenized "American" culture promoted through TV, films, radio and the recording industry. Only a short time remains to catch and preserve the few remnants of this area's special folkloric flavor. However, in order to preserve it for use, it is necessary to recognize it.

Although history and folklore have much in common, there is a distinction between the two which must be stressed at this point. The traditional historian is in constant search for something fixed, i.e. documented proof of actual material, in writing. True folklore, of which folksong is a part, is, on the other hand in a constant state of flux and must be in order to qualify as such. Around a core of truth, or generally accepting information, creative material clings, endless in its variety. A variant is a differing form of a story or proverb. This variation or creativity is the hall-mark of folklore. In order to be folklore, a story or song must circulate and be subject to folk alteration.

The field of oral history may well provide the necessary link between history and folklore which will convince historians that folklore/folksong is a valid area of search. For many years "oral history," collected by a method akin to journalistic sleuthing, was a kind of historic stepchild, mistrusted one supposes because of the frequently too personal nature of its inquiry and response. However, within recent years, the field of oral history has gained the respect and interest of more traditional historians who have assisted in the systematization of the discipline to make its results more palatable by transcription and editing by the collector in cooperation with the donor.

Oral histories, like biographies, journals, and diaries, dependant upon memory and personal bias of individuals contain many of the more "creative" aspects of folklore and legend.

Folklorists and scholar Tristram Potter Coffin holds that "Legends—are born from the *kernels* of *historical fact* and remain legends as long as they are told." He adds that there are three truisms that apply. "That legend tends to seek out the most distinguished figures available; that once these figures are placed in a plot, adjacent facts and incidents tend to rearrange themselves appropriately; and that time and place distortions are easily affected in those *things man recalls within written record.*"[4]

This is the point at which history, oral history and folklore come together. It is perfectly justifiable to question the historical or "factual" accuracy of much of what is found in a folksong. This can also be true of much of what is reported in the newspaper—and offical reports from all manner of institutions. How many "definitive" versions of a tale are written or told by the last one to die, or the one who has the most access to media or even the best and most interesting delivery?

For the sake of comparison—history vs foklore, let us say that there is a murder, the criminal is caught, tried and found guilty. There are court records, newspaper accounts and local gossip to carry the tale forward.

A case in point is Captain William Kidd, our famous Hudson Valley Pirate. In his definitive book of the folklore and song of New York State, *Body, Boots and Britches*, Professor Harold Thompson gives two varying accounts of the death of William Kidd in London in 1701. Going back into history, through documentation in newspapers and court records, it is possible to make a case for Kidd as either a consummate scoundrel or as the not entirely innocent victim of a scheme to build their personal fortunes or Kidd's privateering involving Governor Bellomont, Robert Livingston and several members of the British Royal Entourage. While Kidd's body was still warm and hanging outside Newgate prison, the broadside ballads began to appear that presented the then current public view of the Captain's career and demise.[5]

Of the many variants extant comes this abbreviated version for the singing of Pete Seeger, Beacon Minstrel, who learned it from Steve Benbow in London:

My name is Captain Kidd
(refrain) As I Sailed, As I Sailed
My name is Captain Kidd, As I Sailed
My name is Captain Kidd
God's Law I did forbid
And most wickedly I did
(refrain) As I Sailed, As I Sailed

My parents taught me well (refrain)
to Shun the Gates of Hell
But Against them I rebelled (refrain)

I murdered William Moore (refrain)
And left him in his gore
Forty leagues from shore (refrain)

And being cruel Still (refrain)
The Gunner I did Kill
And his precious blood did Spill (refrain)

My repentance lasted not (refrain)
My vows I soon forgot
Now Damnation is my lot (refrain)

To execution Dock I must go (refrain)
lay my head upon the block
No more the laws I'll mock (refrain)

Which is the true Captain; he who emerges from a trial at which he was not allowed to speak in his own behalf, or the character in the many and differing forms of the story that appear in folksong and lore? The truth is hard to get at.

History and folklore have much in common. They are related in much the way that articles in the *New York Times* and the *New York Post* are related; they start with the same raw material but once the editors and writers have had their way with it, the results are astonishingly different.

Broadsides such as *Captain Kidd* are topical ballads or story songs. Quick reactions to current events; comments, brief accounts and the scarlet headlines of earlier days, they were traditionally hawked, for pennies, as in the case of Kidd's hanging, almost within sight of the event.

Some broadsides, more political in nature, were intended, again as Franklin suggests, as propaganda. "Chester," by William Billings was published as a tune with its first verse in 1770—well before the American Revolution. Even then, it made Billings' position clear.

> "Let tyrants shake their Iron Rods,
> And Slavery clank her galling chains
> We fear them not; we trust in God
> New England's God forever reigns."

During the course of the conflict, Billings added four more verses which chronicled the events of the conflict in a mighty war cry that became a familiar favorite uplifting the spirits of American troops in every quarter of the 'fray.'[6]

Here in the Hudson Valley, the "Ballad of Major Andre," from the singing and family tradition of John Allison, gives quite an accurate account of both the events surrounding the tragic story of Andre and Benedict Arnold and the prevalent attitudes of the public at the time.

> Come all you brave Americans, and unto me give ear.
> I'll sing you now a ditty that will your spirits cheer,
> Concerning a young gentlemen who came from Tarrytown
> Where he met a British officer, a man of high reknown.
>
> Then up spoke this young hero, Young Paulding was his name.
> 'O tell as where you're going sir, and also whence you came.'
> 'I bear the British flag sir,' up answered bold Andre,
> 'I have a pass that takes me through, I have no time to stay.'
>
> The others came around him, and bade him to dismount.
> 'Come tell us where you're going, give us a strict account.'
> Young Paulding said, 'We are resolved that you shall ne'er pass by.'
> And so the evidence did prove the prisoner a spy.
>
> He begged for his liberty, he pled for his discharge,
> And ofttimes he told them, if they'd set him at large,
> 'Of all the gold and silver I have laid up in store,
> but when I reach the city, I will send you ten times more.'
>
> 'We scorn this gold and silver you have laid up in store'
> Van Wert and Paulding both did cry, 'You need not send us more.'
> He saw that his conspiracy would soon be brought to light,
> He begged for pen and paper and he asked for to write.
>
> The story came to Arnold commanding at the fort:
> He call'd for the Vulture and sailed for New York,
> Now Arnold to New York has gone, a-fighting for his King.
> And left poor Major Andre on the gallows for to swing.
>
> Andre was executed, he looked both meek and mild.
> His face was fair and handsome, and pleasantly he smiled
> It moved each eye with pity, and every heart there bled,

146

And everyone wished him released and Arnold in his stead.

He was a man of honor! In Britain he was born.
To die upon the gallows most highly he did scorn.
And now his life has reached its end so young and blooming still.
In Tappan's quiet countryside he sleeps upon the hill.[7]

Songs such as *Captain Kid* and *Major Andre* record history. Songs such as *Chester* make history by influencing public opinion. Songs have been used throughout recorded history to do this. *The Star Spangled Banner* and the *Marseillaise* are political and patriotic documents. Innumerable songs have been written to push a specific point of view in the direction of change. The following is a case in point.

The *Ballad of Big Bill Snyder* was written in 1843 during the period of the anti-rent movements in the Hudson Valley. It was reported first played by the Euterpean band of Rensselaerville at an Anti-Rent Rally on the 4th of July, 1844, at the height of the rebellion. The lyrics, following Franklin's direction, were put to the tune of a currently popular minstrel tune composed by Dan Emmett for his Virginia minstrels. The tune, *Old Dan Tucker,* is still a familiar favorite.

The words spin the tale of a sheriff's deputy, a most unpopular bully named Bill Snyder who ran afoul of a band of Calico Indians while trying to serve his writs on behalf of the landlords. He was tarred, feathered and summarily run back to Albany.

The moon was shining silver bright.
The sheriff came in the dead of night.
High on a hill sat an Indian true
And on his horn this blast he blew.

Chorus:
Keep out the way, big Bill Snyder,
Tar your coat and feather your hide, sir.

Bill ran and ran till he reached the wood
And there with horror still he stood,
For he saw an Indian tall and grim
And he heard a horn not a rod from him.

Bill thought he heard the sound of a gun
He cried in fright 'O my race is run.'
Better that I had never been born
Then come within the sound of that big horn.

The next day the body of Bill was found
His writs were scattered all over the ground.
And by his side a jug of rum,
Told how Bill to has end had come.

Keep out of the way big Bill Snyder,
Tar your coat and feather your hide, sir.[8]

The Indians referred to in the song were tenant farmers disguised as "Calico Indians." The horns upon which they blew were their dinner horns, used in this case to warn their fellows of the approach of the sheriff's men, who sought by arriving in the "dead of night" to surprise the unwary farmers, to serve the landlord's writs and reclaim the lands in question.

Although the tale is not a totally accurate account of what happened, (Bill Snyder was not killed) it does project, even because of its inaccuracies, the depth of feeling of those struggling against what they felt to be great injustices, in terms of their rights as free men. We see, in this context, that the song was a successful rallying cry which did what it was designed to do, excite to political action.

We remember longest those songs that are connected with successful campaigns. Those that are part of a losing issue are more easily forgotten. Martin Van Buren's political career had both its wins and losses and songs to attest to both. This short song written for the 1848 campaign is, nonetheless, full of cultural and political clues for the historian.

Come Ye hearty sons of toil
And cast your ballots for free soil
He who'd vote for Zachary Taylor
Needs a keeper or a jailor
And he who still for Cass can be
He is a Cass without the C;
The man on whom we love to look is Martin Van of Kinderhook

Chorus: Martin Van's the one will go
He is the man for the people, O
I look around and find it so
Just as they said in Buffalo.[9]

Buffalo was the site, in 1848, of the Free Soil Party Convention at which Van Buren was nominated as candidate for President, running on a platform of freedom in opposition to the sectional platform of slavery. Its slogan was, "Free soil, free speech, free labor, and free men."[10] He ran last in a three-way with Zachary Taylor and Lewis Cass. Van Buren continued to be active in politics until his death in 1862 at his home in Kinderhook in Columbia County.

In one brief song sung to the lively minstrel tune, *Dandy Jim from Caroline,* one has the men, the issues and the places of an event, but more importantly, one senses the energy and excitement of the campaign.

In more recent years, songs like *Happy Days are Here Again,* bring to mind the Hudson Valley's best known historical figure, Franklin D. Roosevelt. The Franklin D. Roosevelt Library has an extensive collection of songs written during and about his administration which give a wide view of the presidency and the climate in which the events of his tenure in office took place. They give clues as to public attitude toward his actions—revealing both the anger and the expectations of his constituents, through depression, recovery and war.

Not among the library collection is this song, shared with me for performance purposes by Eileen Mylod Hayden and written by her Uncle, Phillip Mylod, probably in the the late 1920's, prior to F. D. R.'s first election to the Presidency.

It was composed upon the occasion of a legionnaire's convention in Paris c. 1930, and it was understandably a very popular ditty both on the way over and back. The first line can be altered to suit the occasion.

O we're from Dutchess county

or

We're Legionnaires from Dutchess	We're from Dutchess County
And we'd like to have you know	And we'd like to have you know
That Dutchess County is the place	That apples aren't the only thing
Where luscious apples grow.	That Dutchess County grows.
They call us apple-knockers	We've Senator Webb, a Legionnaire
And they needn't take it back,	Of very great renown.
For apple-knockers are the boys	He put the bridge across the Hudson
Who have the apple jack.	Right into our town.
We thought we'de go to New York town	We're from Dutchess County
To show New Yorkers how	Just to make sure that you know
A big parade by Legionnaires	An apple-knocker scaled the heights
Would surely be a wow!	We thought you ought to know
We thought we'd order apple jack	A Legionnaire's Governor now,
But gin was what they sent	A sailor of renown.
So the apple-knockers all came home	We'll tell the world that Franklin D.
Much wiser than they went.	Is the biggest man in town.

The Mylod family has long been active in the political and public life of Dutchess County. The material in this song touches upon the importance of the American Legion as a political and social force. It also refers to the construction of the Mid-Hudson Bridge at Poughkeepsie, giving credit to State Senator Webb for its existence. The final verse links. F. D. R. with the Legion through his stint as Undersecretary of the Navy and dates the song by references to the governorship of New York State. Not only is this a short course in Dutchess County politics, but it also gives clues as to the agricultural economy of the area—the importance of the apple crop and the term "apple-knocker" which is a euphemism for "hick."

Music has been used as a commemorative vehicle as well. In 1825, at the opening of the Erie Canal, a number of such pieces were penned. The following represents an example of such a piece by Samuel Woodworth, who wrote *The Old Oaken Bucket.*

There is not in this wide world a valley so sweet
As the vale in whose bosom the bright waters meet.
O, the last rays of feeling and life must depart
Ere the bloom of the valley shall fade from my heart.

Let the day be forever remembered with pride,
That beheld the proud Hudson to Erie allied.
O, the last sand of time from his glass shall descend
Ere a Union, so fruitful of glory shall end.

All hail! to a project so vast and sublime!
A bond, that can never be served by time
Now unites us still closer—all jealousies cease
And our hearts, like our waters, are mingled in peace.[11]

During the Hudson–Fulton Celebration of 1909, a number of other songs similar in their naive boosterism were written. The Tercentenary of Dutchess County may well be trigger other such expressions of civic pride and historical enthusiasm.

Commemorative songs have also been composed for other occasions. Churches in the Valley have often found anniversaries to be an appropriate moment for such creative out-pourings. The First Presbyterian Church of Newburgh celebrated its centennial in November of 1884, and its pastor, the Rev. Dr. Wheeler, took the occasion to write new words to a well-known hymn written by Lewis Edson of Bearsville, near Woodstock, *Blow Ye the Trumpet Blow*. The following words uncovered by Lyn Burnstine in a program in an old hymnal are now part of the repertoire that we share as performers dealing with Hudson Valley music.

I.   Our earthly years O God are at thy sole command
     And paths by mortals trod are from thy mighty hand.
     Our history a passing dream, a mystery and fitful gleam.

II. One hundred years have fled
     Since here our fathers have wrought
     And lo, their work not dead
     For lives the church they sought
     Thy church O God preserved by thee
     Thy work O God all praise to thee.

Musical material such as we have examined provides the researcher with a rare source of unexpected historical information, often giving a unique view of an event—humor, irony, incitefulness or vengefulness. It occasionally provides geographical data, place names or lore related to places. It may give clues to prevalent attitudes, or attitudes that have been submerged by happenstance or intent. One can also learn much about an informant; the singer or writer of the song. There may be literary or philological clues—words or phrases that indicate either an interesting source or make a cultural connection between one area and another. Moral or value judgements are evident in such material which reveal a cultural or social bias or climate. These songs also give great insight into the creativity of individual Americans. One should not expect accuracy as far as dates or even participants in events are concerned, although it is, as we see, occasionally to be found. What is really to be sought is an enlarged or broadened perspective of history.

In the 1920s students in a class in folklore at Vassar College, under the direction of Martha Beckwith, took upon themselves the task of collecting songs from the older residents of a three-county area of the mid-Hudson Valley—Dutchess, Ulster and Columbia. Constance Varney Ring, a member of the class of 1921, edited the material, which is presently housed in the Vassar Music Library.

In this collection are a number of songs that attest to our Dutch heritage, collected from the descendants of early settlers in the Kingston and Red Hook areas of the valley. Songs such as *Zoo Rid'n de heeren,* which is similar to *This is the Way the Farmers Ride 'Wimble Wamble'*; *Peter Ludlow,* a variant of the song known in the Netherlands as *Pierlala*; and two versions of a Dutch lullabye entitled *The Lire Laatjes* are included among others. These were transcribed by a student, Harriet Stocking with the help of faculty members Gertrude Brown and George S. Dickerson, assisted by Dr. A. J. Barnouw, Queen Wilhelmina Professor at Columbia.

The collection also includes a number of Anglo-American folksongs, game songs and lyrics from 19th century music halls plus several rather sentimental ballads based upon local lore. One of these, *The Johnsville Tragedy,* came originally from a pre–1859 manuscript written by Mrs. Amanda Haight and conveyed to her daughter Mrs. Miriam Wood. It deals with the sad tale of two young farm workers who were struck by lightning in the course of their work and is sung to the tune of *Auld Lang Syne.*

Majestic thunders loud did roar	Into the field with haste they sped
Red lightning doomed to kill	With orders to comply.
T'was called from home to be no more,	A flash of lightning struck them dead,
Two youths from our Johnsville.	Not thinking they must die.
Three horses they designed to take	Young men and maidens of this place
Beneath a spreading tree,	Who that sad scene did view,
When they a sudden flight	Tears start afresh from every face.
did make into eternity.	The call was something new.[12]

Over a century later one may find its sentimental-moralistic tone either quaint or humorous or both. Nonetheless, the editorial-reportorial aspect of the lyric is important. The song establishes the fact that Johnsville, a small hamlet near Fishkill, in the Wiccopee area, was a farming community and the event that it describes is believed to have occurred in the early years of the 19th century. Even if we don't know the names of the two young men involved, we do know that they made a tragic mistake that the writer of the song hoped to avert in the future with a strong warning. Don't stand under a tree in an open field during a thunderstorm! This was undoubtedly an essential message that needed to be understood by anyone involved in out-of-doors farming activities in such a hilly and wooded area as this.

The Ring collection was re-edited and abridged in 1951 by Tristram P. Coffin for his article in the *Journal of American Folklore.* For this article he excluded anything that could not be identified as within the true folkloric-oral-tradition of the Valley. In the distillation process, songs were eliminated that had been composed for political campaigns, any standard forms of widely known songs and a a good deal of popular songs.[13] That which remains represents a three hundred years old chain of traditions, values and lore stretching over ten generations and constitutes one of the most unique and underutilized historical resources of our valley.

From the standpoint of the historian, much of what Mr. Coffin would eliminate for his purposes is still of considerable value and fortunately remains in the library.

Other collectors and carriers of Hudson Valley tradition, folksong, and lore have left us well provided with regional collections. Carl Carmer, Norman Cazden, Herbert Haufrecht, Harry Siemsen, Lawrence Older, John and Lucy Allison, Alf Evers and Yankee John Galusha among others have added to our store of these materials. The search continues even today as those researching specific topics continue to uncover the almost forgotten songs and ballads of yesteryear.

Dorothy Hurlbut Sanderson, teacher and librarian from Ellenville, found a number of songs dealing with the Delaware and Hudson Canal in researching her book, *The Delaware and Hudson Canalway: Carrying Coals to Rondout.*[14] These ditties are often linked to specific places both through text references and language. They give an indication of the rough and ready life of the canalers and also reveal them to have had an equally rough and ready sense of humor.

Mrs. Leslie Symington, a researcher preparing historical materials on the circus for Southeast Museum in Brewster, has unearthed two songs of interest to Dutchess County residents. They both deal with the famous animal trainer Isaac VanAmburgh, who for over a generation, from the 1830s to 1860s astounded both American and European audiences with his courage and control over caged lions and tigers during performaces of this wild animal show.

VanAmburgh's Menagerie, a comic song by Dr. W. J. Witmore, c. 1866, was composed in English music hall style, complete to copying the cockney accent, perhaps in deference to VanAmburgh's success in England where he charmed the Duke of Wellington and Queen Victoria. A later version published by John Wanamaker in 1915 changes the tune, but utilizes essentially the same poetic material. Both versions dwell upon the famous VanAmburgh trick, "He sticks his head into the lion's mouth and keeps it there awhile, and when he takes it out again, he greets you with a smile." Similar material was known and referred to by Henry Noble McCracken in his book, *Blithe Dutchess*.[15]

Music, composed, played and sung in connection with the most important and most intimate occasions in the lives of individuals and communities comprises a reservoir of historical information about our region which continues to replenish itself through new discoveries.

From that lullabye sung long ago by a Dutch mother, to the 19th century minstrel tune, from the ballads, the hymns and campaign songs, the children's games, school songs, and favorite popular tunes of yesteryear, we learn of the struggles, triumphs and daily lives of those who have preceded us here.

When George VI and his queen paid a royal visit to President and Mrs. Roosevelt on the eve of World War II, Eleanor Roosevelt, over the objections of many of her advisors, chose to entertain her guests with the regional folk music, dance and popular song of America.[16] She felt that this was the best and most direct way to reveal the spirit and uniqueness of the American people. The programs for the visit included American Indian prayers, Negro spirituals, cowboy ballads, and play parties sung and danced by traditional performers. They joined collectors such as Alan Lomax and popular and concert artists Kate Smith, Marian Anderson and Lawrence Tibbit in expressing the sour of America.[17]

The deepest and best feelings of a people go into its music and song. Lest we forget—the American Revolution was won with the words of *Yankee Doodle* on the lips of its soliders, and it ended for us in Dutchess, here in Poughkeepsie, to music, as the men of the 2nd New York Regiment delivered their colours and instruments of music to Governor George Clinton early in June 1783.[18]

To paraphrase Franklin, "If you want people to be influenced by your words, write them plainly and pair them with a familiar old tune." The combined power of music and poetry has both expressed and impelled our history. To overlook this is to lose sight of an essential part of the story.

Notes

1. Elie Seigmeister, ed., *The Music Lover's Handbook* (New York: William Morrow & Co., 1943), pp. 667ff.
2. *Ibid.* pp. 671–682.
3. Dr. David Wisnant, "The Politics of Culture in Appalachia" lecture, Vassar College, April 1980.
4. Tristram Potter Coffin, *The Female Hero in Folklore and Legend* (New York: Seabury Press, Inc., 1975) Chapter: Of Ladies and Legends, pp. 5–10.
5. Harold Thompson, *Body, Boots and Britches: Folktales, Ballads and Speech from Country New York* (New York: Dover Publications, 1962) Chapter II: Pirates, pp. 20–32.
6. Seigmeister, *Ibid.*, pp. 664–6: Revolutionary War Verses.

> Howe and Burgoyne and Clinton too,
> With Prescott and Cornwallis joined
> Together plot our overthrow
> In one infernal league combined
> When God inspired us for the fight,
> Their ranks were broke, their lines were forced;
> Their ships were scattered in our sight,
> Or swiftly driven from our coast.
>
> The foe comes on with haughty stride;
> Our troops advance with martial noise,
> Their veterans flee before our youth
> And generals yield to beardless boys.

7. John Anthony Scott, *The Ballad of America—The History of the U. S. in Song and Story* (New York: Bantam Books, 1966).
8. Henry Christman, *Tin Horns and Calico* (Cornwallville, New York: Hope Farm Press, 1978).

9. Vera Brodsky Lawrence, *Music for Patriots, Politicians and Presidents* (New York: MacMillan Publishing Co., 1975), "Martin Van of Kinderhook" p. 323 from "Free Soil Songs for the People" 1848.

10. Richard B. Morris, ed. *Encyclopedia of American History* (New York: Harper Bros., 1953) p. 209.

11. Bob Lusk, *Irish Music of the Catskills and Mid-Hudson Valley* (Ulster County Council for the Arts, 1978).

12. Constance Varney Ring and Martha Beckwith. *Mid-Hudson Popular Song and Verse* (Poughkeepsie, New York: Vassar College, 1937), manuscript.

13. "Mid-Hudson Song and Verse," *Journal of American Folklore*, Vol. 66, January-March, 1953.

14. Dorothy Hurlburt Sanderson, *The Delaware and Hudson Canalway: Carrying Coals to Rondout,* Second Edition (Ellenville, New York: Rondout Valley Publishing Co., Inc., 1969, 74) Chapter 14: Canalers and Their Songs.

15. Henry Noble MacCracken, *Blithe Dutchess* (New York: Hastings House, 1958) Chapter 25, p. 5.

16. Eleanor Roosevelt, *This I Remember* (New York: Harper and Bros., 1949).

17. *Program for the State Visit of their Britannic Majesties,* June 1939, (Hude Park, New York: F. D. R. Library Collection) manuscript.

18. Raoul F. Camus, *Military Music of the American Revolution* (Chapel Hill: University of North Carolina Press, 1976).

Eileen Mylod Hayden, his neice

Phillip Mylod, author of "The Apple Knocker's Song"

The Early Musical Development of Poughkeepsie, NY: 1683–1865

Barbara Biszick
Musicologist

The information presented here is concerned with the rise of the American concert tradition in Poughkeepsie, NY between its settlement in 1683 and the Civil War in 1865. By definition, this would have negated the study of folk music. However, it is impossible to ignore this element since the distinction between art and folk music does not become apparent in Dutchess County until well into the nineteenth century. Therefore, we are obliged to consider any and all musical examples as instrumental in developing a tradition of art music indigenous to this area.

Within this 182 year period, there are less than twenty items whose origins can be linked to Poughkeepsie residents. Admittedly, one can hardly resist the temptation to compare this meager amount to the vast and monumental output of the larger urban centers. But it is precisely this mentality which has inhibited the study of the rise of American culture in rural areas. The small output and the obscurity of sources has led even the most sensitive of historians—the very father of American musicology—Oscar G. Sonneck, to label the Hudson Valley as "practically a musical wilderness."[1]

If we can make any judgement about Poughkeepsie's musical development, it would be to say that, although the output of original material in this period was small, the cultural evolution in this area was consistent. It is herein that the real significance may be found. As more and more small cities are studied they will come to be regarded as constituting a class by themselves. Futile comparisons with large urban centers will be abandoned, and within this new class Poughkeepsie will be seen as a model of musical evolution, much in the same way as it is now regarded as the model of growth and prosperity in the areas of business and education in the nineteenth century. It is this consistent development in a healthy, stable, and fairly peaceful environment that makes Poughkeepsie's fortunate history significant to the study of the American cultural heritage.

This paper is presented in four sections. The topics provide a fairly comprehensive overview of Poughkeepsie's musical development during this early formative period. The topics appear in the following order:

1. Music, Society, and Culture Prior to 1800: The Henry Livingston, Jr. Manuscript.
2. The Impact of Europeans on the Nineteenth Century Musical Scene.
3. Instrument Building in Poughkeepsie.
4. The Rise of Music Education in Poughkeepsie.

Music, Society, and Culture Prior to 1800:
The Henry Livingston Jr. Manuscript

There is a real dearth of material regarding the development of music and the arts in Dutchess County prior to 1800. Since there were no organized efforts to encourage such development at that

n.b.: The preliminary research for this study was made possible by a grant from the National Endowment for the Humanities YOUTHGRANTS Division, 1981.

Ms. Biszick is presently continuing her study of Hudson Valley Music through the Graduate Musicology Program at New York University.

A somewhat more extensive article on Poughkeepsie music appears in the Yearbook of the Dutchess County Historical Society, LXVIII (1983), 128–152.

time, information has remained hidden in seemingly unrelated sources. By themselves, these scattered references to music mean little. And even in light of the very sizable Henry Livingston Jr. music copybook, one can only speculate as to their true meaning. But Dutchess County is indeed fortunate for the existence of this exquisite musical diary which has delivered us from the historian's nightmare of pondering theories about the development of music and its use in this region without the aid of musical examples from the period. It is only through this MS that one might begin to make sense of these sporadic and apparently conflicting references.

Henry Livingston Jr. was born in 1748 and died in 1828.[2] He resided at Locust Grove, now the Young-Morse Historic Site in Poughkeepsie. He was an extremely versatile man and has been the subject of local and regional interest for many years. He drew maps, sketched pictures, is reputed to have played both flute and violin, and was a prolific writer of both prose and poetry.

The manuscript is a sizable compilation numbering 204 pages of handwritten vocal and instrumental music. The variety of selections reflects a broad musical interest. There are folk and fiddle tunes, selections from ballad operas, marches and patriotic songs, and psalm and hymn tunes. Because one quarter of these have been found to exist elsewhere in published sources, it is suspected that the manuscript was a repository for Henry's favorite tunes rather than an exercise book for original compositions.

Although none of the musical examples bear copy dates, tunes such as "God Save The King" where "King" has been crossed out and "Congress" has been added suggests a copy date sometime after the Revolution. Indeed, these pieces are surrounded by many tunes which are found in published sources of the 1780s and 1790s. This really comes as no surprise since these years happen to correspond with Livingston's most creatively prolific period. All but one of the 44 examples of his poetry date from the period between 1784–89. His poetry and prose were published in the *New York Mirror and Literary Repository* between 1791–94. And the magazine even utilised several of his sketches as frontispieces for its issues. Therefore, it is not surprising that Livingston would have devoted himself as diligently to his music during this period.

Music copybooks were not uncommon during the latter half of the eighteenth century. Francis Hopkinson, a noted early American musician and amateur composer, compiled one in 1759.[3] Musical diaries were not inspired by the lack of published music manuals and collections in rural areas. Nor was it due to their excessive cost. Rather they were regarded as a piece of useful memorabilia, an acceptable means of dabbling in music, of practicing the art of notation, and perhaps even of pursuing some amateur attempts at composition.[4] But only through the thorough examination of the entire MS contents and the identification of their origins in published sources will any original pieces come to light. We are encouraged by the fact that, as both a prolific poet and a competent musician, a merger of both of these arts in a creative individual such as Henry Livingston Jr. seems natural.

It is particularly unusual to find any eighteenth century gentleman so thoroughly immersed in music at a time when the appellation "musical enthusiast" meant nothing less than "crackpot."[5] It was socially acceptable—even fashionable—to practice music in one's spare time as long as a firm grip was retained on practical matters. Livingston astounds us with his creative output, the size and quality of which approaches that of a professional writer, artist, and musician. Whether or not he regarded himself as such, the fact that he actively pursued publication indicates a serious and professional approach to these endeavors which likely occupied a great deal of his time.

The cause for Henry's abrupt turn to and almost total immersion in the arts need not remain a mystery. For it is exactly these years that Livingston remained alone after the death of his young wife Sarah in 1783. When he once again married in 1793, his creative output decreased considerably as Henry perhaps turned his attention to the more practical matters of rearing and supporting a large family.

Aside from this, there seems to be evidence of certain personality traits which may have predisposed him to pursue this somewhat eccentric hobby. By nature, Livingston was rebellious and outspoken. This attitude caused his expulsion from a New York City social club just prior to the Revolution. He later served as Major in the Third Continental Regiment commanded by James Clinton which accompanied the Canadian Expedition under Robert Montgomery. Closer to home, it is Henry's church affiliation which may reflect this nonconformist attitude.

Of the two churches existing locally at the time, Henry was associated with the Dutch Reformed—by far the more antiquated in its views of music and amusements. Although the English congregation of Christ Church remained the forerunner of musical development throughout the eighteenth and nineteenth centuries, Livingston may have preferred the Dutch church because of its inherently anti-British sentiment.[6]

The rendering of organized and tuneful sacred music was a concern as early as 1773, when the Christ Church charter conferred upon the rector, the power to appoint a clerk to lead the congregation in responses.[7] Thus evolved the layman's function of choirmaster and a strong tradition of both voluntary and paid choirs was begun. In addition, Christ Church stood alone for some 20 years with the only organ in the town, installed in 1808.

In contrast, music developed much more slowly in the Dutch Church. There is no record of a choir in the early years, and congregational singing was said to be very plain at the turn of the century.[8] The first mention of a choirmaster occurs in 1826 and the only accompaniment was a flute.[9] An organ was not introduced into the service until the late 1840's, and prior to this the use of string instruments in the service was met with considerable resistance. Anthing resembling a "fiddle" was considered the "wiles of the devil" and in 1834, one church elder threatened to put his foot through a cello if it were brought into the choirloft.[10] Such staunchly conservative views among his fellow parishioners and spiritual leaders must have induced some amount of speculation over Henry's musical pastimes, especially since fiddle was one of his favored instruments.[11] While elders debated the appropriateness of instruments as a proper part of public worship, Henry apparently fiddled on. Although the Livinston MS is large, it is by no means a complete representation of musical activities in the county. Livingston can be considered a part of the landed gentry. He owned a farm of some 250 acres and was active in county business and politics. He had been well educated, frequented New York City, and was exposed to the thriving arts community there.[12] As tension built between the trade controlling English and the American colonists, well-to-do families began to migrate northward to the upper colonies.[13] They brought with them genteel manners and leisure time practices that were more refined than the rustic groghouse gossip, cockfights, and horseraces common among the lower class inhabitants.[14] Before long, there was evidence of lively domestic music activity withing the parlors of the elite.[15] The Livingston MS best represents this group of local inhabitants.

The elite seemed to confine their amusements to their parlors and private halls. The little that we know of the common inhabitants—the farmer and tradesman—seems to indicate a conservative view of such pastimes. One incident which is recorded in the local newspaper publicizes a serious warning from the local sheriff to a group of young men and women who had been accused of slating a mixed dance in the village hall.[16] They were told to abandon these plans unless they wished to face criminal charges. The complete lack of public entertainments in this period—be they music, theatre, or otherwise—seems to indicate a strong opinion that among the general populace, such social amusements should be confined to more private establishments.

A portion of the contents of the Livingston MS have been traced to published secular collections common among the gentleman amateurs at that time. The MS consists almost solely of secular music—a curious fact, since the few newspaper advertisements which record the existence of such collections locally are clearly sacred in nature.[17] There is no evidence that secular music was as readily available and it is possible that public pressure was responsible for the limiting of non-sacred music. It is not unlikely that secular music collections circulated freely among the elite and that popular issues were acquired from New York with ease.

The secular music which was common among the blacks in the village may explain some of the lively fiddle tunes found in the MS. The musicality of local blacks is recorded in several newspaper notices describing them for their sale as slaves and the inquiry into their frequent disappearance. Descriptive notices concerning runaway slaves dispel the notion that blacks were musically uneducated and played solely for their own enjoyment. In fact, slaves were considered valuable property and they were encouraged to develop their musical talents since this increased their value and prestige to their masters.[18] Often they would acquire fine European instruments from their masters which would disappear along with them. The descriptive notices would include these details, for it was only a matter of time before the slave would betray himself in public. The earliest records of the musicality of local blacks date from 1791 and 1795, when the *Poughkeepsie Journal* records the disappearance of two local slaves who took their instruments with them.[19]

Before one hastily concludes that all blacks were musical, that all gentlemen amateurs were eccentric, and that all of the common inhabitants thought fiddle music was a sin against God, one must remember that the body of material available during this period is too small to justify generalizations. Rather, the material should be considered along with information concerning the early development of the other arts in Dutchess County—poetry, painting, drawing, and dancing. In this way, the meaning of music in the lives of 18th century Dutchess County residents can become clear within the context of other leisure time activities.

The Impact of Europeans on the Nineteenth Century Musical Scene

After the turn of the nineteenth century, the United States became involved in building an empire. Technological advancement was seen as the vehicle through which to effect change and improve the social condition. Indeed, it was exactly this mentality which, through the efforts of the Improvement Party, raised Poughkeepsie to such heights that it was considered one of the most progressive and prosperous cities in the nation.

Education was afforded special attention by this community group, and during the 1830s Poughkeepsie was known as the "City of Schools" attracting students from as far away as Spain and the West Indies.[20] Before long, music was being considered as a possible addition to the school curriculum. Early in the nineteenth century, it was met with less resistance in the female seminaries, being included as one of the polite arts, along with the French language, dancing, drawing, and ornamental needlework. But as the decades proceeded it became necessary to define music as a science in order to preserve its credibility as a part of the curriculum deemed fitting and proper for young men and women. Musicians referred to themselves as "teachers of the science of music" and the better part of the school catalog was devoted to a lengthy explanation that was little less than an apology for the inclusion of music as a worthy course of study.[21]

In such an atmosphere, it is not difficult to understand why European musicians would dominate the American musical scene. Not only did their backgrounds offer prestige, but their formalized training was grounded in reason and logic, and structured in such a way as to lend credibility to music as a science. Consequently, the native teacher and performer was relegated to a secondary position, unable to compete with their well educated European counterparts.

During the 1850s and 1860s the musical atmosphere in Poughkeepsie was almost exclusively dominated by Germans. Nearly every musical leader was a German by birth and educated abroad. In 1850, a German Singing Society was organized in this city, modeled after the fine community singing groups in Germany, and they performed regularly.[22] The Grube Brothers, Charles and Louis, were local music teachers who advertised lessons on piano, violin, and guitar, and together organized "Concordia," Poughkeepsie's first orchestra.[23] Local German composers were also responsible for three of the six pieces of published sheet music which originated here prior to 1865. Fred Reichardt led the German Singing Society for many years and assisted as a piano accompanist at several public events. His composition is entitled, *The Poughkeepsie Polka,* and was published in New York in 1853.[24] Edward Wiebe was Vassar College's first music teacher at a time when it enjoyed national notoriety as a music conservatory. He was the composer of *Consolation,* a sentimental ballad published in 1853.[25] And Charles Grube was the penman of the *Springside Mazurka,* dedicated to Matthew Vassar and his cottage residence in Poughkeepsie. It appears without a date.

It is ironic that, although European performers were readily welcomed into America, the same cannot always be said for European music. M. E. Barnes-Ostrander in a recent article on domestic music in New York State, points out the relative intolerance of foreign music in America and its notable absence in early New York collections.[26] Two local incidents illustrate this point:

An 1850 report filed by an examination committee for a musical exhibition by the students of the Lyndon Hall School at first praises both the teacher and the students for their musical proficiency and satisfactory execution of the music, but then goes on in the following manner:

> Were we disposed to carp, it would be at the unreasonable quantity of Operatic and other foreign music introduced into the program. This might be very well in a community where a highly cultivated taste for such music prevailed—but in a provincial village where the bulk of inhabitants are comparatively strangers to the intricate and involved compositions of the French and German schools—it were only but right and fitting to indulge the audience with a few native or at least well known melodies."[27]

The young reporter for the *College Hill Mercury* is even less subtle in his dislike for foreign music. Jeams is our reporter who describes a Grube Brothers concert in the third person:

> The first three pieces were played beautifully he thinks, and in such a manner as cannot be surpassed, but when he comes to the fourth, that is, the Aria from *Lucia di Lammermoore*, he begs to particularize a little. He says it was beautifully played and exquisitely sung, that is for those that like it. The fine tremor of the tree toad was blended with the sounding bass of the bullfrog. Senor Ruisenor did infinite credit to himself (at least Jeams supposes so, for he does not understand Dutch)* but he thinks that he would have rendered his articulation cleaner had he removed the bushes from his face.
>
> Now Jeams wants to know if the Americans have no singers among them, and if they are compelled to go to other countries for them, and if English Opera couldn't be written which would supercede the necessity of all this foreign trash that is thrown upon us every year in the shape of Italian music. We profess to possess nearly all the means requisite for a great nation; it is a very singular fact if we can produce no warblers of our own.[28]

The local community apparently had the power to control local music activities. Musicians seemed to devote much of their time to trying to win over their supporting public through newspaper advertisements that were both wordy and sensational. But when they did not deliver what they had promised, they were corrected in short order. The fate of the Beethoven Society is one instance. Principally associated with the Universalist church, it was organized in 1855 as an interdenominational society devoted to the skillful performance of sacred music by amateurs and professionals. Three months after its organization, the society gave a performance which involved virtually every notable vocalist and musician in the area. A portion of the program notes are reprinted here:

June 4, 1855

> It is only three months since the organization of the Beethoven Society, during which time a success entirely unexpected has attended its efforts. . . . Members now number 36 and our expenses . . . have been born by the Gentlemen of the Society. It is hoped . . . ere long, it will result in the permanent establishment of a first class Sacred Music Society.[29]

Within three years, the Society had disbanded. The concert program for the 1855 concert provides a possible clue to its demise. Although claiming partiality to sacred music and advertising "amateurs welcome" the program consisted of some of the most highly virtuosic European secular music available at the time. Pieces included the Finale to *Lucia di Lammermoore* by Donizetti, and selections from *Attila* by Verdi. Although the lighter pieces such as "Hazel Dell and Old Josey" and "Pop Goes the Weasel" are American folk tunes, they were still a far cry from "Nearer My God to Thee." One can speculate that the society fell victim to the criticism of a scrutinizing public who valued truth in advertising, and who tolerated European Opera only in small doses.

Lucia di Lammermoore is an Italian opera by Gaetano Donizetti.

Instrument Building in Poughkeepsie

There appears to have been an active instrument building industry in Poughkeepsie throughout the nineteenth century. There were several piano, organ, and brass manufactories in the 1850s, and the City Directory for 1856–1857 lists no fewer than 10 residents as involved with instrument building. Two family enterprises are notable and it is fortunate that some of their work has survived for study.

The Gunn brothers were makers of violins and organs and their work probably constituted the first local attempt at instrument building. The family was always active in local music. The father, Abel Gunn Sr., was said to have transported the first organ in Poughkeepsie to Christ Church in 1808 by oxcart from Connecticut.[30] Abel Jr. was Poughkeepsie's first native professional musician and organ teacher, and his career as organist at Christ Church spans 53 years. From 1809, at the age of 9, until 1862, Abel performed thunder and lightning every Sunday from the Christ Church gallery.[31] In addition, Abel was a composer of both vocal and instrumental music and was likely the first published Poughkeepsie composer. A sentimental piece entitled *Let Us Love One Another* was published sometime prior to 1840 and another, *The Arabella Waltz,* was published in 1855. Both originated from New York publishing houses, Firth and Hall, and Cleveland and Reed.[32]

The Gunn brothers, Samuel and Joseph, were instrument makers for at least thirty years. Although no examples of Abel's organs are extant, four violins by Samuel have survived, three of which were available for study. The 1820 example is the least professional in construction. Although Samuel was forty-two when this instrument was constructed, he seems to have been in the early stages of his building career. It probably represents a practice or student model. Oddly, it is adorned with an ornate inlaid mother of pearl tailpiece—as though someone were trying to dress up an inferior instrument in order to make up for its shortcomings. The 1848 example is of a more professional construction. It has a rich cherry stain and greater care is taken to the neck and joints. The finest example dates from 1853. It again carries Samuel's signature. The top is spruce and the back and sides are a good grade of maple. This instrument has been studied by both amateurs and professionals over the years. Generally they agree that it can stand on its own merit, with one New Haven Symphony player remarking that it had better tone than his $700 French model.[33]

Another longstanding nineteenth century establishment was the Wiethan Piano Manufactory. Louis Wiethan built pianos in Poughkeepsie from 1837 to his death in 1878 when the business was then taken over by his sons. Wiethan pianos were of greater than local significance. The elder Louis Wiethan enjoyed a wide and favorable reputation for his fine uprights which he distributed both locally and in the South.[34] One example survives in the possession of Vassar College and is believed to be the work of the father. Its construction is more antiquated than what is generally found in a later nineteenth century instrument. It has a small keyboard of 74 keys and two pedals. The hammer structure is quite archaic, and the wound bass strings which extend over the bridge are somewhat reminiscent of harpsichord construction. The bridge, however, is in remarkable condition, attesting to the fine qulity of the materials used and the care with which it was constructed.[35]

The Rise of Music Education in Poughkeepsie

Music education in America became popular in the early nineteenth century. Teachers were usually associated with churches and instruction was largely limited to vocal techniques for the singing of sacred music utilized by church choirs. The first notice of a singing school appeared in the Poughkeepsie Journal, 13 May 1800. It announced that a school had been convened under the direction of Mr. Benham. This instructor must have been operating in this area for some time before this, since a review of a sacred music exhibition under his direction is included in the paper one week later. The performance involved "the several schools of Mr. Benham" which apparently already existed locally, as well as numerous private students that were under his care. The journalist who

Abel Gunn, musician and instrument maker

attended the concert spoke highly of its professionalism and added that "vocal music is a very proper part of public worship, an ornamental accomplishment and more than any of the fine arts, tends to civilize and harmonize society." Incidently, this constitutes the earliest record of a public performance of music within the city.[36]

Other music instructors associated themselves with area schools. As we have already noted, there was a tendency to include music as part of the female seminary curriculum long before any such attempt in the male academy. The impact of music education on two local residents is recorded in two bound volumes of sheet music now in the possession of the Dutchess County Historical Society. Originally the personal collections of two sisters, Sarah and Aletta Ann Ward, the selections indicate extensive musical training which was fairly representative of a young lady's music education at that time. Further, the volumes are useful in comparison since they represent two distinct decades in the manufacturing of sheet music.

The Wards were a fairly well to do family residing for the most part in Pleasant Valley, a small village east of Poughkeepsie. The father owned a mill there, and was assisted by his son, Alson, who kept a diary.[37] From his writings we come to know that the family was active in the village choir, traveling at least once a week to practice, and that the family owned a piano. The sheet music included in the collections was likely purchased at one of the many book and music stores in Poughkeepsie. Since the finer educational institutions were also located in this city, it is possible that the sisters boarded here for school.

There are 104 selections included in the volumes, most of which are missing their title pages. These were probably removed for economic reasons since the binding cost was likely dependent on the number of pages to be bound. Therefore, extraneous pages were removed. With the loss of title pages comes a loss of publishing date, making it difficult to determine exactly when these pieces were purchased. However, the fact that the volumes appear with the sisters' maiden names suggests that the music was purchased and bound sometime prior to their marriage dates.[38]

Aletta Ann's book contains music of the 1830s. Her volume reflects a serious and sentimental nature common to this decade. Selections include excerpts from European opera and sentimental pieces such as *Let Us Love One Another* by Abel Gunn Jr. who apparently was her piano teacher. Several examples of seafaring music are also included which perhaps reflects the local interest in the whaling fleet based here in the 1830s.[39]

Sarah's volume is more frivolous in nature, illustrating music of the 1840s. The many ethnic pieces, especially Irish tunes, reflect the great surge of immigration which took place during this decade. The abundance of minstrel tunes are notable as well. These sensational and versatile performers were the rage during the 1840s and their traveling troupes frequently performed in Poughkeepsie.[40] Several pieces by Stephen Foster are also included, made famous by the celebrated Christy Minstrels.

In the realm of public education, books prior to 1855 contained only words and were called songsters. Each student was provided with one and they were taught the tunes either by ear or on the blackboard. Two local songsters are extant. The first was published by G. W King in Poughkeepsie in 1854. Mr. King is reputed to have been the first public school music teacher here. He was succeeded by Enos C. Andrus who replaced King's book with his own called the *Rural Songster*.[41] But within a year, Andrus became dissatisfied with the "words-without-music" method and adopted a nonlocal publication called the *Robin Redbreast Juvenile Singing Book*. This edition provided both words and music, as well as an extensive preface providing the rudiments of notation and vocal techniques. It continued to be used locally as the principle music manual throughout the mid-century.[42]

Notes

1. Oscar G. Sonneck in M. E. Barnes-Ostrander, "Domesic Music Making in Early New York State," *The Musical Quarterly,* LXVIII, no. 3 (1982), 372.

2. Dr. William S. Thomas, "Henry Livingston," Dutchess County Historical Society *Yearbook,* V (1919), 32.

3. Gilbert Chase, America's Music (New York: McGraw Hill, 1955), 100.

4. *Ibid.,* 100.

5. *Ibid.,* 98.

6. Helen Andrus, *A Century of Music in Poughkeepsie, NY: 1802–1911* (Poughkeepsie, N.Y.: Frank B. Howard, 1912), 2–3.

7. Helen Wilkinson Reynolds, The Records of Christ Church (Poughkeepsie, NY: Frank B. Howard, 1911), I, 199.

8. Andrus, *op. cit.,* 2.

9. Andrus, *op. cit.,* 7.

10. Andrus, *op. cit.,* 11, 12, 18.

11. Helen Wilkinson Reynolds, "Editorial Notes on the Writings of Henry Livingston Jr.," Dutchess County Historical Society *Yearbook,* XXVII (1942), 87.

12. Author not cited, "A Packet of Old Letters," Dutchess County Historical Society *Yearbook,* VI (1921), 51; Thomas, op. cit., 32.

13. Charles D. King, *History of Education in Dutchess County* (Cape May, NJ: Charles D. King, 1959), 32.

14. David M. Ellis, James A. Frost, Harold C. Syrett, and Harry J. Carman, *A History of New York State* (Ithaca, NY: Cornell University Press, 1957), 69.

15. M. E. Barnes-Ostrander, "Domestic Music Making in Early New York State," *The Musical Quarterly,* LXVIII, no. 3 (1982), 353–354.

16. *The Country Journal and the Poughkeepsie Advertiser,* 21 April 1789, p. 3, col. 4.

17. *Country Journal. . .,* 27 December 1786, p. 3, col. 4 and 16 January 1788, p. 1, col. 4 constitute the only references to the sale of music manuals prior to 1789. They are concerned with publications by Daniel Read and Isaac Watts and both consist of settings of sacred psalm and hymn tunes.

18. Chase, *op. cit.,* 76.

19. *Poughkeepsie Journal,* 24 November 1791, p. 4, col. 2. Notice submitted by Godfrey Walwin, Oswego, Beekman Town, 17 October 1795: "Runaway negro, Robert, 23 years old...is a fiddler and took his fiddle with him."
Poughkeepsie Journal, 23 December 1795, p. 4, col. 4. Submitted by Samuel Agustus Barker, Franklin, Dutchess County, 17 October 1795: "Runaway Negro, Zack, 30 years from Connecticut. Plays the fife and German Flute. Has flute with him."

20. King, *op. cit.,* 50; College Hill School, Poughkeepsie, NY, Pamphlets and Catalogs dating from 1837–1864. Courtesy of Adriance Memorial Library Local History Room.

21. *The Rural Repository,* XVI, 15 February 1840, p. 138. Advertisement for the College Hill School: "It was with some hesitation that this branch was introduced as a regular study; but the Principle has the concurrence of many of esteemed judgement, in the opinion which he has formed of the propriety of studying the science, and of the salutary influence which the practice of music may be made to exert over the minds and morals of the young."

22. Andrus, *op. cit.,* 25.

23. Andrus, *op. cit.,* 19.

24. Courtesy of the Andriance Local History Room.

25. Courtesy of Vassar College.

26. Barnes-Ostrander, *op. cit.,* 372.

27. Lyndon Hall School, "Report of Ex. Com. on Music," Poughkeepsie, 25 July 1850. Courtesy Adriance Memorial Library Local History Room.

28. Poughkeepsie Collegiate School, *The College Hill Mercury,* 11 February 1850, n.p.

29. Beethoven Society, Program and Libretto for performance, 4 June 1855. Courtesy of Special Collections Division, Vassar College.

30. From an article which appeared in the *Poughkeepsie Journal,* circa 1936. A copy has been retained by Mrs. Frances Nevers but carries no date. It concerns Frank Gunn, great grandson of Abel Sr. and gives a lengthy outline of family musical activities. It is entitled "Gunn Finishes 25 Years on the Job."

31. Reynolds, *The Records of Christ Church,* II, 315.

32. "Let Us Love One Another" from the bound sheet music collection of Aletta Ann Ward. Courtesy of the Dutchess County Historical Society; "Arabella Waltz" courtesy of The Adriance Memorial Library Local History Room. Aside from the three pieces available locally by German composers and the two cited here by Abel Gunn, there exists only one other piece of music relating to Poughkeepsie from this period. "The Poughkeepsie Quadrilles" are divided into four short dance movements titled for each of the four local counties—Dutchess, Putnam, Orange, and Ulster. They were composed by William Smith and arranged by B. A., published in 1843 by Charles Keith of Boston. It is unclear as to the connection of these individuals to Poughkeepsie. If they were not residents, then they were still rather intimate with the locale. At present, this piece stands as the earliest published music work relating to Poughkeepsie, excepting the possibility of the undated Gunn work which may date earlier.

33. Harold Wynne, Letter to Mrs. Frances Nevers, 5 March 1954. "The work which I possess is too fine to be made by an amateur tinker...."

34. James H. Smith, *History of Duchess County New York* (Interlaken, NY: Heart of the Lakes Publishing, 1981 reprint of 1880 edition), 393.

35. Insights courtesy Mark Moriarty, piano technician, Vassar College.

36. *Poughkeepsie Journal,* 21 May 1800, p. 3, col. 1 recording a concert on 20 May 1800.

37. Courtesy of the Dutchess County Historical Society.

38. Aletta Ann was married in 1840; Sarah was married in 1850.

39. Edmund Platt, *History of Poughkeepsie, NY* (Poughkeepsie, NY: Platt and Plaltt, 1905), 158.

40. Author not cited, "Poughkeepsie Collegiate School, 1848–49: The Diary of a Hudson Student on College Hill," Dutchess County Historical Society *Yearbook,* XXXVI (1951), 39, 40. Excerpts from the diary dated 26 May 1849 and 31 May 1849 cite performances by the "negro minstrels, the Campbells," and the "colored Luca family."

41. Courtesy of the Dutchess County Historical Society.

42. Andrus, *op. cit.,* 29.

MUSIC FROM THE PEN OF CHARLES GILBERT SPROSS

Constance M. Jessup
Musician, Local Historian

The music created by composers is for all time, sentiments for all time. Each composition must be special, like a parent and child. For him the ultimate satisfaction, fulfillment and tribute has to be the performance of his creations and knowing that they will always be enjoyed. So it was for Charles Gilbert Spross, an obscure American composer and the leader of Poughkeepsie's Musical Heritage. Recognition was first accorded him by the musical world outside of his hometown, Poughkeepsie. His professional colleagues knew more about him and his high standards at the height of his career than his fellow townsmen. Today, only his family and close friends remember that he was much more than a Sunday music maker. Besides serving as organist in churches in Poughkeepsie, New York City and New Jersey, he was a prolific composer and a sympathetic, skillful and highly successful accompanist serving in that capacity with such artists as Melba, Fremstad, Jomelli, Schumann-Heink, Homer, Hemple, Caruso, Garden, Case, Ysaye, Gerardy, and others.

Music from the Pen of Charles Gilbert Spross is the title of a brochure cataloguing his compositions. The John Church Publishing Company distributed it sometime after 1935 listing over 200 secular and sacred songs, choral works, anthems, piano, organ, and violin compositions and orchestrations. Five of Spross' earliest songs were published in Poughkeepsie before 1895 by the Dutchess Music Company and distributed by Oliver Ditson Company in New York City. By the time he was 23 years old he had published 18 works and when he died in 1961 he had composed more than 450 compositions including many transcriptions of music of other composers. Only two songs are presently in print at Presser. Eighteen others are on active file but out of print.

Charles Gilbert Spross was born January 6, 1874. Poughkeepsie, at that time, was enjoying a Golden Age of Music. There were a large number of vocal and instrumental soloists and many concerts were given by the local talent. People willingly paid their money to listen to the performances of the musicians of their town without the assistance of outside attractions. Popular music concerts were given to raise money since classical music, as yet, did not attract a very large paying audience. Paraphrases of operatic arias and overtures, brilliant transcriptions of songs and orchestral works were very popular with performers and listeners. The more pyrotechnics they exhibited, the more popular they were. This was the period when the country was slowly recovering from the strain of Civil War. General Grant's administration as President of the United States had just begun. Alexander Bell had just invented the telephone. The electric light was not practical for lighting purposes yet and the automobile was unknown.

Spross' musical talent was inherited from his parents who emigrated from Germany as children. They brought with them the German enthusiasm for choral singing. His father, Michael, had an exceptional bass voice and was a lifetime charter member of the local Germania Singing Society which was founded in 1850. His mother, Alouisa, would encourage her children to sing along with her while doing the family chores. One sister whose pitch was not too accurate was gently encouraged to "follow me and sing low." Apparently Mother Spross was well aware of the importance of the ear for good singing! Many of "Charlie's" brothers, sisters, and cousins were already accomplished musicians by the time he was born, the ninth of ten children. There was always music at family gatherings, and when he became adept enough, Charles Gilbert was always at the piano. He sang in the church choir with a beautiful soprano voice, frequently substituting for the soloist. He pumped the organ for his sister's lessons and after the teacher left he would repeat the exercises while his sister pumped for him.

His first piano studies were with Professor Adolph Kuehn, who had come to this country from Leipzig in 1849 when he was 18 years old. Leipzig was then one of the world's greatest music centers. Riding the train to the end of the line to get away from the big city, he settled in Poughkeepsie, teaching piano at Mrs. Blivens' School on Mansion Street. He organized the Germania Society and except for a short period of time, continued as director until 1911 when he retired at 80 years old. He had to have been a major influence in the musical direction Charles pursued. Spross also studied harmony and organ with Helen Andrus, author of *A Century of Music in Poughkeepsie 1802-1911*. He did not have the "Ivy League" education that many of his peers had. After graduating from Poughkeepsie High School in 1892, he was sent to New York City by his Uncle Elias who had paid for his early music lessons. In New York he became an advanced pupil of Xavier Scharwenka, virtuoso pianist and composer, who had come to this country in 1891 to direct a conservatory of music. Spross also studied with Emil Gramm and Carl Lachmund, pianist and conductor. Lachmund, a student of Liszt, was the only American pupil for whom the master wrote a letter of recommendation. Spross established a studio on 28th street, "the" music area of the city at that time.

It was while studying and playing dinner music with an orchestra in the Majestic Hotel, that Spross' friendships with the celebrated artists began. The Metropolitian Opera Company was formed in 1893 and was well established by the 1900's. Many singers, coming to this country for the first time, stayed at the Majestic Hotel. Mme. Jeanne Jomelli, from Paris, arrived in New York about the same time as Spross. He told his niece, "She was the first Met singer I played for—a superb artist— wonderful voice of rare beauty—perfect control." He played for her in New Orleans, "went all the way for one concert." Considering the mode of travel at that time, it was a very long trip. During orchestra breaks at the Hotel he would write orchestra transcriptions of such popular operatic music as Mascagnis' *Iris*, Puccini's *Tosca*, and the *Sextet* from *Lucia*, as he told his niece, "standing up using the piano for a desk." Anna Case later wrote, "you would write robin songs, wind songs, water and love songs on the train or any old place." He apparently used all that travel time very productively. In a hotel room or at home, he seemed instinctively to recognize the poems and the music flowed from his pen.

The exposure to all the music and musicians he heard in New York City at that time had to have made a profound imprint on the musical foundation he was assimilating. New singers were appearing all the time, among them Tito Ruffo, Benjamin Gigli, Patti, Nordica, Calve, Alma Gluck, Scotti, Bori, Tetrazini, and others. The contemporary composers of the day were Liszt, Wagner, and Tschaikovsky. The singers all came during and after World War I, all anxious to promote their careers in this country. The Metropolitan was their home.

This was a Golden Age of the Song Recital which lasted until the early 1940's. Solo recitals were presented throughout the country in towns large and small, always to large enthusiastic audiences. There was great demand for songs in English, and publishers were eager for any new material that came their way. These programs followed a typical format, including arias and songs with a group of solos by the accompanist. There were plenty of encores and usually at the very last something as familiar as *Home Sweet Home*. The English language songs then demanded real vocalism and genuine audience appeal with pictures, humor, drama, and tears. The audience could relate to them.

Spross became the official accompanist for many of the major choral organizations in the city. There were regular Sunday night concerts at the Met. He and Richard Hageman were the official accompanists, usually without any rehearsals preceding them. In 1911 he was appointed official organist for the New York Philharmonic Symphony. He was a member of the Musicians and the Leiderkrantz clubs. With all these activities he still found time to continue his accompanying in Poughkeepsie for the Euterpe, Rubenstein, and Germania Clubs. "He was always catching a train"— and so his reputation as an accompanist blossomed. In 1908 he was chosen from among many for an American tour with Cecile Chaminade, the Parisian composer and pianist. Together they played her duet compositions for one and two pianos. Spross was the only American to do this. A press notice from New York says that "her most effective work was in the two piano and four hand pieces played with Spross." She later wrote him, "You are a remarkable artist of pure style and brilliant mechanism." This "brilliant mechanism" is reflected in many of his compositions.

From 1912–1929, along with touring and composing, Spross was the minister of music at the First Presbyterian Church in Poughkeepsie. Combining with other choirs in the city, he presented Oratorios including *Elijah, Messiah,* the *Creation,* and *Verdi Requiem* to name a few. He was both conductor and accompanist, engaging many New York soloists. A review of an organ recital presented in Hartford, Connecticut about this time states, "Spross' masterly technique, his highly organized temperament and fine color sense gave his playing charm which held the audience from the first—he brought out all the tonal qualities of the new organ."

In 1915 Spross was guest soloist in a performance by the New York Symphony at the Collingwood Opera House. Under the baton of Joseph Stransky, they played the *Greig A minor Concerto.* A Mason Hamlin piano was sent from New York especially for this performance. The Mason Hamlin was Spross' personal piano for many years. Reports are glowing of this concert and added that eight carloads of Vassar students attended. The "carloads" were trolley cars, of course. From about 1919 he was engaged for the annual Toronto Festival and had several bookings with Mme. Fremstad. The Festivals were forerunners of the Artists Master Classes held today at Berkshire, Saratoga, Aspen, and many colleges. Spross served as official accompanist for those held at Round Lake, New York where Anna Case was often artist-in-residence and at Winona Lake, Indiana with Schumann-Heink as artist-in-residence.

In the early 1920's he recorded many of his compositions and those of other composers for the Aeolian Company's Duo-Art Reproducing Piano. A catalogue published in 1927 lists 40 compositions recorded by Spross. Many of the rolls include his picture with a signed statement, "This music roll is my interpretation. It was recorded by me for Duo-Art and I hereby authorize its use with that instrument." Spross also recorded for the Victor Talking Machine. By the late 1920's the center of musical interest in New York was shifting from the Metropolitan Opera to the Philharmonic Society under Toscanini, who had also come to New York about the same time as Spross. Rudolph Ganz was also another popular accompanist as was the Frenchman Andre Benoit, whose career paralleled Spross' in many ways until 1912 when he devoted his time entirely to accompanying Albert Spaulding, the violinist. There was another popular violinist, Efrem Zimbalist, husband of Mary Garden. John Philip Sousa was touring the country with his Concert Band. Pietro Yon was organist at St. Patrick's Cathedral. Frank LaForge was an equally talented accompanist and arranger. Spross toured with two Belgian musicians during the season they were in America. Eugene Ysaye was considered the world's leading violinist at that time and Jean Gerardy was a leading cellist. Spross became very fond of stringed instruments. In 1933 the premiere performance of his *Sonata for Violin and Piano* was presented from manuscript by Pierre Henrotte, concert-meister of the Metropolitan Opera Orchestra. There is also a *Cello Sonata* in manuscript, dedicated to William Schmitt, who was first cellist with the Philadelphia Symphony.

Of the few anecdotes he repeated over the years, the favorite was probably the one concerning a concert with Mary Garden. She was wearing a lovely gown with a long train falling from the shoulders and as they moved onto the stage, Spross accidentally stepped on it and it dropped to the floor. He very gallantly draped it over his arm and carried it off the stage before beginning the concert. "Garden had an infallible sense of the stage. She loved the exotic in opera and dress. Her characterization of *Salome* was quite a shocker for the time." At a special memorial concert following the Titanic sinking she wore a glittering gown and sang a lively group of French songs. Lillian Nordica, in black, and Caruso also performed with Spross accompanying. On a tour with Amato he received a call at 7pm from Frieda Hemple whose accompanist had not arrived. At 8pm he played the concert for her at sight. On another occasion at Colgate University the soloist failed to appear. Spross presented an impromptu recital playing the piano and organ. For over an hour he played a program that, according to his niece, proved his repertoire-in-readiness was extensive and belied the fact that "he was not a piano recitalist anyway." Spross tells us that Nellie Melba, the Australian soprano, didn't sing a note at rehearsals. "She played along at the piano instead. Didn't sing until the actual performance. Emma Eames was a "great Tosca"; Olive Fremstad was "famous for the roll of Sieglinda." Alma Gluck sang his *Will O'the Wisp* from New York to California. It still sold 5,000 copies in 1960. "She couldn't sing it as well as Anna Case."

There are many newspaper clippings dating from about 1912 about Anna Case and their concerts. Their tours were extensive. They traveled 40,000 miles throughout the United States, Canada, Hawaii, and three trips to London. Charlie Spross was the first musician she met in New York and the only accompanist she ever had. Theirs was a rare relationship between two performing artists, co-workers, not soloist and accompanist. She had studied for only a year and a half when she was offered and accepted her contract at the Metropolitan Opera. "Her singing was a delight to the layman and an inspiration to the musician."

His family and friends felt that he "retired" (about 1930) sooner than he needed to. However, looking at a sample season's schedule tells us what a busy life it was. One season Spross played 90 concerts in four months. He frequently accompanied at the conventions for the Associated Glee Clubs of America. One particular year it was held at Madison Square Garden where Spross led five pianists playing on five separate instruments accompanying 4,000 voices. All travel was by train and even though tours were always under management, many of the details fell on the accompanist as the man in the party. Solo recitalists were of less interest to the concert-going public than orchestra and chamber ensembles. Popular music, Big Bands, and small jazz groups were coming into vogue. Perhaps retiring to composing and organ playing was good timing after all. He was now engaged as Minister of Music at the First Congregational Church on Mill Street in Poughkeepsie, a post he held for twenty-five years, finally retiring in 1955. He played "a thousand weddings," many of them second generation. He was a close friend of the Smiley family and played many concerts for the enjoyment of the Widmere and Cliff House guests at Lake Minnewaska.

Spross took great delight in little things, his niece tells us, things of nature and all the Will O'the Wisps so few people take time to see. All this is in his music. He had an agreeable lack of false dignity, and was reluctant to tell any anecdotes about the artists. He refused a publisher's invitation to prepare a book of memoirs. He claimed his success was due to getting "breaks" wherever he went. He received volumes of amateurs' poetry in the mail. Many of the poems he did use were written by a local woman, Elizabeth Evelyn Moore. Mrs. Moore was a popular elocutionist frequently presenting programs of literature readings in local school assemblies.

Among his published works there are three and four part settings of his own songs for both men's and women's voices as well as several orchestrations which include *Will O'the Wisp, Yesterday and Today, Let All My Life Be Music, Gunga Din,* and the cantata *Word of God.* There are transcriptions and arrangements from the literature of composers from pre-Bach to the contemporary. Mrs. Ethelbert Nevin chose Spross to transcribe and arrange her husband's songs and thus perpetuate the work of a contemporary American whose career was tragically short (1862–1901). Mrs. Nevin felt that Spross was the most sympathetic and knowledgeable of her husband's genius. Spross' music reflects the traditional late German Romanticism. This traditional style of song was established by the German composer Franz Schubert. His form, harmony, and accompaniments transformed a world of poetry into music. By the time Spross began writing, Schubert's songs were a traditional part of most concert programs, and he must have studied and played them for all the artists he accompanied. He demonstrated the same rare genius for establishing a graceful harmony between text and music. Schubert did not, unfortunately, receive the recognition during his lifetime that Spross received. It wasn't until long after his death that a young baritone, Messchaert, championed Schubert's seldom heard songs and aroused enough interest so that soon other singers began to do likewise.

Spross received many tributes during his lifetime. In 1928 Poughkeepsie honored him with a testimonial dinner inviting many of his musical friends. John Philip Sousa came all the way from New Orleans where he was playing on tour. The John Church Publishing Company presented him with seven volumes of his music, a complete edition at that time. He was also presented with a book of letters of congratulations representing every state in the Union. There were telegrams from Mrs. Nevin, Oley Speaks, Frank LaForge, Harriet Ware, Walter Damrosch, Manna Zucca, Edward Johnson, and many others. He was later presented with an Honorary Plaque by the Chamber of Commerce for his many contributions to the cultural life of the city. The Congregational Church, upon his retirement, established the Charles Gilbert Spross Memorial Library. Of all the tributes he received, however, the Honorary Doctorate from Capitol University in 1936 had to be his proudest moment—his crowning achievement!

Spross' music involved his total personality and an artistic honesty, the product of people with old steady ideas. His niece tells us "he could transpose easily and freely, could manufacture what he did not actually memorize and read at sight like *greased lighting*. He could manufacture a piano accompaniment at sight from an orchestral score. In an interview for Musical America magazine in 1913 Spross said, "a good accompanist must be able to make himself an orchestra." Critics wrote: "His was an example of perfect accompanying;" "Calm, self-assured with a touch like velvet;" "Played with skill, taste, and judgment;" "Responding to every demand of the singer." He had to be reassured that the "modern chords and progressions he wanted to use in his Prelude (1929) were not ugly or out of place." He did not add too many *moderns* to his repertoire for performance but that did not preclude an interest in and a curiosity about how the harmonics were put together.

With the Bicentennial celebration of this country came a renewed interest in the history of American music. Surely, the fruits of a lifetime labor of love by Charles Gilbert Spross will not go unheeded or unsung!

Bibliography

1. Gertrude Spross Hart, *Ghosts, Musical and Otherwise, in the Attic of the Spross Family* (Cazenovia, N.Y., 1976). Gertrude, a niece of Charles Spross, was one of the few piano students he had time to teach. She, too, became an accomplished pianist in Poughkeepsie, frequently appearing with her uncle on local programs playing two-piano works. She served as accompanist for the Singers Club, a women's choral organization. Her information was compiled from a box of newspaper clippings Spross had saved over the years and from her recollections and conversations with him.

2. Helen J. Andrus, *A Century of Music in Poughkeepsie* (1912).

3. William E. Doughty, *Lake Minnewaska* (1846).

4. *Duo-Art Piano Music Catalogue* (Aeolian Company, 1927).

5. *ASCAP Biographical Dictionary* (First Edition, 1918).

6. *International Who's Who in Music and Musical Gazetteer* (First Edition).

7. Dietrich Fischer-Dieskau, *Schubert's Songs—A Biographical Study.*

8. *The NATS Bulletin*, May/June 1982.

9. *Spross Music Collection* in the collections of the Adriance Memorial Library.

THE DEVELOPMENT OF AN ART GALLERY
AT VASSAR COLLEGE, 1856–1865

Sally Mills
Curator, Vassar College Art Gallery

When Vassar College opened its doors in September of 1864, not the least of its distinctions was a substantial art museum. Housed on the fourth floor of the Main Building, in a sky-lit room thirty feet wide and ninety-six feet long, this Art Gallery boasted a collection of over four hundred oil paintings, watercolors, drawings, and engravings, accompanied by armor, Roman coins, and a large library of art books. More than one curious journalist who toured the college in its first years saw this room as "the most interesting apartment to the visitor which the building contains."[1]

Vassar was not the first college to own an art collection. In 1811, Bowdoin College received a bequest of colonial American portraits and various European paintings from James Bowdoin III; at least eighteen years earlier, Dartmouth College had started to display portraits of its Trustees alongside archeological and anthropological artifacts. But Vassar College was among the first to provide a separate physical space intended solely for the display of fine art; in fact, the structure of the gallery itself was planned before either Founder or Trustees knew exactly what would fill it. And in 1861, when Matthew Vassar addressed his newly-appointed Trustees and announced a curriculum that would include

> . . . Aesthetics, as treating of the beautiful in Nature and Art, and to be illustrated by an extensive Gallery of Art . . .,[2]

he was introducing the only college art gallery planned coincident with the school building and curriculum itself.

Vassar and others were fond of referring to his college enterprise as one that would provide women with the same opportunities Yale and Harvard bestowed upon their men.[3] But although these men's colleges gave Vassar a ready educational standard to emulate, it is unlikely that they provided him with the idea for an art gallery at his women's college. Harvard, chartered in 1636, owned neither art collections nor gallery to accommodate them until 1895. Princeton, chartered in 1746, did not have an art museum until 1888; Williams, chartered 1785, opened its museum in 1926. And although Yale had possessed a fine art collection ever since 1832, when the artist John Trumbull sold a group of his own works to the college (with the stipulation that the college would build a gallery for the paintings as well as promise to bury Trumbull and his wife directly beneath his famous painting of *George Washington at the Battle of Trenton*), it was not until 1864 that a Yale alumnus agreed to provide the funds necessary to establish a School of Fine Arts and erect a larger building in which art instruction as well as a growing collecction could be housed.[4] Matthew Vassar, however, was thinking of an art collection for his college as early as 1856, shortly after embarking on discussions with Milo P. Jewett on the subject of an endowed college for women. In a letter to Jewett dated December 29, 1856, Vassar discussed several issues involved with their proposed venture, and included mention of a "Cabinet, Paintings, Sculpture" alongside "Furniture, Library, Philosophical Apparatus" and other necessary college equipment.[5] Clearly the men's colleges had not given him a model for an art gallery, nor the easy association of art objects with the other requisite apparatus for a general education. Thus Vassar must have found his precedent for an art gallery elsewhere, and in fact, the prevailing standards for *female* education provide just such a model.

Poughkeepsie itself, "The City of Schools," claimed a number of institutions for female education in the 1850s; among them was the Cottage Hill Seminary. First owned and run by Matthew Vassar's niece Lydia Booth, the school was purchased after her death in 1854 by Milo Jewett. Born in Vermont and educated at Dartmouth College, Jewett came to Poughkeepsie in 1855 from Alabama, where in 1839 he had established the Judson Female Institute, "one of the strong and best-known schools in the South."[6] A Baptist like Vassar, and now the proprietor of a school which had once been close to the retired brewer's heart, Jewett must have found a number of opportunities to turn casual encounters into a close friendship. Jewett soon became privy to Vassar's thoughts about the proper disposal of his considerable fortune; in 1855 these thoughts were tending toward the founding of a hospital such as the one in London erected by his relative Thomas Guy. Jewett successfully persuaded Vassar to drop that idea, pointing out that a hospital in a small city that was not a seaport was unlikely to bring him the lasting fame he desired or even serve the community with the beneficience he wished to bestow. Jewett later wrote that after "a characteristic outburst of impatience [Vassar] petulantly exclaimed 'I wish somebody would tell me what to do with my money! It's the plague of my life—keeps me awake o' nights—stocks going down, banks breaking, insurance companies failing!' "[7] Apparently Jewett seized this moment to suggest that Vassar *endow* a college for women—a college such as he himself would have liked to established had he the financial resources of the Poughkeepsie businessman. Although Jewett does not deserve full credit for the ultimate shape and character of Vassar Female College, he did become its first President and exerted the most important influence on its early development.[8]

Jewett's own school, the Cottage Hill Seminary, advertised instruction in watercolors, drawing, and oil painting from its very beginning in 1855. By 1863, this instruction had become organized into a full "Department of Design," offering

> . . . several original and valuable Paintings, in oil and water color, drawings, pastels and
> crayon studies, by Wier [sic], Cropsey, Church, James Hart, De Haas, Rondel, Hekking,
> Morvillier, and many other excellent Artists, for the study of pupils.[9]

Because by 1863 the Seminary was no longer in the hands of Jewett, it is possible that this particular collection had been organized by his successor or even by the then-instructor of Design, Frederick Rondel (suspiciously prominent among the "excellent Artists" from which the young ladies could study). But such a collection was extant before Vassar's college opened, and it surely was the outgrowth of practices and principles begun under Jewett's administration.

Jewett's course offerings, however, are typical of those offered at other girl's schools in Poughkeepsie, such as the Poughkeepsie Female Academy and the Poughkeepsie Female Collegiate Institute. All three schools offered instruction in art and music as a supplement to the regular course, and the study of these subjects required the payment of an addtional fee. When Vassar College opened, it adopted an identical system: music and art were offered as extra-collegiate studies, and neither credit nor diploma was granted in these subjects. Jewett also permitted the enrollment of students who were solely interested in these subjects:

> Ladies who desire to perfect themselves in this department [of Modern Languages and Fine
> Arts], will be received as day and boarding pupils, and permitted to give it their exclusive
> attention, while increased facilities for practice will be afforded.[10]

Clearly then, such courses were offered to provide extra polish, an additional gloss to the perfection of a young lady's accomplishments. Along with instruction in piano, harp, and/or guitar, penmanship exercises and French lessons, this instruction in the Fine Arts was crucial to a woman's upbringing, but not necessarily to her intellectual development. Jewett admitted as much when he announced in his introductory circular that his Seminary will

> prepare every individual pupil to be a TRUE WOMAN—a woman fitted to meet the duties
> and responsibilities of *every-day* life; to be a dutiful daughter, a prudent wife, a judicious
> mother; a blessing to her own family, an ornament to society.[11]

One suspects that the art lessons Jewett offered were of the variety to make his student a more delightful "ornament" to her own parlor as well as to society in general. It is to Vassar's credit that he avoided such connotations or restrictions to the study of art at his college. He had announced in 1861 that his Art Gallery would illustrate the study of aesthetics, in Nature as well as Art. In doing so, he aligned art instruction with an intellectual exercise and, one assumes, a purpose higher than the acquisition of social skills. Benson Lossing further commended the Founder's insight in this regard when he described the facilities for music and art study at Vassar College:

> The aim of all musical instructions in Vassar College is, as in other departments, in keeping with the expressed desire of its Founder, which is rather to create and devleop a genuine love for all that is good and great in knowledge, and thereby cultivate the heart and discipline the mind of the student, than to spend precious time in the acquirement of expertness in mere recitation, performance, and execution.[12]

To Jewett's credit, it must be admitted that his ideas for a woman's college may have differed from his practices at a girl's school. It is also probable that his own concept of a the role of art in education matured as he talked to other educators in the course of developing Vassar College's curriculum.

Vassar's intention to use an art gallery for aesthetic instruction was not unprecedented, either. Again, such use of art objects can be found in an institution for girls, in particular that one administered by the Presbyterian minister Gorham D. Abbot. Abbot and his two brothers Jacob and Charles had been active in the realm of female education since the 1830s, and in 1843 they founded a "New Seminary for Young Ladies" in New York City. The success of the institution was such that they moved to larger quarters three times before finally settling on Union Square in 1848 and becoming the Spingler Institute. At this time Abbot's school enjoyed "a reputation possessed by no other institution for women in America."[13] Vassar sought Abbot's counsel in the early 1860s, and before this, Abbot was among a number of educators across the country who were polled by Milo Jewett in 1861 and asked to provide opinions on a wide range of topics related to women's education. Citing his pamphlets and the prospectus of the Spingler Institute as further elaboration of his ideas, Abbot answered Jewett's questions in short, pithy sentences. To the question "Best Means of Aesthetic Culture?" Abbot replied, "By Galleries of Art, Lectures & 'clinical,' instructions upon models."[14]

Abbot had in fact just a system in operation at his school. Courses in "linear and perspective drawing" were overseen by Thomas Seir Cummings, the eminent Secretary of the National Academy of Design, although in practice the instruction probably was given more frequently by his daughters Rebecca and Jane.[15] And on the walls of the Spingler Institute hung oil paintings and other works of art:

> In addition to the severer studies Dr. Abbot made much of Music and Art in his educational scheme. Vocal music entered largely into all departments of the school of life. The Chapel and the Halls were hung with exquisite paintings, to familiarize the mind with objects of Art and to cultivate the taste. Choice collections of copies of masterpieces by the eminent Roman copyist, Chevalier Chatalaine, were purchased abroad at a large cost, and made a picture gallery, which was open to all students.[16]

One can assume that the bulk of Abbot's collection consisted of these copies. Such copies of European masterpieces were commonplace in mid-19th century homes, for private collectors purchased copies much as we might buy color reproductions today. The number of art students travelling to Europe was great, and their lessons frequently entailed the specific copying of recognized masterpieces. Many a struggling art student had his Grand Tour financed by a patron back home who was eager to have, and willing to pay for, a Titian or Raphael to hang on his own walls.[17] Some private collectors even purchased copies deliberately, to ensure that they were not paying genuine prices for "Old Master" paintings of dubious origin.[18] Certain European paintings were famous enough even before the age of reproduction to warrant demand for copies in America, and surely Abbot commissioned many such works especially from M. Chatalaine.

Unfortunately, one cannot glean the titles of any specific artworks owned by Abbot from his institution's catalogues alone, although contemporary accounts tell us that they included "some of the choicest works of art to be found in this city."[19] But we do know that Abbot had his particular favorites, for his eulogizers saw fit to remark on the lessons and comfort he took from them. Chief among these was an illustrious cycle by Thomas Cole:

> Some of you will remember what a favorite with him was that peerless pictorial allegory, Cole's Voyage of Life. I have sometimes thought it was because he unconsciously felt in it a prophecy of his own life: the babe coming out of the dark cavernous past, . . . the youth oblivious of his immediate surroundings, and pressing forward, . . . the man, dauntless in the

swift rapids bearing him resistlessly toward, he knows not what new dangers, yet unfearing, because his guardian angel is his God, . . . the old man, waiting on the smooth and open sea, life's perils past, till the heavens shall receive him to themselves.[20]

Thomas Cole had painted this remarkable series of four paintings in 1839–1840 for the New York banker and collector Samuel Ward. Ward died in 1839 and his heirs sold the paintings to the American Art–Union in 1848, where they were offered as the grand prize for its lottery of the next year.[21] The lot fell to the lucky J. T. Brodt of Binghamton, but shortly after winning the four pictures, Brodt sold them to Abbot, who immediately hung them on the walls of the Spingler Institute. In 1852, Abbot decided to have the series engraved for more extensive distribution. After having the paintings copied so that they could be sent abroad to a European engraver, the patriotic decision was made to have an American do the job. James Smillie, the engraver whose burin had so successfully translated landscape paintings by Church, Durand, Kensett and others to the pages of *The Home Book of the Picturesque,* was chosen for the task. With the help of his son James David, he completed the task in four years. Abbot wrote a small pamphlet for the occasion, describing the above circumstances and the paintings' special qualities which merited their wider appreciation. His sentiments in this regard must have been formed in large part by witnessing the effect Cole's paintings had on the girls who passed by them each day:

> The happy influence they were found to exert, by their silent, yet constant teaching, in exercising the imagination, in cultivating and refining the taste, in moulding the sensibilities, and inspiring the soul with exalted and noble purposes of life, suggested the desirability of extending their influence, especially among the youth of our country.[22]

These words form an eloquent testimony to the positive effect of art on the student's development, and in fact, describe exactly the artistic experience that Matthew Vassar hoped to bestow upon his pupils. Abbot's art gallery and the uses to which he put it correspond too closely to Vassar's own for the similarity to be coincidental. Vassar had sought Abbot's counsel before his college opened, while Abbot was making plans for a women's college of his own. However, Abbot did not possess the financial resources of Vassar, and "National calamity [i.e., the Civil War], combined with private misfortune to prevent the consummation of his hope as it reached fruition."[23] Abbot deeded the plans for his college to Vassar, who incorporated them into the structure of his own. The actual content of this transaction has not been determined; but in any case, it was performed after the chartering of Vassar College and thus after the initial efforts of a group of men specifically selected by Vassar to fulfill his intentions for an art gallery.[24]

Although Vassar was not completely ignorant of artistic matters, nor lacking in an aesthetic sensibility of his own, he did not pretend to be an expert in this area. So among the Trustee Committees organized in February 1861 was one devoted to the Art Gallery, and composed of a rather august group of gentlemen. Along with John Thompson and Vassar's nephew John Guy Vassar, sat Benson J. Lossing, one of Dutchess County's first historians, whose publications included a *History of the Fine Arts* (1840), and Samuel F. B. Morse, inventor of the telegraph but also artist and educator in his own right, having helped to found the National Academy of Design in New York and later having served as the first instructor of painting and drawing at New York University. The Chairman of this Committee was the Reverend Elias Lyman Magoon, a Baptist minister from Albany, author of several books as well as a noted patron and connoisseur of art.[25]

The Committee made its first formal report in June of 1861, four months after its inception. Applauding Vassar's decision to include aesthetics in his curriculum and an art gallery among his facilities, they did not yet "suppose it needful, at this early day, to suggest much as to the filling up of the Gallery."[26] Rather, Chairman Magoon used the occasion to comment on aesthetics, nature, and art with his familiar pastorial eloquence. In closing, however, he and his Committee cautioned Vassar to approach the art gallery project carefully:

> Let every specimen be of the highest excellence in subject, material, and style. An original sketch of a dog's foot, however rough, if honest, is more profitable than the most elaborate copy of a saint's head.[27]

Over the next two years, efforts to fill the projected art gallery progressed, often, it seems, with little interference or curiosity from the appointed committee. In fact, the committee's insistence on original art works and their value to a teaching program was not always heeded by President Jewett or the Founder himself. Indeed, it seems that initial attempts for filling the gallery space ran exactly counter to the committee's recommendation, and more in line with conventional galleries of copied masterpieces not unlike Abbot's Roman copies. It also becomes evident that this activity was not always communicated to the proper Trustees, for it eventually became a source of deep contention.

In November of 1861, Matthew Vassar wrote to Sarah J. Hale, editor of the popular *Godey's Lady's Book,* telling her that "The Trustees are also availing themselves of the advantages of these war Times to purchase their Library, Works of Art, Mineral Cabinets, &c."[28] He also mentioned Jewett's tour of various educational institutions, both male and female, implying that the shape of Vassar Female College and its curriculum was not yet firm in all its details.

President Jewett in 1862 embarked upon a European tour, again to compare educational systems. While he was abroad, he also made the acquaintance of a Miss Emma C. Church, an American artist living in Rome. A few years later, in attesting to the necessity of female instructors at his college, Vassar told his Trustees that

> we have the testimony of our President that he finds the most distinguished student and copyist in Rome to be an American woman.[29]

Jewett had apparently gone to Rome in search of a copyist to equal M. Chatalaine, for Matthew Vassar wrote directly to Emma Church in Rome in November 1862:

> Should your first specimens be approved by the Board you may reasonable hope for an order for the Art Gallery of the College of some few thousands Dollars to be executed from Originals representative pictures to show the Characteristic excellency of your greatest master by an American Lady Artist.[30]

Church immediately began work on copying Guercino's *Incredulity of St. Thomas,* then as now in the Vatican Collections, Carlo Dolci's *Virgin and Child* in the Corsini Palace, and a very ambitious 119 x 76 inch canvas of Raphael's majestic *Foligno Madonna,* also in the Vatican.

Charles A. Raymond, another of Vassar's first advisors and in fact a rival for Jewett's position as Vassar's primary counsel, proposed yet another idea to Vassar in February of 1863. James Monroe Taylor (President of Vassar College from 1886 to 1914) describes this idea in his 1912 book *Before Vassar Opened:*

> There must be an art-gallery. A large expenditure, however, would be foolish. Buy a few pictures. Get a good painter as professor of art; engage all his time; let him paint pictures for the gallery. In the course of a few years there would be a fine collection.[31]

Taylor calls this an idea "calculated to appeal to a thrifty, self-made man, though in this case happily ineffective."[32]

By late 1863, however, at least one member of the official Committee on the Art Gallery was active. Samuel F. B. Morse wrote to Matthew Vassar on November 16 to tell him of an offer extended to him by a Mrs. Anne Toffey of Boston. Acting for the estate of E. P. Clark, Mrs. Toffey wondered if Vassar College might be interesting in purchasing his collection of engravings and watercolors. Vassar immediately wrote to Toffey and told her that the subject would be brought before the Executive Committee, whose next meeting would be held the following week. The Executive Committee did not include any member of the Committee on the Art Gallery, and so must have felt poorly qualified to pass judgment on such an important issue. Instead they asked Matthew Vassar to authorize a trip to Cambridge by Chairman Elias Magoon, who should visit the collection and ascertain its value. On November 23, Vassar wrote to both Toffey and Magoon, telling the former to expect a visit, and informing the latter of his wishes and mentioning his progress in securing copies from Emma Church.[33]

Magoon's reply to this request has been lost, but Matthew Vassar's response gives some clue to its content.

> Dear Doctor
> I have yours of yesterday, quite spicy and pointed, I don't blame you abit; I hope you don't me; you have good reasons why you cannot go to Cambridge to look after pictures;

this department has work.[d] bad, but do not blame me, as soon as I could I stop.[d] it, only 2 has come to hand, the other two ordered from Miss Church will not be finished before next fall. At our next meeting of our Board of Trustees I will tell you about matters.[34]

Magoon seemed more upset by Church's commissions than by Vassar's suggestion that he take time away from his ministerial duties to look at a collection of art. Unfortunately, none of Magoon's letters from this particularly delicate time remain, but the extent of the crisis can be inferred from Matthew Vassar's correspondence alone.

Immediately the tone of his letters to Church changed. On December 15, 1863, Vassar confessed to her that "this matter of buying pictures has given me some trouble."[35] Now rather than ordering additional paintings, Vassar told her that henceforth he would assume personally the cost of her third canvas (the copy of Raphael's *Foligno Madonna*), and present it to the College *gratis*. The adjustment in her commissions was indeed due to a misunderstanding concerning "acts that more properly belong[d] to the Committee on 'Fine Arts.' "[36] Magoon (and possibly Morse and Lossing) were upset by the manner in which these copies of European masterpieces had been commissioned and purchased from Church without consulting their Committee or securing its approval. Vassar suggested "jealousy" as a cause of this rift, but actually the character and tone of the projected Art Gallery itself were at stake. Writing to Church nine days later, Vassar told her of his Committee's investigation of the Clark collection (which had since been sold), and another collection of drawings and engravings from the estate of the Duke of Carsano at Naples. He also described "a little disorder in our Committee on 'Fine Arts' originating from trifling circumstances, but widening into a breach, followed by the resignation of the Chairman of that Committee, Doctor Magoon."[37]

Vassar was by no means pleased by this turn of affairs, and he begged Magoon to remain on the Board. Magoon in turn shot back a twelve-page reply to the Founder (again, this letter has not survived), outlining his convictions regarding the proper makeup and uses of a college art gallery. Vassar was impressed. He expressed his wish to pay a visit to Magoon in Albany, and although his health was poor, he managed such a trip on January 13th. Perhaps for the first time on that visit, Vassar cast his eyes upon Magoon's own private art collection—works that must have been hung from floor to ceiling in every room, in such quantity and of such quality that one critic writing for the New York journal *The Crayon* in 1856 deemed it "probably, the best collection in America."[38] Whatever Vassar's impression, the effect was immediate, for he wrote to Magoon upon his return to Poughkeepsie on January 15, 1864:

suffice it to say I want our College to *possess your Collections.*[39]

He also urged Magoon to revise his earlier twelve-page letter and present it as a report at the next Trustee meeting.

And so at that next meeting on February 23, 1864, the Committee on the Art Gallery produced its second formal report, this one prefaced by "a few suggestions on art, on Original Art, and on American Originality in art."[40] Obviously concerned by the amounts of energy and money spent on other college facilities, the report chided:

Large sums have been appropriated for buildings and other appliances, more or less artificial; but not one fostering breath has yet been breathed over what ought to be the central charm of the whole concern. Plaster casts, it may be, or sterile copies, or a mass of dead engravings, are suggested; but living, original, American art is quite out of view.[41]

To remedy this dire situation, the Committee made concrete suggestions.

First of all, we must have at least one hundred oil paintings, by as many different masters as possible, and so diversified in subject and treatment as to exemplify every feature of earth, water and sky, in all seasons and every light. Twenty of them may be choice specimens of Spanish, Italian, German, French, and English art, . . . But at least sixty must be first-rate transcripts of American landscape.[42]

To this core of "living, original, American art," the Committee recommended the addition of

at least one hundred water-color pictures . . . because, out of America, that is the best art intrinsically, and, for female culture, it is the best everywhere. . . . Armor. . . should be in our collection. Etruscan remains, Roman relics, and ancient coins, well authenticated, should likewise form component parts.

We must not only have the best written works on engraving and printing, but original illustrations of the same. . . . All the graver has cut, or the pen traced, to describe events or portray scenes connected with progressive culture, should be arranged in volumes, uniformly bound. . .[43]

Was it only coincidence that Elias Magoon's collection virtually duplicated the prescriptions outlined in this February report? It is possible that Magoon in January simply recommended that Vassar follow the same guildelines in assembling a college art collection that he himself followed when forming a private one. Magoon was later to insist that as late as June 1864, when he visited the College with the Founder and a group of Trustees, that he "had not the slightest intention of offering you my art Collection,[44] and that his final agreement to do so was reached only by "reluctant consent to part with treasures which no wealth can create."[45] Nonetheless, on June 6, 1864, Matthew Vassar paid Magoon $20,000.00 and purchased his full collection, consisting of oil and watercolor paintings—four of these watercolors by James Mallord William Turner—engravings, coins, a substantial library on art and architecture, and—most appealing to our eyes today—a group of some seventy-four landscape and genre paintings by contemporary American artists.

As patron and collector of art, and landscape painting in particular, Magoon quite literally embodied that union of nature and divinity that American artists of the Hudson River School practiced when they re-created the beauties of their native scenery on their canvasses. As images of the moral order and divine purpose that Magoon preached from his pulpit, the art in his collection served as a palpable example of the beauty and harmony that he found in the world and wished to point out to others. He echoed the sentiments of Gorham Abbot when he informed Matthew Vassar that a taste for art was

at once the most engrossing and ennobling, refining the imagination and fortifying the judgment, elevating emotion to the loftiest enthusiasm, and, at the same time, perfecting the critical faculty, under the joint influence of subjugated sense and sovereign reason.[46]

This was precisely the manner in which both ministers, and ultimately Matthew Vassar himself, foresaw the possibility of art "standing boldly forth as an educating force." Sarah J. Hale recognized this intent, and understood it as well as anyone at the time. In an editorial for her magazine in 1864, she applauded Vassar's plan for an art gallery, as it was articulated by Magoon in his Committee's report:

The Art Gallery, projected by the liberal directors, will be a stimulus to the originating mind so peculiarly American, which shows itself in painting and sculpture as well as mechanical inventions. And for those to whom nature has denied creative powers in the beautiful arts, such a gallery is even more necessary; by it, dormant tastes are awakened, and life assumes a new and refined aspect. The richness and beauty of nature are seen and sought for: the mind must go from "nature up to nature's God."[47]

Soon after it opened, the Art Gallery was reviewed in the *Poughkeepsie Eagle* by a journalist who, less poetically but no less admirably, recognized much of Vassar and Magoon's intent:

. . . The most interesting rooms, however, are the Picture Gallery and the Geological Cabinet. The former is hung with oil and watercolor paintings and drawings by some of the best and most celebrated artists in America and Europe, while in a prominent position is a life size portrait of Matthew Vassar, Esq., the founder. The pictures in this gallery, being selected for purposes of instruction, are of every possible variety in style and character, and present beauty of design, accuracy of drawing, clearness and delicacy of finish and richness of color in all their varied and attractive combinations.[48]

Vassar College had opened in September 1864, and its Founder died four years later while delivering his yearly address to the Trustees. But surely Vassar recognized before his death that his own dream to "apply some large portion of my estate to some benevolent object" had been admirably fulfilled, and that, as Magoon had predicted, "among other notable things about VASSAR FEMALE COLLEGE . . . By no means least fascinating are its treasures of Original Art."[49]

Notes

1. *The Yonkers Gazette,* April 25, 1874. Clipping from Vassar College Scrapbook, Vassar College Library.

2. Benson J. Lossing, *Vassar College and Its Founder* (New York: C. A. Alvord, 1867), p. 92.

3. For example, Lossing, p. 81. James Monroe Taylor quotes many of Jewett's letters with similar references (also to Brown and Union Colleges) in his book *Before Vassar Opened: A Contribution to the History of Higher Education of Women in America* (Boston and New York: Houghton Mifflin Company, 1912), pp. 95-6.

4. Jean Harris, *Collegiate Collections, 1776-1876* (exhibition catalogue, The John and Norah Warbeke Gallery Art Building, Mount Holyoke College, 1976), pp. 40-1. A chart on page 66 lists the dates of the establishment of art galleries and museums in U. S. colleges and universities that were chartered before 1876.

5. Matthew Vassar to Milo P. Jewett, December 29, 1856. Original letter in Vassar College Library.

6. Taylor, *op. cit.,* p. 89.

7. *Ibid.,* p. 92.

8. Taylor's book describes Jewett's character and influence in remarkable detail. His account is based on Jewett's correspondence as well as Jewett's unpublished account of the "Origin of Vassar College."

9. *Catalogue of the Cottage Hill Seminary for Young Ladies,* Poughkeepsie, 1863-1864.

10. *Catalogue of the Cottage Hill Seminary for Young Ladies,* Poughkeepsie, 1859-1860.

11. *Catalogue of the Cottage Hill Seminary for Young Ladies,* Poughkeepsie, 1855-1856.

12. Lossing, *op. cit.,* p. 168.

13. "Gorham Dummer Abbot," in *National Cyclopedia of American Biography,* vol. X (New York: James T. White & Company, 1909), p. 356.

14. Gorham D. Abbot to Milo P. Jewett, June 17th, 1861. Original letter in the Vassar College Library.

15. *The Abbot Memorial Book* (Poughkeepsie: Press of A. V. Haight, 1902), p. 55.

16. *Ibid.,* p. 44.

17. Neil Harris, *The Artist in American Society: The Formative Years, 1790-1860* (Chicago: University of Chicago Press, 1982), p. 79.

18. *Ibid.,* p. 104.

19. *The New York Tribune,* August 19, 1860. Quoted in *The Abbot Memorial Book,* p. 45.

20. Reverend Lyman Abbot, address given at a commemorative service for the late Rev. Gorham D. and Mrs. Rebecca S. Abbot, Church of the Covenant, New York, April 23, 1876. Quoted in *The Abbot Memorial Book,* p. 30.

21. Howard S. Merritt, Thomas Cole (exhibition catalogue, Memorial Art Gallery, University of Rochester, 1969), p. 35. Maybelle Mann suggests that the 7,000 new subscriptions to the American Art Union in 1849 were purchased in no small part in hopes of winning Cole's four paintings. See her article "The American Art Union: Missionaries to the Art World," *American Art and Antiques,* vol. 1, No. 1 (July-August 1978), p. 67.

22. Rev. Gorham D. Abbot, *Cole's Voyage of Life, A Series of Allegorical Pictures. . .,* New York, 1860.

23. *The Abbot Memorial Book,* p. 49.

24. The relation between Abbot and Vassar is a topic that would benefit greatly from further research. Though frequent mention is made of the contact between these two men, without knowing exactly when they met, it is impossible to determine the extent of Abbot's contributions to Vassar College. It is intriguing to speculate, however, on possibilities such as the one that Matthew Vassar chose the Reverend Elias Magoon to head his Committee on the Art Gallery in express emulation of Rev. Abbot's example.

25. The life of Magoon and his unique qualities as a collector of art will be explored extensively in the forthcoming exhibition catalogue *All Seasons and Every Light* (Poughkeepsie: Vassr College Art Gallery, 1983).

26. "Fine Art Report" (Report of the Committee on the Art Gallery), June 25, 1861. Manuscript in the Vassar College Library.

27. *Ibid.*

28. Matthew Vassar to Sarah J. Hale, November 13th, 1861. Quoted in Elizabeth Hazelton Haight, *The Autobiography and Letters of Matthew Vassar* (New York: Oxford University Press, 1916), p. 107.

29. Address to the Trustees, February 23, 1864. Quoted in *Communications to the Board of Trustees of Vassar College By Its Founder* (New York: Standard Printing and Publishing Company, 1886), p. 23.

30. Matthew Vassar to Miss Emma C. Church, November 21, 1862. Quoted in Haight, p. 107. All idiosyncracies of grammar and spelling in this and subsequent letters are Vassar's own.

31. Taylor, *op. cit.,* p. 149.

32. *Ibid.*

33. This information is culled from various letters written to and from Matthew Vassar between November 16 and November 23, 1863. Original letters in the Vassar College Library.

34. Matthew Vassar to Elias Lyman Magoon, November 28, 1863. Original letter in the Vassar College Library.

35. Matthew Vassar to Emma Church, December 15, 1863. Quoted in Haight, p. 119-20.

36. *Ibid.,* p. 119.

37. Matthew Vassar to Emma C. Church, December 24, 1863. Quoted in Haight, p. 122.

38. "Sketchings. Our Private Collections," *The Crayon, 3* (December 1856), p. 374.

39. Matthew Vassar to Elias L. Magoon, January 15, 1864. Quoted in Haight, p. 128.

40. "Report of the Committee on the Art Gallery of Vassar Female College," February 23, 1864. Reprinted in *Vassar College Art Gallery, Selections from the Permanent Collection* (Poughkeepsie, 1967), p. xi.

41. *Ibid.,* p. xii.

42. *Ibid.*

43. *Ibid.*

44. Elias Magoon to Matthew Vassar, July 16, 1864. Original letter in the Vassar College Library.

45. *Ibid.*

46. "Report of the Committee on the Art Gallery of Vassar Female College," p. xi.

47. [Sarah J. Hale], "The Art Gallery at Vassar College," *Godey's Lady's Book,* vol. 69, No. 8 (July 1864), p. 84.

48. Poughkeepsie Eagle, January 21, 1865. Clipping from Vassar College Scrapbook (originally kept by Matthew Vassar), in the Vassar College Library.

49. "Report of the Committee on the Art Gallery of Vassar Female College," p. xiii.

From Placentia to Troutbeck, Robber Rocks to Sylvania: Reflections on the *Deus Loci* and Literature in Dutchess County

Harry R. Stoneback
Professor of English, State University of New York at New Paltz

The task of the scholar invited to sketch the literary history of a county, the task of the lecturer who wishes to delight as well as teach, is fraught with difficulty. Such a mission leads over treacherous ground, yet above all, it offers the joy of discovery. The difficulties and joys I shall allude to in the course of these remarks, but I want to say at the outset what my sense of the treacherous ground is: I am here today, in the strictest sense, as an outlander, having come across the river from Ulster County, a terrain, geographical, historical and literary, which I know far better than Dutchess County. Thus this apologia has to do with the sins of omission I am about to commit, should I fail to mention this or that local poet who happens to be the ancestor or cousin or favorite of someone in this audience. Treacherous ground, indeed. So I shall simply say that I am here to celebrate Dutchess County and all of its writers, including all of them in a general blessing, and get on with the ceremony.

The first difficulty one encounters when speaking about such a topic as "The Literature of Dutchess County" is the decision as to just what to discuss. Should one be concerned with literary evocations of the place by travellers and sojourners? Or should one be concerned solely with the work of writers who were residents of Dutchess, even though their work may not in any obvious way reflect the fact? Or should attention be limited to writers who both lived here and in some fashion worked through their sense of place to compose something we might justly call Dutchess County Literature? Moreover, when the region to be discussed is as narrow as a county, are there any writers worth discussing? I am reminded here of the old anecdote about William Gilmore Simms, the prolific novelist and poet of nineteenth-century South Carolina. It seems that just before the Civil War a secessionist convention was meeting in Charleston and the thoughtful confederates there assembled made the following resolutions:

Be it resolved: There *will* be a literature of the South.
Be it further resolved: William Gilmore Simms will be asked to write it.

Now Dutchess County has not had a Simms, and perhaps we are thankful for that, but when I began to work up this address I found myself playing variations on this theme. Resolved: there is a literature of Poughkeepsie. Further resolved: Josh Billings has written it. Or, resolved: there is a literature of Vassar College—Lizzie W. Champney has written it. Yet upon further research and reflection it became apparent that there *is* a rich literary heritage in Dutchess County, and that it is in crucial ways tied to the land, to the county as a numinous place.

Before we look at writers who have lived here, let us remind ourselves that in terms of the nineteenth-century literary milieu Dutchess was very much on the map. The Lyceum circuit regularly brought major writers such as Emerson and Twain, and such immensely popular figures as Artemus Ward. When Ward lectured in Poughkeepsie in 1865 "he took with him on the stage, and let loose in the hall, a number of live mice which scampered in all directions, causing...great consternation among the ladies."[1] This, from the essays of Joel Benton, an important Dutchess County writer. Benton records that Ward's famous *mot* was highly successful in Poughkeepsie: "Brigham Young's religion is singular, but his wives are plural. He is a kind husband, and a numerous father. The pretty girls in Utah mostly marry Young." Benton does not record the presence of Poughkeepsie's own Josh Billings at this lecture, though they were friends, and if Billings was in town, he was surely there. Ward must have been an amusing sight on the waterfront the next day when he boarded the boat for Newburgh. He carried a box fourteen feet long and six inches wide, marked "Artemus Ward—His Valise." There was activity elsewhere in the county, too; Amenia, for example, had an active "literary bureau" and among the figures who lectured there were Margaret Fuller, Horace Greeley, and Mark Twain. Many of these distinguished visitors were entertined at Joel Benton's place in Amenia after their lectures.[2]

Aside from being an important stop on the Lyceum circuit, Dutchess called forth praise from the pens of numerous travellers and visitors. One was the rather remarkable "child-poet," Margaret Miller Davidson, the subject of a biography by Washington Irving. She had this to say of a visit to Dutchess in 1836:

> I write to inform you of our safe arrival at one of the most lovely spots in this beautiful and healthy country. The drive from the boat at Poughkeepsie was delightful; the scenery ever changing, ever beautiful. We arrived at Lithgow...Oh it is a lovely spot...hills crowned with the richest foliage, valleys sprinkled with flowers and watered with winding rivulets and a mild salubrious air as of Paradise.[3]

Incidentally, our child-genius was thirteen years old when she composed that bit of landscape set-piece. For another telling image of Dutchess, later in the nineteenth century, we turn to the autobiographical recollections of Henry James, who had numerous family and social connections in the Hudson Valley. Recalling his childhood visits to a kinsman's home near Rhinebeck, he evoked:

> . . .the house and all its accessories. . .in especial the great bluff of the Hudson on which it stood. . .[we] were surely all gentle and generous together, floating in such a clean light social order, sweetly proof against ennui.[4]

This compelling image, with its Jamesian resonance, provides a touchstone for reflection on the life of one "social order" in Dutchess. James alluded to the county elsewhere in his work, including honorable mention in the title of a neglected story, "Miss Gunton of Poughkeepsie." Of course, the story is not set in Poughkeepsie, since Miss Gunton is yet another American innocent in Europe. But it is in order here to ponder his choice of Poughkeepsie as her point of origin. James had complained in print about the dullness of American place-names, as compared to European place-names, which seemed to spring straight from the soil. Thus his choice here of Poughkeepsie, surely one of the most memorable and telluric place-names in American toponymy. This Jamesian concern with place-names touches directly on one of the implicit themes of this address, as suggested in the title.

For our final image of Dutchess taken from the work of non-resident writers, we turn to Edith Wharton, who had connections and frequently visited here, who, in her novel *Hudson River Bracketed,* gave us one of the best-known images of the region. This novel is, in one sense, a portrait of the artist as a very young, very innocent man. The opening words of the novel identify him:

> By the time he was nineteen Vance Weston had graduated from the College of Euphoria, Illinois...had spent a week in Chicago, invented a new religion, and edited for a few months a magazine called *Getting There.*[5]

Clearly, he is Miss Wharton's candidate for the typical American hero: rootless, pastless, innocent, a callow lover of "Progress." His very name calls up a bemused notion of the West and simplistic ideas of advancement. So he comes east to the Hudson Valley, hoping to make it as a writer in New York. He lives with his cousins in Paul's Landing (probably Fishkill Landing). The first movement of the novel turns on his discovery that there is indeed a past, and that it expresses itself in the Hudson Valley through architecture such as Downing's, through literature, landscape, family and rootedness in place. It is a splendid satirical moment when the future-directed Western boy confronts the old house and all that it represents. Wharton writes:

> It all seemed part of the incomprehensible past to which...the house belonged, a past so remote, so full of elusive mystery, that Vance's first thought was: "Why wasn't I ever told about the Past before?" (p. 61–2)

This scene will serve to remind us that a sense of the past, brooding over the present, informing and shaping the present and the future, is one of the richest treasures in the Dutchess County storehouse of legacies. For the rest, the novel also gives us some of the best architecture and landscape descriptions we have had here, including the memorable sunrise scene high above the Hudson.

Now we must consider writers who have had more enduring associations with Dutchess, who have had deeper intimacy with the *deus loci*, the spirit of this place. James Kirke Paulding, one of the very first important American writers, was born in Dutchess in 1778, grew up around Tarrytown, went off to the great stages of New York and Washington where he enacted the central dramas of his career in literature and politics—as novelist, poet, essayist, Secretary of the Navy—before he established himself as a gentleman farmer in Hyde Park for the last fifteen years of his life. He died at his estate in Hyde Park in 1860. Among his important works are *The Dutchman's Fireside* and his travel tour de force, *New Mirror For Travellers*, a deightful account of manners and scenery in the Hudson Valley. But for our purposes today, I suggest we take a look at the correspondence of Paulding, especially the Hyde Park letters, for these constitute one of the joyful discoveries I alluded to in my opening remarks: nowhere, I think, is there a better evocation of the life of the gentleman farmer in Dutchess County in the mid-nineteenth century.

On the fourteenth of October, 1845, he wrote to his old friend and soon-to-be Columbia County neighbor, Martin Van Buren, another gentleman farmer:

> I have the pleasure to inform you that I have...purchased a place that suits me exactly, except that I have paid a little more for it, than I wished. . .[it] is very beautifully situated at Hyde Park, commanding a beautiful view of your favourite Katskills.[6]

He boasts about his water supply, his view of the river and his "find Bed of Muck;" he declares that he anticipates "making a figure at the agricultural Fair, and gaining a prize for a thumping radish or Mammoth Pumpkin." (p. 408) His next letter to Van Buren answers his friend's many questions about the place:

> It is called Placentia . . . contains fifty acres, all in a lawn lying between the road and the River . . . The House is just what I wanted, and all the out-buildings in good order, and admirably disposed . . . It is about a mile and a half from the village of Hyde Park & the Landing, and there are three or four good neighbors . . . a very charming Spot. (p. 410)

He complains again that he has paid too much for it, though he is immensely pleased with the place. The price?—$19,000. Subsequent letters to Van Buren Provide a full record of the activities of farming and husbandry in Dutchess County in the 1840s. There is much talk of clearing, plowing, planting, weeding, harvesting, livestock-tending and ambitious new land-projects. In high-spirited catalogues of the bounty of his place, he boasts of his salads, radishes, potatoes, mince pies, sausages, head cheese, and above all, his asparagus. Van Buren says he is sending downriver to Paulding twenty bushels of his potatoes, the finest anywhere. Paulding responds, thanking him for the potatoes, and launching into a tall-tale account of the fertility of his piece of the Garden of America:

> We sowed a field of oats, some time ago, and it came up the very next morning...I think of floating You up a Small Raft of Asparagus by Water, as it is too large to go by Land, and I could realize a great profit in it, if it would only make good Boards and Plank. As to our Sallad, You will be I presume not a little envious, when you learn, that when Lazzy Hopper, our Factotum, went to gather some for dinner the other day, he found two of his children, snugly ensconced, among the leaves of one of the heads, where they had sheltered themselves from the rain. (p. 431)

He repeatedly invokes, both seriously and humorously, the notion of *otium cum dignitate*, the classical ideal of the peaceful rural life with dignity and repose, which I offer here as another touchstone for our image of Dutchess County. In one letter, he catalogues misadventures on his farm, complains of lazy hired hands, of Durham calves fattening themselves on muslin curtains, then tells Van Buren:

> I earnestly hope the adverse Fates, who doubtless envied me the possession of such a charming place as Placentia, have let you alone in the mean time, and that you enjoy otium cum dignitate, which means otium come dig potatoes. (p. 417)

Indeed the letters are filled with reminders that rural life is not all a matter of gentlemanly leisure, that bountiful harvests are purchased with blistered hands and "perspiring most gloriously" (p. 434), that the earthy dignity and honor which accompany the *otium* are in fact earned with hard labor. He rails against new farm machinery:

> The accursed Antediluvian weeds brought to life by the infernal Sub-Soil Plough, the inventor of which in my opinion deserves to be obliged to drag his own vehicle through a Carolina Swamp. (p. 486)

He complains about a whole host of afflictions, including especially his immense crop of "*Damned*elions:" "I feel most particular satisfaction in sallying forth with my Gold headed cane, and smiting them sorely hip and thigh." (p. 436) In the winter, however, there is repose and he tells Van Buren that he has passed the happiest winters of his life in Hyde Park. His letters also suggest his sense of community, his relations with neighbors, his church activities at St. James Episcopal, his involvement with county fairs. He urges Van Buren to come downriver while the sleighing is still good, to attend "a great Firemans Ball next week at Hyde Park where we shall have all the Elite of Salt Point, Crum Elbow and New Guinea." (p. 420) In the winter, too, he has more time for his primary occupation: he writes plays, rewrites old novels, assists his son, William Paulding—another Dutchess County writer—in the finish and publication of his work. There are letters to one William Wilson, a bookseller, publisher and poet in Poughkeepsie, concerning literary matters, and similar letters to James Fenimore Cooper. With his old friend Washington Irving, he commiserates over the infernal railroad that is about to destroy their river repose. There are letters, too, to men in the world of public affairs, such as John C. Calhoun, to whom he writes complex letters about the fate of the United States. To James K. Polk, in the White House, he celebrates the richness and fertility, the physical and moral energy of America, asserting in a resonant passage: "The moment in which Columbus first caught sight of this Continent was fraught with consequences, greater and more lasting than ever emanated from any human being since the fall of Adam." (p. 414) What I wish to suggest here is that Paulding's immersion in the agrarian life of Dutchess County was not a retirement from the world of American letters, politics and destiny, but in fact an affirmation of that experience, a deepening of his vision of the American Adam in the Garden of the New World. Indeed, when he writes to Evert A. Duyckinck about the "noble Harvest to be reaped in this New World of boundless space and unexhausted Fertility," when he assails the "sickly affectation" and Europeanizing of most writers of his day, when he asserts "Let [the writer] plant his foot firmly on his own native soil, and he may grow up a Tree of Centuries," Paulding is speaking both as one of the earliest and most eloquent advocates of a truly American literature and as a Dutchess County farmer. (p. 454) Placentia, then, nurtured his vision of the rooted man and writer, the regionalist who knows the only true path to the universal.

Following a path now with some degree of spatial and temporal coherence, we move downriver to Poughkeepsie, where this city's best-known writer, Josh Billlings (Henry Wheeler Shaw), settled in 1854. Billings was a native of Massachusetts, yet his local connections were substantial: he was a real-estate salesman and auctioneer here, and a politician who served as Alderman from the Fourth Ward. He began his literary career in Poughkeepsie, contributing epigrams and essays to the *Daily Press* and the weekly *Poughkeepsian*, at first using the pseudonym "Si Sledlength." He also began his highly successful lecturing career while a resident of Poughkeepsie. Literary fame eventually carried him to New York in the mid–1860s, though the exact date of his departure from Poughkeepsie is variously reported as 1866 or 1867. (Perhaps a closer look at local records would clarify the date and precise nature of his deracination from Dutchess.) At any rate, what concerns us here is that one of the best-known literary humorists of the nineteenth century began his career in the local press. I would suggest, moreover, that his rural wit owes a good deal to his immersion in Dutchess County life and to his pre-literary vocations—what better preparation for a writer who would purvey country wisdom and earthy values than the vocation of real-estate salesman (properly construed, that is)? And what better apprenticeship for a man much concerned with the flavor of folk speech than that of auctioneer? Poughkeepsie, then, figures implicitly and explicitly in his work.

Here are a few Billings aphorisms ("affurisms"):

Cherries are good, but they are too mutch like sucking a marble with a handle tew it.
Peaches are good, if you don't git enny ov the pin-feathers into yure lips.
When bobolinks sing their mouths git as full ov musik as a man's does of bones who eats
　　　fried herring for breakfast.[7]

If such aphorisms may be said to express implicitly the Dutchess flavor of Billings, there are also passages which deal explicitly with the region. Here, in a burlesque advertisement, Billings mocks the real-estate profession:

I kan sell for eighteen hundred and thirty-nine dollars, a pallas, a sweet and pensive retirement, lokated on the virgin banks ov the Hudson...The land is luxuriously divided by the hand of natur and art...The mansion iz ov Parian marble, the porch iz a single diamond, set with rubiz...the floors are ov rosewood, and the ceilings are more butiful than the starry vault of heavin. Hot and cold water bubbles and squirts in evry apartment, and nothing is wanting that a poet could pra for, or art could portray...Here poets have cum and warbled their laze—here skulptors hav cut, here painters have robbed the scene ov dreamy landskapes. . .upward and downward, the eye catches far away, the magesta and slow grander ov the Hudson. As the young morn hangs like a cutting ov silver from the blu brest ov the ski, an angel may be seen each night dansing with golden tiptoes on the green. (N.B. This angel goes with the place). . .For more full deskripshun, read Ovid's Art ov Luv, or kall. . .on Josh Billings, Real Estate Agent. (p. 78)

While the excessive use of "eye dialect," the non-functional cacography, may be distasteful to the modern reader, it was the fashionable mode in his time and, in fact, Billings employed it against his better judgment. Our concern is with the spirit of the piece, which offers an excellent commentary on Dutchess County real estate, a most timely satire of that mode—if you don't think it's timely, read the Dutchess entries in tomorrow's *New York Times* real estate section.

For a Billings composition which echoes another local feature—trout streams—one might have a look at his poem, "Sum Very Blank Verse—The Negro and the Trout," which though cast in his comic cacography is quite an effective evocation of man in nature, and of a pastime dear to Billings, as to many Dutchess fishermen. Even in 1884, the year before his death and many years after he left Poughkeepsie, Dutchess informed his work. An interviewer asked him what his vices were:

"None."
"Have you any virtues?"
"Several."
"What are they?"
"I left them up at Poughkeepsie..."
"What professions do you like best?"
"Auctioneering, base-ball and theology..."
"What is your worst habit?"
"The coat I got last in Poughkeepsie." (p. 28)

Billings is, then one of our own here in Hudson Valley, with a strong sense of place manifested throughout his almanacs and aphorisms and essays, and we should claim him and rediscover him, in spite of the fact that his brand of mangled orthography has long been out of fashion. Indeed the cacography is superfluous to the effects of this work, for he is, at his best, an imagistic poet and philosopher of the rural scene.

Now we must move out Route 44 to Amenia and just beyond to Leedsville and Troutbeck, surely one of the most remarkable places—with its two centuries of agrarian, literary and cultural associations—not just in Dutchess but in any county anywhere. I can scarcely do it justice here, for it deserves several lectures devoted entirely to the spirit of place, to the *deus loci* of Troutbeck. First of all, there are the Bentons: Myron, his brother Charles and their cousin Joel, all of them men of letters with deep Dutchess County roots. Henry Noble MacCracken christened the Leedsville area "Bentonland," and observed that the Bentons attempted to create a little Concord there. Charles published numerous essays and several books, including *As Seen From The Ranks: A Boy in the Civil War,* which has some engaging scenes of recruit camps in Poughkeepsie and follows the 150th N.Y.S. Volunteers, Dutchess County Regiment, through the war. Joel's numerous essays and books include volumes of literary criticism such as *Persons and Places, Emerson As A Poet, In the Poe Circle,* and on a more local note, *Amenia Seminary Reunion,* which reminds us that though he was a figure on the New York literary scene, he was deeply Dutchess County, too. He loved the Amenia area and maintained his residence at Leedsville, in Century Cottage (next door to Troutbeck). Joel Benton's long white hair and his resemblance to Tennyson, as the New York press observed, "made the aged poet a figure to be remarked" in New York literary circles. Yet he was not too busy in the great world of letters to deliver an address and a poem at the Amenia Seminary Reunion in 1906. He spoke of the spell of the waters of the enchanted region—a recurrent motif in what might be called the matter of Troutbeck—and asserted that once you drank of these waters "you were held to the place." He read a poem by one Dr. Horatio N. Powers and one of his own composed for the occasion, both of which celebrated the spell of that "charmed valley."

It is Myron Benton, however, with whom I am most concerned here, the master and namer of Troutbeck. He borrowed the name from one of Coleridge's favored numinous places in the Lake District and applied it aptly to his Leedsville homestead, where the becks, the little brooks, as well as the Webutuck River are indeed trouty, indeed embeckoning. For the better part of a century this numinous place and its presiding genius would nod, summon, truly beckon writers and artists and lovers of nature. The first was Myron Benton, who never published a book in his lifetime, yet from his family farm in Leedsville sent out waves of influence and sympathetic vibrations to the world of letters for half a century: correspondent and acquaintance of Emerson, recipient of Thoreau's last letter, described by Edwin Arlington Robinson as "a true son of the earth in the very best sense," by Sinclair Lewis as one of the "genius loci" of America, by Lewis Mumford as a poet-farmer who "nourished this land with [his] love," who dwelled "in beauty" like a Wordsworth character.[8] The detached literary historian might say that Myron Benton was a competent minor poet and essayist who published in some of the major journals of his day, yet, because of his attachment to the land, his immersion in his rural Dutchess County place, never entered the literary fray with sufficient ambition. John Burroughs, his best friend and famous Ulster County neighbor, corresponded with Benton for forty years and made frequent allusions to him in his work as a kind of ideal, the embodiment of the poet-farmer as genius loci. In addition, Burroughs was an admirer of Benton's poetry, praising in such poems as "Haying," "Embowered," and "The Mowers," a "genuine love of nature, closer and finer observation of her, and a more skillful touch in bringing out her charms" than any other poet of the time.[9] Burroughs also admired the place, what Benton had made of his family farm: "The ideal farm and country home . . . the most beautiful farm I have ever seen."[10] This is in part a function of the place itself, which helps to explain why the Bentons had for many years, in Myron's words, "hugged the soil close...[in an] intense local attachment...fostered through many generations."[11] (One thinks here of Lawrence Durrell's dictum: "Character is a function of landscape.") But the spirit of the place is also the result of Benton's loving work as horticulturalist, landscape gardener, amateur architect and preservationist, in short, composer of the complete milieu of place. Here is Burroughs again:

> Mr. Benton is a poet who writes his poetry in the landscape as well as in books. He is a beautifier of the land. One such lover of nature in every neighborhood would soon change the aspect of the whole country. Planter of trees and vines, preserver of old picturesque cottages, lover of paths and streams . . . historian and portrayer of big trees, collector of local relics and seeker and cultivator of all that gives flavor and character to a place, Mr. Benton is the practical poet of whom the country everywhere needs many more.[12]

He is, in short, a prime candidate for the genius loci of Dutchess County, the presiding spirit of this *locus amoenus.* There is no time here to discuss his work, but I recommend a look at the posthumously published volume, *Songs of the Webutuck,* as well as *Four Days on the Webutuck River,* the delightful account by his brother Charles of a journey they took on that stream, rich with echoes of Thoreau's *Week on the Concord and Merrimac Rivers.* When Benton died in 1902,

Burroughs made this entry in his journal: "A man of fine literary taste . . . a born countryman and lover of the soil . . . a man with the virtues and charm of rural things, keeping their traditions and legends, making much of them."[13] Again, some years later, Burroughs composed what must serve here as benediction for Myron Benton's Troutbeck: "The spirit of the place begat Myron Benton, and he left his stamp upon it in a way that will long endure."[14]

If you will allow me to be personal, as my grandfather used to say, I will add here my testimony that indeed it has endured. One of the joys of preparing this lecture was my discovery of Troutbeck. I had long known about it from reading Burroughs and the Bentons, but I had never sought it out since I thought that it must be all gone by now, even the magical spirit of the place. Thus, I approached the matter obliquely, fearing the worst. On the opening day of trout season, a fine Good Friday morning several weeks ago, I drove over to rural Dutchess in the first light and followed the sunrise road to the upper reaches of the Webutuck, Myron Benton's beloved stream. Taking my pilgrimage to Troutbeck slowly, entering the land with great care and precision, invoking the *deus loci,* I fished my way down that lovely stream, taking two fine trout, and arrived at last at Troutbeck. There I found that the numinous place endures, that it has spoken to a number of other writers since the Bentons—including Joel Spingarn and Lewis Mumford. The net result of that fishing pilgrimage, then, was an affirmation of history and place, a delightful interview with Honor Tranum—Joel Spingarn's daughter—and Joseph Flaherty, the present owner, and contact with Lewis Mumford, who still lives and writes at Leedsville. These names represent the next generations of the matter of Troutbeck.

Joel Spingarn first came to Troutbeck as a seasonal renter but fell so much under its spell that he bought it, enlarged and improved it, extended the farm until it took in nearly a thousand acres. At the beginning of his Troutbeck period, Spingarn was a brilliant young professor at Columbia University, an important literary critic and a minor poet, already having achieved, as Mumford has observed, "something of the immortality that comes with legend."[15] Not long after, he was fired from Columbia, and the ensuing controversy issued in his publication, *A Question of Academic Freedom,* which remains a touchstone on the question. It is tempting to see his retreat to Troutbeck as an escape, a flight from the world of affairs to the rural life of *otium cum dignitate.* But this is not at all the case. In fact, Spingarn had very definite notions about living a life of action, of participating in the *civitas,* the community and the nation.[16] One of his first acts upon establishing himself in Leedsville was to purchase the *Amenia Times,* the local paper which had been founded in 1852 by Joel Benton. Spingarn renamed it the *Harlem Valley Times,* the name it carries today. He regarded this as an essential step in his program of regional and community involvement. He also established the Amenia Field Day, which he described as an experiment in "co-operative recreation . . . managed by the whole community and free for all." [17] This Troutbeck version of a Renaissance Country Fair suggests, according to his biographer, Spingarn's "peculiar desire to combine noblesse oblige with folk democracy." (p. 59) Equally important, and in keeping with his vision of the local and the universal, he remained very much involved in national affairs. In 1908 he ran for Congress and lost. He was one of the founding fathers of the NAACP and was president of the organization until his death in 1939. Numbered among the men, outside the field of letters, who have paid tribute to Spingarn are W. E. B. Dubois and Justice Thurgood Marshall, who lived for a time at Troutbeck. The Spingarn Medal has been awarded annually since 1915 "for the highest achievement of an American Negro." (Recipients have included everybody from Hank Aaron to Jackie Robinson, Alvin Ailey to Paul Robeson, Ralph Bunche to Medgar Evers, and a roll call of the most important black writers, including James Weldon Johnson, Charles W. Chesnutt, Langston Hughes, and Richard Wright.) Among the more remarkable events that have transpired at Troutbeck (where John Burroughs first read Whitman, etc.) was the Amenia Conference on racial problems, convened by Spingarn in 1916. It was something of a grand camp meeting concerned with the direction racial affairs would take in America in the new age. W. E. B. Dubois described the conference as a "landmark in the history of the emancipation of the American Negro." (p. 61) Dubois was impressed with both Spingarn and the spirit of the place: Amenia, he said, was "small, important, complete;" Troutbeck emanated a "sense of utter friendship and intimate memory." (pp. 58–59) Seventeen years later, with the country deep in depression and talk of revolution everywhere, Spingarn called the second Amenia Conference. He was concerned that the movement for racial equlity was falling into the hands of the Marxists, and he detested communism as he did all forms of dogmatism. To many of the Marxists, the newly radicalized liberals and literati at Troutbeck in 1933, he must have seemed something of an anachronism. Anachronistic he may have been, though I rather think not; yet, surely,—and this is more to the point here—he was never anachoristic, never a man out of his place.

But this chapter of his career jumps ahead of the course. He served in World War I, from which he emerged as a lieutenant colonel; he returned to Troutbeck and sank his roots there ever more deeply in the ensuing years. (He was known to his neighbors and is still remembered today in Amenia as "Colonel Spingarn.") He was indeed intensely patriotic, a fact his Marxist friends could not comprehend, a fact which went hand in hand with his profound local attachment. In the 1920s he continued to publish poems, literary criticism and political essays; he also published a series of ten booklets, the "Troutbeck Leaflets," which are, I think, among the most important Dutchess County publications. They were printed in limited editions and each bore Spingarn's characteristic logo: "A series devoted to a single spot of American earth and to those who have touched its life." That is to say, if I may translate, they were published under the aegis of and in tribute to the *deus loci* of Troutbeck. It is a unique series, not just in Dutchess County literature but in American letters. It includes works devoted to John Burroughs, the Bentons, Troutbeck, as well as Charles Benton's *Four Days on the Webutuck River*. In addition, there are works by Lewis Mumford, W. E. B. Dubois, an unpublished essay by Walt Whitman; introductions were written by such eminent writers as Sinclair Lewis, Edwin Arlington Robinson and Vachel Lindsay, all of whom paid tribute to Spingarn's "single spot of American earth" rubric.

As the years passed at Troutbeck, Spingarn fell deeply under the spell of place, if we may judge from his turn in his last decade to horticulture and landscape gardening. He published, for example, an essay on Henry Winthrop Sargent and the early history of landscape gardening in Dutchess County, and a dozen or so scholarly articles on clematis. His literary friends viewed with some alarm this turn in his career; Lewis Mumford thought it somewhat ironic that in the end this poet and philosopher, "this soldier and thinker was known throughout the world as the chief authority on—clematis!" (p. 73) This suggests John Burroughs on Myron Benton, who gave more of himself to his farm and garden than to literature. Such are the dangers, such are the joys, I reckon, of enchanted places. At least this is my reading of Spingarn's career and his love of Troutbeck. One last detail: when he died in 1939 his will left this injunction for his wife Amy to fulfill—erect a memorial to declare their love for Dutchess County. I've not yet located this memorial, but the quest continues.

Of the many writers and artists who came to visit Spingarn at Troutbeck, some of whom stayed in the various cottages and houses in his ideal community, his garden of the creative spirit, the one who stayed the longest and the one who has written the most is, of course, Lewis Mumford. I consider it good policy to avoid capsule statements about living writers, but let us note here that Mr. Mumford, whose bibliography in the National Union Catalog runs to 100 entries, who is known to many of us as an architectural critic, city planner, aesthetician, philosopher, author of a magnum opus on the machine, known to some of us as writer, poet and sometime playwright, and known to others as the "preeminent prophet and ecohumanist" in the world today (as I recently heard him described)—let us make it a matter of record in this year of the Tercentennial, 1983, that Lewis Mumford is *the* Dutchess County writer. It must be the task of some future scholar with an adequate theoretical comprehension of regionalism, with sufficient catholicity *and* local sense, to interpret Mumford's career in terms of his profound attachment to place, to Leedsville, to Dutchess County. I can only assert that if we follow what he has had to say about space and time, architecture and the arts, regionalism and nationalism, sticks and stones, disintegration and renewal, the conditon of man and the conduct of life, we will find that among the articles of his faith for living, to borrow yet another of his titles, we will discover an enduring concern with sense of place, past, community. These crucial senses are suggested by his more than half century's residence at Leedsville, next door to Troutbeck. I do not invite the Faulknerian notion of a writer chronicling the universe through explicit immersion in his "postage stamp" of local soil, since Dutchess County rarely figures explicitly in his work. But I do suggest that some local sense of Dutchess is the presiding genius behind his work. This may be a rather startling claim, and Mumford readers around the country and the world might protest. Let it stand. For it seems to me that his views on the "open synthesis," the "triumph over systems," the "affirmation of organic life," views which, he says, provide the "key to my whole thought and life," are bound up with the rooted notions of past, place, community that I am concerned to elucidate here.[18]

If we wish to hear in Mumford's words what this place means to him, we might turn to his moving biography of his son, *Green Memories,* which evokes the spell of Leedsville. Also there are specifically local passages in his autobiography as well as in an unpublished manuscript entitled "The Story of Troutbeck."[19] There he writes:

> There are places so warmed by human companionship that they have taken on a human character of their own, and their story is a special kind of human biography. Troutbeck is such a place . . . the visible result of a long collaboration between men and nature. Many people have loved this place and each generation has added something to testify to that love. This sense of time past, which hovers like the smell of wildgrape blossoms in the air, gives also a sense of potential lives to come—people who will claim the landscape with the same sort of love and make their own contribution to it . . . (pp. 2, 6)

Like the Bentons and John Burroughs before him, Mumford praises the waters of the celebrated spring and the domesticated trout who dwell there. He salutes Spingarn, who "fell in love not merely with the place but the spirit that pervaded it," who "brought together the living past of this homestead with an equally vital present." Of the house itself, Mumford observes: "After a period of architectural experiment that has turned the dwelling house into a goldfish bowl or terrarium, Troutbeck offers a quality many people are beginning to appreciate again today: it has an interior. Nestling under a hill, secure against even visual intruders, this house cultivates its innerness . . . gives a sense of being snug, protected, inviolate." Yet there are moments when walking around Troutbeck, he says, when "one remembers Chekhov's *The Cherry Orchard,* and wonders whether its fate is to be that of so many country houses in Europe and America: to become the rural outpost of some metropolitan institution, or to be broken up like a suburban subdivision into building lots." I must say that I had the same feeling, the same fear when I visited Troutbeck, for I had heard that it was now "an executive retreat." When I arrived the executives of *The New York Times* were there in force. Yet, after I talked with the hospitable current owners, who acquired it from the Spingarn estate a few years ago, my fears for the future of the place were eased: here were men who loved and respected the place, who were clearly in tune with the *deus loci* of Troutbeck, who would preserve, cherish and nurture it and carry it safely into the next century. I wanted to leave my Webutuck trout as an offering to the *deus loci,* but decided against it, not wishing on that particular day to be taken for one of Shakespeare's lunatic poets.

Before we conclude, a brief excursion to the southeastern corner of Dutchess is necessary, saluting in passing the county's preeminent journalist, the late Lowell Thomas. I would like to be able to say here that Thomas's work was somehow informed by blithe Dutchess, but if it was, I have not yet found the evidence. In a long list of books—*With Lawrence in Arabia, With Allenby in the Holy Land, Seeing Mexico With Lowell Thomas, Seeing Canada,* India, Japan—you name it—with Lowell Thomas—we nowhere find "With Thomas in Dutchess," or "Seeing Dutchess County With Lowell Thomas." Indeed he was, in the words of another of his book titles, a rolling stone. Perhaps the closest he came to the local spirit, was in his *The New York Thruway Story,* and I fear that is the wrong spirit as well as the wrong side of the river.

At any rate, we pass Quaker Hill and go out to Robber Rocks, the old rundown farmhouse where the writers William Slater and Susan Jenkins Brown moved in the 1920s. While there was no formal writers' colony here, this area saw the convergence of a number of important writers, including Hart Crane, Malcolm Cowley, Caroline Gordon and Allen Tate. None of them were locals, none of them were autochthons, "sprung from the land itself"—indeed few Dutchess County writers have been autochthonous. Rather, they were potential anachthons, if I may coin a term, writers seeking a home and a connection to the land. Put more prosaically, they came for the reason New Yorkers have always fled the city and retreated to rural Dutchess: because it was cheap, because it was far enough away yet still close enough to the city to pursue their careers. Here is Susan Jenkins Brown's commentary on the winter of 1925–26:

The Tates had come to Pawling in November and by the time of Hart's arrival in December the Brown and Tate families were settled in for the winter. We enjoyed our country life, even though we were snowed in for months, and the flivver was useless. For long stretches we got our milk, butter and eggs on skis and snowshoes [from neighboring farmers]...But we did not lack company. The Tates had frequent house guests who often arrived from Pawling station in a onehorse open sleigh.[20]

Susan Brown has told me that in those days there was much talk among that group of young ambitious writers of settling there permanently, establishing a community of the arts in Southern Dutchess. Something like that did happen, ultimately, although it did not long include the two major figures—Hart Crane and Allen Tate. Crane loved the rural life, chopping wood, building fires, drinking with local farmers, and he dreamed of buying his own farm there; he even borrowed money, several times, to buy such a farm, but he never did. Given the pattern of his life and his imminent tragic end in the Gulf of Mexico, the longed-for Dutchess home was not to be. Still, Dutchess finds its way into his masterpiece, *The Bridge,* especially in the "Quaker Hill" section of the poem.

As for Allen Tate, the high priest of the Nashville Fugitive-Agrarians, Dutchess never figured in his work explicitly. Yet it is fascinating to contemplate the importance for him of the Dutchess countryside as he brooded over his classic poem, "Ode to the Confederate Dead," as he ruminated his exile from the South and composed poems and essays which issued in that central document of place, community and rootedness—*I'll Take My Stand,* much of this composed in Dutchess County, of all places. A place, to be sure, for the exile to catch the resonance of home. Tate's wife, Caroline Gordon, was a fine novelist who began writing her stories and novels of the South in the Pawling countryside. The Tates might have made a permanent home there, but they didn't have enough money then to buy the old farmhouse they wanted. The price?—five hundred dollars. As Caroline said: "We couldn't buy an extra dinner plate at Woolworth's." Thus Dutchess lost two of its most talented potential anachthons. Conjecture: if the Tates had been able to afford their $500 farmhouse, if they'd stayed, would literary critics and historians and professors all over the land be talking now about the Dutchess County Renascence, the Hudson Valley Renascence, instead of the Southern Renascence? Aside from being another evocative literary place-name, then, Robber Rocks is an important neglected chapter of the county's literary history.

When I began planning and researching this paper, I thought I would spend most of my time by the River. Now I find that I have spent most of my time away from the River, in what someone called the "other" Dutchess County. To round things out, let's return to the River, to "millionaire's row," and glance at another major Dutchess writer, John Jay Chapman. Chapman, of two old New York and Hudson Valley families, the Jays and Chapmans, was a long-time resident of his Hudson River estate, "Sylvania." Well into the 1930s, he was a prolific writer; he produced some thirty volumes of poetry, plays, polemical and critical essays, and translations of the classics. His books included *Emerson and Other Essays, The Maid's Forgiveness: A Play, Deutschland Uber Alles, or Germany Speaks,* and *Notes on Religion.* As these titles suggest he is not in any sense a regionalist, and his work has little to do with Dutchess explicitly. But his life and works embody the notion of the Hudson River Squire, the scholar composing his poems, his plays, his essays on the Greek genius, laboring over his translations from the Greek on the piazza of his Hudson River estate. It is one variation on the theme of *otium cum dignitate,* but it is not quite the Paulding-Placentia mode, nor the Benton-Spingarn-Troutbeck mode. On the whole his work constitutes an engaged study of the American dilemma of extreme dissociation of sensibility, with its marked devotion to dollars and delusory worship of the gnostic myth of Progress. Chapman's quest is for wholeness—physical, moral, aesthetic, intellectual and spiritual. In pursuit of such wholeness he left the city and rooted himself at Sylvania. Yet he assiduously avoided writing anything that might earn him the label, "local colorist." In one essay, he asserted: "A poet must think he is the voice of humanity. He sings and sings and it turns out afterwards that he was the true spirit of the county, not humanity." It seems that Chapman did not quite grasp that one could be both, that in keeping your eye on the universal, on the great abstractions, you were likely to miss the local and the concrete and thus see nothing truly. For is it not true that if you embrace the continent, listen only to

188

the great cosmic song, you're likely to miss the world at your doorstep, the song of the "single spot of earth" where you live? Thus one is neither the "voice of humanity" nor the "true spirit of the county." This may be a summary judgment of Chapman's complex career, but it does suggest, for our purposes here, the drift of things.

John Jay Chapman's youngest son, Chanler, was a wonderful, eccentric Dutchess character and writer. He, too, lived at Edgewater and Sylvania, until his recent death, and was much more the genius loci of the place than his father. He published only one book, *The Wrong Attitude: A Bad Boy at a Good School,* but he wrote essays and poems, and like Joel Benton and Joel Spingarn he published a local paper, *The Barrytown Explorer.* I had the pleasure of knowing Chanler—an accomplished raconteur—and hearing talk about his father, about place and community, life and culture in his corner of Dutchess. I remember the night, after dinner in the stately halls of Sylvania, Chanler told about his father leaning over his mother's grave at her funeral, and a white toothbrush fell out of his pocket and rattled on her coffin. I remember tales about his father laughing as he read Dickens to the children, tales about reading poetry to neighborhood farm children, tales about learning to shoot up among the ruins of the old Livingston mansion. But most of all, I remember and salute madcap Chanler himself—witty, eccentric, outrageous, the ideal candidate for Dutchess autochthon, a remarkable spirit of this place. One night, after all the guests thought Chanler had long since retired, he summoned my wife to his bedroom, where among paintings and murals of sylvan scenes, our panic genius sat on the edge of his bed in silk pajamas and recited flawlessly several of his sonnets. Yes, Chanler Chapman was, *is* memorable, and he belongs in the annals of more than Dutchess County literary history. Indeed one of those mere sojourning writers-in-exile—this one from Chicago and winner of the Nobel prize—secured that place, immortalizing Chanler as Henderson, the Rain King. I refer, of course, to Saul Bellow, a Dutchess sojourner who lived for a time in Chanler's gatehouse and wove the place and the character into his comic masterpiece.

Quite contrary to my initial assumptions, there is indeed a rich literary history in this county, and there are many writers and places we have not had time to mention. We might cite, in passing, the literary criticism of Franklin D. Roosevelt: for example, what I have christened Roosevelt's First Rule of Poetry—never rhyme "knows I felt" with Roosevelt. (Or, if we had time, we could compose an essy or two on how the *deus loci* of Dutchess County informed his work, his achievements, from beginning to end). Allow me to recapitulate. Dutchess County writers have been concerned with a notion of rural repose and dignity, with a sense of the past, place, and community. It is not, for the best of them, a quaint and sentimental affair of local color, issuing in pleasant but ephemeral trivia, but an enduring sense of the concrete values which emanate from past, place, community. It is one thing to speak of the importance of a sense of the past and place in literature. It is quite another thing to speak of the particular history, the particular mysteries of a specific place. Yet they are bound up, each with the other. In ways that we seldom understand, the past, leaning over, gnawing at the present, and place, the lay of the land, signify profoundly. The passing of the rivers and creeks gives shape to our staying, the configuration of the mountains and the buildings, the homes and the gardens, have much to do with the workings of the imagination, the spirit. Here, in Dutchess County, what the Chinese call "earth magic" (*fung shui*) is strong, the telluric mysteries are potent; we are particularly blessed with a past, a place and the mysterious harmonies and joys which spring therefrom. Now, in the late twentieth century, in this Tercentennial Year, these senses are under assault everywhere, receding year by year, in danger of being lost utterly. Yet the *deus loci* of such a numinous place as this is never so lost that we may not recover it, reclaim it, by an act of memory, volition and desire, by particular deeds of planting and pruning, by a thousand daily concrete acts of community, by a larger motion of the spirit. This is my report from the field, as it were, and it is my intent to celebrate the endurance of the spirit of this place. And, as for literature, yes, we have had our Pauldings and Bentons and Spingarns and all the others. Yet still this splendid country, this land, this place, this people, wait for their Balzac, their Hardy, their Faulkner.

NOTES

1. Joel Benton, *Persons and Places* (New York, 1905), pp. 107–9.

2. Charles E. Benton, *Troutbeck: A Dutchess County Homestead,* Dutchess County Historical Society Monographs: No. I (Poughkeepsie, 1916).

3. Washington Irving, *Biography and Poetical Remains of the Late Margaret Davidson* (New York, 1841.)

4. Henry James, *Autobiography,* edited with an introduction by F. W. Dupee (New York, 1956), p. 102.

5. Edith Wharton, *Hudson River Bracketed* (New York, 1929), p. 3. All further references to this work are indicated in the text.

6. Ralph M. Aderman, ed., *The Letters of James Kirke Paulding* (Madison, 1962), p. 408. All further references to this work are indicated in the text.

7. David B. Kesterson, *Josh Billings (Henry Wheeler Shaw)* (New York, 1973), pp. 40–1. All further references to this work are indicated in the text. See also Cyril Clemens, *Josh Billings, Yankee Humorist* (Missouri: Mark Twain Society, 1932).

8. For the Robinson and Lewis references see the Troutbeck Leaflets. The Mumford citation is from an unpublished manuscript, "The Story of Troutbeck," generously supplied for me by Honor Tranum.

9. *John Burroughs at Troutbeck,* Troutbeck Leaflets: Number Ten, ed., Joel Spingarn (Amenia, 1926), p. 9.

10. *Ibid.,* p. 6.

11. *Ibid.,* p. 8.

12. *Ibid.,* p. 10.

13. Clara Barrus, ed., *The Heart of Burroughs' Journals* (Boston, 1928), p. 236.

14. *Burroughs at Troutbeck,* p. 7.

15. Lewis Mumford, *The Human Prospect* (New York, 1955), p. 115. See also Mumford's remark in these pages: "Spingarn belongs among the dark stars in American letters."

16. For the remarks in this portion of the paper regarding Spingarn, I am indebted to Joel Spingarn's daughter, Honor Tranum, who graciously granted me an interview in early April, 1983, as well as to Mumford's published remarks cited above and his unpublished manuscript also cited above.

17. Marshall Van Deusen, *J. G. Spingarn* (New York, 1971), p. 59. All further references to this work are indicted in the text.

18. See *The Human Prospect,* x, and pp. 312–9.

19. Cited above.

20. Susan Jenkins Brown, *Robber Rocks* (Middletown, Conn.: Wesleyan University Press, 1969), p. 26. I am also indebted to Susan Jenkins Brown and to Malcolm Cowley for information concerning Robber Rocks gleaned from conversations with them.

Patrons and the Patronized: The Case of Maria James

William Wilson
Professor of English, Bard College

I am afraid that my title may be misleading, for it suggests first of all a society of "patrons" who encouraged a significant art into existence, and then a class of artist, patronized. In such terms, too, the title suggests that general principles are to be delineated. Neither is certain here. I am going to focus on one isolated incident, significant, I think, though not typical, and what will be evoked is no class with refined aesthetic taste nor the existence of an artist whose talent was needed by the nation. The title would be closer to truth if both words were placed in quotation marks to show the speaker's reservations about the application of these terms in these circumstances, for, as so often was the case in America in those times, the social truth has something of the flavor of Americans playing Europeans.

The "Patrons" were here the river families of Dutchess County, members of what today we would call an establishment, Beekmans, Livingstons, Bards, Astors, Potters, McVickars, and the "Patronized," an immigrant domestic servant, Maria James.

And let me say that central to the problem of this examination—really a retelling of a story perhaps already familiar to some of you—is that it is one sided, and what it reveals is not any whole truth, but the way the articulate class conceived and accommodated its relations to its poet, who is also its servant, for the latter, in spite of her gift of song, is articulate mainly in their terms; it is only by our unreliable imaginations that we can attempt to penetrate these verbal remains to discover some sense of the life beneath.

I want to talk very briefly and I hope very simply about a problem which, it seems to me, must face a historian, and that is, how to listen to the texts. This way of phrasing it confuses the distinction, surely at the center of our thinking now about language, between *parole* and *écriture,* but I do not mean to be mystifying. Although a writer often writes with conscious intention, a historian must often listen to another message in order to approximate a truth about an attitude or even an event.

I have before me several texts which are closely related to one another in intention and in time. Two of them are particularly close, written by two unmarried women, only two years apart in age, the two sharing essentially the same schooling, living in the same household for virtually all of the forty-five years before each wrote, and both on one occasion writing about the same thing. The difference between them is minimal but cleaving. One is mistress, one is servant. Furthermore, the occasion for writing is the prospect of the publication of a book of poems by the servant, and, in consequence, the topic both address is the life of the servant: Maria James writes about herself; Mary Garretson writes about her maid. More pertinently, the topic is one often addressed, the education of the poet. The problem we face is, how can we talk accurately about the relation between mistress, who, with others of her class, is "patron," and the servant, who is, if I may use the form without more than accidental prejudgment, "patronized."

I need to be more circumstantial. In 1800 Maria James, then seven years old, immigrated to America from Wales. Her family gravitated to other Welsh families at the slate quarries on Schultz Mountain on the boundary between Clinton and Rhinebeck. The quarries had been opened in 1798 to provide roofing for the new houses being built along the Hudson, in particular those at Wildercliffe and Grasmere to be inhabited by two Livingston sisters, Janet, the wife of General Robert Montgomery, and Catherine, who had recently married Freeborn Garretson, a Methodist circuit rider whose district ran from Long Island to Lake Champlain, and whose arrival in the Valley signalled the advent of Methodism among the river aristocracy.[1] Maria's mother was, we are told, the only practicing Christian in the little laboring settlement, and one of the few who were literate: she used to assemble others at her house "to read for them, and pray with them in her own language," and she walked regularly the seven miles to the new Methodist chapel. There she came to the attention of Catherine Garretson. Catherine was concerned about her own daughter, Mary, who was "sickly and sedentary" (these are Mary's own words about herself), and when she learned that Mrs. James had a daughter of the appropriate age, she proposed that she enter the Garretson household as a domestic, "an opportunity," as Maria later put it "my parents saw fit to embrace."

The two children were educated together—we will have more of that in a moment—and Maria, whose duties were light, though they increased as she grew older, joined the other children in their games; in not long she was writing poems. Many years later, Margaret Livingston, who was one of those children, remembered "Margaret Astor and Eliza Page when they were children laughing at Maria James writing poetry."

But an American idyl, especially for an immigrant child, tends to vanish at puberty. At fifteen, according to Mary, seventeen, according to Maria, she was apprenticed to a mantilla maker in New York, leaving Wildercliffe, according to Mary, with a sense of excitement and promise, in fact, once in the world, according to Maria, sewing too slowly to be successful. After an essay of nine years "facing reality" (much of the time as nursery maid in a succession of families), Maria returned to domestic service for the Garretsons, with "many sad feelings" Mary supposes, "(though she did not express them.). . . and now set herself down, to be as much as possible a commonplace woman. I doubt," she continues, "if anyone ever more faithfully endeavoured to bring down their manners and tastes to a level with their circumstances . . . a year or two after her return she became decidedly pious, and was united to the church." This psychological drama, of accommodation to reality, of hopes thwarted and ambition suppressed, is Mary's. Maria herself tells nothing of her feelings.

In the years away Maria had published one poem in the New York *American*, "The American Flag," and had signed it deferentially (deferential, undoubtedly, to a Knickerbocker sensibility) "Croaker and Company." She was not to admit to writing poetry again for another fourteen years, when, according to the story which went round and was repeated by Margaret Livingston, Mary asked her for a Christmas hymn for the Sunday School children, which was dutifully delivered the next morning. She was again writing poems after that, this time for an encouraging, if limited, home audience. An "Ode on the Fourth of July" was published (we are now in 1833) in *Album*, one of the typical gift-book publications popular in those decades. By the summer of 1838 the Valley families were astir taking up subscriptions for the publication of a book of her poems. Mrs. McVickar had shown a parcel of poems to her husband, who had shown them to Alonzo Potter, professor of moral and intellectual philosophical and political economy at Union College in Schenectady, later to become Bishop of Pennsylvania, who said they must see the light. *Wales, and Other Poems. By Maria James. With an Introduction by A. Potter, D.D.*, was published in 1839 in New York by *John S. Taylor, Brick-Church Chapel, Opposite The City Hall*, and at the Garretsons' there was a tea for its author in celebration of the occasion. Maria's life had come into its full; it then drops into oblivion, except for one glimpse we have of her five years later through the eyes of Catherine Sedgwick who came to Wildercliffe one day in curiosity to visit the domestic poet who had written a tribute to her for championing the idea that a measure of intellectuality was appropriate to the laboring and domestic classes in her problem novel *Live and Let Live;* and except for the cold notice on her tombstone. Maria James was forty-six when her book was published; she lived to be one month less than seventy-six, and died in service.

When *Wales, and Other Poems* was published, Alonzo Potter provided an "Introduction"; in it he writes to reassure the river families who had subsidized the publication that they had not been guilty of undermining the hierarchy by encouraging domestics to aspire beyond the station allotted them in life. The question was in the air. The poems of Phyllis Wheatley, the eighteenth century Boston slave poet, and Robert Southey's *Lives of the Uneducated Poets* (they were mostly English servants), had both been reprinted the year before. Alonzo Potter argued that talent is distributed equally in all stations, but that such equity does not call the *de facto* social organization into question. He offers his own integrity in gage, assuring us first of all of Maria's humility. "Had I found her eaten up with the desire of praise, writing only that she might have the means of emerging from the obscurity of her station, and in terror or in transport as she anticipated the frowns or smiles of criticism, I should have declined any agency in the publication of this volume." He is further at pains to promote the idea of learning among the working classes, and he sees a new day ahead when, because of universal education, "authorship among labouring men and women, by becoming common, shall cease to appear misplaced," and he goes on to the specific recognition that "such a change will doubtless be long in reaching domestic servants. As a class, they have little command of time; a spirit of self-reliance is not cultivated among them, and their efforts at self-improvement are too seldom encouraged." But, recognizing the facts of the present situation, he further qualifies his position by insisting that "such persons require to be addressed, principally, through the medium of the imagination and the feelings," and instead of books "made up of abstractions, or filled with the hard and dry details of physical science" he urged books which "speak to the understanding through the fancy and the affections," and he finds there the reason Poetry must always occupy a high place "in the literature of the great mass of the people."

A letter from Catherine Sedgwick (champion of the idea that books are good friends to the working man) written in response to Alonzo Potter's solicitation of advice as to the propriety of publishing a book of poems composed by a domestic servant, is also included in the "Introduction." Mrs. Sedgwick was surprisingly cautious about publication:

> I should doubt (I say it to you, sir, with diffidence,) the expediency of presenting Maria James as an example to be followed by minds in her sphere. A mind that like hers has a spring within itself, cannot be repressed within conventional boundaries; and her achievements should be made known to repress the supercilious pride of the privileged and educated, and to raise the courage, and fortify the self-respect of the mute and inglorious in humble life—to prove that as Mad. de Stael said, "genius has no sex"—neither has it any condition. But while I should wish this done—while I should wish the humblest stimulated to the cultivation and enjoyment of their intellectual faculties, I would have them feel that a *dutiful* performance gives dignity to the lowliest office—that a domestic may find exercise for mind and heart in the prescribed duties of her station—and that their intellectual faculties do not run to waste, because they are not devoted to what is esteemed their highest exercise.

The "Introduction" also includes a "Memoir" which consists almost entirely of an autobiographical sketch by Maria herself, in the form of a letter addressed to Mrs. Potter, and signed with a genuflecting and already archaic formality, "Fearing that I have already tried your patience, I will hasten to subscribe myself,/Dear Madam,/Your most obedient,/And very humble servant,/MARIA JAMES." (What irony there might be in that genuflection is one of our problems.) The "Memoir" also contains excerpts from a letter from Mary Garretson, writing Maria's life from her own recollections.

Maria's autobiographical sketch and Mary's recollections are two of our texts. The contents of these two documents, each written, of course, with publication in mind, each addressing the same issue, the education of the poet, and written from a shared lifetime, are as trivial and as poignant, and as hard to "read," as the events I have so rapidly summarized.

What I would like to do now is to examine passages from these two writings carefully enough to see if we can determine what suppositions went into their composition, and what they may reveal to us about the actuality of this relationship. After that I would like to consider a "theme," the relations between the "haves" and the "have nots" which Maria addressed explicitly in her autobiographical sketch and in one of her poems. I am as much concerned with how a thing is said as with what is said.

Miss Mary Garretson, forty-four, remembers Maria's first coming to Wildercliffe and her early education there (which was also her own) in this way:

> Maria came to us when she was about 10 years old . . . as I was a sickly sedentary child.
> (Mamma) thought that if she could get a little girl of my own age to bring up, it would be a

great advantage to my health. She accordingly applied to Mrs. James, and found that her eldest daughter was of a suitable age to be useful in the house, and to be a companion for me, and without seeing her, bespoke her. She was brought, in her striped homespun dress, well instructed by her mother in all the proprieties of her situation, and in all its moral duties—with a pathos and a simplicity, which might have shamed many an elaborate discourse . . . Her work was light,—and when it was finished, with her clean apron on, she always took her seat on a little bench in the parlour, with her knitting, or sewing, while I said my lessons to mamma, or we read. The lessons were very trifling; but we read a great deal. Papa and mamma were very indefatiguable readers, and every interesting or useful book, was read aloud for the good of the whole.

Our imaginations fasten immediately on the striped homespun and the child on the parlor bench in her clean apron, at her sewing, a witness to the lessons, absorbing their literary culture, the discourse of her betters. A pathos and a sympathy are evoked as a means to a humanitarian equalization of persons in spite of differing conditions, or even because of them, and the sentences fall into a rhythm evocative of a mood, a nostalgia for happier times; the writing touches the feelings and encourages us to muse on human circumstance in the web of time and conditon.

Listen now to how Maria James, forty-six, whose book of poems is about to be published, remembers her tenth year when she entered the Garretson household as a domestic servant:

I was now ten years of age, and as an opportunity offered which my parents saw fit to embrace, I entered the family in which I now reside, where besides learning many useful household occupations, that care and attention was paid to my words and actions, as is seldom to be met with in such situations.

I had before me, some of the best models for good reading and good speaking; and any child with a natural ear for the beautiful in language, will notice these things; and though their conversation may not differ materially from that of others in their line of life, they will almost invariably *think* in the style of their admiration.

The difference is not perhaps what we would at first expect. Leaving aside the potentially ironic fact that the "household occupations" were to be "useful," not to a household of her own, but to that of her employers, we notice immediately that Maria's language and style is more "elegant" than Mary's. Gone is the homespun, gone is the clean apron and the sewing, gone is both the pathos and the evocation of times fondly remembered, gone in fact are all those sentiments and those particulars which might attach us to the scene through our feelings and, by way of the senses we all have in common, level us into a common humanity. In their place is a clean, intellectual, abstract diction, and the carefully poised periodic sentence, an eighteenth century correctness which moves very quickly from personal event and physical fact to general principles. This one poet's life participated in the "model" for the developed poetic sensibility, to be discovered in whatever particular situation.

Yet, also typical of an eighteenth century habit of mind, the idea, once thoroughly generalized, is at the end of the second paragraph applicable again to the personal and particular, in this case to Maria's position as a domestic servant. Listen again to the content and poise of the last clauses: "and though their [read, domestic servants who have learned the language of their masters, read Maria James] conversation may not differ materially from that of others in their line of life, they will almost invariably *think* in the style of their admiration." While conceding daily speech to that appropriate to her station, she maintains the prerogative to "*think*" in the style of her betters. The mode thus becomes potentially ironic when the universal idea is re-attached to a person in a particular situation, and a complex exposition of an individual state of mind—no unified personality here—is achieved without either speaking personally or evoking feeling. Notice her stress on *style*, not content; the independence is not rebellion but insistent participation in a higher cultural community of discourse. Mary Garretson was, in a sense, slumming in the feelings of the situation, using a language appropriate to such a sentimental levelling which was, we can see it now, a condescension appropriate to her station. Maria James maintained a decorum which, we might say, by asserting participation in an aristocracy of sensibility determined by taste, reason, and rectitude, puts *her* "inferiors" by these measures on show.

Yet it is Mary, not Maria, who is aware of this class/cultural inversion, and it is she (and the language natural to her) which is free and flexible enough to speak of it explicitly. Mary writes:

> She (Maria) was always imaginative, and her imagination carried her amid European scenes. She was also very aristocratic in her notions. Her pictures of the noble and grand were perfectly unreal; and I well recollect that, in our little disputes as children, she always took the aristocratic, and I the democratic side of the argument.

I do not mean to suggest that Mary *was* more "democratic"—such a judgment is meaningless in such a relationship—but she was disposed to think of herself so, and *her* irony was the privileged irony of bemusement which she shared with her knowing and indulgent peers. Her rhetoric is, as I have already suggested, a rhetoric suitable for a sentimental equality, not an equality of either culture or situation. Mary, we can say, conceded that, beyond differences of class and circumstance, we are all human, and in that, all alike. (Actually, she would have said, we are all equal in the sight of the Lord.) There is not a shred of concession to such notions in what Maria James has written; she does not condescend; she is supremely "humble," but she does not descend from general precept to sentiment; (but I do not suggest, either, that her rhetoric for precept was not a way of speaking at least as commonplace as Mary's).

We are not speaking here of malice aforethought or of deliberate exploitation; even the condescension is that of class attitude, not personal; and as far as we can know all the principals are kindly disposed, considerate, humane, sympathetic, even generous. Wildlercliffe was probably really a safe haven for Maria; an alternate life would more than likely have been more difficult and more dangerous.

"As far as we can know" and "more than likely" must be our qualification. For in effect everything we can know of Maria James and her life comes to us in the voices of her superiors. They are voices we have learned to read; we have heard them often. There are no voices here of slate quarry workers; Maria's mother is mute. We know a great deal about the social functioning of the society her daughter went into service for: its births, marriages, thefts of jewels, masquerade balls, ice boating, flirtations at Saratoga, excursions to Niagara, its ventures into Texas, spring gardening, leasing of lots (to take a loose gathering of subjects from Margaret Livingston's letters for 1838). We know virtually nothing of the life of the workers at the slate quarries; we hardly know they existed except for the fact that someone had to pry out the slabs of slate and split them for roof tiles and table tops.

But what of Maria herself, originating in one world and developing in another? It seems clear from what has been said that Maria's language is acquired in more than one sense. It is a language learned too well. Her prose is more conservative, less appropriate, even, for the articulation of the truth of her situation than that of her social superiors. Surely it is the careful language of aspiration. Mary, in forwarding Maria's autobiographical sketch to Alonzo Potter, said, "Maria has copied until she has taken the spirit from it. The rough draft was far the best, but that she has destroyed."

But what of Maria's poems? In contemporaneous theory, at least, poetry was the medium most appropriate for a direct expression of the self and its feelings. In asking that question we are again raising the further question, how can we know what voice we here is Maria's? Although we may not achieve satisfactory answers, we can attempt them both obliquely and directly, looking for the sources and subject matter of the poems, and by examining closely something of what she wrote.

Maria insists that her tastes were formed on the best models; they are, as she would think them, a domestic in provincial America, elegant, even aristocratic. She tells of the earliest emergence of her poetic sensibility. She remembers that one day soon after her arrival in America, before the family settled in Clinton, she happened to hear a young woman read "Addison's inimitable paraphrase of the 23rd psalm." "I listened," she said "as to the voice of an angel; those who know the power of good reading or good speaking, need not be told, that where there is an ear for the sound, the manner in which either is done will make every possible difference..." (again the particular personal experience is rapidly elevated to precept), and she had thrilled in school in Clinton to hear the elder children read from Timothy Dwight's American epic, *Columbia*. Her own reading at the Garretsons' (in addition, of course, to the scriptures which there, as at home, was "the book of books") was devoted to the predictable *Pilgrim's Progress*, to volumes of the eighteenth century periodical the *Adventurer*, to Hannah Moore's "repository," and to *The Female Mentor*, which she calls "a little epitome of elegant literature." Slim fare, for the most part, for the imagination.

Pilgrim's Progress is also remembered by Mary, who brings it into her own life as a picture of "our own times": "the City of Destruction was behind us and I almost felt as if I was one of the children travelling to Mount Zion, in the train of Christian, and Mr. Great Heart our guide. The house of Gaius wore to me a strong likeness to the houses I was familiar with," and Mary evokes a warm and active life in the Garretson household, with the comings and goings of itinerant Methodist preachers, bringing news of the world to an isolated corner of it:

> Steam-boats and Rail-roads had not then drawn together the ends of the world,—so that we were a very quiet family, seeing, with the exception of our relations, very few persons beside our brethren of the ministry, and of the laity too;—for there was rarely a wandering Methodist (gentle or simple) that did not put up for a night at least, at Father Garretson's. There was much of romance as well as poetry in the Methodist preacher's character in those days. They dropped in upon us, in the midst of storms and cold,—brought us tidings from north and south, the east and west, (our conferences were then very extended), and always sent a thrill of pleasure to our young hearts. The tidings of a "Methodist preacher coming," was echoed from kitchen to parlour, and from parlour to bed-room, until we all were on the watch, and the saddlebags and peculiar joy were discovered.

There may have been the stuff "much of romance as well as poetry" for those in kitchen and for those in parlour in this evocation of a particular corner of provincial life in the Hudson Valley, but Maria did not take the stuff for her poetry from there; it comes from further away. When she first came to write, her imagination "took fire" (the words are hers), not from the doings of the little clan of children at their sports, a Welsh girl among them, and not from the comings and goings of itinerant Methodist preachers (gentle and simple) bringing tidings from north and south, but from the European Wars, accounts of which she remembers filled the newspapers. There is, in fact, among her published poems one in adulation of Napoleon, heroic representative of achievement through individual merit. Actually, most of her subjects in the published poems are usual and predictable. Many are nationally occasional, "The American Flag," "Ode on the Fourth of July," or privately occasional, "Lines Written on a Blank Leaf, on the Life of the Rev. F. Garretson," "On Seeing a Bust of the Late Hon. Edward Livingston," or overtly devotional "Christmas," "Good Friday"; there is a rebus built from Rhine and Beekman; a great many poems moralize from nature, "The Ethiopian Lily," "The Hummingbird," "To the Evening Star"; there is an "Epitaph on a Drowned Boy" (those of you who remember Huckleberry Finn's admiration for Emmeline Grangerford's "Ode to Stephen Dowling Bots, Dec'd." will take notice), and laments by boys, by girls, and by mothers; there is "The Young Soldier" and "The Bride's Welcome." There are seventy-six poems in all, and in fact we are hard put to hear a Welsh immigrant, Maria James, in her time, in her place, in her voice, speaking anywhere among them.

Even in the title poem, "Wales," with its overt attempt to evoke an essential place and a meaningful past, the recollections are of a generalized nature (and how, in fact, could they be otherwise; the child left home at seven), and we hear a familiar "cuckoo's voice"; the particular place is known mainly, or only, by proper nouns, "Snowdon" and "Cymry" (the latter is footnoted), and finally our attention is directed to "her sons of fame, her bards of yore." Maria is correct when she ends with a name only:

> Lord of my fathers! ne'er
> Shall I forget thy name,—
> Oh ne'er while in this bosom glows
> Life's transient flame!

We shall not know what nationality of origin meant for Maria James from such verse. Nor is the American Maria James more directly represented in the patriotic, religious, moral, and familiar poems which follow in the book.

Thus we will look pretty much in vain for the "real" Hudson Valley or the "real" Maria James among the subjects of these poems. The real Hudson Valley, apart from its scenery, would, I think we might agree, for our purposes today at least, be found in the class relations between mistress and servant. But our difficulty, as I have already suggested, is in recognizing the voice of the servant, even if we chance to hear it.

Who, then, is Maria James? What we see of her (besides the scrap of autobiography we have already looked at and another scrap we shall look at in a moment) is seen through the language of those who see her. Maria James, the servant-poet, is *always* described as "humble," blending a "nun-like sanctity and intellectual gleamings with the deferential manner of an English serving woman" (Catherine Sedgwick), a "humbled [one isn't sure of the force of the past participle here] but valued friend . . . proof against the temptations of celebrity" (Alonzo Potter), one who had not known "the sympathies which the peculiarity of her character requires" (Mary Garretson), one whom "the smallest praise the slightest word of approbation sends color to her cheeks and forehead and the tears to her eyes, you remember her little prim formal features mincing step and humble curtsy" (Margaret Livingston). These fit perfectly to Mary's "human" story and Alonzo Potter's need to justify the publication of the poems. They establish the servant-poet in her appropriate humility. There may as well, of course, be truth of character here, but we may also be seeing a redaction of what Maria herself called a speech appropriate to those in her "line of life"; what may be reserved in *thought* is harder to discern. Does the "style" of her "admiration" permit her to express a truth germane to her situation?

The voice in the poems is often humble and deferential as well. With a clear sense of literary (and social) decorum, she does not portray her*self* but maintains a personal distance achieved by recognizable personae, by "poetic diction," and by received forms; she makes a *poem;* she does not presume a *self*-expression. At the same time we do know that she, for all the expressions of pious acceptance of her place in a Christian hierarchy of "duties" sustaining the social organization, *is* aware of a discriminate difference between herself and her "betters," one which has a cutting edge, the one between the "haves" and the "have nots." She learned the difference as a particularly "American" lesson very early—at least one can say that, at forty-six she remembers learning it at seven, along with her first acquaintance with the English language, the language of her achieved life:

> Towards the completion of my seventh year, I found myself on shipboard, surrounded by men, women and children, whose faces were unknown to me: it was here perhaps that I first began to learn in a particular manner from observation, soon discovering that those children who were handsome or smartly drest, received much more attention than myself, who had neither of these recommendations; however, instead of giving way to feelings of envy and jealousy, my imagination was revelling among the fruits and flowers which I expected to find in the land to which we were bound. I also had an opportunity to learn a little English during the voyage, as "take care," and "get out of the way," seemed reiterated from land's-end to land's-end.

This writing is in its way circumstantial enough, and though a familiar story, it has the ring of truth: moreover, Maria James is undoubtedly drawing on the familiarity of these ideas to show that what is important to the future poet is the sublimation of those "feelings of envy and jealousy" emergent from a recognition of the social realities into a dream of the "fruits and flowers" to be found in the new land. The forty-six-year-old woman knows what those "fruits and flowers" of the dream of America have become for her in fact: thirty-three years in service; and we know, as she could anticipate (except for the chance for celebrity the publications of the book could achieve), of the forty-three years in service to come. Again we see that the reapplication of the universal idea to the particular circumstances creates the irony which allows personal statement. There is no overt "protest" in the account, even in the bemused picture of the puzzled child underfoot, but overt acquiescence; yet in the actualities of the situation, the lifetime of servitude (I shift the term slightly for my emphasis) and the chance of, the unrealistic hope for an "American" success, although dependent on patronage, we can guess an alert and not thoroughly acquiescent intelligence, awake, even if effectively mute.

So the idea of the relative fortunes of the "haves" and the "have nots," and the "dreamy" alternative for the latter, is alive in her mind, and it is treated again in one of the few poems in the book which comes close to evoking a sense of an actualized life in a particularized America.

The community of Shakers in Lebanon, New York, made brooms, widely sold, and used, in the Hudson Valley. Maria James herself may not often have used one, more often engaged in other duties. (She is reported to have told a lady who asked "I suppose your poetry often keeps you awake." "No," she replied, "it never kept me awake an hour; but it is often busy with me at the wash-tub—though white-washing is the most favorable.") However that may be, she wrote a poem entitled "The Broom" which I will read to you. It needs to be prefaced, however, as the volume as a whole is, with the "Motto" to the book as a whole, the voice of an indoor domestic accepts as vanity her wishing to mingle with the field workers, "the reaper train" as she says it in eighteenth century "poetic diction":[2]

Motto

I would not ask,—for that were vain,—
To mingle with the reaper train,—
Who gayly sing, as hast'ning by
To pile their golden sheaves on high;
But with the group who meet the view,
In kerchief red and apron blue,
I crave the scatter'd ears they yield,
To bless the gleaner of the field.

It is a conventional subject, but also, in its place, at the head of a book of poems so problematically that of a house servant, pertinent to this argument. A response to the poem develops quickly from any residual actuality into its metaphor for the activity of the poet, retired from the active life, nevertheless making what is gathered from experience by those who live in the world the substance of her poetry, and the situations of domestic house servant and poet are equated. Something more is almost achieved, however, by following the *genre* picture of "kerchief red and apron blue" with an almost aggressive cry of deprivation in "I crave." Yet what is achieved for a moment is conceded the next in the poetical transmutation of the experience gained at second remove into a blessing of the gleaners (or, I suppose of the Great Gleaner himself), and so the initial statement of a resigned humility is reaffirmed.

Something of the same pattern is repeated in "The Broom," though its rhetoric is more complex and the poem itself has more achieved substance:

The Broom

Give me a broom, one neatly made
In Niscayuna's distant shade;
Or bearing full its staff upon
The well-known impress "Lebanon."
A handle slender, smooth, and light,
Of bass-wood, or of cedar white;

Where softest palm from point to heel
Might ne'er a grain of roughness feel—
So firm a fix, the stalks confine;
So tightly drawn the hempen line;
Then fan-like spread divided wove,
As fingers in a lady's glove—
To crown the whole, (and save beside,)

The loop, the buckskin loop is tied.

With this in hand, small need to care
If C——y or J——n fill the chair—
What in the banks is said or done—
The game at Texas lost or won—
How city belles collect their rings,
And hie to Saratoga springs;—
To Erie's, or Ontario's shore,
To hear Niagara's thunders roar—
While undisturb'd my course I keep,
Cheer'd by the sound of sweep, sweep, sweep.

See learned Doctors rack their brains,
To cure mankind of aches and pains,

When half, and more than half, a rise
From want of prudence,—exercise.
The body like a garment wears,

And aches and pains may follow years;
But when I see the young, the gay,
Untimely droop, and pine away,
As if the life of life were o'er
Each day less active than before,—
Their courage fled, their interest cold,—
With firmer grasp, my broom I hold.
Nor is this all; in very deed
The broom may prove a friend in need;
On this I lean,—on this depend;
With such a surety, such a friend,
There's not a merchant in the place
Who would refuse me silk or lace;
Of linen-fine, or broad-cloth dear,
Or e'en a shawl of fam'd Cashmere,
Though prudence whispering, still would say,
"Remember, there's a rainy day."

Hand me the broom, (a matron said,)
As down the hose and ball were laid;
I think your father soon will come;
I long to see him safe at home.
Pile on the wood, and set the chair,—
The supper and the board prepare;
The gloom of night is gathering fast,—
The storm is howling o'er the waste.

The hearth is swept, arrang'd the room,
And duly hung the shaker-broom,
With cheerful smiles and greetings wait
The master entering at his gate.
Let patriots, poets, wind their brows
With laurel, or with holly boughs;
But let the broom-corn wreath be mine,
Adorn'd with many a sprig of pine;
With wild-flowers from the forest deep,
And garlands from the craggy steep,
Which ne'er have known the gardner's care,
But rise, and bloom spontaneous there.

The poem, first of all, is written in tetrameter couplets, arranged in verse paragraphs, a form not usual for Maria James who more typically writes in the more familiar ballad quatrain, popular after Wordsworth established it as appropriate for a humble subject matter, so close to hymn meter or "common particular." At the same time, perhaps it should be said that she does not write in pentameter couplets, the "heroic couplet" of Dwight's *Columbia* reserved, according to eighteenth century codes of decorum, for "heroic" (or, of course, mock heroic) and formally "pastoral" subjects.

The theme here is a variant of the familiar "Vanity of Human Wishes," with an equally familiar Christian Stoicism as the appropriate antidote to those vanities, that tempered by a thoroughly unrealizable dream of wild spontaneity. Yet it concessions are not fully realized, a fact we first notice in the simile in the first stanza which so nicely gathers the straw at the haft of the broom:

> Then fan-like spread divided wove,
> As fingers in a lady's glove

The image not only creates a sense of visual accuracy, it also links the common with the aristocratic and then evokes the human hand beneath the glove. Further, there is a reverberation which begins to hum between the image and the actual hand (not a lady's) which wields the broom, and that body which leans upon it as a security against the unattainable (if realized to be uncertain) goods and pleasures of another way of life. That vision of the active life, of banking, military exploits in Texas, of city belles, their rings and their vacations at Saratoga, and whatever jealousy and envy that vision invokes, are brushed away. The river families *did* summer at Saratoga, did participate in the "game of Texas," as we know from Margaret Livingston's letters, and Niagara's roar *is* something more exciting in fact than the mesmerizing onomatopoeia of "sweep, sweep, sweep." Of course, those who "have" are shown, through want of prudent exercise, to "pine away,/as if the life of life were o'er," a vision which makes the broom holder grasp her broom yet more firmly. A secure position in service, in the fourth stanza, is shown to be steady enough to provide, on credit, just those luxuries, silk and lace and fine linen, broadcloth and even a Cashmere shawl, otherwise denied, if (again, of course) prudence did not remind that "there's a rainy day."

Thus far in the poem a definite contrast is insisted upon between the "I," pretty firmly actualized as a deferentially humble stay-at-home, a domestic servant, in clear enmity to C——y and J——n, who go off to Saratoga and to balls. But there is a problem with the "I." The mode abruptly becomes objective, and *that* "I" disappears into another sweeper. The opening, "Give me a broom, one neatly made," is transmuted in the fifth stanza to, "Hand me a broom, (a matron said,)." We follow into a *genre* picture of a stay-at-home mother, with her children, preparing the hearth for the father's return. There are no servants in this domestic scene; the same womanly retirement from the world, perhaps, the same "useful household occupations," but actualized now in child and hearth and returning father. We know the scene from countless chromos, the picture of a life, not Maria's.

But it is neither in this picture, nor in the earlier evocation of the envious, if resigned, servant, that the fundamental meaning resides, but in the transmutation (who knows how conscious) of the one into the other—the social reality into the unattainable (we are tempted to say forbidden) fruits and flowers of the new land.

Yet the move to yet another stage, and to other flowers, can only be conscious and deliberate. The hearth scene carries four lines into the last stanza until "the matter enters at his gate." Then the discourse switches to a terminal generalization which, in a pattern now familiar to us, in its application to the particular circumstances, becomes sharply ironic. The achievements of both patriots and poets are rejected with the consequently necessary simultaneous identification of the speaker of the poem (and, of course, the author of it as well) as "poet." The laurel is eschewed in favor of the "broom-corn wreath," but this in turn is adorned with pine, with wild-flowers from the forest, with garlands from the crags, with whatever is wild, uncultivated, rising and blooming spontaneously, a fantasized spontaneous self-fulfillment (all, of course, clearly within the control of the formal tetrameter couplet).

Maria James wrote accomplished poems, but they are without a vital center; she wrote in a humble mode determined by an "elegant" decorum; she wrote from a very humble position in a social structure dominated by the reticulation of families close to the center of financial, political, judicial, and cultural power in the United States in the third quarter of its first hundred years. She wrote in a language and in forms rapidly becoming archaic, which in their very nature were both "foreign" and conservative, more aristocratic, if you will, than the language used by her employers, theirs a language in fact better able to accommodate the contradictions between democratic principle and commercial enterprise which was "reality" in America at the time.

In the very act of learning the language of her betters—really, the language of *their* betters, that is their British forebears, which they knew better than to emulate too closely—and in her determination to do *them* one better, Maria James was, of course, defeated, and class and cultural hegemony was once more affirmed. Alonzo Potter needn't have bothered himself with an elaborate apology for the dangerous enterprise of publishing the verses written by a domestic servant. Human nature, the class structure, and the language, did the job effectively.

It is the language of a culture which must—constantly—be renewed along with its other institutions. In America it was still sixteen years before Walt Whitman would sound his "barbaric yawp" over the housetops of America and claim to speak for the inarticulate: "through me all the dumb voices." In 1839, Emily Dickinson was nine years old; she also was to begin with the "common particular" and broke it into a medium for the expression of cloistered but defiant intelligence. Not until the first decade of the twentieth century did an immigrant voice provide the basis for an idiom capable of moving beyond aspiration and condescension in Gertrude Stein's "The Good Anna" and "The Gentle Lena" (though there are problems there as well).

Maria James knew what she had learned on her voyage to America; she remembered it in 1838, that "those who were handsome or smartly drest, received more attention than" those like herself, and she also knew where those "fruits and flowers" are to be found, in the mytho-poetical imagination. She was almost voiceless in telling what she knew, employed, befriended, taught, given refuge, published at last in the new world. She took greedily to herself the forms and conventions for the intellect and the sensibility of a mercantile eighteenth century, and she herself disappeared into them. As I say, she is almost voiceless, and we must use what perspicacity we can (when too often the lenses are dirty) to hear a voice at all.

Or to imagine we hear her. For how can we know we hear *her*, since the very circumstances, the striped homespun, the clean apron on the little girl on the parlor bench, listening, absorbing, with her sewing, on which we base our assumptions of what we *should* hear, are created by the idiom of the employing class itself. It gives us the conversation about the white-wash, and it gives us the rhetoric of the broom as well.

We know its idea of "common humanity" from many places; it is a familiar platitude, that human frailty is the great equalizer, the ultimate democrat. We hear it contemporaneously in a sketch by Nathaniel Hawthorne, and it speaks as ambivalently there as anywhere. Maria, remember, was for a time an apprentice to a mantilla maker; to be a seamstress was one of the very few alternatives to the life she led. Hawthorne, in "The Procession of Life," sees mankind categorized by its diseases, which for him are also the diseases of society.

> But what is this crowd of pale cheeked, slender girls, who disturb the ear in the multiplicity of their short, dry coughs? They are seamstresses who have plied the daily and nightly needle in the service of master-tailors and close-fisted contractors, until now it is almost time for each to bear the burdens of her own shroud. Consumption points their place in the procession.

But those seamstresses are not alone:

> With their sad sisterhood are intermingled many youthful maidens who have sickened in aristocratic mansions, and folk whose aid science has unavailingly searched its volumes and whom breathless love has watched. In our ranks the rich maiden and the poor seamstresses may walk arm and arm.

Ultimately, then, in the language of the established culture, there may be no difference between the "haves" and the "have nots." The sisterhood of consumptive frailty supercedes class distinction. Our hearts (to use a nineteenth century designtion) may acquiesce to such a notion of a common humanity. But it is an acquiescence our heads can no longer tolerate.

Notes

1. Catherine "had already made the acquaintance of the Methodists, a devoted servant in the household at Clermont, who had joined the infant Methodist Church in New York, being instrumental in bringing about her conversion." (Tipple, pp. 80–81) Cf. Sedgwick, *Life and Letters*, p. 296: "She became a Methodist, to the great scandal of her aristocratic family, who were as aristocratic in their religion as in every thing else, and married, at 40, an honest good preacher after the old pattern of Methodism."

2. As my colleague, Mark Lambert, points out, the language of "reapers" and "gleaners" is also reminiscent of *The Book of Ruth* which suggests some significant relations between the situation as well: Ruth is a servant, far from home, gleaning in the fields of Boaz, who takes her to wife.

Bibliography

The accounts of Maria James' life, by herself and by Mary Garretson, as well as the poems themselves, and the "Introduction" by Alonzo Potter, are in *Wales, And Other Poems,* New York, 1839.

An account of the life of Freeborn Garretson can be found in Ezra Squire Tipple's *Freeborn Garretson,* Cincinnati, 1910.

Catherine Sedwick's account of her visit to Wildercliffe is included in the *Life and Letters of Catherine Maria Sedgwick,* edited by Mary E. Dewey, New York 1871, pp. 295–296.

The letters of Margaret Livingston are in the Special Collections of the Vassar College Library.

Henry Noble MacCracken in *Blithe Dutchess,* New York, 1958, pp. 336–339, gives a more circumstantial account of the publication of *Wales, and Other Poems* and of the tea given by the Garretsons for Maria James to mark the occasion. His account is apparently based on letters written by Margaret Livingston. However, her letters for the year of publication, 1839, are missing in the collection at Vassar. It would seem not unlikely that those letters could be found among unsorted papers of President MacCracken currently housed in the Vassar Library.

Letters

To Mrs. K. S. Minot from Catherine M. Sedgwick

Linwood, near Rhinebeck, June 13, 1845

Do you remember my once receiving a letter from Miss G., with some verses, very pretty, from Maria T., (sic., apparently a printer's misreading for "J") a servant of hers, thanking me for having done service to the cause of domestics in "Live and Let Live," and do you remember that I gave her volume of poems to that good old Wesleyan missionary of the St. James? Well, being in the neighborhood of the G.'s, I determined to go and see them, and a few evenings since, when we were taking our drive, the Dr. dropped me at their gate. I approached the house, a modest, old-fashioned structure, by a gravel walk through an orchard covered with old trees, with their shadows sleeping on a bed of the richest clover. As I turned round the house I came to the piazza, and there an erect old lady, "touched (sanctified), not spoiled" by age was standing, explaining to a little girl, such as our Posy will be five years hence, a picture of Daniel and Belshazzar. It was a picture. Roses of all hues in their June bloom were trained about the piazza, a lawn with groups of noble trees before it, and below it a magnificent stretch of the river studded with a little fleet of slopes. I introduced myself to the old lady. Her daughter soon made her appearance, a cheerful, intelligent, excellent person, living a truly godly life here, as far as a glorious scenery can make it so, in the vestibule of heaven. My friend Maria T. soon appeared, to my infinite embarrassment treating me with as much reverence as if her saints had appeared to her. She blends a nun-like sanctity and intellectual gleamings with the deferential manner of an English serving woman—an odd mixture enough! I confess to *you*, dear Kate, that her expressions of gratitude and affection were very precious to me. She came after—to see me, and when she took leave, "God Bless you, Miss S.," she said; "may you never want a servant, friend, or what you may please to call her." I staid to tea at Miss G.'s. She is one of the two last of the old race of L's, a sister of the celebrated E. L., and of the chancellor. There were twelve of them, who lived strong and joyous lives, all having lordly estates in the Manor, with iron physical and rich intellectual constitutions. They ate and drank after the old-fashion—turtle soups, mince pies, and Madeira wine for dinner, hot suppers at night, laughed together over their breakfast tables—*all* lived to slip far beyond the prescribed boundary of man's life, and here is Mrs. G. absolutely unimpaired at 92. Oh, in what blessed ignorance they have lived and died of dyspepsia and nerves! We had tea on the piazza; it was prepared when I arrived, and one refreshing relic there was of the olden time. I heard Mrs. G. tell the maid "to change the tea-cups," and the best china appeared. The old lady presided with a sort of lofty grace, and drank green tea, and ate strawberries and cream "sans peur et sans reproche." She became a Methodist, to the great scandal of her aristocratic family, who were as aristocratic in their religion as in everything else, and married, at 40, an honest, good preacher after the old pattern of Methodism.

To Mrs. Rawlins Lowndes from Margaret Livingston

(New York, between April 14 and April 25, 1838)

Dear Gitty:

You (I?) have enclosed the prospectus with some specimens of Maria James' poetry—The extracts I made from her manuscript and which I intended for you have unluckily been left in the country. Those I now send I procured from Mr. McVickar he was so much delighted with them that he sent a copy of the Fire Fly to Southey. We are all very much interested in procuring subscriptions for her, if you can assist us I know you will. You can show the verses but do not multiply copies as the work will be very small we must not forestal the publication by showing it in manuscript. You can answer for their being the genuine of one whose life has been spent in service—her friends are too conscientious even to alter a word for her—It is curious to hear Maria herself speak of them no vanity no conceit either in tone or manner the smallest praise the slightest word of approbation sends the color to her cheeks and forehead and the tears to her eyes, you remember her little prim formal features mincing step and humble curtsey. The perfect antipodes to any thing poetical or imaginative. Your Papa asked her if she read a great deal? "Oh no she had not time,—how did she manage did she study? No she thought over her subject whilst at her work and never wrote until it was all arranged in her head—but how did she acquire her language her information? she did not know she believed it was by attending to the conversation of sensible people—I remember Margaret Astor and Eliza Page when they were children laughing at Maria James writing poetry—she then abandoned it entirely, about six years ago Mary Garretson asked her one evening for a Christmas hymn for her Sunday school children. The next morning the hymn was laid upon the table Mary was so much pleased with it that she encouraged her to continue and the poems now to be published have all been written since that period, her prose I am told is better than her poetry. I have not seen any of it. She has at Mr Potters request written a history of the progress of her own mind—

Angel and Geraldine have just returned from the Narrows They went down with Robert L. & family his son Robert and wife sailed to day for Liverpool they (sic.) girls have returned very tired and sun burnt. Summer is coming upon us all at once. Yr Papa & Henry went to the country yesterday & I shall go on Saturday—I have been detained here this week to procure servants and am not yet supplied—Your cap is not as pretty as I wished the woman has not exectued my idea Those that have come out this Spring are not becoming and cost from 7 to 10 Dols—. The one I sent you has at least the merit of being cheap all the caps are trimmed flat on the top of the head and full at the sides precisely like that little bead net cap that Mary got from France two years ago—I send you Bulwars two last novels—Your Papa has leased three of your lots at 50 Dols a ps & the taxes—I have not yet exhausted your Feb 7 lr—so do not be afraid to write to me for anything you want

    Your Affet
    Mother ML

Architectural Footsteps: Alexander Jackson Davis

Lea Etta Canter

Once upon a time there really was a 19th Century. In the present tense, that is. Sandwiched in between the end of the great American Revolution and our tragic Civil War, most of the alive and well in the population by 1830 were setting about in pursuit of Life, Liberty and Happiness. A great Romantic spirit of accomplishment as well as talent was about to explode. The future was to prove much more complex than the provincial idiom of the Colonial years.

Within this timeframe, a select group of renaissance men had great plans for the new nation. They were aristocratic, educated elitists, and yes—a sophisticated clique of tastemakers, trailblazers, landscape artists, architects, inventors, and educators. Not only were they all friends but collaborators as they travelled the grand circuit. Wintering, working, promoting in New York City—already considered by the ordinary folk a modern-day Athens revived; summering and retreating on the banks of the sublime lower Hudson Valley; vacationing and walking this hard, rocky but compelling land all the way up to the great Catskill Mountain House—they soon regarded this entire arena as a divine gift from God. This network of exceptional scholars was to embark on a lively voyage of ideas and creative destiny that included a remarkable range of projects under the enlightening new world sun. They became famous, and even more, were listened to! Libraries, public parks, native paintings, literature, poetry, art academies, and of course, architecture emerged.

It must be mentioned again that by 1827, New York City was the only place to be. After the Revolution the eyes of the people shifted from Philadelphia to this exciting, developing metropolis. "There is more life and spirit and variety in one day, than in all other cities put together in a fortnight. How would the people of Baltimore, or the readers of Philadelphia, or the classiques of Boston get along in this world, if they had not New York . . .to show them what is fashionable in politics and pantaloons, in commerce or in coats and corsets? . . . to show them the way of moving and living?" so printed the New York *Morning Courier and Enquirer* in November of 1829. Moreover, the famous as well as the ordinary could and did leave the city's bay aboard a steamboat, take a trip up the Hudson, and view the beautiful land and ledges from a moving deck. A trip up the Hudson caused as much excitement as a voyage to Europe, and cemented ties to the beautiful river valley.

Two paintings of importance, prophetic and remarkably allegorical, reveal the artistic climate of the time. *Kindred Spirits* by Asher Durand is actually a celebration of a Hudson Valley scene of wild grandeur peculiar to our eastern country. Two famous men, spokesmen for their generation, view from a rocky promontory a land never deformed by culture or the axe, and hope this will never be changed in any way. The implication is that they are discussing the ultimate truths in nature preserved, the true meaning to life. One of the men depicted is William Cullen Bryant, who attempted in his own newspaper, *The Evening Post,* to open the eyes of an indifferent public to the physical wonders of their own land. The other figure is Thomas Cole, the celebrated landscape-poet artist of the Hudson River School tradition. He was responsible for the second remarkably revealing painting, The *Architect's Dream.* Reclining atop a huge Doric column, the architect, with encyclopedias at his feet, portfolios of drawings in hand, a classical plan for a temple in the mist, beyond and behind, and to the left the poetical spire of a vertical Gothic church with matching trees, dreamviews his architectural fantasies. The youthful Alexander Jackson Davis could have been a symbolic figure in both renditions. He had been to that native clove many a time, and with these same men. He was easily that architect, dreaming choices atop a Greek classical column. As the junior partner of Ithiel Town, he had access to the largest architectural library in the new world. Town had been shrewd enough to put his fortune from royalties secured from bridge-building patents to use. Davis could consult and research the great buildings of France, Italy and England without a trek to Europe. Leaving young Alex in charge of the New York offices, Town would take that trip on his own, accompanied by Samuel Morse as a travelling companion.

It is thus impossible to freeze this man, Alexander Davis, and his artistic achievements within the borders of Dutchess County without first mentioning that he did become the most prolific architect of his time. How did this happen? Well, he was astute enough to arrive in the right city at the perfect date and just happened to be ready for all the possibilities. Of course, he was also one of the most original and innovative designers as well as an extremely talented and skillful artist with exceptional feelings for the dramatic. The American landscape was still mostly empty. So, it was wide open for development. Plan it! Do it right! Choose well for history and America, for New York and our beautiful Hudson River Valley!

His business card alone is unusual. It read: *ARCHITECTURAL COMPOSER and Landscape Painter*. It is a fascinating idea that is mostly associated with music or poetry. "Designs, enlarges, lessens or copies objects from nature." Interesting. And if you went to the early firm of Town and Davis for the transaction of business, you would state your needs. It could be anything from a warehouse, a church, a cottage, to a villa. Mr. Town sat you down, showed you the partnership's stock in trade, sheets of neat drawings—something suitable for all occasions. If you should express your desire for something unsuitable, you are corrected. He refers to his library, and who had not heard of it? He mentions his trip to Europe and of seeing the originals in original settings. "We will guide you in the proper direction. Something more personal? Mr. Davis, our executive vice-president, plans especially for you. There will be a slight extra charge, since he is in charge of production—say, thirty-five dollars for the working drawings, ten for a pair of elegant gatepost plans, . . . a fence to go with them?" (A price list for such quotations still exists from 1848 in Davis' handwriting in the Newton-Avery Library at Columbia University.) This was the New York City establishment of Town and Davis, first on number 4 Wall Street, later at the Merchant's Exchange, and finally on Washington Square in a Gothic tower built for New York University and designed by Town and Davis, naturally.

On free days, weekends probably, and to escape the commotion of the already congested New York City, Davis would leave that developing metropolis of Gotham and travel north, first by stagecoach, then by sloop and steamboat, then engage a horse and carriage, and finally free to hike on foot the beloved land with sketchbook in hand. For over fifty years of his long life he visited influential friends who became clients. Already a recognized success, he met and collaborated with a man who shared the same initials, middle name, and importantly kindred ideas—Andrew Jackson Downing, the famous romantic looking landscape and writer theorist, influencer, great tastemaker and horticulturist from Newburgh, New York. He was a famous man who was not only honored in his own birthplace, but would be elected to the Royal Botanic Society of London, in the land of ancient country houses, elegant country gentlemen, sublime gardens, and parks of high cultivation. Even Berlin, the Low Countries, and Denmark acknowledged him, and he visited there, with a brief visit to Paris, where he saw first hand their sights and sounds.

Alexander Jackson Davis, the artist-architect, with his partnership and offices, the only true "modern" establishment around in the only city that really mattered, never took that ocean voyage. He remained to upgrade the architect on the road to professionalism, not merely a superior tradesman. As already suggested, he worked on a fee basis per drawing, partial and full services at percentages. And he did some collaboration with Downing.

Davis and Downing, with regard to the Hudson River Valley, both agreed that a civilized man of means should want and must have a dwelling on this particular place, where he could watch the traffic flow up as well as down the liquid artery from a proper home landscaped and designed by them. Smiling lawns, romantic grounds with artistic embellishments surrounding homes painted in prescribed subdued hues. Never white! This picturesque ideal, believe it or not, was a protest against the confining restraints of symmetrical classicism. A search was on for a truly original American homestyle. What developed was a castellated architecture considered most suitable for the Highlands of the Hudson, pointed Gothic, a borrowed style, for the romantic intervals above and below, and the Italianate villa modified style for clear and sunny glades.

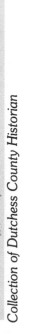

Design for an improved country home from *The Horticulturist*

If any of Downing's ideas have come down to us today, it is for those of us who know enough to want to lead harmonious lives in tasteful surroundings. Davis was to live out a long artistic life. Downing was not, and perhaps that is the reason why there remain more superb examples of Davis' creations in this 20th century.

So, let us embark on a trip, and follow in Davis' energetic, creative footsteps.

It is fitting to begin at Sunnyside, the home of Washington Irving, best remembered as America's first internationally successful author and diplomat. Irving called on Town and Davis in 1838 to remodel but retain the original character of his "snuggery." It originally was a tenant farmer's cottage built in the 17th century on the 52,000 acre Philipsburg Manor. The first remodeling had been accomplished by Irving and George Harvey, neighbor and friend. A Dutch step gable, ancient weathervanes along with some Gothic and Romanesque features were added. Davis and Town wisely added another stepped gable over a new porch and wings, changing the chimney top to a cluster of stacks in the Tudor style. They added Gothic dormers, porches, and casement windows capped with dripstones. The result was a harmonious ensemble of Eclecticism. Sunnyside is one of the most picturesque homes in America. Irving used to view the Hudson and the activity on it from his livingroom window or landscaped summer lawn. The grounds are still beautiful with ancient trees, orchards, gardens and wooded paths. It still looks the same as when Davis last visited its charismatic owner.

Moving a bit to the north, nearer Tarrytown, we can drop by at Lyndhurst. It was here that Davis was called upon to draw up plans for a Gothic villa. A country mansion in the pointed style, a dream castle for tycoon knights and their lovely ladies. Downing wrote, ". . . The eye is struck by the picturesque outline of towers, turrets, gables and pinnacles and with pleasing variety afforded by the windows decorated with stone mullions and tracery." Lyndhurst is Davis' masterpiece and one of the great houses of America, unrivaled as an example of American Gothic Revival. The romantic setting, sweeping vistas, long curving driveways, and great ancient trees are only a part of the grey-white exterior constructed of Sing Sing marble. The interior, also designed by Davis, awaits with gracefully ribbed ceilings on the first floor. The dining room with bay windows (said to be an invention of Davis) and the great timbered ceiling of the library still looks out upon the lordly Hudson through a huge mullioned window. Lyndhurst has had three owners: William Paulding, a general and former mayor of New York; George Merritt, merchant and wealthy from a Patent Car Spring; and Jay Gould, one of the most powerful railroad men of America. In 1838, Paulding called upon Davis, then thirty-five years old, to turn his home into a country seat. Davis, in his studio beneath the turreted tower of the great new Gothic building at NYU, drew his sensitive, painstakingly skillful, and exquisite plans, drawings and sketches. When the house was completed, it became known as Paulding's Folly by some who considered it too large for a home. However, George Merritt, the second owner, called upon Davis to enlarge the house for his sizable family. In 1864–67, Davis raised the roofline, added a northern wing, a new porte-cochere to the east, and a great tower to the west. The Merritt children's initials are whimsically perpetuated there high up on the cornice beneath the battlements. When Jay Gould purchased the Knoll, or Lyndhurst, as it is now known, he changed little. The original vaulted ribbed celings, the original corbels and bosses, even the furniture designed by Davis, and the chimney pieces are there to be seen today. Lyndhurst is a monument to American architectural history, and is further enhanced in its authenticity by the numerous documents and remarkable drawings by the architect.

In November of 1841, Philip Paulding, the son of seventy-year old William, wrote to Davis: "If you see anything offensive to your gothick eye (concerning some mantels to be sent) . . . put your veto on it. They are extremely elegant and I wish them to be correct specimens of the style. How the ladies will dote on them!"

Lyndhurst must have been a childhood dream come true for Davis. As a precocious lad, he stole to the attic of his parent's home to read Gothic novels about unhappy heroines. He drew for them romantic castles, arranging trapdoors, subterraneous passageways and drawbridges. Lyndhurst looks as if exceptional men and women talked, laughed and loved to live here. One sees the grand and the beautiful. A complex elegant pile. Rich in color, sensuous, and as light burst dramatically through stained glass windows, the experience gives anyone the feeling of the religious in this cathedral of a home.

Leaving Lyndhurst, our next visit is to Locust Grove in Poughkeepsie. We find ourselves in the heartland of Dutchess County. Originally, this was the home of Samuel Finley Breese Morse, another brilliant 19th century friend—an inventor, artist and founder of the National Academy of Design. Here was the meeting place of Downing, Davis, and Matthew Vassar. Morse bought this North River property in July of 1847. It had been part of the Livingston Manor. "But far superior," wrote Morse, "100 acres and house for $17,000. I am almost afraid to tell you of its beauties and advantages. Its capabilities, as the landscape gardeners would say, are unequalled. There is every variety of surface: plain, hill, dale, glen, running streams, and fine forests. The Fishkill Mountains toward the South, the Catskills towards the North. The Hudson with its variety of rivercraft, steamboats of all kinds, sloops, etc., constantly showing a varied scene. Delightful neighbors and friends. The new railroad will run at the foot of the grounds, probably on the river and brings NY within two hours of us . . . Good markets, churches, schools."

Morse invited Davis in 1852 to remodel his peaceful retreat into the style of a Tuscan Villa. Morse had returned from his European trip with Ithiel Town and had admired the styles he had seen in Italy. Davis, under the watchful eyes of fellow-artist, Samuel Morse, added the present porte-cochere, the hexagonal-porched and latticed centered portion, and the tall tower to the riverside. Morse spent the warmer months of every year here, until his death in 1872. (He had a townhouse and offices in the north corner suite of rooms upon the fourth floor tower above those of Town and Davis.) The grounds and gardens, and intertwining wisteria, another 19th century must (can be seen blooming at both Sunnyside as well as at Lyndhurst), were planned in the style of Downing. Today, 20th century traffic and snarls speed past its unruffled calm every day of the week. The somber tan house will remain much as it was, for the property is a National Historic Landmark. You can visit and feel the gentle pull

Locust Grove, home of Samuel F. B. Morse in Poughkeepsie

Dutchess County Historical Society Yearbook 1932

of the mannered generation, walk the gracious grounds, notice the black locust trees that Jane Livingston, wife of Henry Jr., planted along the driveway in the 18th century. You can even enter the house, and see the interior and furnishings, including drawing plans by Davis.

Travel now on to Rhinebeck, that historic village founded in 1688. Here is my favorite house of all, and the inspiration for the original interest in research of who was this person A. J. Davis. Whenever I am in the vicinity and know that I will be passing this charming dwelling, I find myself sitting a little straighter, straining to see its condition, determined not to miss that sight. Well, it is safe and sound, the Delamater House, and in a state of perfect preservation even though 140 years old. Davis designed it for the founder of Rhinebeck's First National Bank. A list of architectural details of this beautiful cottage would read like a textbook for the proper small house in the Carpenter's Gothic manner. It is now a guesthouse of the Beekman Arms. George Washington did not live long enough to sleep here, but you can. The center gable, with delicate ornamental bargeboard, large porch with elaborate "gingerbread" woodwork and rope-hanging swings, diamond paned windows, and projecting bays, and paired chimneystacks should delight you. But it is the board and batten siding that typifies and integrates the various shapes and textures by emphasizing the verticality of them all. A Davis hallmark. The scrolls and finials are bandsawed from wood, where at Lyndhurst these are cut from stone. Here we have come a long Gothic way: a condensed size, in wood, not stone, a house available to a less wealthy man, still romantic, still special and even religious, reaching a kind of architectural perfection. This style spread out through the entire 19th century New England, and as far west as the Mississippi. A very contagious style and idea were born. Perhaps ordinary men with some means could live in such a house and way. The interior of the Delamater House is now as authentic as its exterior and gives the visitor an idea as to furnishings of years past. Davis' plans and lovely architectural drawings are mounted on the wall of the central hallway.

Travelling further north, still in Dutchess County, and onto the campus of Bard College, there is an enchanting hexagonal gatehouse. It is really in a class all its own. Atop a grassy knoll, surrounded by huge embracing pinetrees, this small example of perfection, now painted white, houses the administrative offices of the college. An architectural gem. Once inside, there are three floors. The offices are windowed slices of its geometric form. To reach them there is a central spiral stairway in its very center. It was originally built from Davis plans, including a manor house called Blythwood, that no longer exists (circa late 1830–40). The gatehouse's projecting roof with supporting brackets are typical features of Hudson Valley architecture of the 19th century era, and seems to also show the influence of Orson Fowler and his interest in using the geometric shape as a perfect form to be lived in.

Thomas Jefferson, our only architectural president, sighed over Roman ruins while in France and came home and built Monticello and designed the University of Virginia, both after the classical style. He greatly influenced the early character of America and Washington D. C. "I am," he confessed to Madison, "an enthusiast on the subjects of the arts, but it is an enthusiasm of which I am not ashamed." He was our first national tastemaker.

Generations later, another president, Franklin Delano Roosevelt, Dutchess County-born, who when he retired had expressed the desire to spend those years as a Hyde Park historian with an emphasis on local architecture. In 1942 he acquired a little 9 × 12 sketchbook that now resides in the Roosevelt Library. It can be seen anytime, opened in its showcase. Our 32nd president and neighbor, who lived in an interesting manor house of his own overlooking the Hudson, assembled this collection of 59 drawings because he knew it for what it is. An historical artistic gem. The landscapes and buildings therein are drawings by A. J. Davis, sketched by him on hiking trips up and down this river valley. They are enveloped in an atmosphere of 19th century beauty, evoking a special texture and light. But it is not just any old light, not any old place, any old time. They are actual sights Alex Davis looked upon, the still unspoiled slopes of the Hudson Valley and River, all drawn in his lovely linear line, watercolor wash, or both. There is a summer riverbank scene, quietly rendered in a breathless beauty of trees and watercolor. On the flyleaf is Davis' name penciled in his own lovely handwriting. On another page he has written in the names of proper flower plantings for a lady's garden. Several quick sketches in hazy misty colors depict: Anthony's Nose, Down Poughkeepsie-Up-Catskills, West Point, Downstream-Highlands, "Shakespeare's Temple at Garrick's House"—a classical pretty cameo against American greenery. There are pencil sketches of Gothic chairs at Lyndhurst. One is called the wheelchair, its back designed as the rose windows of a stained glass design taken directly from the great Gothic cathedrals of Europe and England. There is an exquisite rendering of the gatehouse at Bard, delicately drawn floorplans for an oval house in tipped-in watercolor, and one delightful oriental-like gazebo—a romantic enclosure, a shelter from the sun, but for viewing river traffic, landscape, sky, trees, even sunsets. This bears the title of Montgomery Place-Shore Seat. Behind the gazebo, but not seen, still stands the elegant house twice remodeled by Davis. He designed the east portico with its classical ornamentation and roof balustrade. It is a magnificent and famous estate, and was owned by Mrs. Edward Livingston during the picturesque 19th century. One interesting scene reveals three tiny figures laboring up a wooded mountain incline toward a little gazebo. To the right, a bubbling stream tumbles downward. The men hiking could be Davis himself, with Thomas Cole, Asher Durand, William Cullen Bryant, or even Downing!

The sketchbook is usually opened not to a Dutchess County scene, but to a delightful fairytale rendition of Davis' own house, a summer lodge he called Wildmont. Perched atop 25 acres on the cliffs above West Orange County, New Jersey, beyond the tidal swamps and undulating lowlands, overlooking New York Bay, its turrets, towers, gables, bays and chimneys abounded. The view was southeast and was part of a remarkable early experiment in group suburban living (circa 1878). Homes were planned and set on 300 acres of gardenlike surroundings, complete with planned and winding carriage roads. A Davis gatehouse still guards the timeless rhythms of a God-given nature. In the clear 19th century air, the panoramic view from his castle extended 100 miles onto the church spires of Brooklyn. Davis could look out and see a forest of ship's masts of New York City. I like to imagine that he could also, in his own board and batten, stuccoed brick ensemble, turn and gaze out a northern bay window and see the County of Dutchess beckoning him to return.

There is a portrait of Davis, by a George Freeman dated 1852. He is seated, a serious, small featured, light-haired gentleman, formally attired in his proper black suit. 1852 Is the year Downing died. Davis lived on to 1892, eighty-nine years old, in a simple cottage that in the end replaced Wildmont after it burned down. The Gothic era was really over. America had tired of it all and was onto new architectural styles, but Davis had shown how romantic forms, though borrowed in the beginning, could in the end have native and poetic expression.

And here is the message from the past. From preserved architecture one can learn more history, philosophy, art and lifestyles than from reading books. Alexander Jackson Davis, one great artistic spirit from the 19th century, a truly unique period of opulence and studied manners, gives much for us to dwell upon in this computerized 20th century as we rush mindlessly on to the next toll booth or plaza.

Thank you, Mr. Davis!

BIBLIOGRAPHY

Andrews, Wayne: *Architecture, Ambition, and America;* The Free Press; 1964
Davies, Jane: "Llewellyn Park;" January 1975, pages 142–58
Davis, Alex J.: *Sketchbook:* Roosevelt Library of Research; Hyde Park, N. Y.
Landmarks of Dutchess County, 1683–1867; Architecture Worth Saving; 1969
Lynes, Russell: *The Tastemakers,* Dover Publications, Inc.: NYC; 1980
Morse, Edward Lind: *Samuel F. B. Morse, Letters & Journals;* Two Volumes
National Trust for Historical Preservation: *Lyndhurst;* Booklet: April, 1965
Newton, Roger Hale: *Town & Davis, Architects;* Columbia University Press; 1942

A very sincere thanks to the Roosevelt Library Research staff and slide department and Dr. Teichman.

THE TWENTY MILE LONG MUSEUM

William F. Gekle

The story behind this Tercentenary observance actually began in the year 1664 when the English almost casually deprived the Dutch of what had been called New Netherland. They did not seem very much interested in all of the territory that had been claimed by the Dutch, but only in that part through which the Hudson River flowed. The Duke of York, whose province it became through the generosity of his brother, King Charles, relinquished or, more accurately, abandoned most of the eastern portion of New Netherland to the Puritans and Quakers of New England. This included much fine land as well as a number of small islands clustered below Cape Cod. That portion of the Dutch claim between the Hudson and Delaware Rivers, the Duke presented to two of his close friends. This was a long, narrow strip of fertile land which, despite the fact that it ran due north and south, came to be known as East Jersey and West Jersey and collectively as The Jerseys.

As to the wilderness north of Albany which extended, for all anyone knew at the time, westward to the Pacific Ocean, the Duke gave it very little thought. He seemed quite content that the Province of New York should consist almost entirely of the Hudson River Valley and its contiguous mountains. The Duke considered, as did everyone else at the time, that the Hudson River ran to the north all the way to the St. Lawrence, and that it ran through a vast wilderness that had been briefly explored only by a Frenchman named Champlain. The French might therefore be said to have some claim to this land and the English were not minded to dispute it for the present; they were having trouble enough with the French as it was. They decided to bide their time until the "Domino Theory" would toss the wilderness into their lap and the Province of New York would extend to the very border of Canada. Unless, of course, Canada tumbled as well.

The Province of New York therefore consisted, in practice and in principle, of Long Island, which gave New York as much coastline as it would ever need, and the Hudson River Valley between New York and Albany. In the year 1683, the Province was divided into twelve counties for the praiseworthy purpose of establishing a framework of government under the supervision of the Crown. Actually, New York was at the time so sparsely inhabited in most regions that there was almost no one to govern. Nevertheless, counties were established and named for various branches of the royal family and its dependencies. One of the counties was designated "The Dutchess's County" in honor of the Duke of York's wife, another was called "Ulster County" in the hope and belief that the Irish would very shortly be brought to heel—or at least to show some signs of deference to the Crown.

What was it like, we may wonder, three hundred years ago? What did the Hudson River Valley look like in the year 1683—the year we celebrate in our meeting here today? It looked almost exactly the same then as it does now. Fortunately, there has been preserved for us a very good picture of it, live and in color. To see this picture, we have but to walk out to the very middle of the Mid-Hudson Bridge, which one can very easily do, although at the risk of being regarded with some suspicion.

Standing on the bridge and looking to the south, all that one can see is a great, green world of forested hills and smoothly rounded promontories through the center of which runs the Long Reach of the Hudson River. This green world is what one would have seen in 1683 or, for that matter, in 1609 when Henry Hudson first sailed up the river. It is well to keep one's eyes on the horizon ahead, where the green meets the sky, and not to permit one's eyes to stray to either side beneath the bridge where it is anchored in sheer cliffs of solid rock. There, on both sides of the river, as far as the eye can see, there is no sign of human habitation, nor of man's machinations, nor of corporate enterprise.

We may know very well that somewhere down there are the blasted hills and the enormous quarried hole that mark the graves of the hamlets of Camelot and of Clinton Point, but they are hidden

213

from view. Mine Point conceals what Lone Star Industries hath wrought, just as, a little further down, Blue Point and other headlands conceal the power plants at Danskammer and Roseton. To the north, toward Crum Elbow where the Long Reach ends and the river turns to one side, the same view persists from this vantage point. The same rolling waves of green, broken only by the corner of a dormitory at Marist College and the cupolas atop the former Jesuit stronghold that now houses the CIA. [Lest anyone suspect a Jesuit Connection for that sometimes sinister organization, let us recall that CIA thus applied means merely the Culinary Institute of America.]

How does one explain this seeming miracle? How can there possibly exist this great green place in such close proximity to the concrete sprawl of megalopolis at the mouth of the river? Surely man has helped to preserve what God has so generously given him. The fact, the statistical fact, is that even today, in this troubled year of 1983, more than three-fifths of New York State, the former Royal Province, is covered with trees. Sixty-one percent, according to the New York State Forest Preserve in its current report, is still forest primeval. And the Hudson-Catskill region is one of the most thickly forested in the state, with more than two million, three hundred thousand *acres* of tree-covered land. But greenery is not best expressed in statistics, nor can percentages describe what the eyes can see: the great, green world of the Hudson River Valley. A miracle indeed!

Miracles defy explanation, but there is an explanation for this one. It is one of many paradoxes we will encounter as we consider the twenty-mile stretch of the river to the north of Crum Elbow and Hyde Park. The miracle and the explanations all have their origin in the year 1683 when the Duke of York established the river counties. Almost immediately thereafter, another layer of royal initiative was superimposed upon this pattern of counties. This took the form of manorial grants, of enormous tracts of land given by the Crown to a handful of carefully chosen individuals. The Lords of the Manors thus created assumed all of the rights and privileges accorded them, including the right to hold courts-leet and courts-baron, which gave them almost absolute control over the lives of all who lived or came to live upon the lands they owned. Moreover, economic control was also built *into* the system for, whether those who lived on the land as tenants paid for it in fee-simple or through leasehold, they were in effect the vassals of the Lords of the Manors.

One final layer of royal benevolence was interposed between the land and the people. This was the granting of Royal Patents to individuals who bought or otherwise acquired land from the local Indians. The patents were usually quite extensive tracts of land, not as large as the manorial grants but comfortable enough for the one or two individuals to whom they were given. It should be quite obvious that these various layers constituted one of the most effective forms of population control ever devised by man. It should be equally obvious that we who live here on the Hudson are, in many respects, the ultimate beneficiaries of these policies of royal retardation.

We have no knowledge of what plans the Duke of York might have had for the future of the Province of New York because, in 1685, he became King James the Second of England. From that time on, his own future became uncertain and his plans were subject to change without notice. His was not a happy reign. It is ironic that, having evicted the Dutch from New York, he was himself evicted from London by a Dutchman who then became King of England in his place. William of Orange, for all his romantic appeal and historical fame, did nothing to encourage the growth of the Province of New York. As a result, it remained the least populous of England's dominions across the sea. This was because less than two dozen Lords of the Manor and Royal Patentees owned too much land, leaving too little for those who might have wished to come here. This is another of the paradoxes mentioned earlier: the governors frequently outnumbered the governed.

This was made quite clear in a report, dated January 2, 1700, made by the Earl of Bellomont, Governor of New York, to the Lords of Trade in London. The Governor complained that men of initiative were not satisfied to settle where they could never hope to own the land they cultivated, and that New York was steadily losing what little population it did have to the Jerseys and Pennsylvania where land was available almost for the asking or taking. As an example of this, Bellomont pointed out that Robert Livingston, whose grant was 16 miles long and 24 miles broad, owned more than one hundred and sixty-three thousand acres. On all this land, said the Governor, there were only four or five families who worked for him and who remained too poor ever to become farmers on their own. He cited also the situation on the Manor of Cortland. The Cortlands were, of course, related to the Livingstons and Beekmans, and perhaps as a matter of family policy, they accommodated an equally small number of poor families.

The years that followed Lord Bellomont's report to London were the most turbulent ever experienced in this magnificent mid-region of the Hudson Valley. The Lords of the Manor became more powerful politically and economically. Their hold on their land and their tenants was virtually feudal. There were uprisings and riotings among the tenants and there were wars with the French and the Indians. This warfare was not as disruptive here as it was elsewhere, but that was only because there were so few combatants to be encountered here. It was not until the reign of Queen Anne that an effort was made to encourage emigration to the Royal Province. Some three thousand Palatine refugees were sent here with the promise of land and freedom. The Provincial Government had purchased six thousand acres of pine forest from Robert Livingston. The Palatines were to settle here, and to set themselves up in the manufacture of naval stores for Her Majesty's growing fleet. The tall trees would provide masts for her ships, and pitch and turpentine for the caulking and painting thereof. Unfortunately, the pine trees turned out to be of the wrong kind and the Palatines fell into vassalage of the Manor or escaped into vacant lands across the river and into the mountain valleys of the Catskills.

Then, close on the heels of the French and Indian Wars, the great American Rebellion against England began. It was not until 1783, exactly one hundred years after the event we celebrate here today, that a treaty of peace was signed and we had won our independence. The last British troops sailed for home, the lands of the Loyalists were seized, and peace settled down upon the Hudson Valley. These intimations of history are important to us, not only because they are a part of our heritage, but because, however tedious they may be when recounted in detail, they explain how population growth and the problems of progress were held at bay for so many years. Perhaps they also explain that pleasantly peculiar sensation one so often feels in Hudson Valley, of being suspended in time.

Let us return, for a moment, to the report of Lord Bellomont. In it, you will remember, he mentions the sixteen mile length of Livingston Manor that lies along the east bank of the Hudson River. It is that stretch of land that is central to our history here in Dutchess County, as well as to the delivery of this paper and what it proposes. We are, most of us, familiar with that sixteen mile stretch. We know, for example, that in March of 1979, the National Register of Historic Places recognized its importance and designated it as the Sixteen Mile Historic District. In May of the same year, it was decided by the National Register to add to it the Clermont Estates and thus created an eighteen mile stretch of contiguous shoreland properties - the longest historic district in the entire nation. Not to be outdone by the Federal government, the State of New York, in the following year, increased this shoreland area from eighteen miles to twenty miles and designated it as the first State Scenic Area. We have thus followed the traditional pattern of superimposing one layer of protection and governance upon another. It is, of course, this very same area to which I refer in the title of this presentation as "The Twenty-Mile Long Museum" . . . for that is exactly what it is—a museum.

There is nothing quite like it anywhere else in the country, and perhaps not in the world. Here on the east bank of one of the world's most beautiful rivers, is a living museum of our national history, an environmental miracle almost untouched by devastation, pollution and paving-over. It has, thus far, been protected and preserved as few places in the world have been. It has been the subject of more books, brochures and articles than most places in our country. It has been written about for the past two hundred years by almost every great American author and by dozens of world-travelers: admired, praised and almost endlessly described. Even Henry James, that distinguished expatriate, when he saw it again after many years absence from his country, noted that there were here the signs of a great and gracious civilization.

A contemporary writer recently observed the "The middle portion of the Hudson River Valley is an area that is ostensibly located between New York City and Albany, but on closer inspection turns out to be situated somewhere between the eighteenth and nineteenth centuries." What a delightful thing to say, no matter how disparagingly he may have meant it! But it is a great deal more than a museum. It is a place where people have lived for more than three centuries, a full hundred years before the nation itself existed. These were a people who accomplished much for themselves, and who did more than their share in shaping the future of the nation they helped to establish.

There are, within this short space of twenty miles, some three dozen estates, large and small. On most of them were built what have come to be known as the Great Houses, the River Houses. They are monuments, perhaps memorials is the better word, living memorials, of what has been described as the "quasi-manorial character of Hudson Valley land tenure that was unique in the United States." They are called the Great Houses because they are simply that—houses that were built as the homes of the large families that occupied them for generations. They are not the "show-places" such as were built in later years by the merely rich in Newport and Palm Beach, nor are they the elegantly restrained town-houses one sees in such citadels of urban civilization as Boston and Philadelphia, Charleston and Savannah.

These houses existed in a kind of feudal enclave, if you will, inhabited by a class of people who came as close to being an aristocracy or landed gentry as we have ever had in this country. This manorial system persisted well into the early years of the great democratic republic to which, paradoxically, these families contributed their sons, their fortunes and, as the phrase went in those days, their sacred honor. Most of the Great Houses face to the west, looking out over the river to the blue mountains beyond. They began as rather plainly designed and solidly built houses, standing foursquare and strong against the elements and the uncertainties of life on a frontier. Later, after independence had been won and enemies pacified, they were enlarged and embellished. They sprouted wings and porticoes, added towers and turrets, pillars and columns. They became, as did their owners, centers of political, economic and cultural power.

The people who lived in these houses continued, somewhat astonishingly for all they were considered aristocrats, to use their power for the common good. Among them were members of the first Continental Congress, framers and signers of the Constitution of the United States, field officers by the dozen in the army that fought and won the war with England. They outfitted privateers to carry on the war at sea, and if some of the privateers became pirates it was only because the pirates saw it as their patriotic duty to do so. It was a Robert Livingston (there seems always to have been at least one Robert Livingston in the family) who arranged the Louisiana Purchase—and who built the first steamboat before he had ever heard of Robert Fulton, and it was a Roosevelt who helped him in this work. The men who married into the Livingston family managed, most of them, to live up to Livingston standards. There was Richard Montgomery who captured Montreal and who became the first American hero of the war when he was killed in the assault on Quebec. There was General Armstrong who, having failed to make George Washington the King of America, settled for a president and became another Minister to France. There were Livingstons at the Battle of Saratoga and at West Point when the treason of Benedict Arnold began to unravel.

The Livingston women were no less remarkable. Consider Margaret Livingston who, after the British burned Clermont in 1777, asked General George Clinton to release from army duty the carpenters and stone masons she needed to rebuild the house—and got them. And Janet Livingston Montgomery who built Montgomery Place after her husband had been killed at Quebec. There were Livingston women who married Astors, Chanlers and Aldriches who bore new generations of Livingstons, Astors, Chanlers and Aldriches. It was all of these men and women who helped to create the history and the legends surrounding these great estates and the houses that still stand, suspended in time, in this National Historic District.

But this must not and cannot be construed as merely a foolish and futile exercise in ancestor worship, nor a celebration of great wealth. We must consider also that which they created here, and the contributions they made in shaping this great national asset. They gave such men as Andre Parmentier, the man who landscaped the estate of Dr. Hosack in Hyde Park, the scope he required to do his work. And to Andrew Jackson Downing whose theory of landscape gardening was born along the Hudson and who carried out the landscaping of Montgomery Place and Blithewood and many other estates on the river. And Hans Gustav Ehlers who helped to create the broad vistas and the intimate gardens in this historic district. Nor can we forget men like Alexander Jackson Davis, Calvert Vaux and Stanford White who were employed here to create and develop a truly American style of

Ogden and Ruth Livingston Mills Mansion, Staatsburg, New York

217

architecture. And who does not know that the first school of painting in America had its home here in the Hudson Valley?

All of these things taken together contribute to the museum-quality of this place where the Great Houses stand beside the great river. Their very names are evocative of this place and their time. There are the English and Scottish names of Clermont, Calendar House, Teviot, Montgomery Place, Rokeby, Maizefield, Leacote, Ellerslie and Ankony. The pastoral-sounding names of Rose Hill, The Pynes, Blithewood, Ferncliff, Edgewater and Sylvania. The names that seem to have come from Gothic romances: Marienruh, Ravenswood, Wildercliff, Wyndcliff and Wilderstein. All of these names are expressive of this place and these people and of the ambience they created here amid a setting of river and mountains that inspired a new school of painting and a new way of looking at the world around us. These names are a litany of praise of a very special place, and there is a note of sadness in the recital because the Great Houses and the land upon which they stand now face a very uncertain future.

The houses are old and in need of repair and restoration. Some of them have already disappeared, others have been destroyed by fire and ravaged by vandalism. The Great Houses no longer house large families—nor produce them. It is only the meek who plan to inherit the earth. Death and taxes enact their historic roles and exact their traditional tools. The cumulative effects of land taxes, inheritance taxes and the costs of maintainance and necessary repairs create problems never before faced by the Great Houses. They are a great national resource, they are unique in their very existence, and that existence is threatened—or will be in the coming years. The question is a very simple one: what will become of them? The answers to that question should be of concern to all of us because we are talking about a national asset that could be forever lost to us.

The question we have posed is complicated by the diversity of present ownership as well as by the condition of some of these houses and the practical uses to which they might be put. Some of the houses are still owned and occupied by descendants of the original families. Some have been acquired by institutions. The useful life of any of them cannot be predicted, and so the problem grows rather than diminishes, or can be diminished by individual effort. This is not because the problem has been ignored. As we have seen, there has been a tremendous amount of national, state, and regional concern over the preservation of this historic district. Plans have been drawn up by the National Trust for Historic Preservation and by the State of New York. Local communities have created a Hudson River Shorelands Task Force and the State formed a Heritage Task Force to study the problem and come up with solutions. County commissions, local municipal governments and half a dozen historical societies have conducted studies and made surveys and enacted resolutions. The problem has attracted wide attention and good intentions - but the problem has avoided or eluded solutions. That we must find the answers is obvious. The manner in which we do so is not at all clear.

The first thing to be taken into consideration, naturally, is the present ownership of the land in this region. Having supported their heritage for so many years, having improved their houses and lands, and having been generously taxed for as many years, the owners cannot be expected to donate or otherwise dispose of their property except on favorable terms. Most of them are torn between their desire to see their possessions properly preserved and the temptations offered by developers. The State of New York cannot be expected to purchase all of them and at the same time relinquish the taxes they would yield.

Also interested in the ultimate fate of the Great Houses and the almost priceless land upon which they stand are the developers, the carpet-baggers and urban gorillas who are always ready to move in with their bulldozers and wrecking-balls. Their vision runs to how many look-alike houses can be crowded into any given amount of acres and how many high-rise condominiums can take advantage of the riverviews. Most important to them is how many banks and zoning-boards they can persuade to share their visions. We are fortunate that there is a lower-level but longer lasting and more accountable layer of local government that has, at least until now, steadfastly rejected the wooings of the most ambitious developers. The officials in the towns, villages and counties involved are as history-oriented and preservation-minded as their citizens and voters want them to be.

It must be realized, however, that institutionalization carries with it as many dangers as carpet-baggery and Levittownery. There are those who see large houses on large expanses of land as ideal for the establishment of so-called "half-way" houses for the rehabilitation of the drug-addicted, the wayward, and other classifications of social misfits. Such establishments have their place in our society, but not necessarily in a place of such historical and environmental importance. Some of us will remember a time when the Catholic Church acquired a number of these estates for seminaries, convents and monasteries. They made excellent neighbors, to be sure, were well-behaved and quiet except for occasional bell-ringing, but their day seems to have passed, alas, or is passing.

I asked John Delafield one day, as we stood on the lawn fronting his Montgomery Place estate: "What will become of all these beautiful houses and their lands?" He shrugged, and then said he thought they might become museums and state parks. I suppose it was this that first set me to thinking about a twenty-mile long museum. There is some precedent for this: Clermont is already a state park and a small museum. The Ogden Mills mansion, once called Endekill and one of the earliest of the Livingston estates, is now a museum. The Roosevelt estate has become one of the most important museums within the region and the State of New York. Wilderstein, owned by Margaret Suckely, will become a museum by the wish of its owner. Miss Suckely is an archivist in her own right and her collection of family papers and library form the basic foundation for a house museum. So, too, do Rokeby and Montgomery Place with their libraries and records of three hundred years. But we cannot realistically think of creating more Williamsburgs and Sturbridge Villages throughout the country. A twenty-mile long museum seems, on the face of it,, unrealistic indeed. But there is the nagging thought: is it unrealistic? Have we not the possibility, and the potentials for turning this great national asset into a great national museum?

Almost every commission or organization that has ever surveyed and studied this region has mentioned the possibility of one or more museums here, and of archival centers. Starting with the Hudson River Valley Commission, which issued a preliminary inventory in January of 1969, and continuing with the Heritage Task Force, and the Hudson River Shorelands Scenic District, and the National Historic District, reports and brochures have been produced to this end. The primary purpose of all of them can be summed up in this one sentence: "To assist the present and future landowners in programs to maintain, preserve and restore their properties in a way that is sympathetic to the overall historic and cultural character of the regional landscape."

All of these organizations and their programs agree on one thing: the setting up of a master plan, one that has the force of some authority behind it. Most of these organizations have been over-lapping and under-financed, but the most serious defect in them and their greatest weakness is that their life expectancy seldom exceeds four years—a time span that happens, unfortunately, to coincide with that of political administrations, on the national as well as the state level. What is needed, of course, is a carefully balanced program, a master plan, to be continuously administered by state and Federal governments and through the cooperation and contributions of the private and public sectors.

With this in mind, I would like to present a proposal, a potential program, for the express purpose of establishing a twenty-mile museum or, if you will, a National Historic Preserve. The United States Department of the Interior, under the present direction of the zealous Secretary Watt, has already launched an ambitious program for the sale of extremely large tracts of Federally owned land. There are millions of acres of such land scattered throughout the country, and there is no doubt that it is public land. There should also be no doubt as to who should benefit from their sale. It would probably take an act of Congress to stipulate that the entire proceeds of these land sales be placed in a National Trust Fund or, more specifically, a National *Public* Trust Fund. The Act should further stipulate that no part of this Fund is to be used by this or any other administration to reduce its deficits, cut taxes, bolster up any other sections of the economy, provide subsidies for any class of individuals, crops or corporate endeavor. The Fund would be used only for the benefit of the public at large. It should be used for the purchase of lands and facilities to be used by the general public, now and forever. This would include national parks, seashore areas, barrier islands, wildlife preserves, wetlands and endangered ecosystems. It could be used for the establishment and operation of libraries and museums and the maintenance thereof.

The sale of thousands, perhaps millions, of acres of sagebrush and cactus, desert and inaccessible mountain areas would establish a National Public Trust Fund with millions or billions of dollars in cash which, properly invested, would provide more dollars. This proposal is not, please note, an effort to liquidate the assets of the United States, which seems to be the intent of Secretary Watt. On the contrary, it would make a great deal of sense to trade off vast areas of virtually useless land in exchange for land and facilities of greater public benefit. Some of these more isolated public lands could be sold to those industries who create nuclear and chemical wastes: others for the creation of enormous solar-power stations under public ownership.

The National Public Trust Fund would be administered by a Board of Trustees, at first appointed or nominated by a Congressional or Senate Committee and subject to Congressional approval. Members of the Board would be scholars, historians, certain kinds of businessmen who would be free of conflicts of interest, professionals in certain fields of study, as well as former holders of public office whose service to the nation had always been beyond reproach. Such a Board of Trustees could purchase the entire Twenty-Mile Historic District and make of it a National Historic Preserve. This would not be a campsite, a wilderness for the pleasures, such as they are, of backpackers. There would be no convenience food purveyors, service stations or muffler repair shops within the Preserve—there is plenty of room for these facilities on the state and county highways nearby.

Provisions would be made for the continued residence of the present owners on their properties. There already exist a number of ways in which landowners in this district can donate portions of their land for preservation and tax exemptions. The most immediate result of the purchase, restoration and maintenance of the District would be a tremendous increase in the one industry suitable to it—the tourist trade. More important, because it would be a year-round rather than a seasonal facility, a number of scholars and research historians would be drawn to the area. This is already true of the Roosevelt Library and Museum in Hyde Park. Other uses suggest themselves: some of the present buildings might be leased to become corporate seminar or research centers, others would be houses of study operated under lease by colleges and universities. Some of the present houses might become guest houses for visiting scholars, or open to tourists and charging admission. The land could still support its orchards and such private enterprises, all under lease to the Trust, as the raising of cattle and horses. In thus reverting to the traditional leasehold arrangement, further revenues would be paid into the National Public Trust Fund.

The National Historic Preserve could also acquire, through purchase or donation, many kinds of valuable historic material and documents. Many of these documents have already been acquired by universities and museums in distant parts of the country. The University of Texas, for example, and the Huntington Museum in California, with their enormous budgets and great thirst for the records and artifacts of earlier civilizations, such as the one that flourished herein the eighteenth and early nineteenth centures, already hold too many treasures that should one day be brought home. The Trust could also publish and sell books and brochures of the history and art that was created here, and biographies of the people who lived in the great houses and of the great houses themselves.

There is no doubt that the cities, towns and villages in the surrounding areas would benefit from the great attraction of the Historic Preserve. Hotels, motels, restaurants and businesses of every kind would benefit, as would the taxing authorities, even though the properties themselves might be removed from the tax rolls. This is not an impossible dream: the land, the stage-setting, the backdrops are in place—all that is needed is for the action to begin. Public awareness, interest and support are already considerable; it needs but be channeled and directed by a master plan. The Twenty-Mile Long Museum is possible, and it could and would become, to a large extent, self-supporting and even profitable.

Whether or not some or all of these things are done in the next few years, whether this great public asset is permitted to be destroyed by development or allowed to decay, this much is certain: the Twenty-Mile Long Museum already exists. Most of it is still privately owned, and we owe much to those who have preserved and protected it for so many years. The owners must be compensated fairly and gratefully. The owners would be pleased, and they would, no doubt, cooperate in efforts to see their heritage become ours through public ownership. It is the only reward they will have had for their patient and expensive stewardship, and the only assurance we will have that this place and all that it represents will remain forever preserved in the public interest.

This will take a lot of doing—even if the proposed National Public Trust Fund comes into existence through an Act of Congresss, and even if the Public Trust Fund were to find itself awash in millions. There would remain the problems of acquisition, organization and administration. Fortunately, there is a workable model for us to follow. The British National Trust has saved many of the stately homes of England—and made them pay. We could look to the British for help—especially since they are also observing 1983 as the anniversary year of their having lost their finest American Province.

We also have for our guidance the work of the several task forces and their recommendations. Scenic Hudson has developed a fact sheet with suggestions concerning such things as tax abatements and the advantages of transfer of title to various organizations that have been established for just these purposes. Local libraries and historical societies have copies of a book published several years ago through a New York State grant. Entitled *Saving Large Estates,* the book describes what has been done and outlines realistic programs for use wherever there is enough interest by citizens and local governments in establishing their own preservation projects. Nowhere in this country is there as much to be preserved and protected than on this twenty-mile stretch of the east bank of the Hudson River. Let us, therefore, begin . . . and carry through.

PLURALISM AND THE CATHOLIC COMMUNITY IN 19TH CENTURY POUGHKEEPSIE

Louis C. Zuccarello
Professor of Political Science, Marist College

The reality of pluralism has been a key factor in more recent attempts to understand and describe the development of American society from its colonial origins to its contemporary configuration. Particular attention has been paid to the identification of major ethnic, racial and religious groups and to the study of their interactions over the years. Others have focused on the attempts of minority groups, different at different stages of our history, to negotiate with the dominant culture to arrive at mutually acceptable accommodations. The historical debate over what constituted the major accommodation patterns continues to the present day—some suggesting that the final accommodation approximates an amalgam of the contributions of the groups involved; while others argue that the dominant culture indeed dominates and is satisfied only by a type of unconditional surrender by the minority. Melting pots, salad bowls, peeled onions are some of the clever symbols that have been used to illustrate the varying views on how America has dealt with the reality of cultural pluralism.

While at one time it would have been correct to say that much less attention was paid to problems of pluralism within groups, today there seems to be a growing body of literature which seeks to describe more fully intra-group diversity. This is certainly true in studies of American Catholicism. Starting out not only as a different group, colonial Catholics often found themselves deprived of full citizenship and confronted by laws which declared some of their central acts of worship as criminal. Through the eighteenth century and in spite of growth and some accommodation in the nineteenth century, American Catholicism and American Catholics were continually forced to deal with questions about their allegiance to the Republic and the compatibility of Catholicism with Americanism (forced to deal with these issues well into the twentieth century.) Second, as an immigrant Church, American Catholicism shared in the difficulties and suspicions visited upon its immigrant members and leaders. Finally, the governance style, the erection of Ecclesiastical hierarchical institutions and the establishment of educational and social service bodies which paralleled secular/public bodies generated another level of tension and conflict between Catholics and the non-Catholic society.

However, as the American Church attempted to steer its way through these issues, it simultaneously struggled with the problems of pluralism within its own organization. Ethnic and racial tensions and conflict within the Church grew through the nineteenth century and still surface in the second half of the twentieth century. Debates that centered on Church governance and leadership styles evoked diverse views and empassioned advocacy among Catholic leaders. Doctrinal issues were contested as were strategies for dealing with non-Catholic neighbors and public officials, who, in most nineteenth century communities, reflected not only a cultural dominance but also a numerical dominance. The pressure of these internal conflicts and tensions within the Church spread beyond the borders of the nation to Rome itself and forced the highest levels of the Church to intervene in particular controversies, e. g., the McGlynn affair in New York, and ultimately to attempt to lower the voices of dissent within American Catholicism in general.

This preface should underscore the need to see American Catholicism in the nineteenth century, not as the unified monolithic body which some superficially use to describe the Church, but rather as a minority body which faced serious challenges not only from forces external to it but, perhaps even more importantly, from within its own ranks. Nineteenth century Poughkeepsie reflected some significant dimensions of both internal and external struggles. In some respects, Poughkeepsie's Catholics were part of some significant chapters in American Catholicism. In other respects, they were typical of the many other Catholic communities in the country as they struggled with issues of pluralism both within the Church and, more importantly for most, outside the Church. This paper attempts to provide an overview of nineteenth century Catholicism in Poughkeepsie and to identify examples of the effects of ethnic diversity within the city's Catholic community and examples of how Poughkeepsie Catholics attempted to deal with their non-Catholic neighbors in the city.

Catholics in the colony of New York were objects of the discriminatory legislation which followed the removal of Governor Dongan as head of the colony. The anti-Catholic spirit was reflected in the oaths required of office holders in Dutchess County. As Platt reports: In 1729, the shortest of them read:

"I _____, do swear that I do from my heart abhor Detest and abjure as Impious and Heretical, that Damnable Doctrine and position that Princes Excommunicated or deprived by the Pope or any authority of the see of Rome may be deposed or Murdered by their subjects or any other whatsoever, and I do declare that no Person Prelate State or Potentate has or ought to have any Jurisdiction Power Superiority Preeminence of authority; Ecclesiastical or Spiritual within this Realm. So help me God."[1]

There is little evidence of any significant Catholic presence in Dutchess until the 1830's when a group of Catholics sought to replace the occasional meetings in their homes with missionaries from New York, with a permanent church which might be able, someday, to support a resident pastor. In fact, when Father Michael Riordan arrived in 1844, he succeeded a line of pastors whose short stays in Poughkeepsie prevented the growth of real stability in the congregation. His predecessor, Father Burke, told the parishioners to work with the new priest but " . . . if the parish proved to be too small or too poor as yet to support a pastor the young priest would be sent elsewhere until such time as the diocese became stronger and the priests more numerous."[2] This was said twelve years after the 32 founding members of the church agreed to initiate the project (1832) and seven years after the Church was dedicated by Bishop DuBois (1837).

The scraps of evidence available suggest that these were difficult times for Poughkeepsie Catholics. There were reports of threats to destroy the church which prompted Dr. Pyne, a non-Catholic, to offer the Catholic Association a small cannon to protect the church.[3] In the same week that the Poughkeepsie papers carried an invitation by the Catholics to their " . . . Protestant friends" to attend the Bishop's consecration of the church, they also carried announcements of the lecture by Rev. Dr. Brownlee.[4] "This distinguished champion of Protestantism will, with divine permission, deliver a lecture on the subject of Romanism, in the Reformed Dutch Church on Tuesday October 31."[5] Rev. Brownlee was a well known opponent of Catholics and his speaking in Poughkeepsie less than a week before the dedication of the Catholic Church was clearly no mere coincidence.

During the 1840's as the stream of Irish immigrants increased in the country, Poughkeepsie too noticed an increase in its Irish population and as a result in its Catholic population. Proportionately, Poughkeepsie did not attract as many immigrants as other inland cities.[6] Still, Father Riordan was able to write his Bishop Superior, Hughes, in July of 1845, that his congregation numbered approximately " . . . 500 grown people."[7] Although the church debt was not large ($30.36), there were other problems; poverty (Riordan writes " . . . the revenues of both churches arising from pew-rents and Sunday collections amounts to only $692 yearly; a considerable part of which can never be collected both on account of poverty as well as the disagreeable temper of the people."); conflict within the church (Riordan again, "It will be difficult when the rules can be applied to find two persons to discharge the duties assigned them especially that of Treasurer; those who would at all be competent are persons who had sufficient difficulties heretofore with which you have been made acquainted. At my arrival here I found two contending drunken parishes without faith, hope, charity, or a spirit of Christianity in any form—by exerting myself . . . with the grace of God I succeeded in introducing some order and harmony among them; in this respect though, a great deal remains to be done.")[8] Platt noted: "The Catholic Church at this time was under the able rectorship of Rev. Michael Riordan who steered it safely through the Native American or "Know-Nothing" agitation and brought it to greatly increased strength and respect. He had unbounded influence over the Irish laborers who were building the railroad, and more than once quelled what threatened to be serious riots among them."[9]

The face of prejudice against Catholics appeared in many forms. Those Catholics who could read, were treated to regular columns of "Paddy" jokes. The *Dutchess Intelligencer* in December 1832 carried two interesting pieces: "An Irishman recently told the President of the United States that he liked the country so much that he believed he should become a *native*."[10] A week earlier the paper had observed:

> "Catholic Chaplain—The Rev. C. Constantine Pine, a Roman Catholic clergyman, was on the 11th instant [of December] chosen Chaplain of the United States Senate, for the present session. This strikes us as a somewhat singular selection in this country."[11]

The attacks on Catholics were stepped up in the larger cities in the middle of the decade of the 1830's and the work of Samuel Morse, who would become a neighbor in Poughkeepsie, was very instrumental in warning of the dangers posed by the increasing tide of the Roman Catholics. What Louis Scisco notes, could probably be applied to Poughkeepsie: "The natives regarded the Irish of 1830 as responsible for costs in almshouses, in penitentiary; lawless; tending to be clannish with little desire to learn American ways."[12] The growth of nativism in the 1840's expressed itself in many ways. The Native American Party was established in Dutchess in 1845, and garnered 11% of the Dutchess votes in 1846. In 1846, Augustus T. Cowman founded and published the *American,* and in 1847 a chapter of the United Order of American Mechanics was established. Both, active in Poughkeepsie, were clearly anti-Catholic.

The rise of nativism prompted the *Poughkeepsie Journal* to denounce, " . . . the odiousness of nativism! . . . They seek by publishing the lists of the names of new arrivals to stir up antagonism against the immigrants. This was to be the land of the free and a refuge for the oppressed which these people would make worse than the worst despotism."[13]

It was at this time that Poughkeepsie noted a new wave of immigrants, from Germany, many of them Catholics. Settling "on the south side of Main Street, west of Market. . . .," it was not long before their church was completed on Union Street.[14] Although the *Poughkeepsie Journal* does record some incidents of conflict between Irish and Germans at the time, Platt's history notes that both Irish and Germans contributed to the building of the German church which would come to be known as Nativity. Located fairly close to each other, each church served distinct ethnic populations. In downtown Poughkeepsie, in the middle of the 19th Century, one had a microcosm of the new forces in the American Church, each reflecting a distinct way of responding to the cultural and religious pluralism with which they were confronted.

In some respects, it seemed that the natives were happier with the Germans than they were with the Irish—seeing in them, if not higher social class, at least those virtues underscored by the "Puritan Ethic." The *Poughkeepsie Journal–Eagle* commenting on the new German immigrants stated:

> "The increase of German immigrants in all parts of this country within a few years past has been very great and we are not certain but that there are now as many of them among us as any foreign nation. As a general rule no better citizen need be desired for a more industrious, orderly, thriving, and intelligent class of people can hardly be found. As soon as they learn our language, manners and customs, they become in everything but name Americans and in all respects prosperous and useful."[15]

One almost suspects that the natives had greater expectation of assimilation by the Germans than by the Irish who had been here longer and started with a better knowledge of the language.

The story of the recurring tragedies of the poor in this case, the immigrant poor, is reflected in an incident where a baby girl slightly more than a year old was left at home by her German parents and died in a fire. The *Poughkeepsie Telegraph* noted: "It is a common thing for people to condemn parents for leaving children thus alone . . . But said a woman at the fire, poor people who have to go out to work for a living, don't always have someone to take care of their children and they can't take their children with them."[16]

225

Although the Irish and German Catholic Churches were no more than a mile apart, they developed distinct patterns. We can assume that some of the factors noted regarding Germans and Irish in the national experience may have had some validity in Poughkeepsie. Robert E. Curran writing about this subject:

"There was a fierce cultural pride about the Germans that the Irish found threatening. So conscious of their ambiguous status in American society, the Irish tended to resent the German's clinging to an alien culture which (in the Irish view) only heightened the suspicion that Catholics were less than fully American. The Germans, for their part, often vied with the English in their contempt for the Irish."[17]

German Catholics and Irish Catholics in Poughkeepsie seem to have adapted distinct ways of dealing with their neighbors. Technically, both functioned under the authority of a single Bishop, but he was 70 long miles away in New York City. Distance, the relative independence of parish units and the youthful character of the American Church permitted a good deal of diversity.

The Irish response to questions about their ethnic character and their Catholicism in Poughkeepsie seems to have been shaped by what eventually would be called "Americanizing Strategies" by Nelson Callaghan.[18] While scholars have usually identified two distinct strategies by which 19th century Catholics dealt with the larger society, Callaghan suggests a third. The first, heavily employed by the German leaders and sometimes referred to as Cahensleyism after Peter Cahensley, a leader in asserting German interests in an American Church dominated by an Irish hierarchy, sought emphasis on national ethnic parishes rather than territorial parishes and a "major emphasis on preserving the language culture and custom of their people."[19] Curran refers to this strategy as marching under the banner, "Language Saves Faith."[20] The fight over this matter would reach such proportions that John Keane would warn Cardinal Manning from Rome in February of 1887 that the "social and the German . . . questions are the two wedges with which the devil is trying to destroy the unity of the Church in our country. Pray that he may not succeed. . . ."[21]

The second strategy, that of the Americanists led by Archbishop Ireland, was based on a belief that ethnic Catholics should seek full status as Americans as quickly as possible and give up the cultural values and practices of the old world. The third strategy which Callaghan identifies, is that of the Americanizers, and he includes among them Father James Nilan, pastor of St. Peter's in Poughkeepsie from 1877 to 1902. While they "valued highly the culture of the United States and saw in this culture great hope for the future of the church . . . they also saw the value of the culture the European immigrant brought to this country. They had no desire to suppress that culture, for like the "Europeanizer" they knew that culture and faith were closely linked . . . the Americanizers dreamed of a day when the immigrants would melt into one great and new Church which would reflect the free institutions of the United States. Unlike the Americanists, they believed in gradual assimilation; were concerned that the American Church was being bound by an Irish model; did not seek a power base in the large urban centers."[22]

In Poughkeepsie, it was clear that the Germans of Nativity parish " . . . most self-consciously attempted to preserve both a distinctive religion and culture, viewing the strength of one as dependent on the strength of the other."[23] The authors, Clyde and Sally Griffen, go on to note that they showed more tendency than German Protestants to insulate themselves from native Protestants. In spite of this, by 1897, Father Bruder, the German pastor, complained that the younger generations were losing the German ways and culture. German Catholics in Poughkeepsie ran their own school, set up their own religious and benevolent societies and eventually sought their own cemetery, choosing not to use the Catholic cemetery of St. Peter's on Salt Point Road.

This last request was approved by Archbishop Corrigan prompting Father Nilan of St. Peter's to object. (Archbishop Corrigan had been a classmate of Father Nilan's at the newly opened American College in Rome and both were ordained priests at the same ceremony. Their careers would develop quite differently and lead to repeated confrontations over a series of important issues.) In this clash, Nilan reminded the Archbishop that opening a German cemetery in town directly carried out the spirit of Cahensley's plan, which he regarded as regressive. Nilan noted that two German priests already had monuments in St. Peter's Cemetery which, Nilan assured the Archbishop, was "large enough."[24]

Reverend James Nilan, D.D., pastor of St. Peter's Church, Poughkeepsie

Father Nilan, after assuring the Archbishop that he had no self-interest and would have preferred not to meddle, made another important point which reflected a key concern of church leaders in Poughkeepsie and elsewhere. There were unpleasant complaints about opening a cemetery so near to Vassar College. He advised, "There is no wisdom in exciting hostility against our religion."[25] Nilan's concern about his German neighbors was expressed a week later in his expression of disbelief that Archbishop Corrigan was quoted as allowing the sale of beer at an outing of the St. Michael's German Society. In addition to spawning a request from the Fabian Society, Corrigan's action " . . . hurts our effort to contradict the habit of drinking."[26] Nilan's concerns and views seem consistent with the posture of his less learned but influential predecessor Father Michael Riordan. An early theme struck by those seeking acceptance by the American majority was that Catholics had to prove themselves, especially regarding those questions and criticism which seemed to arise most frequently in the minds of their neighbors. These included questions of patriotism, temperance, and separatism.

Early in the century, Bishop Dubois' stress on sophistication and on the importance of eloquent preaching, especially " . . . to stand the criticisms of Protestants of the highest class and best information," was echoed through the speeches and writings of leading intellectuals like Orestes Brownson who seems to have had little patience with what he regarded as the crude manners of his immigrant fellow believers who were quickly coming to dominate the image of American Catholics.

Father Riordan, pastor from 1844–1870, was praised and remembered for resolving conflicts among factions in his congregation, for his dedication to the cause of temperance and for his displays of patriotism. At an 1894 dinner for the visiting Apostolic Delegate Satolli, Mayor Ketcham recalled Riordan's devotion to the Republic—"When the nation called for men to save its life, well do I remember what the then pastor of St. Peter's church, Rev. Michael Riordan, said at a meeting in the opera house. He was pale, emaciated and ill at that time, and his voice was weak and tremulous. He raised his hand and said, 'When I came to this country I made this country's flag my flag. I have seen no reason to change my allegiance to it and I only wish I could lay down my life for that flag now, if so poor an offering were needed.' It was a brief speech but it did more than any other speech that was made to arouse the men of this city to the defense of the republic."[27] Even as late as the celebration of the 75th Anniversary of St. Peter's, the history of the parish printed in the *Journal* devoted special attention to listing those killed in the service of their country, noting, "The members of St. Peter's and Nativity parishes were unselfish in their loyalty and devotion to this (in most instances) their adopted country."[28]

Attention to temperance also earned praise for Catholic leaders. MacCracken's *History* extols Riordan's St. Peter's Total Abstinence Society "as a most worthy cause."[29] The Griffens cite the "role of the Catholic Church in Poughkeepsie in encouraging emulation of Protestant respectability, especially temperance and literary cultivation . . . ."[30] The *Commemorative Biographical Record* remembers Rev. James Nilan in this way.

> Dr. Nilan's pronounced temperance principles, his warm sympathies with the humblest of his flock and his frank acceptance of all the responsibilities of citizenship have combined to give him an enviable position, not only with members of his parish, but in the community at large."[31]

In fact, Msgr. Cohalan, a contemporary church historian relates that Nilan's devotion to the cause of temperance was such that he served no wine but only ginger ale at the visit of the Apostolic Delegate in 1894 and only added, by so doing, to Satolli's annoyance with some of the practices he found in Nilan's church liturgy.

In addition to responding to the suspicions and the bias of some of their neighbors, Catholics, especially during the tenure of Father Nilan at St. Peter's and Father McSweeney at St. Mary's, were encouraged by the example and actions of these priests to move out into the wider community and participate in collaborative efforts. This contradicted the more separatist tendencies of more conservative church elements, who preferred to stay with their own. Both Nilan and McSweeney were active members of the Vassar Institute and frequently presented papers in the literary section. The *Transactions of the Institute 1881–1894*, notes approximately seven presentations by Nilan and two by

McSweeney who was transferred early in that period. The topics included religious subjects, some of which might be considered quite controversial.[32]

In an essay written on Luther, Nilan noted that only at the insistence of and with the assurances of respected Protestant clergymen that the discourse is not offensive, did he agree to have his talk (read at regular meeting of Vassar Institute, March 14, 1982) printed.[33] In another essay one year later, Father Nilan, speaking of European persecutions of Catholics by Protestants and of Protestants by Catholics, declared:

> "The atrocity of the one was to be reprehended no more lightly than the injustice of the other. And let us hope that the time shall never return when man shall have it in his power to intrude by law or otherwise into the sanctuary of the conscience of his fellow man."[34]

Perhaps the boldest evidence of the cooperative spirit in Poughkeepsie was to be seen in the "Poughkeepsie Plan" as it was called. Denounced by Catholics and non-Catholics alike, it generated sufficient support to last from 1873 to 1899. The "Plan" turned over to the Poughkeepsie Board of Education two former parochial schools. They would be run and supervised as public schools, being leased for $1.00 a year, and would be staffed by the nuns and lay people who had previously taught in them as parochial schools. In the same year the "Plan" began, 1873, readings from the St. James version of the Bible were discontinued at the high school, a practice which may have discouraged some Catholics from sending their children to the high school. German Catholics in Poughkeepsie continued to operate the Nativity School, in part reflecting the views of a German Catholic Congress which, meeting in Buffalo in 1891, condemned the Poughkeepsie school compromise as "unwise and dangerous."[35] Since the very start of the "Plan," Catholic critics worried about dealing with a Board of Education composed mostly of enemies—"Freemasons besides being Protestant."[36] They reminded proponents of the Poughkeepsie Plan that Catholics had supported their own schools in harder times than these.

Yet in spite of the criticism of powerful figures like editor and publisher MacMaster (a convert brought into the Church, ironically by Father Riordan) and Bishop McQuaid of Rochester who feared the results of Catholic children mixing with non-Catholic in a secular environment ("It is the indifferentism with regards to all religious beliefs we most fear.")[37] The "Plan" came to be a model which drew national attention and was actually adopted in a number of other communities. Archbishop Ireland of St. Paul praised the "Plan" at the 1890 meeting of the National Education Association and encouraged its adoption in two communities in his diocese.

There is evidence that both the lay leaders and the clergy who implemented the "Plan" thought well of it. Criticism by the German Congress led Nilan to speak sharply. ". . . the "Plan" has worked admirably for 18 years . . . it satisfies all intelligent people. But those who do not understand it condemn it. It is safe to say that not one of those foreign priests ever visited our schools. Some of them cannot comprehend the lesson in the first English reader. Their condemnation is a eulogy."[38] Yet the "Plan" eventually came to an end. Writing to Archbishop Corrigan in January of 1898, Father Nilan noted that objections to the Sister's garb was the critical issue. Charging that one of the board members was active in the Anti-Catholic American Protective Association, Nilan concluded: "No one is willing to come out and be known as hostile to us but hostility exists. J____ F____ of Boston denounced us in a small Methodist Church here last Sunday."[39]

As the century drew to a close, significant developments had taken place in the Catholic community and in its relations with non-Catholic neighbors. Some measure of accommodation and assimilation had taken place, but separatism, prejudice and the arrival of new immigrant Catholic groups would continue to test the ability of Poughkeepsians to deal with issues of religious, ethnic and racial diversity. Presiding over the last years of the century as one spokesman of Poughkeepsie Catholics, Father Nilan was aptly described as one who:

> " . . . represented in his temperament and career the compromise theory, which in our mixed conditions has a larger practical value than the conservatives are willing to admit. He mingled freely and easily with all classes, lectured at Vassar and other advanced institutions, possessed a sarcastic humor well-suited to his peculiar position, made himself entirely objectionable to the opposite party and lived and died an irreproachable priest."[40]

St. Peter's Catholic Church, Poughkeepsie

Aware of the unresolved problems of the older Irish and German churches, Nilan took a special interest in attempting to assist the new Catholic immigrants, especially the Italians and Poles who headed the numbers of the new immigration. Almost as soon as they arrived, Italians were objects of the same suspicions as visited upon earlier Catholics, especially the Irish. The *Poughkeepsie News-Telegraph,* on May 21, 1887, attempted to quiet some of the economic concerns:

> "There are about one hundred Italians employed by the Bridge Company. They have to do hard and mean work. There was no necessity for a complaint as published in a city newspaper to the effect that the Italians crowd out deserving working men in this neighborhood. None but Italians could or would do the sort of work given to them. The Italians are by no means drawing princely salaries. The best of them do not get more than $1.50 a day and the majority get from $1.00 to $1.25."[41]

Father Nilan's fluent Italian served him well in his attempts to accommodate the new immigrants and allowed him to serve as spiritual director of the Italian Benevolent Society. The first Italians who settled at 109 Mill Street were not named in the early Poughkeepsie directories but simply listed at the address as "Italians." Not until 1904 did the Italians have special services by an Italian priest. Father Iacobucci from Mother Cabrini's Home in West Park, was invited to say mass in the basement of St. Peter's Church by the new pastor, Father Livingston. Father Nilan's awareness of the growing needs of a new group, the Polish people, led him to urge Archbishop Corrigan to send a Polish priest to minister to their needs.[42]

In each case, Nilan was sensitive to the need for gradual assimilation accomplished by sensitivity to the culture of the group—a process he hoped would create a new American Church based not on any one culture, not divided into many cultures, but rather the product of the fusion of old world elements with American principles of democratic governance, participation and sensitivity to an enriching rather than divisive diversity—principles which he believed to be not only American but also consistent with the truest principles of Catholic Christianity.

However, Nilan's was not the only vision of how to deal with pluralism both inside and outside of the Catholic community. Nineteenth century Poughkeepsie Catholics and non-Catholics interacted in a variety of ways and while the twentieth century has witnessed the election of a Catholic as a President and the dramatic changes of the Vatican Council, one suspects that, even today, Americans still have some issues to resolve.

Notes

1. Platt, p. 24.
2. *Poughkeepsie News-Telegraph,* "Satolli visit," March 14, 1894.
3. F. Cohalan, History of Regina Coeli Parish, Commemorative Booklet, 1964.
4. *Poughkeepsie Telegraph,* Nov. 1, 1837.
5. *Poughkeepsie Telegraph,* Oct. 25, 1837.
6. Griffen, *Newcomers and Natives,* p. 3.
7. Archives of Archdiocese of N. Y. (AANY), M. Riordan to Bishop Hughes, July 7, 1845.
8. *Ibid.*
9. Platt, p. 147.
10. *Dutchess Intelligence,* Dec. 26, 1832.
11. *Dutchess Intelligence,* Dec. 19, 1832.
12. Scisco, Louis, *Political Nativism in New York State,* 1901, Reprint by A. M. S., p. 21.
13. *Poughkeepsie Journal.,1 May 22, 1847,* p. 2.
14. *Platt, p. 146.*
15. *Poughkeepsie Journal—Eagle,* Aug. 11, 1849.
16. *Poughkeepsie Telegraph,* Dec. 28, 1852.
17. Curran's *Biography of Archbishop Michael Corrigan,* p. 138.
18. Nelson Callaghan, Preface to the edited publication of the Diary of Richard Burtsell, p. XVII.
19. *Ibid.*
20. Curran, *op cit.,* p. 168.

21. *Ibid.*
22. Callaghan, *op cit.,* p. xviii
23. Griffens, *op cit.*
24. AANY, Nilan to Corrigan, July 31, 1891.
25. *Ibid.*
26. AANY. Nilan to Corrigan, Aug. 3, 1891.
27. *Poughkeepsie News-Telegraph,* March 14, 1894.
28. *Poughkeepsie Journal.*
29. MacCracken, p. 99.
30. Griffens.
31. *Commemorative Biographical Record.*
32. *Transactions of the Vassar Institute, 1881–1894.*
33. James Nilan, *Essay on Luther,* preface.
34. James Nilan, *Essay on Oliver Plunkett,* 3/18/83.
35. Pratt, p. 263.
36. AANY, "Sacerdos" to Bishop McClorkey, March 19, 1875.
37. Zwierlein, *Letters of Archbishop McQuaid,* Vol. 3, McQuaid to Pope Leo XIII.
38. Pratt, p. 263.
39. AANY, Nilan to Corrigan, Jan. 13, 1898.
40. Smith, J., *History of the Catholic Church in N. Y.,* Vol. 2..
41. *Poughkeepsie News-Telegraph,* May 21, 1887.
42. AANY, Nilan to Corrigan, Aug. 9, 1899, Aug. 11, 1899.

VIEWS OF THE POUGHKEEPSIE PRESS: 1783–1883–1983

Judy Clark

The transformation of the Poughkeepsie press from the year 1783 to 1883 and then to 1983 was a reflection of a phenomenon that was national in scope. Competition between two or more daily newspapers in a city of under 100,000 people by 1976 had become virtually non-existent.[1] Poughkeepsie was no exception.

More than thirty newspapers existed separately, in competition with each other, or merged together in the 18th, 19th and 20th centuries in Poughkeepsie and its surrounding localities.[2] But newspapers, like the men and women who get them out, have had to go through some hard times. Economic realities, from the rising cost of newsprint and technological advances in printing, to the more important competition for circulation and advertising revenues, have killed too many fine newspapers.[3] The result is a decline in the number of newspapers and an increase in the concentration of ownership.[4]

Often, those of us who experienced the 114-day New York newspaper strike of 1962 and 1963, look back with nostalgia to the good old days when we could count on the New York *Herald Tribune, World Telegram and Sun, Journal American,* and *Daily Mirror* as comrades, or at least competition. It was the longest strike in the history of the American newspaper business.[5] And, like the deaths of loved ones, losses weren't necessarily apparent right away, but became more real as the weeks and months, and even years, rolled by.

But it doesn't do any good to cry about the loss of newspapers that will never return. It may, however, be therapeutic and moreover revealing to look back to the newspapers that once existed. Unlike the fleeting moments of radio and television, newspapers leave a written record that can be held and read again and again.

The record of the past that was preserved in the Poughkeepsie newspapers of 1783 and 1883 is telling when compared to the present. There are not only obvious differences, but striking parallels.

Although the champion of Sam Adams and the Sons of Liberty, John Holt, printed the New York *Journal* in Poughkeepsie before 1783, no record of it exists for that year.[6] Most likely Holt moved it back to New York after the Revolution. Copies of Samuel Loudon's weekly *New York Packet and the American Advertiser,* however, do exist for the year 1783. Loudon printed his paper in Fishkill, most likely to be close to New York, where he, too, eventually returned after independence.

In the June 12th issue of the four-page paper, datelined Poughkeepsie, June 7, 1783, it is reported that: "The colours and Committee of officers from the 2nd New York regiment were escorted to Poughkeepsie by the infantry company. The officers of the regiment dined with the Governor, and in the evening a very splendid ball was given by his Excellency." (That very same "ball" will be re-enacted on June 4th of this year.) In the same issue a report from Westchester County states there was a celebration on May 15th "for the purpose of devoting the day to joy and mirth on the occasion of a cessation of hostilities between America and Great Britain." The banquet was held "under a spacious bower of green purposely erected,—where nigh two hundred gentlemen and ladies dined; previous to dining, 13 cannon were discharged. . . ." Further, "13 toasts were drank." The first was to the "U.S.A." and the last to "A speedy exit and perpetual exclusion from this state of all tyrants and tories, and then peace to all the world." If the phrase "peace to all the world" sounds familiar, the avowed patriotism of the freeholders and inhabitants of Poughkeepsie precinct appears to parallel the phrases used by some of our present government leaders: "The spirit of '75 still beats high and *must* beat high, or American freedom is no more."

But in 1783, freedom was not extended to everyone. In copies of Samuel Loudon's paper that still exist there are four advertisements announcing slaves for sale.[7] Yet in the June 26th issue "from a late Boston paper" is an impassioned plea for the estate of a loyalist from his slave, Belinda, who: "For 50 years" has "been compelled to ignoble servitude for the benefit of an Isaac Royall, until, as if nations must be agitated, and the world convulsed, for the preservation of that freedom which the Almighty Father intended for all the human race, the present war commenced. The terrors of men, armed in the cause of freedom, compelled her master to fly and breath[e] away his life in a land, where lawless domination sits enthroned, pouring bloody outrage and cruelty on all who dare to be free."

The *New York Packet,* however, had a lighter side. It is revealed in a number of advertisements that would most likely not be printed in the *Poughkeepsie Eagle* of 1883 or the present-day *Poughkeepsie Journal.* A few eyebrows would raise when the "young gentlemen of 23" advertises that he "is desirous of settling himself for Life by entering into the Bands of Hymen with any lady . . . Provided her Circumstances will enable them to live in that happy State of Mediocrity . . . ."[8] In another issue, a frustrated advertiser is offering a five-dollar reward for an apprentice: "I took him 5 years next Sept., when no one would have him, as he was naked, lousy and had the itch."[9] Moreover, the standard format for the present-day classified ad, "I, Joe Glutz, will no longer be responsible for the debts other than my own," appears dull when compared to the *Packet's* version. "Whereas, my Wife . . . Has eloped from my bed and board and has behaved in a very unbecoming manner without any just cause . . . I will pay no debts of her . . . ."[10] Most of the advertisements in the *New York Packet* offered horses for sale, or rewards for horses that were stolen. One advertiser offered a reward for a silver spur lost in the Beekman precinct.[11] Real estate advertisements also appeared frequently. But ads for patent medicines and "perfumeries" were certainly not as frightening as those that appeared in the *Poughkeepsie Eagle* of 1883, or as banal as those that appear in the *Journal* today.[12]

Perhaps the most significant feature of the *New York Packet* is the amount of foreign and national "news," or, more accurately, "newsletters." It appears that Samuel Loudon had his own team of correspondents in London, Paris, Rome and Dublin abroad, and Philadelphia, Boston, Savannah and Charleston at home.

But even as the *Packet* appeared to have a bevy of correspondents, it was essentially a one-man operation. Loudon was the printer, the publisher, the editor and more often than not, the reporter. He took the advertisements, kept track of the books and swept the floor. He sold everything from Bibles to men's shoes at the printing office, and even once offered for sale "a new and accurate map of the 13 United States agreeable to the boundaries settled by the late treaty of peace."[13] There were no headlines in the *New York Packet,* and more important, no editorials. Every piece of news was editorialized, for the purpose of the newspaper was to support the cause for independence. And what was most impressive about Samuel Loudon's paper, unlike the *Poughkeepsie Daily Eagle* or the *Poughkeepsie Journal,* is that it appeared to contain not a single typographical error.[14]

The *Poughkeepsie Daily Eagle,* was in 1883, a morning newspaper published by Platt and Platt. It was a large 8-column, 4-page newspaper which claimed to have "a bona-fide paid circulation more than double that of any other daily published in this City." Further, it went "to people who valu(ed) it highly enough to pay for it." The publishers claimed it was "an independent Republican Journal with an opinion on every subject, firm in its advocacy of freedom, equal rights and just laws for all men; outspoken in its opposition to the abuses and follies of the day, in favor of progress and improvement everywhere and especially devoted to the interests of Poughkeepsie and vicinity."[15] What little competition the *Eagle* had came from the democratic *News Press* and *News Telegraph,* two separate newspapers before 1883, and an afternoon newspaper established in August of 1883, the *Evening Enterprise.*[16]

The *Poughkeepsie Daily Eagle* in its stories, claims and advertisements reflected the era that would later be called the "Age of Excess."[17] Headlines informed readers that there was an "Exciting Indian Fight." Better yet, "A Plucky Woman," and in the subheading, "Catching a Midnight Robber in a Blanket while Her Husband Slept."[18] In an odd combination of headlines that ran across the top of the May 25th edition, we are treated to "The Arson Case," "The Stone Throwers" and last, but not least, "Boy Drowned." Readers could find out on February 13th that a John Sheffield was "a dissolute character . . . who fired his house." Under "The Gossip of the Town," the "Crispy News Item" of the day is: "They are getting up all sorts of queer things for the annual fair of the YMCA." Finally a rather puzzling item appears under "State News": "Some of our wealthy businessmen want rest, but it is the rest of the earth." It is difficult to discern why that particular tidbit appears under "State News."

In the edition of the *Eagle* published the day before, however, the importance of the opening of the Brooklyn Bridge is clearly reflected in nine separate headlines, each appearing under the other. Without reading the body of the story itself, the local Poughkeepsie resident can find out at a glance that the bridge was open, that there were "rejoicings" in New York and Brooklyn, a military and civilian procession, many distinguished "persons" present, ceremonies on the bridge, a dinner at Mayor Low's residence, fireworks, and "a splendid scene in the harbor." To the left of the story is a small, perhaps more interesting paragraph, the last sentence of which reads: "We congratulate our neighboring villages down at the mouth of the creek on their enterprise and pluck and success, and hope we can invite them up here to just as big and as important a Bridge celebration of our own some day." (Perhaps it would be fun to send that item off to Mayor Koch for the forthcoming centennial celebration of the Brooklyn Bridge.)

If news items sometimes appear humorous to us in the *Daily Eagle*, advertisements often seem hilarious. On the very top left hand corner of the front page of the February 13th edition appear the words: "teeth extracted without a pain a specialty." In the same edition falling just below the masthead, a prominent ad proclaims a "Sale of Ladies' Muslin Underwear! at Lucky Platt." We can feel assured that "Mary Stuart Face Powder . . . contains no Arsenic, Lime or White Lead." Better yet, it only costs "25¢." And, finally, the advertisement which must be seen to be appreciated, appears in both the April 30th and May 21st editions: The "R. V. cable patent corset" is printed upside down.

And so, the *Poughkeepsie Daily Eagle* which claimed to be "neutral in nothing" offered a little bit of everything, from a public opinion column to features. In looking back upon it today, however, what it really offers to us is not only a reflection of time and community, but a lot of entertainment. In fact, to date, I believe the *Eagle* is the most entertaining and humorous newspaper I have read.

In 1983 we have come full circle to the familiar *Poughkeepsie Journal*, the only local newspaper in town. Now owned by the Rochester-based Gannett Corporation, the *Journal's* ancestry dates back to 1785. The citizens of Poughkeepsie and the surrounding localities are treated to foreign and national news (usually provided by the wire services), opinions of syndicated columnists, advice to working mothers, comics and other features too numerous to mention. But the *Journal's* value is not based as much on its foreign or national news or syndicated features as it is on how well it covers local news. In 1983, with respect to coverage of local news, there are two rather interesting items that are worthy of mention.

On April 9th, the *Journal* ran a front-page story about former Poughkeepsie attorney, Barry Grandeau, who was sentenced from one to four years in state prison for stealing $115,000 from his clients. A photograph of Grandeau leaving the courtroom with his family appeared with the story. In this instance I believe the Journal editors lacked discretion in using that particular photograph. One would certainly not question using a photograph of Grandeau, the subject of the story. But the question ought to have been asked whether it was necessary to use a photograph that included his wife, and more important, his adolescent son. They were not guilty of any wrong-doing or criminal act. Often, although it was not necessarily intended to do so, a photograph can imply guilt by association. In the future, one would hope that the *Journal* editors would be more sensitive to the feelings of people who have already experienced enough grief through no fault of their own.

In the second instance, some nine days later, a correction was written by columnist and editor Larry Hertz. Instead of being obscured in some insignificant place on page two, it was placed in the top left-hand column of the "Area" news section. Hertz acknowledged making a mistake in the process of writing his column. He confused the names of two women, one who had a drinking problem and the other who was the caseworker. Although it was a grave error, the *Journal* editors and Larry Hertz, in particular, showed by their actions and words that the only newspaper in town can be sensitive to the feelings of others. Moreover, it is possible for the only newspaper in town to be a responsible force in the community, despite qualms about chain-ownership and the negative effects of automation. It is

235

after all, the local newspaper that serves us by leaving a record of where we've been and providing news of where we are. It even reports the most intimate facts of our lives—our births, our loves, and ultimately, our deaths. We're damned lucky to have the *Poughkeepsie Journal* in our community.

But then, as that newspaperman of newspapermen, A. J. Liebling, once said: "Everybody knows what it is that one swallow doesn't make, but I am an incorrigible optimist about newspapers."[18]

Notes

1. Edwin Emery and Michael Emery, *The Press and America, An Interpretative History of the Mass Media* (Englewood Cliffs, 1978), p. 437.

2. Edmund Platt, *The Eagle's History of Poughkeepsie From the Earliest Settlements, 1683 to 1905* (Poughkeepsie, 1905), p. 323 and *passim*.

3. Emery and Emery, p. 437.

4. Emery and Emery, p. 437.

5. A. J. Liebling, *The Press* (New York, 1964), p. 289.

6. At least not at the Adriance Library, Poughkeepsie, N. Y. Perhaps it might turn up among the newspapers in the Clinton House that have not yet been indexed. Although it is doubtful.

7. *The New York Packet and the American Advertiser,* #308, March 20, 1783, p. 4, and *passim* through numbers 329, Aug. 14, 1783. Published in Fishkill by Samuel Loudon.

8. *N. Y. Packet,* #307, March 13, 1783.

9. *N. Y. Packet,* #315, May 22, 1783. Also appeared June 5.

10. *N. Y. Packet,,* #307, Mar. 13, 1783 and *passim.*

11. *N. Y. Packet,* #315, May 8 and May 15, 1783.

12. *N. Y. Packet,* #303, Feb. 13, 1783 and *passim.* Compare to *Poughkeepsie Daily Eagle,* 1883, *passim.* and *Poughkeepsie Journal, passim.*

13. *N. Y. Packet,* #329, Aug. 14, 1783, p. 4 and *passim.*

14. Compare *N. Y. Packet* to *Poughkeepsie Daily Eagle* to *Poughkeepsie Journal,* 1783, 1883, 1983 respectively. *Passim.*

15. The *Poughkeepsie Daily Eagle,* printed by Platt and Platt, Vol. 23., No. 6862, Feb. 13, 1883, p. 1.

16. Platt, *Eagle's History of Poughkeepsie,* p. 240.

17. For an excellent account of the time see Ray Ginger, *Age of Excess* (New York, 1975), *passim,*

18. Liebling, *The Press,* p. 293.

Panel 9
"Of Government and Politics"
  Chair: William Emerson, Director, Franklin D. Roosevelt Library
    1. F. Kennon Moody, Dean of Community Services, Dutchess Community College
F.D.R.: Neighbors and Politics in Dutchess County
    2. I. Jack Lippman, Professor of Political Science, Dutchess Community College
Dutchess County Adopts a Charter
    3. William Bartles, Town Supervisor, Hyde Park
County Government in Transition

Session 5-Sunday April 24, 1983   3PM-5PM
Panel 10
"Dutchess County's Musical Heritage"
  Chair: Edward Reilly, Professor of Music, Vassar College
    1. Barbara Biszick, recipient, NEH Youth Grant
Poughkeepsie's Musical Heritage
    2. Joyce Ghee, Dutchess County Historian
Songs That Tell Our History: Music as a Historical Resource
    3. Constance Jessup, Local Historian, Musician
Music from the Pen of Charles Gilbert Spross

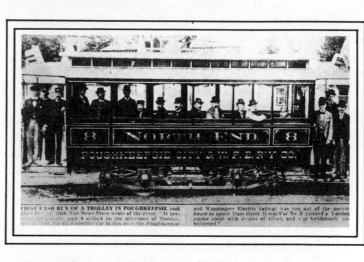

FIRST CASH RUN OF A TROLLEY IN POUGHKEEPSIE took place [...] 1894. The News-Press wrote of the event: "At [...] minutes past 4 o'clock on the afternoon of Monday, [...] the first electric car to run over the Poughkeepsie and Wappingers Electric railway was run out of the power-house in upper Main street. It was Car No. 8, painted a London smoke color with stripes of silver, and was handsomely upholstered."

Panel 11
"Doing Local History"
  Chair: Cortland P. Auser, Director, Yorktown Museum
    1. Kevin Gallagher, Librarian, Local History Collection, Adriance Library
Problems in Local History Research
    2. Jacob Chaput, Teacher, Arlington Elementary School
Teaching Local History in the Primary Grades
    3. Joseph Lombardi, Teacher, Arlington High School
Teaching Local History in the Secondary School

Panel 12
"Red, White and Black"
Chair: Maurice Lee, Director, Higher Education Opportunities, Bard College
    1. Jack Campisi, Professor of Anthropology, SUNY, Albany and Lawrence Hauptman, Professor of History, SUNY New Paltz
Neighbors and Intruders
    2. Louis Zuccarello, Professor, Political Science, Marist College
Pluralism and the Catholic Community: 19th Century Poughkeepsie
    3. A.J. Williams-Myers, Chair, Black Studies, SUNY, New Paltz
The African (American) in the Mid-Hudson Valley

Closing Ceremony and Reception-Sunday April 24, 1983   5PM-6PM
    1. "The Future of Dutchess County"-Dutchess County Planning
    2. Closing Remarks-Joyce Ghee, Dutchess County Historian

Registration: The conference fee $20.00 includes registration, a luncheon on Saturday and a wine and cheese reception at the close of the conference. The attached registration form and a check made payable to Dutchess Community College should be sent to the Office of Community Services, Dutchess Community College, Pendell Road, Poughkeepsie, NY 12601. **Registration Deadline April 15, 1983. All sessions will be held in Dutchess Hall and Drumlin Hall.**

- -

CREDIT-FREE COURSE AND SPECIAL PROGRAM REGISTRATION

Please Print
MR. ☐
MS. ☐

Last Name   First Name   Middle Initial

Social Security Number*   F

Street Address (Abbrev. if necessary)   County

City and State   Zip Code

Area Code/Home Telephone No.   Area Code/Business Phone

Detach and Mail With Check to:
Office of Community Services
Dutchess Community College
Pendell Rd., Poughkeepsie, NY 12601

Please use one registration form per person.
For additional registration forms please duplicate this form.
For further information call
Office of Community Services at 471-4500/Ext 240.
Tuition must accompany Registration Form.
*Not required by Federal Law; however, colleges use SS# to process registrations.
•All refunds must be processed before first class or beginning of event.

COURSE NUMBER	SECTION	COURSE TITLE	FEE
XCH981-01			$

Total Fee $

TWENTY FIVE YEARS • DUTCHESS COMMUNITY COLLEGE • 1957 ★ 1982
EDUCATION FOR A DEMOCRACY OF EXCELLENCE
1957

Dutchess County Tercentenary
Advisory Committee

Honorable Lucille P. Pattison, Member, ex-offico

Mrs. Joyce C. Ghee, Dutchess County Historian and Director,
  Dutchess County Tercentenary, Chairman

Mr. Richard Birch, Vice-Chairman

Mrs. Elizabeth Carter

Dr. Jonathan Clark

Dr. Colton Johnson

Mrs. Emily Johnson

Mr. Joseph Lombardi

Mr. Zinas Mavodones

Mrs. Sally Mazzarella

Mr. Donald McTernan

Mrs. Caroline Reichenberg

Mrs. Constance Smith, Secretary

Dr. Thomas Toler

Miss Louise Tompkins, Honorary Member

Mrs. Joan VanVoorhis

Mrs. Carolyn Wilson

Dutchess County Tercentenary
Advisory Committee

Honorable Lucille P. Pattison, Member, ex-officio
Mrs. Joyce C. Ghee, Dutchess County Historian and Director,
    Dutchess County Tercentenary, Chairman
Mr. Richard Birch, Vice-Chairman
Mrs. Elizabeth Carter
Dr. Jonathan Clark
Dr. Colton Johnson
Mrs. Emily Johnson
Mr. Joseph Lombardi
Mr. Zinas Mavodones
Mrs. Sally Mazzarella
Mr. Donald McTernan
Mrs. Caroline Reichenberg
Mrs. Constance Smith, Secretary
Dr. Thomas Toler
Miss Louise Tompkins, Honorary Member
Mrs. Joan VanVoorhis
Mrs. Carolyn Wilson